T0239007

IFIP Advances in Information and Communication Technology 429

IFIP – The International Federation for Information Processing

IFIP was founded in 1960 under the auspices of UNESCO, following the First World Computer Congress held in Paris the previous year. An umbrella organization for societies working in information processing, IFIP's aim is two-fold: to support information processing within its member countries and to encourage technology transfer to developing nations. As its mission statement clearly states,

> *IFIP's mission is to be the leading, truly international, apolitical organization which encourages and assists in the development, exploitation and application of information technology for the bene t of all people.*

IFIP is a non-profitmaking organization, run almost solely by 2500 volunteers. It operates through a number of technical committees, which organize events and publications. IFIP's events range from an international congress to local seminars, but the most important are:

- The IFIP World Computer Congress, held every second year;
- Open conferences;
- Working conferences.

The flagship event is the IFIP World Computer Congress, at which both invited and contributed papers are presented. Contributed papers are rigorously refereed and the rejection rate is high.

As with the Congress, participation in the open conferences is open to all and papers may be invited or submitted. Again, submitted papers are stringently refereed.

The working conferences are structured differently. They are usually run by a working group and attendance is small and by invitation only. Their purpose is to create an atmosphere conducive to innovation and development. Refereeing is also rigorous and papers are subjected to extensive group discussion.

Publications arising from IFIP events vary. The papers presented at the IFIP World Computer Congress and at open conferences are published as conference proceedings, while the results of the working conferences are often published as collections of selected and edited papers.

Any national society whose primary activity is about information processing may apply to become a full member of IFIP, although full membership is restricted to one society per country. Full members are entitled to vote at the annual General Assembly, National societies preferring a less committed involvement may apply for associate or corresponding membership. Associate members enjoy the same benefits as full members, but without voting rights. Corresponding members are not represented in IFIP bodies. Affiliated membership is open to non-national societies, and individual and honorary membership schemes are also offered.

Birgitta Bergvall-Kåreborn
Peter Axel Nielsen (Eds.)

Creating Value for All Through IT

IFIP WG 8.6 International Conference
on Transfer and Diffusion of IT, TDIT 2014
Aalborg, Denmark, June 2-4, 2014
Proceedings

 Springer

Volume Editors

Birgitta Bergvall-Kåreborn
Luleå University of Technology
Department of Business Administration,
Technology and Social Sciences
Luleå, Sweden
E-mail: birgitta.bergvall-kareborn@ltu.se

Peter Axel Nielsen
Aalborg University
Research Centre for Socio+Interactive Design
Aalborg, Denmark
E-mail: pan@cs.aau.dk

ISSN 1868-4238   e-ISSN 1868-422X
ISBN 978-3-662-51544-0 e-ISBN 978-3-662-43459-8
DOI 10.1007/978-3-662-43459-8
Springer Heidelberg New York Dordrecht London

Typesetting: Camera-ready by author, data conversion by Scientific Publishing Services, Chennai, India

Printed on acid-free paper

Springer is part of Springer Science+Business Media (www.springer.com)

Preface

This book developed from the collaborative effort of the IFIP Working Group 8.6, a working group dedicated to the study of diffusion and adoption of information technology innovations. The book contains the proceedings of the IFIP Working Conference on Creating Values for All Through IT held in Aalborg, Denmark, in June of 2014.

The theme of the conference was "Creating values for all through IT" and was intended to encourage researchers to reflect on future technologies that create value by transferring and diffusing new functionality, features, and capability, in new forms, and to larger groups of users and customers. New phenomena that have the potential to extend our perspective on value creation include: platforms for third-party development, Internet of things, green IS, smart cities, social media, and cloud computing. Contexts in which IT is used become increasingly complex, uncertain, and differentiated. These are just a few examples. The conference provided a forum for consideration and evaluation of new and radical innovations and allowed researchers to consider values and value creation in the context of advanced utilization of future and enabling information technologies.

The conference employed a public call for papers and attracted a total of 37 submissions. These included 28 full research papers, and eight other papers, research-in-progress papers, experience reports, and panels. The conference Program Committee refereed the submissions in a blinded review process. Ultimately, we selected 18 research papers, five research-in-progress papers, two experience reports, and one panel.

The Program Committee was active in shaping and promoting the conference and they played a key role as reviewers and selectors of the contributions to the conference and to this book.

A conference and the production of a book is never possible without the commitment and hard work of the Program Committee and many others. In addition to the Program Committee we want to thank IFIP and the sponsors and in particular the organizers who were responsible for the implementation of the program and for setting up a facilitating environment during the conference.

March 2014

Birgitta Bergvall-Kåreborn
Peter Axel Nielsen

Organization

General Chair

Tor J. Larsen   Norwegian Business School

Program Co-chairs

Birgitta Bergvall-Kåreborn   Luleå University of Technology, Sweden
Peter Axel Nielsen   Aalborg University, Denmark

Conference Organization

John Stouby Persson   Aalborg University, Denmark
Ivan Aaen   Aalborg University, Denmark
Merete Wolder Lange   Aalborg University, Denmark

Program Committee

Deborah Bunker   Sydney Business School, Australia
Frada Burstein   Monash University, Australia
Kieran Conboy   National University Ireland Galway, Ireland
Linda Dawson   University of Wollongong, Australia
Yogesh Dwivedi   Swansea University, UK
Andreas Gadatsch   Hochschule Bonn-Rhein-Sieg, Germany
Robert Galliers   Bentley College, USA
Helle Zinner Henriksen   Copenhagen Business School, Denmark
Netta Iivari   Oulu University, Finland
Karl Kautz   University of Wollongong, Australia
Pernille Kræmmergaard   Aalborg University, Denmark
Lars Mathiassen   Georgia State University, USA
Jacob Nørbjerg   Aalborg University, Denmark
Markus Nüttgens   Hamburg University, Germany
John Persson   Aalborg University, Denmark
Jan Pries-Heje   Roskilde University, Denmark
Tero Päivärinta   Luleå University of Technology, Sweden

Table of Contents

Creating Value through Applications

Panel

Research in Progress

Experience Report

Value Creation from Public Healthcare IS

An Action Research Study in the Faroe Islands

Bjarne Rerup Schlichter, Per Svejvig, and Povl Erik Rostgaard Andersen

Department of Business Administration, Aarhus University, Denmark
{brs,psve,ros}@asb.dk

Abstract. The obtainment of value from IT is a recurring theme that has diffused into healthcare information systems (HIS). Having completed the implementation of an integrated HIS, the Faroese Health Service (FHS) has started discussions regarding the obtainment of value from its IT investment which is the subject of this paper. Based on an action research project focusing on the improvement of the stroke process, this paper reveals that it is not possible to distinguish between working processes and HIS and that the realization of value in this context has a much broader significance than mere financial value. During the project, specific key performance indicators (KPIs) were identified and a baseline was established for the stroke process. The outcome is a framework for measuring IS public value as: professional, organizational, patient-perceived and employee-perceived quality as well as learning. Selected non-financial measures for each dimension and their development are presented, e.g., a decrease in mortality.

Keywords: Healthcare information systems, IS business value, IS public value, action research, value realization, stroke process.

1   Introduction

The creation of value through the use of IT has received increasing attention in recent years. The debate concerning the value of IT also has diffused into healthcare [1, 2], and is closely related to a more wide-ranging discussion regarding the performance measures of healthcare organizations [3-6] and public organizations in general [7, 8]. The general discussion concerning the value of IT and the broader discussion regarding the performance measures of healthcare organizations motivated us to start an action research project in the Faroe Islands. The Faroese Health Service (FHS) completed the implementation of an integrated healthcare information system (HIS) in 2010; it was then time to consider reaping the value of the system.

We initiated an action research project with the objective of creating (more) value from the newly implemented HIS. It soon came to our attention that one of the major challenges in this project was to establish a shared and sound understanding of what actually constitutes value in the healthcare setting and how to measure any status or

B. Bergvall-Kåreborn and P.A. Nielsen (Eds.): TDIT 2014, IFIP AICT 429, pp. 1–15, 2014.

progress that is rooted in the ongoing development of the processes. Also, we observed that FHS had defined no targets for value in the initial implementation of the HIS project (i.e., no business case was available).

This paper addresses the need for a more fine-grained framework for measuring (or evaluating) the creation of value in HIS settings. This is a response to Breese [9], who stated in a recent paper that there is a need for the development of theories regarding the creation of value "which are based on in-depth analysis of practice, and acknowledge and incorporate ambiguity and uncertainty." Several studies have explored value creation methods [e.g. 10, 11] characterized by the functionalist, rational model that so often dominates the project management community [12], and that, to some extent, lacks the complexity experienced in practice [9]. The paper provides a framework for measuring the IS public value realized in a healthcare setting and demonstrates how the framework was used in practice; thus, it shows the actual value created by a present framework of multidimensional value categories and identifies the key differences between governmental and for-profit organizations. Hence, it shows that different approaches to the measurement of value are needed.

The paper proceeds as follows. The next section reviews the literature regarding value in a public sector context. This is followed by a section describing the action research method applied and the concrete activities in the two action research cycles. We then present the actual creation of value in the project with the offset in an empirically derived structure of value and quality dimensions. We conclude with the implications for research and practice.

2   From IS Business Value to IS Public Value

The economic consequences of IS investments have been a recurring theme for many years (at least from the 1980's to the present) [13-15]. The terminology and notions vary when 'value,' 'benefit,' 'outcome' or 'worth' [16] are the terms used and linked to benefit realization management [9-11], value management [17] and beyond. Different semantic understandings are put forward [16]; some focus on financial and productivity measures [18], while others pay attention to both financial and non-financial measures, intangibles such as organizational capabilities [13] or strategic impact [19].

A fairly general understanding of value could be described as follows [20, p 140]:

[Value is] the relationship between the satisfaction of need and the resources used in achieving that satisfaction...Value is not absolute, but relative, and may be viewed differently by different parties in differing situations.

Value might be positive or negative for specific stakeholders depending upon the benefits or disadvantages that accrue to them. A more specific definition of IS business value is presented by Schryen [16, p 141]:

IS business value is the impact of investments in particular IS assets on the multidimensional performance and capabilities of economic entities at various levels, complemented by the ultimate meaning of performance in the economic environment.

The definition of IS business value presented above has multiple facets that have been elaborated further by several scholars in various settings [e.g. 21, 22]. We adapt the following classification in this paper [adapted from 6, 21]:

Table 1. Multidimensional value categories

Value category	*Description*
Strategic value	To change the nature of how a company competes
Informational value	To provide information for decision making in the company
Transactional value	To enable cost savings and support operational management
Transformational value	To change the organizational structure of a company as a result of the implemented IT systems that provide a greater capacity for further future benefit realization. This is typically a longer term effect (lag effect)
Unplanned/emergent value	A result of a transformation or change of process

These value categories underline the multidimensional nature of IS business value as suggested by Schryen [16]. Seddon et al. [22] elaborate on differentiating between short-term and long-term values. Short-term values are seen as being connected to the project level and tied to the immediate realization of an IT system while long-term values are connected to the organizational level.

Despite the very comprehensive literature that addresses IS business value [e.g. 13, 14, 16], it appears to be incomplete when it comes to public organizations. We therefore suggest an alternative concept for public organizations coined 'IS public value' instead of continuing to stretch or force the IS business value concept into the public domain [23].

IS public value research identifies key differences between governmental and for-profit organizations, which naturally leads to other means of evaluating the value of information systems in this sector. The differences are summarized in Table 2 below [24, 25]:

Table 2 shows that the public sector needs alternative measures, especially with regard to non-financial measures. However, the public sector might also subscribe to traditional financial measures such as cost savings from the optimization of processes [7]. The IS public value concept has formed the theoretical foundation for this study.

Table 2. Key differences between governmental and for-profit organizations

	For-profit sector	*Public sector (i.e., health-care)*
Normative goal	To maximize shareholders' wealth	Achieve social mission
Principal source of revenue	Sales of services and products	Tax appropriations
Measure of performance	Financial bottom line	Efficiency and effectiveness in achieving the mission
Key calculation of improvements	Find and exploit distinctive competence of firm by positioning it in product/service markets.	Find better ways to achieve mission

3   Methodology

We initiated an action research study in the Faroe Islands to fulfill the objective of creating value in the FHS's implementation of a HIS. The action research began in 2010 and is expected to come to an end spring 2014. Below, we introduce action research in our context, provide an overview of the research setting and present a detailed description of the actual research process.

3.1   Action Research

Action research involves close cooperation between practitioners and researchers to bring about change. It essentially consists of the analysis of a social situation followed by the introduction of changes and the evaluation of the effects [26]. The action research process can be defined as a number of learning cycles consisting of predefined stages; each starts with a diagnosis, a process that involves the joint (practitioner and researcher) identification of problems and their possible underlying causes. Action planning specifies the anticipated actions that may improve or solve the problems identified and action taking refers to the implementation of those specified actions. Evaluation is the assessment of the intervention and learning is the reflection on the activities and outcomes (adapted from [27]).

Action research has become widely accepted [26] and work has been done to conceptualize the approach to enable understanding of and enhance the different elements of action research practice (problem-solving and research activities) [28]. In two action research cycles, we diagnosed, planned and executed change. The final part of each action research cycle was the evaluation of the problem solving based on both process and outcome. Our action research is theoretically premised on an abductive inference style [28] as the project was initiated by a theoretical discussion regarding the obtainment of value from the implementation of a HIS but challenged and enlightened through observations from the case [21, 22].

3.2   Research Setting

The Faroe Islands are a self-governing territory within the Kingdom of Denmark with approximately 48,000 inhabitants. The FHS is a relatively small organization consisting of three hospitals and 27 general practices (GPs). In 2005, the FHS began the implementation of an integrated HIS covering hospitals and GPs. The project faced many problems during its first years, even to the point that discussions were held considering the termination of the project, particularly due to the high costs that had been incurred (financial as well as personal) and doubts regarding the value realization [29]. However, the project continued and 530 healthcare professionals are currently using the HIS, which covers all areas of the hospitals and GPs.

Based on the initial implementation process, an evaluation report was prepared that drew on DeLone and McLean's success model [30]. The users were satisfied with the solution, which greatly supported their clinical work, but no initiatives aimed at harvesting the potential value had been planned or implemented [31]. Thus, it was concluded that more needed to be done to obtain proper value and payoff.

3.3   Research Process

The action research project was initiated in the fall of 2010 and is expected to come to an end spring 2014. The present part of the project, which focused on how to structure and realize value in a (public) healthcare setting, was prompted by management's wishes to realize value from the previously implemented HIS-system. The researchers have had a high degree of interaction with FHS [32] and have used a variety of research methods related to diagnosing, action planning, action taking, and evaluation and learning. As a result of meetings with staff and observations of the processes in action, it was determined that the first obstacle was to actually *define* what 'value' means in the present setting and how to actually *achieve* it based on the limited transformational capacity in FHS. It was then decided that the Good Stroke Process would be replicated to *explore* and *demonstrate* the potential for value realization at the medical ward.

During the first action research cycle, it became increasingly difficult to distinguish between the information system (HIS) and the associated working processes; they are like Siamese twins [33] with regard to value creation. Also, it came to our attention that the creation of value in healthcare has a much broader scope than mere financial value [13] and can be divided into three main areas: (1) professional quality (e.g., mortality rate after six months), (2) organizational quality (e.g., length of stay in hospital), and (3) patient-perceived quality (e.g., level of information about the course of disease).

The first workshops helped an understanding to emerge among the healthcare professionals of the need to document the present stroke process in detail. During the very detailed discussions of the process, several KPIs were identified to establish a baseline for the measurement of future improvements and a search for the KPIs was performed.

In the second action research cycle, we observed that the new HIS made it much easier to collect and calculate KPIs, thus making the measurement of improvements possible. Many KPI candidates emerged during the analysis. While the first cycle of the project identified three value dimensions: professional quality (the clinical treatment of diseases and cure – effectiveness), organizational quality (the optimal use of resources – efficiency), and patient perceptions of quality (customer/patient satisfaction), the second cycle of the project revealed that there was a lack of consideration of the "voice" of the employees. Based on the analysis described above, a baseline of observations and measurements was prepared by FHS staff under the supervision of the researchers, changes in processes were realized and, during the final part of action research cycle two, the measurement and collection of other data was repeated and evaluated against the baseline.

Table 3. Summary Table of Research Cycles

Cycle	Goal	Learning
First action research cycle	Define value measures	Value in healthcare has broader scope than mere financial value
		Understanding of need to document processes
Second action research cycle	Achieve value	New HIS made it easier to collect KPI
		The lack of the voice of the employees revealed
		Framework for IS value in healthcare setting established

The results were presented and discussed during a series of workshops held on the Faroe Islands in October 2013 that included the participation of staff from wards, management and members of the HIS-implementation organization.

4   Value Creation from the Good Stroke Process

During the two action research process cycles, which are mentioned above, we have been challenged in discussing IS public value at FHS. The first action research cycle revealed three value dimensions (benefit areas): (1) professional quality, (2) organizational quality, and (3) patient perceived quality. These quality dimensions are based on the Danish Healthcare Quality Model [34] and can be linked to specific measures.

However an additional dimension to the three abovementioned was found during the second action research. The healthcare professionals (nurses, doctors, therapists and secretaries) showed an understanding of quality/value which is not covered by the three dimensions 'Employee Perceive Quality' was added.

Fairly late in second cycle we decided also to include learning as an important value dimension due to the fact that projects are an arena for learning [35, 36], which is of future value to organizations although typically with a lag effect.

The more or less empirically derived dimensions are mentioned below:

Table 4. Empirically derived quality/value dimensions

Empirical derived dimension	Example
Professional quality	Mortality rate after 30 days for stroke patients
Organizational quality	Length of stay at hospital
Patient perceived quality	Level of information about course of disease
Employee Perceived Quality	The satisfaction of the employees, i.e., do they believe that the process is well taken care of
Learning	The capability to work in cross-functional teams

Table 4 indicates five fairly broad areas which all can be related to IS public value in HIS settings. The following sections will describe these five dimensions in more detail and present selected measures for these dimensions.

4.1   Professional Quality

The measures for professional quality are based on indicators from The Regions Clinical Quality Development Program [37]. These indicators have been defined and produced by a group of professional clinicians representing the public hospital owners and the Danish Government. At Danish hospitals these indicators are obligatory. The hospitals at The Faroe Islands were not using the standardized indicators for measuring the quality in different settings and different diseases as they are not obligated to, but to gain more easy compatible data it was decided to use the indicators for stroke patients for measuring the professional quality in the project. Only some of the indicators were relevant in the actual setting. In table 5 a subset of indicators for the treatment of stroke patients is shown. More indicators are in play in the project, but the validation of the values has not been completed yet.

The year of 2011 is defined as a baseline for our measures. The baseline values have been calculated through an audit of the patient records. Most of the values were picked up from the text based electronic patient system. In the beginning of 2012 more features were added to the HIS system, which means that several templates were set up in the HIS so the registrations of specific events – e.g. assessment done by the physiotherapist (indicator 3 in Table 5) - were more user friendly and precise.

We faced different challenges in the work with clinical data from the electronic patient system. One was the data quality. For example proper registration of different events in regards of time; it could be the time registered for the physiotherapist assessment. Is it the time for the registration or is the time for the assessment? Another challenge was access to the data in the system. Did we get the right data from the database? It is an important question due to the fact that the data model for the system is not documented.

In accordance to those two challenges we put a lot of efforts into the data validation. One important initiative in that respect is presenting and discussing the data with the relevant group of clinicians.

Four of the indicators in Table 5 are process indicators, dealing with treatment and care processes. The last one is an outcome indicator, the only one in our measures. It deals with mortality, and measures the proportion of stroke patients who die within 30 days after admission. This value is interesting as it is below the limit value in 2012 and 2013. We are in the process of trying to get an explanation of that circumstance.

There is a positive trend in the proportion of patients who were admitted to a stroke unit (indicator 1 in Table 5), but still (in 2013) it is below the limit value of 90%. The reason for the positive trend is that in the beginning of 2012 one specific unit has been set up as a stroke unit

The second indicator in the table, the proportion of patients getting blood dilute pills shows values below the limit value and indicates and improves process for this area.

Table 5. Measures for a subset of indicators of the professional quality

Indicator	Type Standard/	Base-line/ 2011	2012	2013, until mid-October
1. Proportion of patients who are admitted to a stroke unit no later than the 2nd day of hospitalization	Process >= 90%	28%	61%	80%
2. Proportion of patients with acute ischemic stroke without atrial fibrillation where treatment with antiplatelet inhibitor is initiated no later than the 2nd day of hospitalization	Process >= 95%	58%	91%	87%
3. Proportion of patients who undergo a CT/MR scan on the first day of hospitalization	Process >= 80%	**79%**	Missing	Missing
4. Proportion of patients assessed by a physiotherapist no later than the 2nd day of hospitalization in order to clarify of the extent and type of rehabilitation and time for initiation of physiotherapy	Process >= 90%	45%	Missing	Missing
5. Proportion of patients who die within 30 days of admission for acute stroke	Outcome <= 15%	Missing	8%	7%

4.2 Organizational Quality

We have focused on one main indicator for the organizational quality, which is the length of the hospital stay. We have the data, but still need to do data validation. There is big dispersion in the data because a small number of patients stay a very long time at the hospital for different reasons. Therefore it is needed to make a journal audit and make adjustments in order to give a suitable and detailed picture of the length of stay in hospital for stroke patients.

4.3   Patient Perceived Quality

To contribute to the baseline and identify areas for improvement, interviews were held with two stroke patients. The interviews showed that the patients were quite happy with their experiences. One patient said: *"I have received good information and I am very satisfied with the stay, I have to admit that…"* (Patient 1, 60-year-old male, in his fifth month of hospitalization). We have not been able to conduct interviews with patients after the different initiatives for the stroke patients were implemented.

4.4   Employee Perceived Quality

Two surveys were conducted in September 2011 and in September 2013. They were based on a questionnaire and completed by the involved health professionals. The number of participants was respectively 24 in 2011 and 25 in 2013[1]. The questionnaire can be seen in appendix A. The questions in the questionnaire were related to informational and communicational issues.

At the same time a number of interviews were completed with the heads of the departments involved. The subject was the work processes related to the treatment of stroke patients and the collaboration between the different professional groups. In the interviews conducted in 2013 questions related to the project process were added because it was relevant to discuss learning from the process itself.

The data from 2011 from both investigations constitutes the baseline for the voice of the clinical staff. In figure 1 the answers from to two questionnaires are depicted. There is a positive tendency in the answers from 2011 to 2013. The average for answers on all 16 question is a bit below the neutral value of 4 in 2011, while in 2013 the value is very close to 5, thus above the neutral value. The difference between the average in 2011 and 2013 on all questions is 1.2 which is a significant difference.

The questions can be divided into groups. The group with the biggest gap between 2011 and 2013 can be labeled 'Well formulated goals and plans for stroke patients' (question B6, B7, B8 and B9). The smallest difference in answers is related to 'Use of data from other profession groups' (question B13). Here we see a high score above 5 in 2011 as well as in 2013. This means that employees are and were satisfied with the data they can get from other profession groups. These data are and were available through the HIS.

---

[1]   The survey has not been conducted as a pairwise study. Some of the respondents are identical; every answer is given anonymous. In 2011 nearly 80% of the population (all clinicians participating in the treatment and care of stroke patients) participated and in 2013 100% of the population participated.

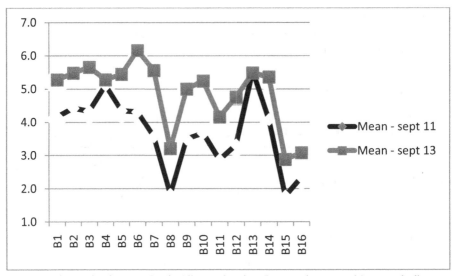

Answers have to be given on a 7-point Likert scale, where 7 = strongly agree and 1 = strongly disagree.

Fig. 1. The voice of the clinical staff related to informational and communicational issues in 2011 and 2013. Exact questions are given in annex A.

4.5   Learning

The project has created a lot of learning, especially with respect to the process of running a cross-functional project. It was a new way of working for the employees from the different departments. The project manager recognized that the success of the whole initiative (working with this type of interdisciplinary tasks) was caused by the fact that it was set up and completed as a project with a steering committee, a project group and project manager:

"The first things you should clarify is: What you wish to achieve, And if you are approaching it with interdisciplinary and not mono-disciplinarily: Who is in charge?, That there is an action behind it whenever you do something...I think that it has helped that a steering committee, project group and project manager was appointed. Otherwise it would never have worked." and *"I feel that the project has been understood. It has been supported which has been great"* (Project manager).

Supported by the executive consultant:

"There are some things that you wish to improve because the patient is not feeling well. We are not there yet, but we have come a long way. But if we agree now that we will give this to [the board] and the management group will give this to day-to-day operations. Then we need some kind of management of this, which we have discussed a bit. We have discussed checklists and regular management meetings,

where we will address if there are any issues where something is insufficient, is there something we need to be updated on etc. You could say that we took ownership back then (when the project started) and we are holding on to this." (Executive consultant).

But other issues were also present on the learning agenda. The usefulness of clear goals and plans for the treatment of stroke patients is recognized by the clinicians working with stroke patients.

"Well I think the difference is that now it is a bit more established in terms of goals and plans etc. All patients are now being taken care of and we try to set goals for all patients." (Therapist).

The measures set up for the project were also addressed in the interview with the project manager, who was not satisfied with the measures and indicators set up for the professional quality. In her opinion it only covered a limited part of the professional quality. She argues that it is important also to have measures regarding life quality for the stroke patients:

"We have NIP-measurements [the indicators in table 5]. And that is in principle what they are interested in, the board. And every aspect of quality apart from that, we have actually not set any measures for. I believe we should have other measurements as well. It cannot be right that the only measure you have is whether people die or not. That is not quality in my world. You should measure life quality and find out if they get the information needed. You should, in my opinion, move towards this. I know it is hard to measure something like this on patients. They were just super pleased" (Project manager).

Defining value in relation to organizational change never ends. It is important to be open-minded in order to pick up or plan harvesting new benefits in a never ending process when implementing it-projects or other organizational change. The project manager recognizes this and is ready for the challenges related to emergent value.

5   Discussion and Concluding Remarks

During the action research project it has been shown how value in a public sector HIS context can be conceptualized and selected actual measurements of baseline values have been provided (2011). Values was measured in 2012 and 2013 after the establishing the baseline showing how value were created by the use of the newly implemented IHIS thus fulfilling one of the objectives of the action research project In this section we will discuss the empirical derived quality/value dimensions using the structure of multidimensional value categories presented earlier in the paper.

Table 6. IS Value in a Healthcare Setting

Value Category	Professional quality	Organizational quality	Patient-perceived quality	Employee Perceived Quality	Learning
Strategic	(1)	+	+	+	+
Informational	+	+	(3)	+	+
Transactional	+	(2)	+	+	+
Transformational	+	+	+	+	(4)
Unplanned/emergent	+	+	+	(5)	+

Table 6 indicates how IS value can be understood using a two dimensional structure consisting of measured qualities and category of values. For illustrative purposes we have described one example from each cross of rows and columns below following the structure of the Value Categories.

Strategic value (1) can in the context of The Good Stroke Process be related to the main objective of FHS to provide high *professional quality* treatment of patients. In our case one of the measurements was the 'proportion of patients who are admitted to a stroke unit no later than the 2nd day of hospitalization' which showed improvement by rising from 28% to 80% during the project.

Informational value (2) can, naturally, be exemplified by the obvious fact that the structuring on what to measure also created possibility to actually do it and hence provide information for decision making in the FHS. Another example is the *Patient Perceived Quality* where interviews indicated a fairly high satisfaction which was highly appreciated by the ward management and used to support self-confidence among staff.

Transactional value (3) was shown by addressing *organizational quality* when measuring the 'length of stay in the hospital' which by the FHS management is seen as an important enabler of cost saving and supporting operational management. Quite interesting this was one, out of many, examples on how difficult it is to agree on concrete definitions due to difficult traditions, procedures and possibilities in the same organizational system of FHS as the project could not provide reliable figures for this indicator.

Transformational value (4) has been achieved by the *learning* done in the FHS and HIS organization. As such FHS is now in a better position of facilitating new IS value creation projects in the future.

Unplanned/Emergent value (5), which is result of a transformation or change process, was observed when the need to include *employee perceived quality* came up hence highlighting the importance and potential of including the voice of the employees in the IS value creation process.

The present research indicates the need and the many challenges to conceptualize both a more fined grained framework for IS public value creation and to assure the actual measurements in a HIS setting. We suggest that the presented framework can be used as a foundation for further research of IS public value in the given context but acknowledges the limitations and need for refinement and challenging of findings in related contexts thus coming closer to the call by Breese [9].

Acknowledgments. The project was done under and with support from Center for IT Project Management and Innovation at Aarhus University and support from the Faroese Ministry of Healthcare. We are thankful for the open doors, friendly interaction and professional discussions provided by the clinical staff (doctors, nurses and therapists at the medical ward) and staff from the HIS unit.

References

1. Devaraj, S., Kohli, R.: Information technology payoff in the health-care industry: A longitudinal study. Journal of Management Information Systems 16(4), 41–67 (2000)
2. Friedman, C., Wyatt, J.: Evaluation methods in medical informatics, vol. 19. Springer, New York (1997)
3. Murray, C.J.L., Frenk, J.: Ranking 37th - Measuring the Performance of the U.S. Health Care System. New England Journal of Medicine 362(2), 98–99 (2011)
4. Reeves, D., et al.: Analysis: How to identify when a performance indicator has run its course. BMJ 340, c1717 (2011)
5. Bend, J.: Public value and e-health. Institute for Public Policy Research (2004)
6. Sapountzis, S., et al.: Realising benefits in primary healthcare infrastructures. Facilities 27(3), 74–87 (2009)
7. Cole, M., Parston, G.: Unlocking Public Value - A New Model for Achieving High Performance in Public Service Organizations. John Wiley & Sons, Hoboken (2006)
8. Coats, D., Passmore, E.: Public Value: The Next Steps in Public Service Reform. The Work Foundation (2008)
9. Breese, R.: Benefits realisation management: Panacea or false dawn? International Journal of Project Management 30(3), 341–351 (2012)
10. Bradley, G.: Benefit Realisation Management, 2nd edn. Gower, Farnham (2010)
11. Ward, J., Daniel, E.: Benefits management: How to Increase the Business Value of Your IT Projects. Wiley, West Sussex (2012)
12. Morris, P.W.G., Pinto, J.K., Söderlund, J.: Introduction: Towards the Third Wave of Project Management. In: Morris, P.W.G., Pinto, J.K., Söderlund, J. (eds.) The Oxford Handbook of Project Management, pp. 1–11. Oxford University Press, Oxford (2011)
13. Kohli, R., Grover, V.: Business Value of IT: An Essay on Expanding Research Directions to Keep up with the Times. Journal of the Association for Information Systems 9(1), 23–28, 30–34, 36–39 (2008)
14. Melville, N., Kraemer, K., Gurbaxani, V.: Information Technology and Organizational Performance: An Integrative Model of IT Business Value. MIS Quarterly 28(2), 283–322 (2004)
15. Parker, M., Benson, R., Trainor, H.: Information economics: linking business performance to information technology. Prentice Hall, Englewood Cliffs (1988)

16. Schryen, G.: Revisiting IS business value research: what we already know, what we still need to know, and how we can get there. Eur. J. Inf. Syst. 22(2), 139–169 (2013)
17. Association for Project Management, APM Body of Knowledge. 6 ed, Buckinghamshire: Association for Project Management (2012)
18. Brynjolfsson, E., Hitt, L.M.: Computing Productivity: Firm-Level Evidence. The Review of Economics and Statistics 85(4), 793–808 (2000)
19. Irani, Z.: Information systems evaluation: navigating through the problem domain. Information & Management 40(1), 11–24 (2002)
20. European Standard 12973-2000, Value Management (2000)
21. Gregor, S., et al.: The transformational dimension in the realization of business value from information technology. The Journal of Strategic Information Systems 15(3), 249–270 (2006)
22. Seddon, P.B., Calvert, C., Yang, S.: A Multi-Project Model of Key Factors Affecting Organizational Benefits From Enterprise Systems. MIS Quarterly 34(2), 305-A11 (2010)
23. Svejvig, P., Schlichter, B.R., Andersen, P.E.R.: From Business IT Value To Public IT Value – An Action Research Study of Healthcare in the Faroe Islands. In: MCIS 2012, Proceedings. Paper 18. Guimarães, Portugal (2012),
   http://aisel.aisnet.org/mcis2012/18
24. Moore, M.H.: Managing for Value: Organizational Strategy in For-Profit, Nonprofit, and Governmental Organizations. Nonprofit and Voluntary Sector Quarterly 29(suppl. 1), 183–208 (2000)
25. Moore, M.H.: Creating public value: Strategic management in government. Harvard University Press, Cambridge (1995)
26. Baskerville, R., Myers, M.D.: Special issue on action research in information systems: making is research relevant to practice–foreword. MIS Quarterly 28(3), 329–335 (2004)
27. Myers, M.D.: Qualitative Research in Business & Management. Sage Publications, London (2009)
28. Mathiassen, L., Chiasson, M., Germonprez, M.: Style Composition in Action Research Publication. MIS Quarterly 36(2), 347–363 (2012)
29. Schlichter, B.R.: Development of trust during large scale system implementation. Journal of Cases on Information Technology 12(2), 1–15 (2010)
30. DeLone, W.H., McLean, E.R.: The DeLone and McLean Model of Information Systems Success: A Ten-year Update. Journal of Management Information Systems 19(4), 9–30 (2003)
31. Andersen, P.E.R., et al.: Effektvurdering af EPJ/THS i det færøske sundhedsvæsen. Aarhus School of Business: Aarhus (2010)
32. Svejvig, P., Andersen, P.E.R.: Setting the stage for benefit realization of healthcare IS: The voice of health professionals. In: OASIS Pre-ICIS Workshop, Shanghai (2011)
33. Alter, S.: The work system method for understanding information systems and information system research. Communications of the Association for Information Systems 9(1), 90–104 (2002)
34. Regions, D: Indicators and Standards in The Danish National Indicator Project (2009),
   http://www.nip.dk/files/Subsites/NIP/Om%20NIP/About%20NIP/DN
   IP_Acute_Stroke_idicatorform_20100820.pdf (cited March 18, 2012)
35. Hällgren, M., Wilson, T.L.: Mini-muddling: learning from project plan deviations. Journal of Workplace Learning 19(2), 92–107 (2007)
36. Packendorff, J.: Inquiring into the temporary organization: New directions for project management research. Scandinavian Journal of Management 11(4), 319–333 (1995)

37. Apopleksiregister, D.: Indikatorskema for Dansk Apopleksiregister (October 01, 2013), http://www.kcks-vest.dk/files/Subsites/KCKS%20vest/ De%20Kliniske%20Databaser/Apopleksi/ Apopleksi_indikatorskema_fra%201%20%20september% 202013_F_26072013.pdf (cited November 20, 2013)

Appendix A: Questions from the questionnaire completed by the clinicians in September 2011 and in September 2013.

Answers were given on a 7-point Likert scale, where 7 = strongly agree and 1 = strongly disagree.

B.1 I find that I have the necessary information about the patient in connection with **receiving** the patient.

B.2 I find that I have the necessary information about the patient in connection to **treatment** (during hospitalisation)

B.3 I find that I have the necessary information about the patient in connection to **caretaking** (during hospitalisation)

B.4 I find that I have the necessary information about the patient in connection with **discharging** the patient.

B.5 I feel that my knowledge about the disease stroke is good and sufficient enough to treat and nurse patients suffering from this disease.

B.6 I find that there is a well-formulated plan for what acute precautionary measures and examinations should happen to patients with stroke symptoms upon arrival on the ward.

B.7 I find that there is a well-formulated plan for what should happen in terms of treatment and caretaking of the stroke patient in connection to hospitalisation on the ward.

B.8 I find that there is a well-formulated plan for the stroke patient after being discharged from the hospital.

B.9 I feel well-informed about the goals and plans for treatment of stroke patients.

B.10 I find that an individual care- and treatment plan is formulated for every single stroke patient.

B.11 I experience that the entire course of treatment of stroke patients is well managed and coordinated.

B.12 I experience the treatment of stroke patients as being good.

B.13 I find that I have good use of other profession groups' records about stroke patients in my own treatment of patients.

B.14 I experience that I can give patients continuous good information about treatment and caretaking.

B.15 I find that the physical surroundings are good and appropriate in connection to treatment and caretaking of stroke patients.

B.16 I find that the ward is sufficiently staffed to treat and take care of stroke patients.

The Challenges of Creativity in Software Organizations

Frank Ulrich[1] and Shegaw Anagaw Mengiste[2]

[1] Department of Computer Science, Aalborg University, Denmark
frank@cs.aau.dk
[2] IT University of Copenhagen, Denmark
sanm@itu.dk

Abstract. Managing creativity has proven to be one of the most important drivers in software development and use. The continuous changing market environment drives companies like Google, SAS Institute and LEGO to focus on creativity as an increasing necessity when competing through sustained innovations. However, creativity in the information systems (IS) environment is a challenge for most organizations that is primarily caused by not knowing how to strategize creative processes in relation to IS strategies, thus, causing companies to act ad hoc in their creative endeavors. In this paper, we address the organizational challenges of creativity in software organizations. Grounded in a previous literature review and a rigorous selection process, we identify and present a model of seven important factors for creativity in software organizations. From these factors, we identify 21 challenges that software organizations experience when embarking on creative endeavors and transfer them into a comprehensive framework. Using an interpretive research study, we further study the framework by analyzing how the challenges are integrated in 27 software organizations. Practitioners can use this study to gain a deeper understanding of creativity in their own business while researchers can use the framework to gain insight while conducting interpretive field studies of managing creativity.

1   Introduction

Creativity has inherently become an important part of software development and use because the creative mindset is the pre-requirement in any innovation effort [23]. As Florida and Goodnight [19;131] noted: "The creative economy is here to stay, and companies that figure out how to manage for creativity will have a crucial advantage in the ever-increasing competition for global talent". Successful IS development companies such as Google and SAS have incorporated creativity as an important part of their strategies to create lasting innovations by creating creative environments, clear incentives for their employees, and a culture of social creativity where the contributions from each employee become important [19, 30]. Companies like LEGO have successfully created a business model that involves creative interactions with their customers through collaborative virtual worlds and online communities [45]. However, as Couger [15;230] argued, creativity is often treated as a "dangerous opportunity" that requires leadership and willingness to take risks. Hence, creative endeavors

B. Bergvall-Kåreborn and P.A. Nielsen (Eds.): TDIT 2014, IFIP AICT 429, pp. 16–34, 2014.

are not always equal to massive success, and organizations will often experience organizational challenges when embarking on creative endeavors [15].

To understand the challenges of managing creativity in a software setting, we define software organizations as information systems (IS) organizations, information systems development (ISD) organizations, and clone organizations (clone). In this paper, we treat IS organizations as those that use IT as a strategic driver for business operations and must be creative when implementing existing technologies, exploring new business opportunities, and enhancing their existing business in a competitive market [15]. ISD organizations are those that develop IT for others and must be creative when designing and creating innovative products or services [13]. Hence, IS and ISD organizations use time and effort in creating novel ideas for new market innovations to strategize their efforts for optimizing organizational performance, gaining competitive advantages, and attracting talented employees [19]. In between IS and ISD organizations, there are clone organizations. These are a mix between the IS and ISD organization because they develop IT as ISDs, and at the same time use this IT for internal and external business operations as an IS organization would. Regardless of the typology, however, software organizations are driven by continuous innovation to obtain and maintain their competitive advantages. As Couger clearly indicated, creativity has proven to be an important driver for IS, ISD, and clone organizations [15]. Moreover, creativity enhancing software has already proved useful for companies that are unrelated to IS or ISDs. As Rose [48] explained, creativity enhancing software have been developed for businesses in the areas of art, medicine, and chemistry. Likewise, creativity techniques originally developed for non-IS development have proven useful when software organizations are developing or exploring novel ideas for innovative software [15].

We wrote this paper upon a previous literature review [40]. This paper is a contingency of the original review where we address the subject of managing creativity challenges in software organizations. This paper differs from the original review by including literature we excluded from the original review. We examined the literature through a systematic process and provided interpretations to create a new framework of creativity management in software organizations. Moreover, we supplemented the literature with practical experiences collected through multiple empirical sources.

We structured the paper as follows: We initially provide a short research perspective for the study. Then we explain our research strategy, collection methods, and analysis. Next, we provide initial data analysis and describe in detail 21 challenges that software organizations experience when embarking on creative endeavors. We divide these challenges into seven different factors of creativity management and add our empirical findings. Finally, we collect our findings into a comprehensive framework for software organizations and explain how our study can help research and be deployed into practice.

2   Research Perspective

Understanding creativity in software organizations has since the early 1990's been a subject of IS research. This research surrounds the understanding of human-computer interaction [49, 59], proper training of individuals or groups [16], and techniques for facilitating creativity in the organizational setting [14, 15]. Moreover, the organizational environment's influence over creativity [5, 15] and creating working strategies for creativity [61] have also proven important when enhancing creativity in software organizations.

Rhodes [46] suggested a framework of four interconnected components influencing creativity. These consist of press (environment), person (individuals and groups), product (creative results), and process (training and management) - each explaining aspects of creativity in the organizational context. We follow Rhodes' [46] track by examining a similar framework of interconnected factors and their underlying challenges.

The general consensus on creativity is that it is individuals' or groups' ability to come up with novel and useful ideas or solutions to problem [3, 4, 14, 15]. However, there is somewhat of a misconception of what a creative individual or group is in a software setting. Innovative software individuals or teams are typically viewed as either software designers or system developers [6, 13, 31]. Nonetheless, creativity in IS or ISDs is a conjoined effort by the entire organization and consists of many different factors and roles beyond the traditional software designer or system developers, as technology users can be equally creative [42]. Creative software individuals or groups can consist of customers, system developers, software designers, business analysts, portfolio managers, marketing managers, web designers, university researchers, computer and traditional artists, sourcing experts, project managers, CIOs, security experts, network analysts, customers, users, SPI specialists, etc. They all contribute with their own creative ideas for innovations to happen in the software organization, and they all use different practices, where creativity is needed and beneficial. Each profile must be taken into consideration when exploring the challenges of creativity in the software organization. Hence, our perspective on creativity management is the ability to understand the creative potential of the entire organization, by knowing how each organizational factor contributes to creating novel ideas, to identify them, to implement them, and finally to commercialize them into working innovations. This paper revolves around these factors of organizational creativity by examining those challenges that software organizations experience when they embark on creative endeavors. As such, our research subject is focused on the organizational aspect of creativity and not a study of creativity in a specific software setting (e.g. [63]. Hence, our research approach is guided by this overall question for inquiry: "What are the challenges of creativity in software organizations?"

3   Research Approach

To answer our research question, we used an adaptive multi-strategy approach [35] by providing interpretations from both quantitative and qualitative sources. According to Layder [35] the multi-strategy research approach offers several advantages over traditional research, as it increases the strength, density, and validity of the research by incorporating many data sources and strategies to approach the research subject, which enables the researcher to create more "robust" theoretical perspectives [35]. Hence, we divided the data collection between a survey in 27 software organizations and six interviews with employees of two of the organizations that participated in the survey.

We constructed the survey around a cross-sectional research design [8, 54, 62], as the survey is consistent with more than one case and is fixed to a single point in time [8]. Moreover, we used a systematic and standardized approach for collecting data and examining relationships between variables [8]. This approach enabled us to view the integration of creativity management practices in software organizations and their relation to the literature reviewed by Müller and Ulrich [40].

For the interviews, we used an embedded case study design [62] by collecting data from different subunits in the organizations (e.g. departments, projects or management levels). This helped us to analyze different management perspectives in correlation to the challenges and factors from the literature.

Analytically, we worked interpretively both in our use of theory and in our data collection, whereby the theory and data played an equally vital role throughout the study when providing interpretations. For the interpretative approach, we used Walsham [55–57], who emphasized collecting and interpreting key concepts from the participants' social reality. However, when creating new interpretations, we analyzed all the data with a "healthy skepticism" [56]. This approach enabled us to support new ideas and concepts created during the analysis of the data provided by triangulating the findings [35] from the two data sources, which we transferred into a framework for creativity management at end of the paper. Moreover, these interpretations make the study highly inductive, as we locate management practices from the empirical data, rather than testing existing theoretical frameworks.

3.1   Data Collection

We collected the data through a survey of 31 managers and business analysts in 27 Danish software organizations. In addition, we conducted interviews with the CIO, a project manager, and a business analyst from the IT-department in a local Danish municipality, and the CIO, the head of innovation, and the head of product management in GameSim, a medium sized subunit of a much larger private and international organization. GameSim specializes in high tech computer game development for the private sector. The participants from the interviews also participated in the survey - listed as cases 1-3 and 21-24 in Table 1.

Table 1. Participating organizations in the survey

Case	Organizational size	Public / private organization	Type of organization
1-3	Medium	Private	Computer game developer (same organization)
4	Very large	Public	Local municipality
5	Very large	Public	Local municipality
6	Very large	Public	Government organization
7	Medium	Private	E-learning software developer
8	Very large	Public	University college
9	Medium	Private	AV equipment distributor
10	Very large	Public	Local municipality
11	Medium	Public	Knowledge organization in IT-research
12	Very large	Private	IT-infrastructure developer
13	Medium	Private	Administration software developer

Table 1. (*Continued*)

14	Very large	Private	Major international software and hardware developer
15	Very large	Private	International process equipment engineering company
16	Medium	Private	Medical device data systems developer
17	Small	Private	Medical devise developer
18	Medium	Private	Hardware and software reseller and developer
19	Very large	Public	Local municipality
20	Very large	Private	Major internet service provider
21-	Very large	Public	Local municipality (same organization)
24			
25	Large	Private	Healthcare software developer
26	Very large	Public	Local municipality
27	Small	Private	E-learning software developer
28	Very large	Public	Government organization
29	Very large	Public	University college
30	Very large	Private	Major information systems developer
31	Large	Private	International developer of labeling equipment and software

Organizational size = Small (1-9 employees), Medium (10-99 employees), Large (100-499 employees), Very Large (501+ employees)

For conducting the survey, we used the social networking site Linkedin to locate participants. As Table 1 demonstrates, representatives from several types of software organizations chose to participate in the survey. In total, 38 chose to participate and complete the survey. However, we removed seven participants due to lack of credentials in the software sector or for not providing personal or company information.

We asked each participant to rate the integration of creativity management within the underlying challenges of the seven factors. In addition, participants were asked to provide information about their organization size (very large, large, medium, small), type of organization (private or public), management level they represent (CIO, project manager, or business analyst), IS use (developing for others, developing for themselves, or using IS developed by others). Moreover, we asked them if their organization uses IS to support creativity (use specialized IS, do not use IS for creativity, or use IS for creativity that is not designed for the purpose).

We asked each participant to rate the integration of creativity management within the underlying challenges of the seven factors. In addition, participants were asked to provide information about their organization size (very large, large, medium, small), type of organization (private or public), management level they represent (CIO, project manager, or business analyst), IS use (developing for others, developing for themselves, or using IS developed by others). Moreover, we asked them if their organization uses IS to support creativity (use specialized IS, do not use IS for creativity, or use IS for creativity that is not designed for the purpose).

3.2   Data Analysis

We analyzed the survey using SurveyXact, by conducting measurements on data frequency and the average distribution of data. Moreover, we calculated cross references between average distributions of data through Excel. We analyzed the survey results to establish casual relationships [54] between the factors of creativity and their challenges and the other groups of variables. These variables are organizational size, type of organization, management level, IS use, and use of creativity-enhancing software.

We analyzed the interviews using section transcription by providing in-depth notes for each interview [8]. We labeled each note with time, subject, and respondent, which provided a quick overview of the combined interview data. This approach enabled us to collect relevant key concepts when we interpreted and triangulated the survey and interview data.

4   Mapping the Challenges

To operationalize the challenges within the technology, environmental, institutional, individual, group, leadership, and external factors, we first identified each challenge by examining the existing literature. Second, we placed each challenge within a complementary factor. Specifically the work of several researchers [5, 13, 15, 19, 22] worked as guidelines, as they each provide a normative emphasis on the challenges of creativity in software organizations or provide emphasis on creativity challenges applicable to any organization regardless of internal structure or commercial output. However, most creativity challenges in the literature were descriptively operationalized by rigorously reviewing each challenge after reoccurrence in the literature and adding their normative guidelines to our in-depth description of each challenge. Finally, we connected the theoretical finding with our empirical findings. Hence, to clarify our observations from the survey and the interviews, we initially present our preliminary data findings in section 4.1 below. We then review the literature for each factor and connect our data findings in the subsequent sections for each factor.

4.1   Preliminary Data Findings

The survey elaborates how different managers in Danish software organizations have integrated the diverse challenges related to creativity in their organizations. The data collected in the survey demonstrates that the average integration score across the challenges is just below average. Their integration is aligned with the comments from survey and interview data. Our data demonstrated that Danish software organizations still face a range of challenges when integrating creativity management practices in their organizations. In addition, 45% (14) of the managers and business developers participating were within public organizations and 55% (17) were within private organizations. Moreover, there is little difference between private and public organizations when integrating the different creativity management challenges. The difference between the combined replies from private and public organizations is 3.6%. Furthermore, when viewing employment among the participants, 23% (7) of the participants were employed within top management as CEOs or CIOs, whereas, 64% (20) were employed as mid-level managers such as project managers or department heads. Finally, 13% (4) were not employed within management, but were business developers. This finding demonstrates that the survey provided wide perspective within public and private software organizations.

In the area of use and deployment of IS, 26% (8) of the respondents answered that their organization developed IS for other organizations (ISD organizations). Also, 48% (15) deployed IS as a part of their daily business, but did not develop it themselves (ISD organizations), and 26% (8) deployed IS as a part of their daily business and developed the systems themselves (clone organizations). Furthermore, clone organizations were 16.7% less likely to integrate management practices to deal with challenges in creativity than IS organizations, and equally 16.7% less likely to do it than ISD organizations. This finding demonstrates two different possibilities: ISD and IS organizations have a higher need for managing creativity; they are more likely to be driven by communities of creative practices as they are more engaged in creative behavior on a daily basis.

To our surprise, only one of the organizations had deployed specialized creativity support systems, and 29% (9) used IS for supporting creativity that were not designed for that purpose. In comparison, 65% (20) did not use any form of IS driven creativity support. One did not know if their organization used it or not. The fact that the majority who used IS driven creativity support have chosen to use existing systems to support it is somewhat strange, because specialized systems could provide better possibilities. However, when interviewing the CIO of the local municipality the reason became apparent. As he stated:

> "After an innovation management course we conducted for the managers in the municipality, we deployed a specialized tool to get people to work with idea development. However, people only partially used it because it was not a part of their daily workflow and they had to remember to use it. When people got back to work, they started to go back to use Outlook instead."

Hence, the reason for using existing systems to support creativity may be due to employees' and customers' preference to be creatively engaged in systems they use in their daily work activities.

4.2   The Technology Factor

Technology makes information and communication flow between stakeholders and is an important factor in organizational creativity [61]. When managers seek to increase organizational creativity, they can deploy computerized tools to support creative processes in organizations. Greene [24] demonstrated several characteristics of creativity software tools including: being exploratory in a sandbox mode; being engaged with content to advance learning and discovery; and being able to support collaboration, iterations, and challenging tasks. Creativity tools should also be domain-specific for the given task and make it easy for users to store, classify, relate, and retrieve things [24]. However, deploying or developing creativity tools or systems is not without challenges. When designing creativity tools or systems, developers must include the challenge of human-computer interaction by encapsulating user preferences, playfulness, interaction between design, and task-specific appliances [49, 59]. Hence, before development, business analysts must set design requirements that capture the organizational necessities and include business benefits from existing system portfolios through specific business plans [31, 58]. In addition, implementation of new IS requires user acceptance [18]. Users frame and make sense of technology differently within their own social and work-based arenas, which often collide with the implementation efforts [44, 60]. Thus, when implementing new IS (including creativity supported IS), managers must consider the social setting and users' preferences and take proper action when needed [20].

Findings.
Our findings showed that focus on human-computer interaction was less significant in organizations that develop creativity enhancing IS for themselves than in ISDs. Human-computer interaction was, however, slightly less integrated in clone and ISD organizations than IS organizations. Similar in technology acceptance, integration in clone organizations tends to be significant at a lower level than in ISDs, and somewhat lower than IS organizations. These findings demonstrate that ISD and IS organizations have a closer relationship to suppliers and customers and are more likely to collect management practice experiences and new system ideas when implementing and developing new systems. Another explanation can be a closer interaction with their business and an increased knowledge of organizational management practices when developing IS for creativity enhancement. Moreover, IS and ISD organizations prefer to implement creativity enhancement within their existing IT-portfolio. This increases technology acceptance, as employees and customers are more likely to use creativity enhancing software when it is included in systems they know and use.

4.3   The Environmental Factor

The environment in software organizations influences the creative output by providing social spaces for creative individuals and teams, which enables them to be inspired and construct ideas [14]. The physical environment in organizations have proven to have an impact on creativity efforts when developing new IS [5, 15]. Likewise, substantial evidence indicates that virtual environments in creativity enhancing software increases organizational creativity by creating social spaces for developers to share thoughts, find inspiration, compile relevant information, and conjoin creative efforts [1, 2, 25, 29, 32–34, 37, 39, 41, 50]. Moreover, when organizations are embarking on creative endeavors, managers must be aware of existing institutional practices and cultural norms that could create barriers for organizational creativity [15, 36]. Hence, they must create an organizational culture that supports creativity through direct strategies and leadership [5, 61].

Findings.
Our findings demonstrated equal medium integration in IS, ISD, and clone organizations when creating physical and virtual environments for creativity. For physical environment, some participants in the survey stated that their organization lacked proper equipment and facilities, which decreased creative thinking. When interviewing the business developer in the municipality it was also apparent that they had the proper equipment for enhancing creative thinking. However, the technology had technical difficulties, and they lacked training:

"We have this smart board as a part of a test for the schools, but we primarily use it as an overhead projector... It is not properly calibrated... It is simply faster to do it with pen and paper and then take a picture and send it by mail... The school teachers are much better to use it than we are... the learning curve is simply too high."

This problem is also apparent with virtual environments. Most organization uses analog devices, such as group brainstorming and pen and paper techniques, instead of software based solutions. However, some organizations use online idea boards in existing knowledge management systems. Here, employees share new ideas or save them for later use.

Private organizations are more likely than public organizations to create social environments for creativity. However, Danish public organizations are only just beginning to think in creativity and innovation, due to new policies for the public sector. Hence, they must continuously reform their business to save money while keeping or increasing the overall service level. Private organizations, however, have done this for years to gain competitive advantages. As the CIO of the municipality explained, they focused increasingly on creativity and innovation. To achieve their goals, leaders from the schools, nursing homes, and all other business areas of the municipality had to undergo innovation training and were included in the overall innovation efforts.

4.4   The Institutional Factor

Institutional barriers include negative perceptions towards new ideas and creative employees, not sharing relevant data, autocratic leadership, lack of task support, and fear of the unknown in creative processes, all of which negatively affect the outcome of organizational creativity [9, 15]. Also, employees can have different creative styles, which place barriers on an individual level [15]. To reduce institutional barriers, managers must understand their employees' creative styles and create change-strategies for removing institutional barriers that poses negative influence on the creative output [15]. Moreover, Cooper [13] argued that creativity requires proper structures to be successful. Clear development goals reduce misplaced efforts by employees and groups and encourage productivity. However, tight control over creative processes will reduce autonomy and motivation of employees and negatively affect the creative outcome [9]. Managers must seek a balance between structure and over-the-edge autonomy ([13]. Agile development techniques such as extreme programming (XP) and the dynamic systems development method (DSDM) has proven to capitalize on employees' strengths [11], and give goals and constraints that provide boundaries for creativity to flourish instead for running amok [28]. However, creative endeavors in organizations are not without costs. Training and deployment strategies within the physical and virtual environment requires allocation of resources when enhancing the creative abilities in employees and leaders [5, 14, 15].

Findings.
Institutional barriers still provide a massive problem by preventing creative people from being creative and exploring their potentials. Our findings revealed that both in the municipality and GameSim, many barriers were related to working in top-down

governed organizations. These included strong expectations to get returns on investments, lack of possibilities to experiment without providing strong business cases for support of projects, lack of time to be creative, political trends influencing decision-making, expectations of continuous growth and system functionality, and lack of creative visioning in top management. However, this was much more apparent in GameSim, where traditional top management dictated the development strategies of the sub-unit. There was a better linkage in the municipality between the IT-department and the political leadership, which provided an increased ownership over projects and opened opportunities for experimentation without requirements of return of investment.

Defining structures for creativity is equally important. As one participant from a private developer in the survey stated:

> *"The waterfall model is our approach to project management … This kills the creativity in the projects. The employees fight against this, which equal positive results. However, this process is very ad hoc when we have the time and resources."*

Development processes in GameSim were equally very ad hoc. The creative process would stop when the requirement specifications were defined for a given project. In the municipality, they acted differently by strategizing projects as implementations projects. Requirements were either set in advance or defined as "next practice projects". Next practice projects included continuous creativity and experimentation during the entire project life cycle to provide more benefits and increase organizational knowledge in new areas. Hence, availability to experimentation is a valuable resource when embarking on creative projects. In GameSim, they created a system due to a larger certification. However, there were loosely defined requirements for the system, and government funding provided the proper time and resources for conducting the project. This provided GameSim room for developing new ideas by continuously interacting with their customers over a two-year period. The result was a very innovative product that both GameSim and their customers benefited greatly from.

4.5   The Individual Factor

To increase the creative output of the organization, employees require continuous education for developing their creative skills [16]. IS organizations also thrive from the individual's ability to be creative and create new ideas for continuous innovation ([19]. However, several factors influence individual impact on creative output. Creative employees are especially known for being exceptionally difficult to manage. They often know their own worth, have expert knowledge, and have A-type personalities and behavior that often results in conflicts with authorities [19, 22]. Managers must create an environment that not only empowers creative employees, but also attracts them to the organization [9].

Findings.
There is low overall integration in the challenges connected to the individual factor in comparison to the challenges connected to the other six factors, which indicates that the participating organizations have little emphasis on training their employees in

creativity and manage creative people. However, our analysis showed many different approaches to provide training for creative employees. Some organizations would provide individual courses for employees, while others would hire external consultants for enhancing the overall creativity and innovation ability in the organization. Some would not provide any training at all and would rely on their employees' natural ability to be creative. However, training in creativity provides many benefits for organizations. In the municipality, a creativity and innovation workshop helped the employees to think differently and engage in experimentation, which provided solutions for a range of problems they faced.

Equally, in the daily management of employees, empowerment was important. Where the municipality used empowerment to encourage creativity for the employees, employees in GameSim were already empowered. The employees engaged in the creative development were some of the few specialists within their field. As the head of product development argued:

> *"Our employees are small kings within their own field and there is not a lot of team spirit"*.

Hence, the challenge in GameSim was not to enable creative empowerment in their workforce, but to control the highly creative employees, as the individuality of these specialists often collided with the needs of the customers. Consequently, one of the job specifications for the head of product development was to enable communication between customers and the creative employees to provide encouragement for the employees and to insure business value to the customers from their new ideas.

4.6   The Group Factor

Creative activities are often conducted in teams. As Cooper [13] argued, IT-specific knowledge is an important capability in development teams. It enables them to act creatively according to the organizational context. Professional differences in development teams are thus important for the composition of development teams and overall success of projects [13]. Moreover, when giving tasks to creative individuals or creating creative teams, an important consideration is that individuals are different in their cognitive abilities, knowledge, behavior, and personality [5]. Equally important is the demographic, cultural, and social composition. Creative development teams perform better when they are composed of employees with different experience and education levels [5, 13, 21, 53]. However, teams are less creative when they are comprised of employees with different social or cultural backgrounds, or different sexes [52]. Managers must understand these factors and their employees when they create development teams composed of individuals with different professional, social, and cultural backgrounds [5, 13, 52]. When teams are comprised of employees with different backgrounds and experiences, they require a higher level of communication and interaction to collaborate. As Cockburn and Highsmith [11;132] argued "Interestingly, people working together with good communication and interaction can operate at noticeably higher levels than when they use their individual talent". Hence, managers are required to use increased time and effort to create working development teams and to facilitate mediated communication and interaction in the teams [52].

Software organizations are also an entity of different communities of practices that influence organizational culture and norms, which results in learning and innovation, defines organizational structures, and creates institutionalization of those practices [7]. When creating creative groups, communities of practices are important for transferring organizational knowledge from individual to individual [15, 38]. In managing for creativity, managers must understand the existing communities of practices in the organization and actively use these in the knowledge creation processes, when changing culture and norms, and when transferring knowledge to create a shared understanding of problems.

Findings.
Creativity workshops can do a lot when attempting to increase organizational creativity. During a creativity and innovation workshop in the municipality, leaders across the organization were divided into groups. The purpose of the workshop was to place the participants out of their normal comfort zone and encourage them to think in digital solutions for their everyday problems. During the workshop, the leaders would then change groups and further develop the problems within a new group of people. This approach of constantly changing the leaders' environment broke down cultural differences and enabled the leaders to think differently, which resulted in novel ideas for digitalizing problems across the organization. Moreover, the survey showed that IS and ISD organizations have a similar integration of communities of practices, while clone organizations had a lower integration. This cause of difference can be related to a higher inclination in IS and ISD organizations to institutionalize existing practices through software use and development (e.g., [43, 44]).

The importance of mediated communication is also apparent. Without proper communication between team members and between departments, actors will lose important information that they can use as a source of inspiration of novel ideas. In both the municipality and GameSim they solved this problem by using IS for mediating the communication and information sharing process. GameSim used an intranet solution for their developers and business analysts, which contained design and development ideas and other relevant information provided by the employees. The municipality, alternatively, used an open intranet solution that allowed departments across the organization to view detailed information from digitalization projects in other departments.

4.7   The Leadership Factor

Managers' leadership abilities in software organizations are an important and often overlooked factor in the organizations' goal of increased creativity [19]. Managing IS does not only include delegating tasks and resources or creating of business plans for projects. IT also requires clear leadership, which involves individual human empathy and empowerment of employees [5, 9, 15], and a clear understand of the group dynamics in development teams [13, 38]. Managers must be willing to take risks when needed [9, 15, 51]. Fear of failure in top management discourages employees and decreases the flow of novel ideas [15]. Moreover, managers must deploy creative techniques when needed and create incentives and motivation for employees and groups to enhance the creative output [14, 15], while being able to include employees' personal characteristics when transferring techniques to system use [10]. Hence, managers must strategize and conceptualize the creative endeavors in IS organizations with the existing business processes, by providing plans for implementation of systems and change, training, evaluation, and diffusion of creativity tools and techniques [14, 15].

Findings.
The integration of incentives for creative development was the lowest of all the challenges despite it being a powerful motivator for increasing organizational creativity [15]. In our survey, 48% (15) answered that this challenge was not very well integrated in their organization, and only 6% (2) replied that it was very highly integrated. Hence, these software organizations lack a leadership culture that provides incentives. However, the findings from the interviews demonstrate a positive culture for empowerment, as employees and managers are encouraged to take ownership over projects.

Our findings also showed that there is some kind willingness to take risks with new ideas in software organizations. However, private organizations had a substantial higher integration than public organizations when it came to practices in risk-taking. The cause of this difference can come from Danish public organizations being subject to government laws, which prevent them for hiding their failures. This exposure to their customers' opinions (politicians and citizens) can make them less inclined to take risks, which affects their overall ability to engage in high-risk creative projects.

Deploying creativity techniques IS and ISD organizations were mostly on ad hoc initiatives. In the municipality, they would hire outside consultants to conduct their workshops, and when asked about the techniques deployed, they would only provide sporadic information about them. In GameSim, the same problem was apparent. The managers utilized creativity techniques such as brainstorming, but they had no defined approaches or predefined knowledge for deploying different creativity techniques.

The integration of strategizing creativity in the organizations was almost equally below average in both private and public organizations. The interviews somewhat explained this finding. In the municipality, they had only recently created a strategy for creativity and innovation one year prior to this study. In GameSim, a similar strategy was created only four months prior. However, this finding also indicates that both private and public organizations increasingly attempts to integrate creativity management practices in their organizations by defining overall strategies for creativity and innovation.

4.8   The External Factor

User and customer involvement are an important factor in system development [17]. As customer do not always know their needs, it is important to understand the user to make requirements [6]. Hence, for new business opportunities to emerge, novel ideas must be evaluated and screened before implementation [15]. Florida and Goodnight [19] recommended locating a balance between creating novel ideas and allocating customer needs through relationship building and testing schemes. However, analyzing customer needs in creative processes requires a culture of constructive criticism to deliver continuous quality [19]. This also requires a culture that emphasizes that some projects just fail. Organizations who punish employees who fail with projects will remove any incentives to be creative [5].

Using quality assurance schemes such as Software Process Improvement (SPI), Lean, and Six Sigma are common practices in software development to provide product and service quality and standardization of business processes for continuous customer value [12, 27]. However, the discipline aspect of quality assurance schemes have been criticized for inhibiting creativity [47]. Conradi and Fuggetta [12] and Herbold [26] argued that organizations should balance their quality assurance efforts between discipline and creativity, where discipline support inspections and standardization of business processes, and creativity and collaboration support engineering and software design.

Findings.
Data from the survey and interviews revealed that organizations' business primarily use business cases before and after software implementation to evaluate novel ideas. Business cases have the advantage of providing a quick determination of business value for a given idea (e.g. [58]). In the two organizations in which we conducted interviews, they measured the quality of new ideas by level of business value. They would rarely use strict management methods, such as Lean, Six Sigma, and SPI, to ensure quality control of new ideas, which could be the cause of low integration in creating quality assurance schemes. Instead, their employees was encouraged or simply told to determine business value for each new idea before implementation. However, in the municipality, they would follow up on the business cases during implementation. This ensured that new ideas could emerge and add additional business value over the project's life cycle.

In most of the software organizations, user and customer involvement was important to insure business value for creative ideas. However, user involvements in the private organizations were significantly higher than in public organizations. In the municipality, the CIO agreed that they were good in involving their own users and suppliers in new digitalization project. However, they lacked a clear emphasis on involving their customers (the citizens). In GameSim, the customers were highly involved in the creation of new products, as they were a source of novel ideas during the requirements specification of new products and services. Moreover, the survey demonstrated a clear contrast to the overall integration of user and customer involvement between ISD, clone, and IS organizations. ISDs were far better at integrating user and customer involvement than IS organizations and somewhat better than clone organizations.

5   A Framework for Creativity in Software Organizations

From our synthesis of the literature and the empirical evidence, we constructed a framework consisting of the seven identified factors for creativity in software organizations. Moreover, we identified 21 challenges in creativity management within the seven factors.

The schematic representation of our proposed framework is presented in in Figure 1 and demonstrates how multiple challenges can unfold themselves in software organizations. These challenges exist within seven factors in the creative context of organizational creativity. The framework also demonstrates the mutual influence from each of the seven factors on a software organizations creative output (ideas generation). Each factor has individual challenges attached that are illustrated with unbroken lines between the challenges and their factors. The challenges define the factors, which in return affects the creative context and ultimately the creative output of software organizations. For example, a challenge can be the demographic composition of creative development teams in the group factor, or the challenge of organizational barriers in the institutional factor.

Inspired by Rhodes' (1961) thinking, no individual factor of creativity stands alone, but all are connected in unity. Hence, the different factors can impose influence over other factors. For example, creativity support systems can influence the creativity in individuals and groups, while individuals can affect how groups function. Moreover, leadership influences the creative environment, while external factors like idea evaluation schemes and relationships with customers can influence the institutional structures of the organization. Hence, this area of influence represented in the middle of Figure 1, demonstrating how each factor influences the organizational context through interaction with other factors. This interaction between factors also defines the creative context of the organization. As illustrated, this mutual influence and interaction between different factors ultimately outlines the creative output of the software organization.

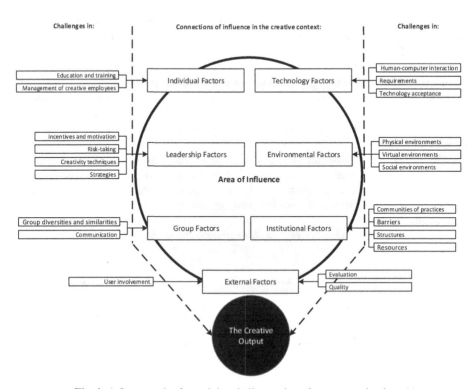

Fig. 1. A framework of creativity challenges in software organizations

6   Conclusion

Creativity management has become an increasingly important factor in conducting product and service innovation in software organizations. Creativity management involves increasing expertise in techniques, leadership, strategies, evaluation, and human-computer interaction in order to break down management challenges and achieve the necessary benefits of organizational creativity initiatives.

In this paper, we asked ourselves the following research question: "Which challenges of creativity does software organizations experience?" To this end, we created a framework that influences creativity management in software organizations. We identified seven organizational factors of the technology, environment, institution, individuals, groups, leadership, and external issues. Moreover, we identified 21 common challenges within the different factors and provided a combined framework with a comprehensive theoretical foundation and an interpretive research study to support it, which demonstrates how managers in software organizations practice creativity management. The framework also shows that organizational creativity is a combined entity consistent of different factors, which impose mutual influence on each other. Managers and researchers must be aware of this mutual influence and are encouraged to provide new initiatives for practice and research that support organizational creativity as a combined entity.

The research provides several insights for creativity management in technology-driven organization. For example, our results showed that managers or employees often conducted creativity in practice through ad hoc initiatives rather than doing it in a structured form. However, the study also provided valuable insights into creativity management practices that are transferrable to normative guidelines for creativity enhancing software that practitioners could benefit from. As such, it became clear that creativity enhancing software requires a number of different features, including integration in the existing IS-portfolio, integration of knowledge management systems, and information awareness, design usability and training, mediated communication, pre-selection of tools, empowerment through incentives, and computerized evaluation of new and novel ideas. In addition, it requires additional management practices including clear strategies for creativity and innovation before implementation, culture building, and empowerment trough ownership of projects and freedom for experimentation. Such experimentation must include allocation of the necessary resources and clear leadership from top management when taking new risks.

However, when writing this paper, we also realized that creativity encompass a far wider complexity across a software organization than this paper is able to present. Hence, researchers can use our findings to gain a better understanding of how these factors and challenges are interconnected and influence the complex and often chaotic endeavor of creating novel and useful ideas for new software innovations.

References

1. Abrams, S., et al.: QSketcher: An environment for composing music for film (2002)
2. Aiken, M., Carlisle, J.: An automated idea consolidation tool for computer supported co-operative work. Inf. Manag. 23(6), 373–382 (1992)

3. Amabile, T., et al.: Affect and creativity at work. Adm. Sci. Q. 50, 367–403 (2005)
4. Amabile, T.M., et al.: Assessing the work environment for creativity. Acad. Manag. J. 39(5), 1154–1184 (1996)
5. Amabile, T.M.: How to kill creativity. Harv. Bus. Rev. 76(5), 76–87 (1998)
6. Beyer, H., Holtzblatt, K.: Contextual Design – Defining customer-centered systems. Academic Press, London (1998)
7. Brown, J.S., Duguid, P.: Organizational learning and communities-of-practice: toward a unified view of working, learning, and innovation. Organ. Sci. 2(1), 40–57 (1991)
8. Bryman, A.: Social Research Methods. Oxford University Press, New York (2004)
9. Catmull, E.: How Pixar Fosters collective creativity. Harv. Bus. Rev. 86(9), 64–72 (2008)
10. Cheung, P.K., et al.: Does knowledge reuse make a creative person more creative? Decis. Support Syst. 45(2), 219–227 (2008)
11. Cockburn, A., Highsmith, J.: Agile Software Development: The People Factor. Softw. Manag. 34(11), 131–133 (2001)
12. Conradi, R., Fuggetta, A.: Improving software process improvement. IEEE Softw. 19(4), 92–+ (2002)
13. Cooper, R.: Information technology development creativity: A case study of attempted radical change. MIS Q. 24(2), 245–276 (2000)
14. Couger, J., et al.: (Un)structured creativity in information systems organizations. MIS Q. 17(4), 375–397 (1993)
15. Couger, J.D.: Creativity & Innovation in information systems organizations. Boyd & Fraser, Danvers (1996)
16. Couger, J.D.: Creativity: Important addition to national joint undergraduate IS curriculum. J. Comput. Inf. Syst. 37(1), 39–41 (1996)
17. Davenport, T.H.: Process Innovation – Reengineering work through information technology. Havard Buisness School Press, Boston (1993)
18. Davis, F.D.: Perceived usefulness, perceived ease of use, and user acceptance of information technology. Mis Q. 13(3), 319–340 (1989)
19. Florida, R., Goodnight, J.: Managing for Creativity. Harv. Bus. Rev. 83(7-8), 124–131 (2005)
20. Gallivan, M.J.: The influence of software developers' creative style on their attitudes to and assimilation of a software process innovation. Inf. Manag. 40(5), 443–465 (2003)
21. Gero, J.S.: Computational models of creative designing based on situated cognition (2002)
22. Goffee, R., Jones, G.: Leading clever people. Harv. Bus. Rev. 85(3), 72–+ (2007)
23. Govindarajan, V., Trimble, C.: The Other Side of Innovation: Solving the Execution Challenge. Harvard Business School Publishing, Boston (2010)
24. Greene, S.L.: Characteristics of applications that support creativity. Commun. ACM 45(10), 100–104 (2002)
25. Hailpern, J., et al.: TEAM STORM: Demonstrating an interaction model for working with multiple ideas during creative group work. In: Proceedings of the 6th ACM SIGCHI Conference on Creativity & Cognition, pp. 193–202. ACM, Washington, DC (2007)
26. Herbold, R.J.: Inside Microsoft - Balancing creativity and discipline. Harv. Bus. Rev. 80(1), 72–79 (2002)
27. Hicks, B.J.: Lean information management: Understanding and eliminating waste. Int. J. Inf. Manage. 27, 233–249 (2007)
28. Highsmith, J.: What Is Agile Software Development? J. Def. Softw. Eng. 15(10), 4–9 (2002)
29. Hori, K.: A system for aiding creative concept-formation. IEEE Trans. Syst. Man Cybern. 24(6), 882–894 (1994)

30. Iyer, B., Davenport, T.H.: Reverse engineering Google's innovation machine. Harv. Bus. Rev. 86(4), 58–68 (2008)
31. Kappel, T.A., Rubenstein, A.H.: Creativity in design: The contribution of information technology. IEEE Trans. Eng. Manag. 46(2), 132–143 (1999)
32. Kerne, A., et al.: CombinFormation: Mixed-Initiative Composition of Image and Text Surrogates Promotes Information Discovery. Acm Trans. Inf. Syst. 27(1) (2009)
33. Kletke, M.G., et al.: Creativity in the organization: the role of individual creative problem solving and computer support. Int. J. Hum. Comput. Stud. 55(3), 217–237 (2001)
34. Kohler, T., et al.: Co-creation in virtual worlds: the design of the user experience. MIS Q. 35(3), 773–788 (2011)
35. Layder, D.: Sociological Practice - Linking theory and practice. Sage Publications Ltd., London (1998)
36. Leonardi, P.M.: Innovation Blindness: Culture, Frames, and Cross-Boundary Problem Construction in the Development of New Technology Concepts. Organ. Sci. 22(2), 347–369 (2011)
37. Maccrimmon, K.R., Wagner, C.: Stimulating ideas through creativity software. Manage. Sci. 40(11), 1514–1532 (1994)
38. Malhotra, A., et al.: Radical innovation without collocation: A case study at Boeing-Rocketdyne. Mis Q. 25(2), 229–249 (2001)
39. Massetti, B.: An empirical examination of the value of creativity support systems on idea generation. MIS Q. 20(1), 83–97 (1996)
40. Müller, S.D., Ulrich, F.: Creativity and Information Systems in a Hypercompetitive Environment: A Literature Review. Commun. Assoc. Inf. Syst. 32, 175–200 (2013)
41. Nakakoji, K., et al.: A framework that supports collective creativity in design using visual images (1999)
42. Nambisan, S., et al.: Organizational mechanisms for enhancing user innovation in information technology. Mis Q 23(3), 365–395 (1999)
43. Orlikowski, W.J.: The duality of technology - Rethinking the concept of technology in organizations. Organ. Sci. 3(3), 398–427 (1992)
44. Orlikowski, W.J.J., Gash, D.C.C.: Technological frames - Making sense of information technology in organizations. Acm Trans. Inf. Syst. 12(2), 174–207 (1994)
45. Piller, F., et al.: Overcoming mass confusion: Collaborative customer co-design in online communities. J. Comput. Commun. 10(4) (2005)
46. Rhodes, M.: An analysis of creativity. Phi Delta Kappan 42, 305–310 (1961)
47. Roger, W.H., Martha, M.G.: Lean Six Sigma, creativity, and innovation. Int. J. Lean Six Sigma. 1(1), 30–38 (2010)
48. Rose, J.: Software Innovation - Eight work-style heuristics for creative system developers. Software Innovation, Aalborg (2011)
49. Shaw, T., et al.: The effects of computer-mediated interactivity on idea generation - An experimental investigation. Ieee Trans. Syst. Man Cybern. 23(3), 737–745 (1993)
50. Shneiderman, B.: Creativity support tools. Commun. Acm. 45(10), 116–120 (2002)
51. Sutton, R.I.: The weird rules of creativity. Harv. Bus. Rev. 79(8), 94–103 (2001)
52. Thatcher, S.M.B., Brown, S.A.: Individual creativity in teams: The importance of communication media mix. Decis. Support Syst. 49(3), 290–300 (2010)
53. Tiwana, A., McLean, E.R.: Expertise integration and creativity in information systems development. J. Manag. Inf. Syst. 22(1), 13–43 (2005)
54. De Vaus, D.: Research Design in Social Research. Sage Publications Ltd., London (2001)
55. Walsham, G.: Doing interpretive research. Eur. J. Inf. Syst. 15(3), 320–330 (2006)

56. Walsham, G.: Interpreting Information Systems in Organizations. Wiley, Chichester (1993)
57. Walsham, G.: Interpretive case studies in IS research: Nature and method. Eur. J. Inf. Syst. 4(2), 74–81 (1995)
58. Ward, J., et al.: Building better business cases for IT investments. MIS Q. Exec. 7(1), 1–15 (2008)
59. Webster, J.: Microcomputer playfulness: Development of a measure with workplace implications. Mis Q 16(2), 201–226 (1992)
60. Weick, K.E., et al.: Organizing and the process of sensemaking. Organ. Sci. 16(4), 409–421 (2005)
61. Woodman, R.W., et al.: Toward a theory of organizational creativity. Acad. Manag. Rev. 18(2), 293–321 (1993)
62. Yin, R.K.: Case Study Research - Design and Methods. SAGE Publications Ltd., London (2003)
63. Aaen, I.: Essence: Facilitating software innovation. Eur. J. Inf. Syst. 17(5), 543–553 (2008)

Diffusing Best Practices: A Design Science Study Using the Theory of Planned Behavior

Richard Baskerville[1] and Jan Pries-Heje[2]

[1] Georgia State University, USA
Baskerville@acm.org
[2] Roskilde University, Denmark
janph@ruc.dk

Abstract. Both the practice and the research literature on information systems attach great value to the identification and dissemination of information on "best practices". In the philosophy of science, this type of knowledge is regarded as technological knowledge because it becomes manifest in the successful techniques in one context. While the value for other contexts is unproven, knowledge of best practices circulates under an assumption that the practices will usefully self-diffuse through innovation and adoption in other contexts. We study diffusion of best practices using a design science approach. The study context is a design case in which an organization desires to diffuse its best practices across different groups. The design goal is embodied in organizational mechanisms to achieve this diffusion. The study used Theory of Planned Behavior (TPB) as a kernel theory. The artifacts resulting from the design were two-day training workshops conceptually anchored to TBP. The design theory was evaluated through execution of eight diffusion workshops involving three different groups in the same company. The findings indicate that the match between the practice and the context materialized in the presence of two concordant factors. On the context side, the qualities of the selected opinion leader were necessary to provide the subjective norm described in TPB. On the best practice side, the technological qualities of the best practice itself were necessary to instill the ideal attitude (belief that the behavior will be effective). These two factors were especially critical if the source context of the best practice is qualitatively different from the target context into which the organization is seeking to diffuse the best practice.

Keywords: Diffusion, Best Practice, Theory of Planned Behavior, Action Case.

1   Introduction

While there is much work regarding the content of best practices, there is remarkably little work that considers that nature of best practices and in particular the diffusion of best practices in general. The definition of the concept best practice is regarded as subjective. The term is rarely defined in the literature. For the purposes of this paper, we will adopt the following as our working definition, "best practices are leadership, management, or operational methods or approaches that lead to exceptional performance." [1, p. 334]

B. Bergvall-Kåreborn and P.A. Nielsen (Eds.): TDIT 2014, IFIP AICT 429, pp. 35–48, 2014.
© IFIP International Federation for Information Processing 2014

This general conceptualization of best practices is flavored by its anchors to the concepts of professionalism. Professionals encourage the diffusion of best practices among their professional colleagues. Often this encouragement takes the form of professional certifications or accreditation. While accreditation, such as professional accreditation, is often intended to diffuse best practices. However, studies have shown that it actually has only limited effects in this regard [2]. Such studies suggest a critical suspicion of the concept of best practice diffusion might be fair.

Diffusion of best practices by professionals is sometimes driven by commercial interests. Commercial pressure to converge on a set of best practices in global strategic management arises from international competition and capital markets. Improved communications and professionalization often presses for dissemination of best practices worldwide. However, this idea downplays differences in national systems and cultures as sources of competitive advantage. More nuanced strategy formulation is necessary that a radical convergence on a single, global set of best practice [3]. Such differences, and the need for nuanced diffusion of best practices, may help explain why the effects of professional diffusion of best practices are so limited.

The need for professionals to adapt or "nuance" the best practices as they diffuse is a continuing theme in the research in this area. Consultants and experts deliver practices to their companies and their clients. These professionals operate with conflicting roles, creating a dilemma. In one role, as professionals, they adhere to an epistemic community; in another, they adhere to a community of practice [4]. Professionals enacting a role as an expert interacts more with their epistemic community, privileging their creative processes. To convey the value of these proposed best practices, the professional must convince top management to change their strategic vision. Professionals enacting the role as a consultant interacts more with their community of practice, privileging the diffusion of best practices across the firm to enhance routine operations. These professionals (consultants and experts) often operate globally. As a result, any diffusion of best practices can involve inter-industries, cross-cultural, international, inter-disciplinary and trans-disciplinary links [4]. Professionals are knowledge carrying agents who diffuse best practices into diverse organizations.

Sluggish diffusion of best practices can sometimes be explained simply. For example, diffusion is known to increase "when the actors involved are perceived as being similar, when the diffusing practices are theorized as similar, and when the practices are theorized to be modern." [5] But the conceptualization of diffusion of best practices can be overly naïve. Best practice diffusion often involves a dependence upon the transfer of primarily explicit knowledge. Many professionals admit that such explicit coding of a best practice will lack its important implicit aspects. Such explicit best practices may provide a foundation for practicing in the setting at hand, but adaptation is usually necessary. Consequently, in real-world usage, a best practice will incorporate an emergent property. A coded best practice represents the starting point for a process of improvement [6]. In this sense, diffusion of best practices is not necessarily dissemination of knowledge. Rather it is a process of improvement. In this process, the actors in the field are not just receivers of a best practice, but are co-constructors of this best practice. In other words, the best practice must be co-constructed by the actors in the new context [7].

The need for best practice co-construction in the diffusion process means that certain kinds of best practices may seem to diffuse more easily than others. For example, with reference to new product development, best practices for strategy-setting (product selection, goal-setting, technology, etc.) seem to diffuse more widely than best practices for control (process control, metrics, documentation, etc.) [8]. It is not uncommon to blame limited best practice diffusion on motivational factors, like resistance to change. However, diffusion of high-value best practices are related to internal stickiness [the inability to reset a practice, 9]. Sticky best practices have a higher incremental cost of best-practice diffusion. Studies have shown that the central barriers to the diffusion of a best practice are the recipient's lack of absorptive capacity, causal ambiguity in the practice itself, and an arduous relationship between the source and the recipient [9].

The diffusion of best practices is therefore not as simple as declaring new process rules. For example, there is a known dialectical tension among the key principles in international business regulation. Harmonization and mutual recognition often oppose national sovereignty and low cost location. Such rule compliance opposes diffusion of best practices, continuous improvement, and best available technology [10].

The concept of a best practice implies a motivation to diffuse such a practice. However, the literature suggests that this diffusion is problematic. There are at least six aspects to these problems:

1. Diffusion of best practices can be motivated as part of a professional identity, and such diffusion may disregard the suitability for such practices in different settings.
2. In their efforts to diffuse best practices, experts and consultants can overly regard their own epistemic community and marginalize the community of practice that contextualizes the practices.
3. Diffusion of best practices sometimes disregards the innate advantages of national systems and cultures.
4. Best practices sometimes diffuse in an incomplete form: the explicit knowledge aspects are disseminated without the tacit knowledge aspects. New settings require adaptation, which can mean deconstructing and re-constructing/co-constructing the practice as an outcome of its arrival in a new setting with different actors.
5. Diffusion of highly valuable best practices can encounter internal stickiness making the diffusion costly.
6. Diffusion of best practices varies depending on the subject matter of the practice.

These issues lead to the research question addressed in this paper: Why do organizations fall victim to the innate problems with diffusion of best practices; how can an organization ideally enable such diffusion?

We use a design science research approach to explore this question. We develop a procedural artifact (a process or method artifact) that aims to avoid the known problems above and effectively diffuse best practices. Our kernel theory is Theory of Planned Behavior as (TPB). A kernel theory is a natural or social science theory that governs design requirements [11]. We selected TPB because the initial framing of the problem was given as resistance to change. This abductive selection arose because TPB is perhaps the most widely acknowledged model for describing the decision-making process that results in behavioral stasis or behavior change. (See the discussion of TPB in the next section.) We report results in a case where TPB was used as an intervention to diffuse a procedure for (improved) project management. A workshop was carefully designed using TPB as a basis. Forty managers in this workshop reported strongly increased intention to use immediately after the workshop. Furthermore observational data indicated a majority of the managers actually used the procedure months after the workshop.

2   Theory of Planned Behaviour (TPB)

TPB is a predictive model of human behavior in specific situations [12, 13]. It is an extension of the theory of reasoned action.   Ajzen is probably correct when he states, "Judging by the sheer number of investigations it has stimulated, the TPB is perhaps the most popular of the reasoned action models" [14, p. 454]. As an extension of the theory of reasoned action, TPB is anchored in the human attitude toward a behavior, often modeled as an expectancy of value. Such attitudes have a cognitive component (beliefs) and an affective component (evaluations). The causality presents actions as dependent on attitudes, and attitudes as dependent on beliefs and evaluations.

TPB regards an individual's intention to perform a given behavior as a central factor. A strong intention is expected to increase the likelihood of an actual behavior. However, the degree to which an intention leads to a behavior is conditioned by the degree to which an individual actually has volitional control (whether the individual can actually decide to perform the behavior). Behavioral achievement depends on intention (motivation) and ability (behavioral control) [15].

Behavioral control regards the extent to which people possess the information, skills, abilities, emotions, compulsions and the absence of external barriers to perform a given behavior. In TPB, the actual behavioral control is less important that the perceived behavioral control. That is, the degree of their belief in their behavioral control. It is very similar to the notion of self-efficacy. " Behavioral control is linked both to behavioral intention and behavioral achievement [14].

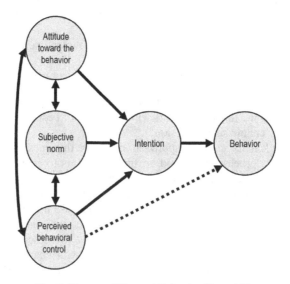

Fig. 1. Theory of Planned Behavior [from 15]

Motivation is partly comprised of a trait possessed by the individual: a general disposition to succeed that is not dependent on the situation at hand. This general disposition combines with a situational expectancy of success. A third situational factor is the incentive value of the expected success. Together with behavioral control, these factors combine to make three determinants of behavioral intention. The first determinant is the attitude toward the behavior. It embodies the degree to which the individual has a favorable or unfavorable evaluation or appraisal of the behavior. The second determinant is subjective norm, a social factor referring to the perceived social pressure to perform or not to perform the behavior. The third determinant is perceived behavioral control [15]. Figure 1 illustrates the TPB.

3   Research Method

The case methodology applied here is described as an action case [16]. An action case is a hybrid research approach that combines action research and interpretive case approaches. It combines intervention and interpretation in order to achieve both change and understanding. It is a form of soft field experiment with less emphasis on iteration and learning and more on trial and making. The approach is holistic in philosophy, and prediction is not emphasized. The intervention in this case was that of a designer introducing a previously well-published theory – the theory of planned behavior (TPB) – as a strategy for solving a problem diffusing a best practice. The case at hand is a setting in which an international company in the energy sector faced problems. For anonymity reasons we will refer to this company as ENKACE.

ENKACE is an old company headquartered in Europe but working with projects all over the world. Recently ENKACE has grown considerably mainly through mergers and acquisition. They had started to gather "lessons learned" from projects and realized that improving their project management would have a huge positive influence on their results. For example, better forecasting of their potential problems through early risk management brought the potential of saving millions of Euros. Another example is better stakeholder management, which together with early communication about expectations would have saved a number of projects from costly failure.

But in some projects, ENKACE had found that everything had worked out successfully. Based on these successes, the quality department had developed a *best practice procedure*. This procedure was carefully written so that problems that had been encountered in ENKACE projects could have been coped with. ENKACE quality managers from all parts of the world had been involved in the development of the procedure, hence it was covering *best practice* in ENKACE. The first version of the best practice procedure was aimed at project managers managing energy projects at sea. Their challenge in diffusing these best practices was to improve the professionalism of some 40 project managers for at-sea operations.

One author of this paper was presented with ENKACE's best-practice diffusion problem. Using TPB as grounding, this researcher suggested the design of an intervention to deliver these best practices as ideal professional conduct for the project managers. The design idea implied within TPB is to diffuse both explicit and implicit best practice to build on the project managers general disposition to succeed. The design process began in early 2013 with a brainstorming and knowledge transfer session at ENKACE headquarters. Following the brainstorming session, the researcher created an initial design. This design was then discussed in several video-based sessions involving participants from ENKACE worldwide. The final design was framed as a 2-day workshop for project managers.

Data consisted of field notes and documentation. The documentation centered on the evolving design of the training program and the evaluation of the various events in the training program. Like other forms of action research, action case methodology is often iterative. In ENKACE, the iterations coincided with a sequence of training events (e.g., in Asia, Europe, and North America). Learning acquired in each event conditioned the subsequent events. Some of these training events were collaborations between a professional trainer and the researcher; other training events were conducted by the trainer alone.

4   The Design

The kernel theory for the design was TPB. A number of company-based examples were chosen to influence the attitude of project managers. The rationale for choosing the examples involved illustrating for the participants how unfortunate project outcomes could have been prevented or avoided by using a particular best practice (in this case, the Project Management Procedure).

Influence over subjective norms involved recruiting an influential Project Manager as a co-trainer in the workshop. This individual is seen among colleagues as a respected opinion leader. The co-trainer not only influences (group) normative beliefs in the group of project managers participating in the workshop, but also encourages others in co-construction of the best practice. Co-training by someone perceived as a peer participant can relax other participants about interactively offering content adjustments. Hence this part of the intervention was built on Rogers' Diffusion of

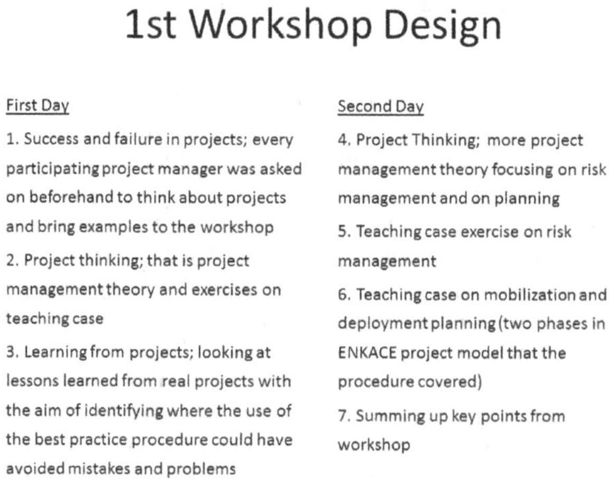

1st Workshop Design

First Day

1. Success and failure in projects; every participating project manager was asked on beforehand to think about projects and bring examples to the workshop

2. Project thinking; that is project management theory and exercises on teaching case

3. Learning from projects; looking at lessons learned from real projects with the aim of identifying where the use of the best practice procedure could have avoided mistakes and problems

Second Day

4. Project Thinking; more project management theory focusing on risk management and on planning

5. Teaching case exercise on risk management

6. Teaching case on mobilization and deployment planning (two phases in ENKACE project model that the procedure covered)

7. Summing up key points from workshop

Fig. 2. First workshop design

Innovations theory [17] using the idea that early adopters have the highest degree of opinion leadership.

The workshop included training in risk management, stakeholder management, and planning. This training is intended to influence perceived behavioral control. A teaching case built on realistic projects was developed. Exercises incorporated in the teaching case gives participants the feeling that they have the necessary information, skills, abilities, etc., to exercise volitional control to shape their behavior and their behavioral intentions.

See Figure 2 for the overall workshop design.

The Design Rationale behind the workshop design was the following (numbers referring to Figure 2):

1. The workshop begins with a focus on the attitude of the participating project managers. This session unfreezes the participants' attitude about their past behaviors and the behavioral norms. Attitudes are opened to the relevance of doing something different. This attitudinal shift arises in telling the failure stories from their own projects. Simultaneously participants contribute their own best practices for their peers to consider. Such a discussion of the success stories reveals implicit knowledge within the community of practice that is present in the workshop.
2. The workshop participants shift to a learning mode by studying best practices from other companies and from the professional community of project managers. This process should help move subjective norms closer to the best practices.
3. The first day concludes with a further focus on the attitude of the project managers. A sense of motivation is communicated helping participants realize that the use of the best practice procedure could have led to the prevention of unfortunate previous outcomes.
4. The second day begins with a continuation of the learning mode to help reset to subjective norms.
5. The centerpiece of the second day is a teaching case to provide the participating project managers an understanding of how they could apply the best practice in a professional way. This activity increases the belief in their behavioral control.
6. The emphasis on improving a belief in behavioral control continues. The co-trainer from ENKACE participates intensely in the discussion of the case thereby influencing both the belief in behavioral control and the subjective norm within the community of practice among ENKACE project managers. By witnessing the co-construction of the best practice at the hands of a peer project manager (the co-trainer), the belief in behavioral control re-freezes the best practice as behavioral intention.
7. The final session of the workshop evaluates the results of the workshop process. The participants critically assess "Did it work?" and "How do you perceive the best practice procedure now?"

4.1   Iteration One

The first instance of the workshop was held in Asia early May 2013 primarily for Asian project managers. An author of this paper worked as the main trainer. A known strategy for overcoming resistance-to-change is to involve an opinion leader as a change advocate [17]. An experienced project manager – now working in Quality Assurance (QA) at ENKACE – was enlisted as co-trainer in the workshop. Before having the workshop the author and the enlisted co-trainer had a virtual meeting a month before and a physical meeting the day before the workshop. These two meetings were spend re-designing and improving the workshop. For example the meetings resulted in the specific choice of cases for learning (bullet 3 in Figure 2) and in the specific presentation of the teaching Case (bullet 5 and 6 in Figure 2).

The presence of the opinion leader as co-trainer succeeded. Commencing with the project manager's own successes and failures also succeeded in making the participants receptive to the best practice and its concomitant professional knowledge. Learning from past projects, especially a demonstration of exactly where the new best practice procedure would have helped, was also successful. The discussion of each case clearly brought forward knowledge that was not explicitly stated in the practice, but was implicitly known by the experienced members of the group.

At the end of the workshop people were enthusiastic about the best practice procedure. This practical outcome suggests that this first test run of using TPB as kernel theory for designing a workshop was a success: The participants found it useful and gave it high scores for utility.

The two next instances of the workshop were held in Europe in May and June 2013. Both workshops were small in terms of the number of participants: 8 and 10. As with Asia, the workshop setup worked well. Participants noted that the time allocated for the workshop (ten hours over two days) was too brief. In one of the workshops the co-trainer from Asia could not participate. Instead the senior project manager in the company (in terms of the longest tenure) was trained to take on the role as opinion leader and contributed to the case projects to look at (bullet 3 in Figure 2)

The workshops were also evaluated using a questionnaire. Table 1 lists the items on this questionnaire.

Table 1. Evaluation questionnaire items

- How important do you believe that project management skills and understanding are in relation to your position?
- Is the PM procedure adequate?
- How well does the approach the workshop takes using a mix of PM theory and exercises work?
- How well does the workshop in your opinion reinforce the use of the PM procedure for ENKACE operations?
- Workshop trainer?
- Workshop material?

The participants were asked to rate questions on a scale from one to five, with one being poor and five being excellent. On average answers in the three workshops ended up at 4.2 - 4.3. The highest scores in the two workshops were given to question no. 4 on how well the workshop reinforced the use of the best practice procedure. Based on the experience and the participant responses, our conclusion is that TPB is suitable as a kernel theory for designing a workshop to diffuse best practice.

The learning that developed from this iteration centered on the role played by the opinion leader. While enlisted as an advocate for change (in order to overcome resistance-to-change), this individual demonstrated how essential it is to situate the best practices within the practical context of the participants. This role must be richer than merely advocating for change, but became as well essential for helping the participants to learn how the best practices would operate in their own context.

4.2   Iteration Two

The second iteration and intervention took place in another part of ENKACE. The three workshops in Iteration One covered most of the project managers in that part of the company. This second iteration was then aimed at project managers for land operations in a mature market. The aim of the undertaking was to create buy-in for two of three best practice procedures and to deliver information about a third. Procedures – again – had been written by QA based on best practices identified throughout the company. The three procedures regarded: (1) Starting a project; (2) Running a project; and (3) Creating a Project Quality Plan.

Based on the experience from Iteration One, and because three best practice procedures were diffusing, it was decided to add three hours each day making it an 16 hour workshop in total. In order to expand the focus on local context, new topics were covered including stakeholder management and even more emphasis was placed on planning. A new teaching case (with exercises relevant to the context of the new group of project managers) was developed and incorporated. The teaching case allowed the participants to experience a project situation that could easily have been their own project. This new case context was important to give the participants the perception of behavioral control through

The first workshop in Iteration Two was held in August 2013 in North America, the second in September (Europe), a third in October (Europe), and a fourth in the beginning of November again in North America. Learning from the first iteration continued through the workshops in the second iteration. In the first workshop, the new teaching case was not fully successful in building in the participants' own context. More work was needed to attract the participants to picture themselves as working with just such a project. Between the first and the second workshop the teaching case was updated. It was important to get it exactly right so that the participants could picture themselves in it as if it was their own project.

Another limitation concerned the co-trainer's ability to command a role as opinion leader. The co-trainer in Iteration Two had many years' experience in industry but only one year experience in ENKACE. While well-equipped to contextualize a new best practice, this co-trainer lacked corporate-level experience with this particular new practice itself. This clearly led to limitations in the co-trainer's ability to take on the role both as opinion leader for the new practice, and as contextualizing expert to help the participants situate the new practice in their own projects.

4.3   Iteration Three

In parallel with the latter part of Iteration Two another target group of project managers were identified. This third target population for the best practices was land operations in immature markets. Again, the aim of the workshop was to diffuse the use of best practice procedures, e.g. in dealing with the immature market and the risks incurred by it.

In Iteration Three a very experienced co-trainer with many years at ENKACE was engaged. This co-trainer also took on a more active role in the workshop. Where the division of work in the first two iterations had been 70-30% between the trainer/researcher and the co-trainer/ENKACE-er, in Iteration Three the division of work was fifty-fifty.

In October 2013, the first instance of Iteration Three opened. The timing was again eight hours a day for two days. The participants fell in two groups; Old with more than 20 years' experience (on average), and Young with about five years' experience (on average).

An interesting observation was that the intended behavior (the buy-in) by the Young group was higher than the Old group. The attitude from some of old group was, "just let me keep doing what I have been doing all the time; why bother with a new best practice procedure? To me my practice is good enough."

Another interesting observation was that the co-trainer had been training some of the Young group four-five years ago when they first came to the company. This history strongly influenced the co-trainer's ability to function as opinion leader among these people. They simply accepted straight away what was being taught as best practice. In contrast, the Old group needed to see several examples before becoming convinced that they were confronting a best practice.

4.4   The Effect of the Interventions

In the first iteration there was very clear buy-in (behavioral intention) to the procedure immediately after the workshop. An interesting question is (of course) whether that behavior intention yielded behavioral achievement. (In other words, did this buy-in last?) Preliminary indications are positive. The Iteration One co-trainer observed improved use of the best practice had continued months later. However, no exact figures have been gathered yet. So it is still too early to measure an effect (for example as a lower percentage of failing projects).

In the second iteration there was clear behavioral intention toward two out of three best practices. For the first two instances the buy-in was not directly measured. But then we developed an instrument specifically for measuring buy-in (behavioral intention). The questions asked for the first best practice procedure (on starting projects) are shown in Figure 3.

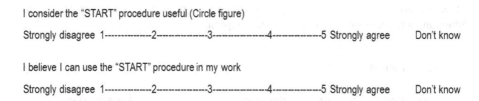

I consider the "START" procedure useful (Circle figure)

Strongly disagree 1--------------2--------------3--------------4--------------5 Strongly agree   Don't know

I believe I can use the "START" procedure in my work

Strongly disagree 1--------------2--------------3--------------4--------------5 Strongly agree   Don't know

Fig. 3. Best practice "buy-in" questions for determining behavioral intention

Similar questions were asked for the "CONTINUE" best practice procedure on ongoing project management and for the Project Quality PLAN procedure.

The buy in for the three procedures after instance 3 (the third best practice) was reasonably good. On a scale from 1 to 5 (with 5 being "Strongly Agree") the scoring is shown in Table 2.

Table 2. Behavior intention (buy-in) for three best practices after instance three

N = 14	START Useful	START I can use	CONTINUE useful	CONTINUE I can use	PLAN useful	PLAN I can use
Average	3.57	3.57	3.46	3.54	3.71	3.71

The buy-in for the three procedures at the end of the training was quite good and noticeably higher than in instance 3. On a scale from 1 to 5 with 5 being "Strongly Agree" the scoring at the end is shown in Table 3.

Table 3. Behavioral intention (buy-in) at the end of the intervention

N = 15	START Useful	START I can use	CONTINUE useful	CONTINUE I can use	PLAN useful	PLAN I can use
Average	4.00	3.36	3.86	3.50	4.07	3.93

There was a change between workshop instance 3 and workshop instance 4. We gave the participants an exercise for each best practice/procedure: "Make a critical review of the procedure and come up with at least one observation e.g. on something missing or superfluous". This exercise seems to have a positive influence possibly linked to participants' perception of control over the procedures and ability to influence it.

In the third iteration three instances has taken place. The measured buy-in effect of the first instance workshop was good. Seven out of nine rated the effect "Good", one rated it "Fair, and one rated in "Inadequate". The one rating it inadequate pointed to the lack of relevance of the procedures to the individual himself as the main cause.

Overall, however, there was a high measured positive effect of the workshop on participant behavioral intention (buy-in) to adopt the best practices.

5 Discussion

The learning that developed across iterations one and two shifted our perspective on the essential practical problem. We initially framed the problem as "resistance-to-change". Across the iterations, we reframed this problem as "not-invented-here".

This re-framing arose as the role of the co-trainer evolved. In keeping with Roger's (2003) theory that opinion leaders can help overcome resistance to change, the initial role of the co-trainer was pronounced as an opinion leader. As the iterations evolved, a further critical role emerged: that of contextualizing expert who helped participants see themselves using the new best practice in their own projects. The importance of both roles became evidence in the comparison of the iterations. In iteration one, the co-trainer was both opinion leader and contextualizing expert. In iteration one, the outcome of the TPB-based training program was positive. In iteration two, the co-trainer was well prepared as an opinion leader, but a weakly prepared as a contextual expert. The outcome of the TPB-based training program was less positive. In iteration three, the co-trainer was more carefully chosen to strongly suit both roles. The outcome of the TPB-based training program was very positive.

The research question at hand is, "Why do organizations fall victim to the innate problems with diffusion of best practices?" Our work first reveals that there are two essential innate problems involving behavioral planning: (1) resistance-to-change, and (2) not-invented-here. Problem one is a deeply human issue involving both psychological and cognitive components. Grounding training in TPB provides an avenue to resolving this problem. In our research setting, however, the second problem is also a facet of decentralized organizations. It is a tension between centricity and diversity in the sense that widespread adoption of best practices assumes sufficient organizational coherence to permit distributed adoption of the practice. But in decentralized organizations, such an assumption may only hold in the most central part of the organization. Diffusion of a best practice requires the engagement of experts who can help adopters situate the practice in their own specific context. Such experts address the not-invented-here problem but do not obviate the resistance-to-change problem. Also needed are opinion leaders.

Organizations fall victim to innate problems of diffusion of best practices because there is a problem dualism confronting such diffusion: resistance-to-change and not-invented-here. Such diffusion is aided when both opinion leaders and contextualizing experts are engaged in the process.

The results reported in this paper has some likeliness to the work of Mathiassen et al. [18] on Software Process Improvement. In Chapter 1 they discuss how important it is to focus on real problems to motivate improvements [18, p. 4]. That is exactly the mechanism used in the workshops at ENKACE. Mathiassen et al. [18, p. 11] also emphasizes that "Participation makes improvement happen" which is exactly why it was so successful involving co-trainers in the workshop.

6   Conclusion

Research that considers the nature of best practices and in particular the diffusion of best practices is remarkably sparse. This may lead to a critical suspicion that the diffusion of best practice is difficult or nearly impossible. However, at the core of being professional often lies the notion of being able to apply best practices. In that sense professionals are knowledge carrying agents across or within organizations.

In this paper we have described an Action Case study with the aim of using TPB as the kernel theory for a design of a method for diffusing best practices within the case organization ENKACE. In short we found that it is possible to use TPB for guiding a design. And we found that the resulting design actually diffused best practice within ENKACE. In more detail we found:

Diffusion of best practices can be motivated as part of a professional identity within an organization especially through the systematic engagement of opinion leaders to influence subjective norm.

It is important to allow the described best practice to be adopted into the community of practice that contextualizes the practices. One possible vehicle for achieving this diffusion is the discussion of lessons learned from relevant, completed projects.

Lessons learned from prior projects can be used for co-constructing a practice – building on the best practice – in a new setting with different actors. Internal stickiness that makes the diffusion costly is hard to avoid. But using TPB as kernel theory for the design can help considerably.

Best practice diffusion often involves a dependence upon the transfer of primarily *explicit* knowledge. But the transfer of *implicit* aspects is also an important part of working professionally. Actors in the field are not just receivers of a best practice, but are co-constructors of this best practice. The workshop design applied here (cf. Figure 2) allowed for this.

Furthermore, our findings from ENKACE indicate that the match between the practice and the context materialized in the presence of two concordant factors. On the context side, the qualities of the selected co-trainer / opinion leader were necessary to provide the subjective norm described in TPB. On the best practice side, the technological qualities of the best practice itself were necessary to instill the ideal attitude (belief that the behavior will be effective). These two factors were especially critical if the source context of the best practice is qualitatively different from the target context into which the organization is seeking to diffuse the best practice.

References

1. Ungan, M.C.: Manufacturing best practices: Implementation success factors and performance. Journal of Manufacturing Technology Management 18(3), 333–348 (2007)
2. Teodoro, M.P., Hughes, A.G.: Socializer or Signal?, How Agency Accreditation Affects Organizational Culture. Public Administration Review 72(4), 583–591 (2012)
3. Carr, C., Pudelko, M.: Convergence of Management Practices in Strategy, Finance and HRM between the USA, Japan and Germany. International Journal of Cross Cultural Management: CCM 6(1), 75–100 (2006)

4. Creplet, F., et al.: Consultants and experts in management consulting firms. Research Policy 30(9), 1517–1535 (2001)
5. Gooderham, P.N., Nordhaug, O., Ringdal, K.: Institutional and Rational Determinants of Organizational Practices: Human Resource Management in European Firms. Administrative Science Quarterly 44(3), 507–531 (1999)
6. Gonnering, R.S.: The Seductive Allure Of "Best Practices": Improved Outcome Is A Delicate Dance Between Structure And Process. Emergence: Complexity and Organization 13(4), 94–101 (2011)
7. Komporozos-athanasiou, A., et al.: Policy as a struggle for meaning: disentangling knowledge translation across international health contexts. Knowledge Management Research & Practice 9(3), 215–227 (2011)
8. Dooley, K.J., Subra, A., Anderson, J.: Adoption Rates and Patterns of Best Practices in New Product Development. International Journal of Innovation Management 6(1), 85 (2002)
9. Szulanski, G.: Exploring internal stickiness: Impediments to the transfer of best practice within the firm. Strategic Management Journal 17, 27–43 (1996)
10. Hargrave, T.J., Van De Ven, A.H.: A Collective Action Model of Institutional Innovation. Academy of Management Review 31(4), 864–888 (2006)
11. Walls, J.G., Widmeyer, G.R., El Sawy, O.A.: Building an information system design theory for vigilant EIS. Information Systems Research 3(1), 36–59 (1992)
12. Fishbein, M., Ajzen, I.: Belief, attitude, intention, and behavior: An introduction to theory and research 1975. Addison-Wesley, Reading (1975)
13. Ajzen, I., Fishbein, M.: Understanding attitudes and predicting social behavior. Englewood Cliffs, Prentice-Hall (1980)
14. Ajzen, I.: Theory of planned behavior. In: Van Lange, P.A.M., Kruglanski, A.W., Higgins, E.T. (eds.) Handbook of Theories of Social Psychology, pp. 438–459. Sage (2011)
15. Ajzen, I.: The theory of planned behavior. Organizational Behavior and Human Decision Processes 50(2), 179–211 (1991)
16. Braa, K., Vidgen, R.: Interpretation, intervention, and reduction in the organizational laboratory: a framework for in-context information system research. Accounting, Management and Information Technologies 9(1), 25–47 (1999)
17. Rogers, E.M.: Diifusion of Innovations, 5th edn. The Free Press, New York (2003)
18. Mathiassen, L., Pries-Heje, J., Ngwenyama, O. (eds.): Improving Software Organizations. From Principles to Practice. Addison-Wesley, Boston (2002)

Digital Innovation and Social Dilemmas

Maria Åkesson and Michel Thomsen

Halmstad University
Sweden
{maria.akesson,michel.thomsen}@hh.se

Abstract. Digital innovation is rapidly reshaping society, affecting fundamental aspects of our everyday activities and lives. This development is accompanied with benefits as well as social dilemmas. In this paper we approach this class of challenges in IS digital innovation research. We investigate how social challenges are attended in research agendas, and reflect upon social challenges emerging from a digital service innovation project. Based on the empirical case, we present a scenario that illustrates how social challenges can unfold in digital service innovation. The case exemplifies three conflicts of interest that are used to discuss implications for the research agendas for digital innovation. We propose that explicit attention is paid to social and ethical challenges, taking a large scale and interdisciplinary approach on social and ethical challenges in digital ecosystems.

Keywords: Digital innovation, research agendas, social and ethical challenges, social dilemmas.

1   Introduction

Digital innovation is continuously reshaping everyday activities, affecting many aspects of our lives. Innovative digital services are designed and implemented in a variety of contexts, targeting new user groups and application areas. For example, digital services have been developed to promote independent living for elderly [1] and for medical support in homes for people with diabetes [2]. Innovative digital design is also implemented in numerous products. Newspapers and books are being digitized, cars have novel digital capability, shoes have embedded chips counting steps and measuring blood pressure, etc. The rapid development of digital technology enables innovative digital services, expanding design into new contexts, confronting us with new social dilemmas.

While digital innovation indeed enables novel values to large groups of people, others are left behind. As Walsham [3, p.91] pose, it is important to ask – Who benefits, and who is missed out? Walsham´s question clearly has bearing on digital innovation and design. Within IS research more assessment of social consequences has been emphasized [4]. Laying out a future agenda for the IS field, Walsham suggests use of critical approaches and strong ethical goals in IS research. Let us give an example of a social dilemma. Imagine a tourist bus equipped with an intelligent remote

B. Bergvall-Kåreborn and P.A. Nielsen (Eds.): TDIT 2014, IFIP AICT 429, pp. 49–61, 2014.

diagnostic system (RDS). The RDS predicts a break failure before entering downhill on Timmelsjoch-Hochalpenstrasse (Fig. 1), and a potential accident is luckily avoided.

Fig. 1. Timmelsjoch-Hochalpenstrasse

This digital innovation clearly has benefits for safer bus transportation. Now, imagine the difference RDS can make in developing countries with limited resources, and where traffic accidents are common due to technical failures. So, how do we approach this class of challenges in digital innovation, affecting individuals, groups of people and society at large?

Since the millennium, digital innovation has been recognized as an important IS research theme. IS scholars like Kalle Lyytinen, Youngjin Yoo, Richard Boland and Ola Henfridsson have published proposals for research agendas, calls for research, and commentaries on digital innovation. In this paper we investigate how social challenges are treated in these publications, and reflect upon social dilemmas that emerged in a digital innovation project in the vehicle industry. In this project an intelligent RDS is developed with a vehicle manufacturer that seeks to expand business by adding digital services to their vehicles. There are technical and organizational challenges associated with this ambition, however in this paper we pay particular attention to the social challenges. We adopt a broad view on social challenges by referring to the world agenda for sustainable development, including aspects such as social responsibility, social justice and equity [5]. Using a scenario based on the RDS project, we illustrate potential benefits and social dilemmas in this project. A social dilemma emerges when actions or decisions impair, or has the potential to impair the wellbeing of an individual or group. Social dilemmas, or what Walsham [6] refers to as ethical issues, impact on the moral well-being of organizations and are important to IS scholars. The aim of this paper is to discuss and empirically illustrate social and ethical dilemmas accompanying digital innovation, and to contribute to the agenda for future research on digital innovation.

The paper is organized as follows. We start with an overview of challenges addressed in calls for research and research agendas on digital innovation. We then present the empirical context, the RDS project, and an empirically grounded scenario illustrating how social dilemmas can unfold in digital service innovation. Finally, we discuss social dilemmas and ethics in digital innovation research.

2   Calls for Research and Research Agendas on Digital Innovation

Digital innovation is a sub field in IS which captures the innovative capacity driven by the rapid development of digital technology. In general terms, innovation refers to an outcome perceived as new, weather it is an idea, object, or process, as well as to the process of creating this newness [7]. The newness may be a recombination of old ideas challenging the present order in such a way that it is new to the people involved [8]. Digital innovation refers combining digital and physical components in new ways making products programmable, addressable, sensible, communicatable, memorable, traceable and associable [9]. Such digitization distinguishes digital innovation from non-digital innovation. The generative capacity of digital technology enables refinement, expansion and recombination of digital services [10]. To its nature, digital innovation is distributed because the control over product components is distributed across multiple firms, and the product knowledge is distributed across heterogeneous disciplines and communities [10]. Accordingly, digital innovation spans beyond single stakeholders control [11], creating a paradox of change and control in digital innovation, see e.g. [12]. This in turn, continuously leads to new emergent and fragmented design situations [13].

By digital service innovation we refer to services enabled by digital innovation. To give an example we use the RDS. In this case, buses are digitized by embedding sensors, processors, wireless transmission and algorithms for prediction of faults in the buses. This digitization of buses provides a platform for digital services innovation. An example of a digital service enabled by the RDS is a real-time monitoring service of a fleet of buses offered to bus operating companies. This type of digital service innovation brings new business opportunities for manufacturing companies, expanding their business with digital services afforded by digital innovation [14].

Within the IS sub field of digital innovation a number of calls for research and research agendas on digital innovation have been published since the millennium. We have reviewed central research themes, and how social and ethical challenges are articulated in these publications (summarized in order of appearance in Table 1).

Table 1. Digital innovation research themes and challenges

Theme	Emerging research agenda
Information Systems Research - The Next Wave of Nomadic Computing, Vol. 13, No. 4, December 2002, pp. 377-388 Lyytinen K. and Yoo Y. - Research Commentary [15]	
The authors analyse nomadic information environments based on their prevalent features of mobility, digital convergence, and mass scale, along, with their mutual interdependencies.	A research framework that organizes research topics in nomadic information environments at the individual, team, organizational, and interorganizational levels and is comprised of both service and infrastructure development, we assess the opportunities and challenges for IS research (see Table 1 p. 381)

Table 1. (*Continued*)

Attention to social and ethical challenges
Na - The authors mention e.g. "At the level of services, IS researchers need to address the design, use, adaptation and impact of (digital) services." (see Table 1, theme 2, p. 381). Infrastructure for individual level – Governance and control address access privileges, privacy, and visibility of personal and public knowledge.

Communications of the ACM - Issues and challenges in Ubiquitous computing, 2002, Vol. 45, No.12, pp. 63-65. Lyytinen, K. and Yoo, Y. - Special issue article [16]

The authors suggest that radical improvements in microprocessor cost-performance ratios have, in 40 years, transformed the early large "computing machines" into compact devices that enable, mediate, support, and organize our daily activities.	The authors suggest that the shift toward ubiquitous computing poses multiple novel, social, and organizational challenges. Technical level issues of computer architecture and configurations on a large scale. "… the emergence of truly integrated sociotechnical systems will create a wide array of research and policy issues that deal with social organization, impact, and the future of work, organizations, and institutions." (p. 65)

Attention to social and ethical challenges
The authors put forward questions that concern previously, unexplored (social) challenges that will emerge at the border between the technical and the social some issues are to be left outside the technical implementation to be addressed by social negotiation and due process; other issues should be addressed during technical design.

Organization Science - Organizing for Innovation in the Digitized World, Vol. 20, No. 1, January-February 2009, pp. 278-279 Yoo, Y., Boland, R., Lyytinen, K. and Majchrzak, A. - Special issue [17]

The authors suggest that many challenges related to rapid and radical digitization will dominate the concerns of managers in this century. Studying the full impact of digital technology on innovation requires cross-disciplinary dialogue, richer vocabularies, diverse theoretical perspectives, new research methodologies, novel data analysis techniques and increase the breadth of research.	Research questions relating to: - Convergent and generative characteristics of pervasive digital technology - Organizational innovation with pervasive digital technology

Attention to social and ethical challenges
Na - One question is: What are the social and material characteristics of digital technology that enable radical innovation?

Information Systems Research - *The New Organizing Logic of Digital Innovation: An Agenda for Information Systems Research* Vol. 21, No. 4, December 2010, pp. 724-735. Yoo, Y, Henfridsson, O and Lyytinen, K.-Research Commentary [10]

Pervasive digitization gives birth to a new type of product architecture: *the layered modular architecture* A conceptual framework describing the new organizing logic for digital innovation	A conceptual framework of a new IS research agenda with digital innovation including research themes relating to: - New strategic frameworks - Cooperate IT infrastructure

Attention social and ethical challenges
Na

Table 1. (*Continued*)

Information Systems Research - Digital Infrastructures: The Missing IS Research Agenda Vol. 21, No. 4, December 2010, pp. 748-759. Tilson, D., Lyytinen, K. and Sørensen, C. - Research Commentary [12]	
Use of e.g. mobile services creates decentralized work organizations. Understanding these new dynamics will necessitate the field paying attention to digital infrastructures as a category of IT artefacts.	Three research directions: 1) Theories of the nature of digital infrastructure as a separate type of IT artefact 2) Digital infrastructures as relational constructs are shaping all traditional IS research areas. 3) Paradoxes of change and control as salient IS phenomena. Suggestions on feasible methods for studying large scale sociotechnical phenomena.

Attention to social and ethical challenges
Na

MIS Quarterly - Computing in Everyday Life: A Call for Research On Experiential Computing Vol. 34 No. 2, pp. 213-231, June 2010 Yoo, Y. – Issues and opinions [10]	
As the rapid development of digital technology continues to make computers and computing a part of everyday experiences, we are once again in need of a new discipline of the artificial. The author argues that the IS community must expand its intellectual boundaries by embracing experiential computing as an emerging field of inquiry in order to fill this growing intellectual void.	An experiential computing design science research encompassing both behavioural and design sciences Six research opportunities are suggested to the IS research community relating to e.g. sociomateriality, generativity, group experience, and hybrid networks.

Attention to social and ethical challenges
The author does not discuss topics like social challenges, ethics or "who is missed out?" in any detail. However he suggest research opportunities that relate to e.g. social challenges and integration of digital infrastructures with existing cultural infrastructures.

Information Systems Research - Report on the Research Workshop: "Digital Challenges in Innovation Research" 2010. Yoo, Y., Lyytinen, K., Boland, R. and Berente, N. - Research workshop to guide future research on digital innovations. [18]	
The authors suggest that ubiquity of digitalization is one of the primary forces behind innovations across a wide range of product and service categories.	Participants were asked to address four questions; one is What are the organizational, technological, social and economic implications of these issues, and what generative processes of innovation and change emerge from them? Six recommendations for future research: Multi disciplinary research, Design scholarship, Taking data seriously, Infrastructure, and Theorizing digital technology.

Attention to social and ethical challenges
Na, One question deals with organizational, technological, social and economic implications of these issues, and what generative processes of innovation and change emerge from them.

Table 1. (*Continued*)

Organization Science - Organizing for Innovation in the Digitized World. Vol. 23, No. 5, September-October 2012, pp. 1398-1408. Yoo, Y., Boland, R., Lyytinen, K. and Majchrzak, A. - Special issue [19]

Pervasive digital technologies change the nature of product and service innovations. The organizational research implications of these three digital innovation traits.	An analysis of convergence and generativity observed in innovations reveals three traits: (1) the importance of digital technology platforms, (2) the emergence of distributed innovations, and (3) the prevalence of combinatorial innovation. Identification of research opportunities for organization science scholars.

Attention to social and ethical challenges
Na – one article in the special issue deals with the consequences of digitalization of tools, in the context of car development. The authors (Bailey, Leonardi and Barley *"explore how the increased dependence on more realistic digital tools to simulate, visualize, and test new complex products and their "crashability" leads to unintended consequences of separating physical objects and people from the virtual representations of design objects. They also show how the use of these highly realistic digital tools leads to recon-figurations of jobs and tasks and design outcomes are not always desirable. Finally, they point out that placing too much trust on digital tools can backfire, and the likelihood of casting blind faith on digital technology increases as its power and capacity to represent the world grows*. Their finding provides a contrarian perspective to existing stream of research.

MIS Quarterly – Digital Innovation as a Fundamental and Powerful Concept in the Information Systems Curriculum. Forthcoming 2014-2015. Fichman, R. G., Dos Santos, B. L. and Zheng, Z. E. – Issues and opinions [20]

Potential teaching themes related to IS core class. Examples: IT for competitive advantage, IT assimilation, digitally infused products, Ethical issues an IT, IT driven industry transformation, IT architecture, and interface design.	Suggestions to the IS research agenda for digital innovation: - Broaden innovation research - Focus more attention on distinctiveness and heterogeneity - Focus more attention on how digital technology transforms innovation

Attention to social and ethical challenges
Ethical issues an IT is mentioned as a pedagogical theme, but not discussed

Table 1 shows that most themes relate to technical and organizational challenges, and that digital innovation is addressed as a large scale phenomenon. It also shows that central themes are the characteristics of digital technology, infrastructure and platforms, conditions for innovation and processes, and the general organizing logic of digital innovation. The table shows, however, that explicit attention is put to the nature of digital technology, while ethical considerations are articulated in only few of these publications.

3   Empirical Context – The R2D2 Project

To illustrate how social challenges can unfold in digital innovation research, we zoom into a collaborative research project in the vehicle industry. The R2D2-project started in

April 2009 and was finalized in December 2013. The participants were a global vehicle manufacturer and a group of researchers in computer engineering and informatics.

The overall goal of the project was to develop an intelligent RDS that diagnose the health status of individual vehicles while in traffic. The RDS detects deviating patterns of vehicles with sensor technology in for example a fleet of city buses, and wirelessly transmit information about the buses while in traffic. This digital technology enables digital services such as prediction of faults, maintenance and traffic planning. In exploiting potential digital services enabled by the RDS, public bus transport organizations and bus operating companies were engaged in activities in the project as they are potential customers.

The incitement for the vehicle company to explore this innovation path is grounded in an ambition to expand their business with digital services coupled with their vehicles. The vehicle company has offered services to support the function of vehicles since 1985. This has been regarded as a post market and not a core business. In 2009, the company decided to prioritize servitization of their products, taking digital innovation initiatives such as the R2D2 project. This expansion brings technical, organizational and social challenges that were addressed in the project.

The rationale of an intelligent RDS, if successfully implemented and adopted, is benefits for traffic safety, reduced maintenance costs, increased life length of vehicles, increased up-time of operation, better work environment for bus drivers, improved service quality for public, etc. In other words, there are many potential benefits for large groups of bus riders, public transport companies, bus operators, and other stakeholders in the transport ecosystem. The project is therefore relevant in relation to the question – who benefits, and who is missed out.

The project was organized in two parallel parts. The first part involved the technical development of the RDS including diagnostics and prediction of maintenance, with a focus on methods for diagnosing and predicting faults. The second part involved digital service innovation enabled by the RDS. This included studying the RDS ecosystem, business potential and customer value of such services. While the first part started in 2009 and ended 2013, the second part started in 2010 and ended 2012. This paper is based on the second part where three informatics researchers and two service developers from the vehicle company participated. In this part of the project, the researchers interacted with different company representatives and external stakeholders. In Table 2 we present a summary of activities in the project.

In the monthly project meetings, participants from both project parts gathered to inform about and discuss project progress. These meetings were generic and cross disciplinary including technical as well as service innovation issues that emerged in the project. The meetings with service developers were planning meetings for the second part of the project and related to the digital service innovation. The interviews with the vehicle company representatives aimed at capturing the internal vision of RDS, and to get a deeper insight into the company reasoning on challenges associated with the digital services. The interviews with stakeholders outside the vehicle company aimed at exploring potential digital services based on the RDS. The workshops were explorative and aimed at creating scenarios for future digital services. In addition to meetings, interviews and workshops, there were group discussions in order to gain a holistic understanding of public bus transport. Finally, the data from these activities is complemented with documents such as minutes of meetings, project newsletters and project reports.

Table 2. Summary of sources, activities and participants

Sources, activities and participants (2010-2012)	Duration	Number
Project meetings		
Monthly project meetings	2-3 hours	20
Service development meetings with company service developers	2-3 hours	30
Interviews		
Vehicle company business managers	1-2 hours	3
Vehicle company service development manager	1 hour	1
Vehicle company technology development manager	1 hour	1
Vehicle company repair and maintenance manager	1 hour	1
The vehicle company project manager	2 hours	1
Public transport organization traffic manager	2 hours	1
Bus operating company manager	2 hours	2
Workshops		
Workshops with vehicle production managers	4 hours	3
Future workshop with bus company representatives	4 hours	1
Scenario workshop with company representatives	4 hours	1
Group discussions		
Visit and group discussion at bus company site	3 hours	1
Visits at bus company testing the RDS	2 hours	2
Documents		
54 Weekly project newsletters	---	54
Minutes and notes of meetings	---	50
Project reports (including scenarios and service concepts etc.)	---	4

When interpreting and reflecting on the activities and interactions in the R2D2 project, we identified social dilemmas observed as conflicts of interest. We exemplify three of these conflicts in an empirically grounded scenario. The scenario is a means to bring life to the sociotechnical context and social dilemmas when RDS is implemented in a public transportation system.

4   The Public Bus Transportation System in Cityville

Alan is responsible for repairs and maintenance planning in BusOp, a bus operating company with the contract for public transport in Cityville. There are 65 vehicles of the brand SmartBus and 15 of the brand Riveras in the fleet of buses in Cityville. In high frequency traffic 78 of these buses are needed in operation, while in low frequency traffic there are about 50 buses in traffic. There are a two hours at nigh when the busses are out of operation. Alan's responsibility is to make sure that there are enough buses available at different times, and to reduce the risk of bus failure while in traffic. This is a complex task.

BusOp has a contract with the vehicle manufacturing company SmartBus for regular maintenance performed according to a schedule every 12 weeks on each individual bus. BusOp also has its own garage where they do checkups and some repairs work. At these occasions parts are, for preventive reasons, also exchanged even if they function. This is costly, but it is weighed against the risk of breakdowns while in traffic, which is a priority to avoid.

The high frequency timeslots are the bottlenecks in Alan´s planning, but the biggest challenge is that individual buses do not have the same pattern. For some busses the 12 week regular maintenance is enough, but other buses might need it every 8 or even 6 weeks. There is even one bus that is seldom in traffic since the engine for some reason suddenly stops and the driver cannot start it again. Because of the individual differences Alan keeps journals on each individual bus.

Disturbance in operation happens every day. It can be anything from a door not closing, or flat tire, to break failure and electrical problems. In some cases the problem is easy to solve by a mechanic that drives to the bus and fixes the problem. In other cases a replacement bus needs to be put in, and the bus that has broken down is towed to the garage. These types of failures are disruptive and disturbing for the bus riders, and the situation is uncomfortable for the bus driver and other employees in BusOp. An even worse situation, that luckily happens less often, is when the break down causes an accident. The most common breakdown causing accidents is break failures.

SmartBus is an innovative company that in collaboration with researchers has developed a new intelligent RDS, enabling to predict faults such as break failure before they actually happen. The overall function of the RDS is to model and characterize operation for a fleet of buses, and to predict their maintenance need over a lifetime. The system is built on an architecture where sensors are embedded in different parts of the bus. The sensors generate on-board data that the system continuously mines. The information is sent to a back office server where it is analyzed for deviating patterns by comparison to reference data. This enables to detect faults early and to estimate the lifetime of parts (see Figure 2).

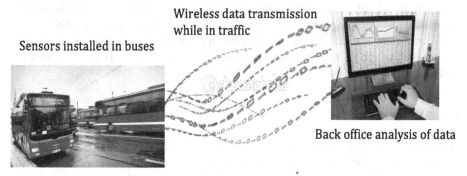

Fig. 2. The overall principle of the RDS

SmartBus is now offering a set of digital services enabled by the RDS to BusOp. The service offer builds on a monthly payment for continuous monitoring of the health status of the buses. Alan thinks this service is a great help for his work. Now he can monitor the buses in real time while in traffic. He can better match maintenance with needs for individual buses. Alan can also prevent break-downs with help of the predictive information which in turn improve the overall up-time of the bus traffic. Most importantly, Alan really hopes this will make the zero accident goal of BusOp possible.

There is just on thing he is not so happy about. The RDS service is only available for the SmartBus vehicles, hence the Riveras buses cannot be connected to the service. Bob, the traffic planning manager, finds this challenging. He thinks it is difficult to decide what routes to put the now safer SmartBus buses and what routes to traffic with the Riveras buses. He has taken the Riveras out of school bus operation and now looks at statistics of traffic, passenger numbers etc. in order to make an as good a decision as he can.

Bob also works for the bus operating company BusGo in a neighbor city. BusGo drives only SmartBus vehicles equipped with RDS technology, but they have not found room for the RDS service in their budget. When Bob planes the school bus rout he cannot help thinking that the information in the system could prevent accidents. However, BusGo cannot does not get that information since they are not paying for the service. This makes Bob feel uncomfortable. He wonders what the parents would say if they knew this.

Alan really likes the RDS service. At a public transport convention Alan did a presentation together with Jessie from SmartBus. They explained the RDS and Alan spoke in very positive terms about it and how it contributes to better up-time for BusOp. Jessie explained how this is a new business opportunity and a how SmartBus now can have a more service oriented relation to BusOp. They can now work together to develop more digital services enabled by the RDS. At the convention a representative from the national transport administration asked about the type of data that the system mines. She asked if this perhaps is important information that can help develop new routines for roadworthiness, tests etc, in turn contributing to a safer traffic environment for all. "If your data shows that a part should be examined in roadworthiness tests it is of public interest that we have that information". Jessie hesitated, and realized that opening the system for public organizations would have implications for future business cases. She recognized that there is also a dilemma since the data mining enables analyzes of the weaknesses of SmartBus vehicles. This is of course of confidential nature for the SmartBus company.

5   Discussion and Conclusion

In this paper we empirically illustrate social and ethical dilemmas accompanying digital innovation. We discuss that digital service opportunities bring social and ethical challenges. We show how this class of challenges is treated in IS research agendas for digital innovation, and we show how social dilemmas can emerge in digital innovation initiatives.

The review of calls for research and research agendas on digital innovation give at hand that the technical re-orientation in IS is well covered, while social challenges are articulated less explicit. Since digital innovation is diffused to new social contexts, it is reasonable to expect that a) potential teaching themes [20] more emphasis on social challenges and ethics, and b) social and ethical issues to be well mirrored in the research agendas.

The investigation into the digital innovation project showed how such challenges can unfold, in this case conflicts of interest. In summary, the scenario shows how third parties stakeholders such as bus riders might have different value perceptions and interests than what is inscribed in the service design. This was illustrated with the example of school buses and the bus operating companies' restrained budgets. Another conflict of interest was related to the challenge of balancing safety and risk in traffic planning, and the relation to business model interests of service provision. This is portrayed with the example of how the RDS was locked-in by the bus manufacturer for exclusively for their brand. Finally, the scenario gives an example of how public interest of data mining as a source for societal improvement, in this case improved traffic safety, potentially can be in conflict with the interests of companies building up data mines as a resource for digital service innovation.

Acknowledging the nature of digital innovation such as stakeholder heterogeneity, generativity, multi layered logic, distribution of knowledge, the paradox of change and control, see e.g. [9, 10, 11, 12], we suggest there are implications when addressing social challenges in digital innovation. As highlighted by the scenario, it is overpowering to one single actor to overview and control the chain of possible social consequences in large scale digital ecosystems. It is not always evident who is to take responsibility for, or to coordinate, the systematic application of moral principles in distributed innovation settings. Furthermore, the complex nature of digital innovation continuously creates new research and design situations. As a consequence new and multi disciplinary social challenges rapidly emerge in digital innovation settings. Without doubt, the fragmented nature of digital innovation adds to this complexity.

There certainly are important research themes addressing technical and organizational challenges in the research agendas for digital innovation. As illustrated in the scenario there is a complex maze of business opportunities and ethical challenges when digital innovation is diffused to new social contexts. The social dilemmas observes in the RDS project unmistakably point to social dilemmas that can emerge in digital service innovation when apprising value of services from different stakeholder´s perspectives. The interest of one stakeholder can clearly lead to decisions that can impair the wellbeing of people. We propose that explicit attention is paid to social and ethical challenges, for example with collaborative analysis of consequences and models for shared ethical responsibility.

In the research agendas in reviewed, digital innovation is mainly addressed as a large scale phenomenon. Our understanding is that the structures and architectures on large scale have ethical implications that pervasively span everyday human activities. We therefore propose taking a large scale approach also to social and ethical challenges in digital ecosystems.

As suggested by e.g. Walsham [3] and Majchrzak et al. [4] this class of challenges cannot be solved by simple interventions – today's sociotechnical challenges encourage for multidisciplinary research initiatives. Consequently, we suggest that there is a need to find efficient ways to articulate and share our experiences and insights with researchers in relating disciplines to contribute to strong ethical goals in the future digital innovation research agenda.

References

1. Frantzidis, C.A., Bamidis, P.D.: Description and future trends of ICT solutions offered towards independent living: The case of LLM project. In: Proc. of PETRA (2009)
2. Kanstrup, A.M., Bertelsen, P., Glasemann, M., Boye, N.: Design for more: An ambient perspective on diabetes. In: Proc. of PDC, pp. 118–127 (2008)
3. Walsham, G.: Are we making a better world with ICTs? Reflections on a future agenda for the IS field. Journal of Information Technology 27(2), 87–93 (2012)
4. Majchrzak, M., Markus, L.M., Wareham, J.: ICT and Societal Challenges, Call for Papers Special Issue. MIS Quarterly (2013)
5. Report of the World Commission on Environment and Development: Our Common Future, http://www.un-documents.net/ocf-02.htm#I (retrieved November 21, 2013)
6. Walsham, G.: Ethical theory, codes of ethics and IS practice. Information Systems Journal 6(1), 69–81 (1996)
7. Slappendel, C.: Perspectives on Innovation in Organizations. Organization Studies 17(1), 107–129 (1996)
8. Van de Ven, A.H.: Central Problems in the Management of Innovation. Management Science 32(5), 590–607 (1986)
9. Yoo, Y.: Computing in Everyday Life: A Call for Research On Experiential Computing. MIS Quarterly 34(2), 213–231 (2010)
10. Yoo, Y., Henfridsson, O., Lyytinen, K.: Research commentary - the new organizing logic of digital innovation: An agenda for information systems research. Information Systems Research 21(4), 724–735 (2010)
11. Henfridsson, O., Bygstad, B.: The Generative Mechanisms of Digital Infrastructure Evolution. MIS Quarterly 37, 907–931 (2013)
12. Tilson, D., Lyytinen, K., Sørensen, C.: Research Commentary - Digital Infrastructures: The Missing IS Research Agenda. Information Systems Research 21(4), 748–759 (2010)
13. Thomsen, M., Åkesson, M.: Understanding ISD and Innovation through the Lens of Fragmentation. In: Dwivedi, Y.K., Henriksen, H.Z., Wastell, D., De', R. (eds.) TDIT 2013. IFIP AICT, vol. 402, pp. 467–480. Springer, Heidelberg (2013)
14. Akram, A., Bergquist, M., Åkesson, M.: Understanding Tensions in Incumbent Manufacturing Firms – A Study of Digitalized Product. HICSS'47 (January 2014)
15. Lyytinen, K., Yoo, Y.: Research Commentary: The Next Wave of Nomadic Computing. Information Systems Research 13(4), 377–388 (2002)
16. Lyytinen, K., Yoo, Y.: Issues and challenges in Ubiquitous computing. Communications of the ACM 45(12), 63–65 (2002)
17. Yoo, Y., Boland, R., Lyytinen, K., Majchrzak, A.: Organizing for Innovation in the Digitized World. Organization Science 20(1), 278–279 (2009)

18. Yoo, Y., Lyytinen, K., Boland, R., Berente, N.: The Next Wave of Digital Innovation: Opportunities and Challenges: A Report on the Research Workshop 'Digital Challenges in Innovation Research (June 8, 2010), Available at SSRN:
    http://ssrn.com/abstract=1622170 or
    http://dx.doi.org/10.2139/ssrn.1622170
19. Yoo, Y., Boland, R., Lyytinen, K., Majchrzak, A.: Organizing for Innovation in the Digitized World. Organization Science 23(5), 1398–1408 (2012)
20. Fichman, R.G., Dos Santos, B.L., Zheng, Z.E.: Digital Innovation as a Fundamental and Powerful Concept in the Information Systems Curriculum. MIS Quarterly (forthcoming 2014-2015)

Generating Sustainable Value from Open Data in a Sharing Society

Thorhildur Jetzek[1], Michel Avital[2], and Niels Bjørn-Andersen[3]

[1] Copenhagen Business School
`tj.itm@cbs.dk`
[2] Copenhagen Business School
`michel@avital.net`
[3] Copenhagen Business School
`nba.itm@cbs.dk`

Abstract. Our societies are in the midst of a paradigm shift that transforms hierarchal markets into an open and networked economy based on digital technology and information. In that context, open data is widely presumed to have a positive effect on social, environmental and economic value; however the evidence to that effect has remained scarce. Subsequently, we address the question how the use of open data can stimulate the generation of sustainable value. We argue that open data sharing and reuse can empower new ways of generating value in the sharing society. Moreover, we propose a model that describes how different mechanisms that take part within an open system generate sustainable value. These mechanisms are enabled by a number of contextual factors that provide individuals with the motivation, opportunity and ability to generate sustainable value.

Keywords: Sharing society, Sustainable value, Value generating mechanisms, Open data.

1 Introduction

The impact of the digital revolution on our societies can be compared to the ripples caused by a stone thrown in water: spreading outwards and affecting a larger and larger part of our lives with every year that passes. One of the many effects is the emergence of an already unprecedented amount of digital data that is accumulating exponentially. Moreover, a central affordance of digitization is the ability to distribute, share and collaborate, and we have thus seen an "open theme" gaining currency in recent years [18]. These trends are reflected in the explosion of Open Government Data (OGD) initiatives around the world: governments striving to open access to various data-sources and making them available for use and re-use for commercial or other purposes. However, while hundreds of national and local governments have established OGD portals and are being followed by similar initiatives by international institutions, civil society organizations and even businesses, there is a general feeling that the open data initiatives have not yet lived up to their true potential. This feeling

B. Bergvall-Kåreborn and P.A. Nielsen (Eds.): TDIT 2014, IFIP AICT 429, pp. 62–82, 2014.

is not without good reason; the recent Open Data Barometer report highlights that strong evidence on the impacts of OGD is almost universally lacking [11].

This lack of evidence might, however, not be as surprising when we consider the complexity of the task at hand. How do we measure and evaluate something as complicated as the value of open data? And if we cannot show that value is generated – how can these initiatives be sustained? Our take on this dilemma is that before we even start trying to evaluate, we need to develop a deeper understanding of *to what ends* (what it is we want to accomplish with open data) and *by what means* (how this can possibly happen). And due to the embryonic nature of the open data phenomenon, research on open data impacts and affordances is still lacking (see, for instance, [59]).

Our goal with this paper is to contribute to this gap in knowledge by developing a theory on how open data can generate sustainable value. We build on the notion that the world is at an inflection point, where technological advances and boundary-crossing social challenges have come together to create a paradigm shift. This notion was very evident at the 2014 Annual Meeting of the World Economic Forum in Davos, where the shift towards the sharing economy and the current social challenges faced by our societies were repeatedly mentioned. These social challenges are numerous and urgent, and both social, environmental and economic in nature. They range from economic inequality, unemployment and poor social conditions to chronic diseases and climate change.

Given the complexity and cross-boundary nature of these challenges, a new approach is necessary. In particular, we need an approach where social and technological progress co-evolves in order to generate value [37]. We would like to contribute towards such an approach through addressing the following research question: "How can use of open data stimulate the generation of sustainable value?" The definition of sustainable value represents a move away from the previously dominant economic value focus and moving towards a focus on proactive, concerted efforts of businesses, government institutions and the overall community in addressing social challenges in innovative and holistic ways that generate social, environmental and economic value for all stakeholders and future generations [50].

This theory development paper is structured as follows: We first elaborate on the recent trends discussed earlier based on a review of the literature, after which we build theoretical foundations. We propose that we are experiencing a paradigm shift in how people make decisions in their quest for creating and appropriating value enabled by the transformative power of information technology. These recent technical and social developments call for a re-interpretation of the behavioral assumptions used in some of our most prominent value theories. We proceed to discuss four value generating mechanisms that describe different paths through which the use of data can be transformed to value. Our contribution here is a framework that adds a new network-based dimension to the well-established market-based mechanisms of efficiency and innovation (exploitation and exploration). We propose that all four mechanisms interact within an ecosystem we call the *sharing society*, and that the interaction between the private and the public sectors via the different mechanisms can generate the synergies that are necessary to tackle the highly complicated social challenges we face. Finally, we visualize our theory with a nomological network that shows the relationship between the main antecedents that can enable and stimulate value genera-tion from data, the value generating mechanisms and the resulting, sustainable value.

2 Open Data Empowers the Sharing Society

The industrial economy was primarily based on production, where Gross Domestic Product (GDP) was the key measure of economic activity, and buying and selling goods and services on the market became the basic foundation for the value generat-ing mechanisms. A dichotomy of the state and the market was one feature of the in-dustrial economy [38]. The state´s responsibility was to create a structure around the goods that did not fit the market mechanisms, so-called market failures. However, continuing advances in digital technologies have started to disrupt the status quo by altering the way people think, live and work, and by rearranging value pools [30]. This development has led to entirely new forms of products and services that, in many cases, are based on data collection, data re-use and data sharing. The digital revolu-tion, including the digitization of nearly all media, the ubiquity of Internet access, the proliferation of mobile phones and the growth of the Internet of Things, has created multiple affordances which subsequently require a change in the basic assumptions that are used when discussing value maximizing behavior.

First, the digital revolution has led to an explosion in the generation and availability of data. Digitization has affected two important features of data: 1) when data become easily accessible to more than one person at a time, they acquire the feature of non-rivalry and; 2) when marginal costs incurred by re-production and distribution are drastically reduced, re-use of data becomes economically feasible [35], [44]. Second, following the advent of the "open theme", data that have traditionally been locked up in closed repositories are now increasingly becoming open and available for use and re-use [18]. Openness has changed one important feature of digital data, namely, mak-ing them non-excludable. Accordingly, when opened up, digital data become a shared resource - a public good or what has been termed 'digital commons' [19]. Open data, particularly government data, have generated a great deal of excitement around the world for its potential to empower citizens, change how government works and im-prove the delivery of public services. The economic value potential from open data has also been celebrated, and recently estimated as the equivalent of 3 trillion USD per annum globally [29]. In short, computing and networking capabilities combined with openness are expected to drive massive social, political and economic change [24].

Most of the open data initiatives today are driven by governments around the world, the most important driver seemingly being their expectation that open data will stimulate the generation of considerable social, economic and environment value for their societies [22]; [58], [51]. These initiatives have either been fuelled by the politi-cal ideology of Open Government [25] or been focused on economic value genera-tion, highlighting the potential of re-use of data for innovation and efficiency [21]. However, despite this interest, there is still not much evidence of value generation, probably as most of the open data initiatives are still in their infancy [11], [20], [59].

Thus far, most of the published material on value generation is based on predictions and hypotheses, and there is still considerable confusion regarding what needs to be done, who should do it and how (*by what means*), as well as why we are doing it and for whom (*to what ends*). For instance, the technological availability and accessibility of data need to be conceptually separated from the political openness required to drive transparency and accountability [57]. One is concerned with the usability of the resource; the other is a mechanism whereby data are being used for specific purposes.

Interestingly, in the 77 countries surveyed in the Open Data Barometer, less than one in 10 datasets (or 71 out of the 821 public datasets reviewed) were truly open, i.e., available online, in bulk, and under an explicit open license [11]. In most cases, datasets are provided in aggregate formats (often in XLS or CSV), or are not machine readable (PDF files). The Open Data Barometer report also points towards important issues of data quality and trustworthiness. Of the 113 datasets that were available in machine-readable and openly licensed form, researchers found 15 where the sustainability was questionable and 20 that were not up-to-date or published in a timely fashion [11]. Moreover, while recent developments with open data offer unprecedented access to large scale data sets on a huge variety of topics, successful use of such data requires a new set of technical skills and data literacy, that are currently in short supply. Finally, while technology enabled services are key to harnessing the value of data, they are often limited by problems with usability, searchability, language, sufficiency of technological infrastructure and availability of computers and Internet access for many segments of the general population [4]. We conclude that governments still have some way to go: from embracing the value potential of open data to actually implementing the required value generation enabling structures.

Our aim with this paper is to contribute to an improved conceptual clarity in this discussion by presenting an open system we call the sharing society. We define the sharing society as an *open economic and social system in which information technology is leveraged to empower individuals, corporations, non-profits and governments with data that are shared, reused and transformed to sustainable value through different mechanisms.*

Following [6], we assume that the goal of the social system is to maximize utility or what we have defined as sustainable value. We use Coleman's framework as a meta-theory to explain the micro to macro level relationship between use of open data and the generation of sustainable value. Coleman's framework underscores the mediating role of individuals in linking macro-level variables such as social structure and the behavior of the social system [31]. A theory which can generate macro-level empirical generalizations as specific propositions may be thought of as "a theory of individual action, together with a theory of how these actions combine, under specific rules, to produce systemic behavior" [6], p. 20. But how is the sharing society conceptually different from the industrial economy? In the following sections, we outline the basic assumptions for our theory on how open data can generate value in the sharing society.

3   Behavioral Assumptions for Value Generating Mechanisms

Any theory comprises a set of assumptions from which empirical generalizations have been derived [32]. In the social sciences, a satisfactory explanation must ultimately be anchored in hypotheses or assumptions about individual behavior [12]. By making a set of explicit, behavioral assumptions, we can highlight that all macro-level, societal phenomena are inherently derived from human beliefs and actions, and that certain mechanisms mediate these actions between the initial conditions and the observed outcome. Since the core behavioral assumptions of a theory often form the foundation of its mechanistic explanations, it is crucial that these assumptions are explicitly defined and tested during the early stage of empirical research [49].

The classical economic model of strategic interaction assumes that people are (a) only concerned about bettering their own material situation, and (b) able to calculate the optimal strategy for doing so. However, new results from behavioral economics have cast doubt on these assumptions, as evidence shows that people are, in fact, concerned with unobservable payoffs such as reputation, fairness or the well-being of others [45]. Furthermore, people are also concerned with how actions taken today might affect their future well-being. Accordingly, we must consider the wider social impact as well as the sustainability of our current actions [9], [45], [47]. A number of dimensions that can make classical models of rationality somewhat more realistic, while sticking within the vein of fairly rigorous formalization are described in [46]. These include: (a) limiting the types of utility functions, (b) considering the possibility of people having a "multi-valued" utility function and (c) recognizing the costs of gathering and processing information.

The general willingness of people to generate sustainable value is not really contested, but measures have remained elusive, and hence the emphasis on material wealth in economic theory. However, while monetary based indicators offer a convenient way to measure and compare value, there is a cross-disciplinary consensus that we need a more inclusive measure of welfare or wellbeing [47]. In the field of economics, a number of initiatives propose a move beyond using Gross Domestic Product as a measure of a country's progress. Renewed attention has been given to the concept of public value in the e-government and public policy disciplines. The public value framework is based on the premise that public resources should be used to increase value, not only in an economic sense but also more broadly in terms of what is valued by citizens and communities [2], [33]. These trends have resulted in the development of new, broader measures, such as OECD's Better Life Index.

At the organizational level of analysis, the concept of shared value presents a similar ideology. The premise behind shared value is that by including the generation of social value in their strategies, private companies can improve their competitive advantage at the same time as they contribute to society [38].

While most of us would like to act for the good of society, we do not always have the means or the cognitive capability to do so. Most people have limited attention, suffer from status quo bias and choice overload, and are prone to procrastination [45]. Moreover, people typically do not apply sufficient cognitive effort to calculate an optimal strategy, resorting rather to heuristics which can be influenced by context [46].

Rationality of individuals is limited by the information they have, the cognitive limitations of their minds, and the finite amount of time they have to make a decision.

Bounded rationality is "behavior that is intendedly rational but only limitedly so" [46], p. xxiv. So construed, bounded rationality takes exception with the analytically convenient assumption of hyper-rationality but does not preclude a predominantly rational approach to the study of complex economic organization [56]. Given that people face a multi-dimensional value function with complex relationships between individual and social wellbeing and that we as individuals have limited cognitive ability to rationally choose between different options, we can conclude that collection and dissemination of different types of data and the conversion of these data to information and insight are a key resource.

As a foundation for our theory, we make two assumptions. The first is that individuals in general want to go beyond increasing their own material wealth in their value generation efforts. We assume that individuals will strive for sustainable value, including social, environmental and economic value, for all stakeholders and future generations [50]. Sustainable value generation can be the result of collaborative efforts or it can happen through traditional market exchange, but the context in which decisions are made must provide the *motivation*, *opportunity* and *ability* for sustainable value generation to happen.

The second assumption we make is based on the notion of bounded rationality. People will be able to make decisions closer to an "optimum" if provided with the right kind of information about the situation they face. Access to the right kind of information can therefore push the boundaries of our ability to choose rationally and contribute to the generation of sustainable value. This assumption goes across all the proposed value generating mechanisms, i.e., we assume that provided with new data and information, people will choose differently, and this will lead to a sustainable value generation that will happen via different but interlinked mechanisms.

4   A framework of Four Value Generating Mechanisms

In order to frame the different value generation strategies, we have formulated a taxonomy/framework consisting of four archetypical value generating mechanisms. The mechanisms are organized after two dimensions, as seen in Figure 1. The x-axis dimension categorizes value mechanisms on whether data are used predominantly to do things better (exploit current resources) or to do new things (explore new opportunities). The y-axis represents our contribution to this traditional classification. The market-based mechanisms are an offspring of the traditional monetary economy, but the "new" network-based mechanisms revolve around information sharing. Market based mechanisms have traditionally been focused on the generation of economic value, either through lower costs or increased profits and are based on classic economic theories of the likes of Williamson and Schumpeter [42], [55], [56]. However, all mechanisms in the sharing economy to some extent focus on generating sustainable value. All are important and all depend, to a certain degree, on collaboration of people, across the boundaries of organizations and sectors.

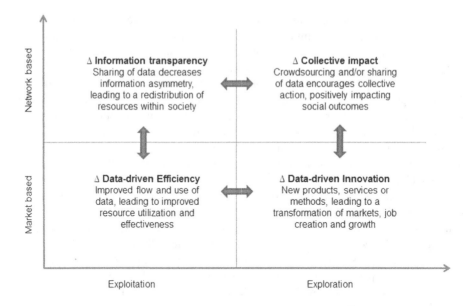

Fig. 1. A framework of four archetypical mechanisms that transform data to value

In the following list we summarize how these mechanisms work:

- Information transparency is gained if the data are available, accessible, accurate and trustworthy, and shine a light on a certain subject. The transparency mechanism generates value when individuals acquire new information that result in actions that further lead to a redistribution of resources.
- The collective impact mechanism generates value when a large group of individuals use data to collectively contribute to a common cause, positively impacting social outcomes.
- The data-driven efficiency mechanism generates value when stakeholders use data to improve productive efficiency and effectiveness, which can result in direct cost savings, saved time and effort, as well as improved quality of services.
- The data-driven innovation mechanism generates value when novel use of data leads to new innovative products, services or methods that transform markets and industries while generating jobs, profits and multiple other affordances, thus resulting in the generation of sustainable value.

5   Generating Sustainable Value from Data in the Sharing Society

Figure 1 shows the four archetypical mechanisms we propose that can transform data to value. We have, however, not explained how we can *enable* this value generation to happen, depending in all circumstances on the context in which the value generation happens. The model we present in Figure 2 is based on the macro-level model in [23], but it is extended to incorporate the findings from behavioral economics that explain the role and impact of individual behavior. A class of behavioral theories, based on the Motivation-Opportunity-Ability (MOA) framework, shows how motivation, opportunity and ability to perform certain tasks impact the behavior of individuals (see, for instance, [5] and Rheinolds et al., 2011). These models are commonly used in relation to social marketing and information processing [26], [40], public relations [15], knowledge sharing in workplaces [39], [43] and consumer behavior [60]. Broadly speaking, motivation can be defined as goal-directed arousal [26], [40]. In the context of this model, high motivation implies that individuals have the incentive to allocate resources to generate value from data; opportunity refers to the environmental or contextual factors that enable action; and ability represents the power or capacity to act [40].

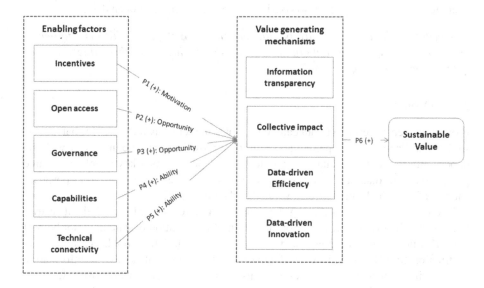

Fig. 2. A model of the sharing society – transforming data to value

We propose that policy makers can influence the motivation of users by offering incentives and the opportunity for value generation not only by supporting open access to data but also by providing risk-free and sustainable, high-quality data resources for internal and external users. Policy makers should also pay attention to the general ability of individuals to use these data by focusing on the availability of technical infrastructure as well as the general capabilities in society (although these two factors are, of course, also dependent on the provision of the market). We now briefly explain these enabling factors.

5.1   Incentives

The organizational leadership literature has shown that employees who are aware of the positive impact their behavior has on others are more motivated to make a pro-social difference, and that inspiration, a compelling vision and intellectual stimulation, likely enhances employees' motivation to actively engage in knowledge sharing [39]. Motivation can also influence companies to change institutions in order to support social practices, as can be seen in the many nonprofit organizations recently established by for-profit companies [53].

Following [53] and [45], we maintain that people not only chase visible carrots, but they also tend to consider the bigger societal-level impact of their actions, and are willing to participate in the "larger quest for the invisible gold at the end of the rainbow." We propose that by creating the right incentives, policy makers can motivate different stakeholders to use data to generate sustainable value. We have already seen a number of such efforts, most notably the relatively widespread Hackathons and Datapaloozas, which have been hosted by various municipal and state governments in order to encourage people from all sectors to consider the potential value of open data.

Proposition 1: Incentives positively influence the motivation of individuals to generate sustainable value from data in the sharing society, hence positively affecting each of the value generating mechanisms

5.2   Open Access

Providing open government data can be seen as a matter of availability, format, accessibility and license [10]. Opening access to data provides everyone in society with the opportunity to use these data to generate value. Openness is a key enabler for value generation from data, as it allows various users to re-use data for different purposes and therefore unlocks the intrinsic value that data hold [29].

The basic belief behind making the data available to external uses without restrictions is that the originator, owner or custodian of information or data may not be best placed to understand the potential future uses of the data they hold. Waste and the destruction of value could occur if government set rules of access to information which fails to recognize the requirements of unforeseen users and uses. In other words, too tight rules of engagement may unintentionally constrain the beneficial use by third parties or eventual end-users in the process of the diffusion of innovation. Moreover, openness should combine unrestricted availability of data with accessibility and technical interoperability [48]. Therefore, in addition to the general availability, an important dimension to open data is that there should be no legal or technical barriers to use and re-use. Use of open licenses and open data standards can facilitate the re-use of these data.

Proposition 2: Open access positively influences the opportunity for individuals to generate sustainable value from data in the sharing society, hence positively affecting each of the value generating mechanisms

5.3   Governance

When opened up, data become a common, shared resource, available for use within an open network of public and private stakeholders. However, this resource is still governed by the main collector or creator of the data. Therefore, we include governance as a construct that is intended to reflect the importance of data governance for the value that can be extracted from the resource. Based on [23], we conceptualize governance as a construct that describes the quality and sustainability of the data resource, where sustainability means that the common resource must meet the current needs of many individuals without compromising the ability of future generations to utilize the resource [19].

Data governance must consider data quality, data management, data policies, business process management and risk management. Data governance ensures that data can be trusted and that privacy is guarded. Making data accessible and ensuring it is fit for re-use are not insignificant challenges and such efforts raise a wide range of complex questions, including questions on how and when sharing is appropriate [18]. Without governance, the risks of using the data resource for mission critical purposes might become too high, and the data might not come at the right time or be in the right granularity to be of use for information purposes.

Proposition 3: Governance positively influences the opportunity of individuals to generate sustainable value from data in the sharing society, hence positively affecting each of the value generating mechanisms

5.4   Capabilities

As open government data are common, shared resources, the generative ability of the value generating mechanisms depends on certain capabilities in society. A capability can be defined as a measure of the ability of an entity to achieve an objective. In our case, it is the collective ability of individuals and organizations to use and re-use the data. Following [19], we emphasize the need for equitable use of the data resource. Citizen's access to the Internet and their ability to utilize the provided information are considered important for ensuring equitable dissemination [4], [16]. The digital divide can be broadly defined as the gap between those who have access to technologies and those who do not; however, there are, in fact, multiple divides that can exist, of which access to technology is but one. These issues include technology literacy as the ability to understand and use technology, as well as the ability of persons with disabilities to access the content through adaptive technologies [4]. Without the capabilities to access, use and make sense of data, the generative ability of the mechanisms becomes limited.

Proposition 4: Capabilities positively influence the ability of individuals to generate sustainable value from data, hence positively affecting each of the value generating mechanisms

5.5   Technical Connectivity

The current trend towards a massive increase in the generation of data, as well as wider access to different kinds of data, has important implications for both public and private organizations. This trend is supported by recent advances in technology: the technical ability to manage and openly disseminate big and small datasets; the ability to analyze, mash up and make sense of different types of data; and the networking capabilities to access and link data from various sources. Research suggests that the scale and scope of changes brought on by use of data are set to expand greatly as series of technology trends accelerate and converge. To capture value from data, public and private organizations will have to deploy technologies that can help individuals and organizations to integrate, analyze, visualize and consume the growing torrent of available data [28].

Technical connectivity is conceptualized as a construct that describes the availability of technologies that allow users to store, access, combine and analyze the data. The construct consists of three dimensions: 1) the infrastructure that facilitates data exchange between government agencies, private sector firms and the public, 2) dissemination of software, including data organization management software, as well as analytics and discovery software and 3) access via multiple platforms, such as mobile and web-based platforms.

Proposition 5: Technical connectivity positively influences the ability of individuals to generate sustainable value from data, hence positively affecting each of the value generating mechanisms

5.6   The Generation of Sustainable Value

Following is a short description of the main premises of our suggested model:

- Due to the complexity and cross-boundary nature of today´s social challenges, societies need to support various different value generating mechanisms.
- These mechanisms account for the way in which sustainable value can be generated from the use of data. All of the mechanisms are dependent on some sort of collaborative efforts, but these can either be network based or market based.
- All of the mechanisms are dependent on the motivation, opportunity and ability of people to generate value from data.
- While the mechanisms function independently, they can and will interact within an ecosystem of mechanisms called the sharing society, and this interaction can generate valuable synergies.
- The sharing society is defined as an open economic and social system in which information technology is leveraged to empower individuals, corporations, nonprofits and government with data that are shared and reused and transformed to sustainable value through different mechanisms.
- The mechanisms contribute to the generation of sustainable value by creating different types of value: increase GDP through means such as corporate profits, job creation and tax payments; contribute to society by improving the general wellbeing of individuals through means such as better health, education, social inclusion or equality; or contribute to the livability of the environment through means such as reduced emissions, less traffic congestion or access to clean water.

Proposition 6: Sustainable value is generated through a system of value generating mechanisms within the sharing society, both directly and through synergies between the mechanisms

6   Discussion: The Transformative Power of Data

We face many social challenges in this world. While none of the challenges has simple solutions, or can be solved by individual stakeholders or groups, there are ways to overcome many of these challenges – if we utilize the power of the sharing society. The market, by itself, oftentimes lacks the incentives and appropriate models to solve many of these issues, often called market failures. The payback in most market transactions is defined by an implicit or explicit contract, and its timing occurs closely behind, or simultaneous to, the initial contract. Within areas such as public health and social issues, the monetary payback, however, is often vague, uncertain and in the distant future [40].

Market failures are thus currently considered to be either the responsibility of the state or of civil society [38]. However, in many cases the silos of government departments are poorly suited to tackling complex problems that cut across sectors and nation states. Civil society might also lack the capital, skills and resources to take promising ideas to scale [34]. We thus propose that an informal collaboration between the public and private sectors, enabled by openly sharing and re-using data and information can positively influence the generation of sustainable value.

The model of the sharing society shows the potential progress from using data under different contexts, to the mechanisms that explain how the value generation happens, to the actual impact or output – the sustainable value that is generated. We wish to suggest a potential answer to the *to what ends* question, by highlighting the social challenges we are facing today and by showing how different governments and companies have together addressed some of these challenges by using open data. We also wish to delve deeper into the question of *by what means* by pointing out that use of data can generate value through different mechanisms (although these mechanisms interact and influence each other) and by highlighting the importance of the context in which value generation happens. Thus far, there has not been much scientific evidence to support the hypothesis of a link between opening access to government data and value generation. However, the relationship between use of data, the enabling factors, the different mechanisms, and value generation and appropriation can be illustrated with anecdotal evidence. This will be provided below, where we are suggesting possible value generation potentials to four of the largest societal challenges.

6.1   Challenge Number 1: Economic Inequality

One of the most acute social challenges we face today is the issue of economic inequality within or between nations. While economic inequality might primarily be seen as a violation of social justice, research shows that growing economic inequality since the mid-1970s has contributed to dysfunctional economies. It has even been linked to the recent economic crisis with devastating effects [14], [52]. Inequality is crystallized in a skewed allocation of resources, where the majority of society´s resources belongs to certain groups enjoying more opportunities than do others.

To a certain degree, uneven distribution of resources is a part of the capitalistic society's market-based mechanisms. However, in some cases, resources are not allocated in a socially optimal way due to behavior such as opportunism and even corruption. Such outcomes are usually possible where there is an asymmetry of information between people, undermining accountability. Information asymmetry conceals skewed resource allocations which too often prioritize the interests of business, political and military elites over development priorities of the majority of the population.

Transparency and Accountability to Combat Inequality

Transparency refers to the absence of asymmetric information. Information transparency is a characteristic of governments, companies, organizations and individuals that are open to the clear disclosure of information, rules, plans, processes and actions.[1] Information transparency can contribute to improved social outcomes by generating incentives and reducing uncertainty. Increased transparency in an organization´s operation increases the outside stakeholders´ capacity to hold the insiders accountable and provides stakeholders with information they can use in their own decision making. The transparency mechanism is essentially network based, as it depends on multiple instances of sharing and receiving of information between stakeholders. Eventually, increased transparency should facilitate equitable and effective allocation of resources across boundaries. In the context of accountability, transparency-enhancing mechanisms involving a multitude of stakeholders throughout society can be thought of as creating millions of "auditors" [3]. This "auditing" can mobilize resources from being used where they benefit few at the cost of many, to being used in a more socially responsible manner.

One such transparency agenda for tackling poverty in the global economy was presented by the British Prime Minister, David Cameron, in the G8 meeting at the World Economic Forum in Davos in January, 2013. The plan was to tackle illicit financial flows, the hidden company ownership that makes such flows possible, and land grabs in developing countries. The claim is that citizens in developing countries are regularly robbed of the benefits of their countries' mineral wealth through poorly negotiated or corrupt backroom deals. Collective global action is essential to improve the transparency of land transactions, thereby attracting more responsible investment that will contribute to sustainable economic growth and reduced poverty.[2] In this case, open access to government data on company ownership, natural resources and taxes enables greater cross-border transparency. Interestingly, key datasets such as Land Registries and Company Registries are least likely of all the datasets reviewed in the Open Data Barometer to be available as open data, suggesting that OGD initiatives are not yet securing the release of politically important datasets that can be vital to

---

[1] http://www.transparency-initiative.org/about/definitions

[2] https://www.gov.uk/government/publications/uk-g8-presidency-report-2013

holding governments and companies accountable [11]. However, as a part of the G8 transparency agenda, the UK has committed to establishing a publicly accessible central registry of company beneficial ownership, and is undertaking a wider review of corporate transparency.

6.2   Challenge Number 2: The Climate Challenge

Climate change has emerged as one of the most important economic policy issues of the early 21st century. The pollutants that contribute to global warming are commonly known as greenhouse gas emissions. Carbon dioxide (CO_2) is probably the best known greenhouse gas, representing 85% of all greenhouse gasses in the U.S. Electricity production is the largest single source of global warming pollution in the U.S., responsible for nearly 40% of greenhouse gas emissions[3]. A McKinsey report published in July 2009 estimated that there was a huge potential for energy-efficiency increases in the U.S., and that a 23% reduction in energy usage was possible by 2020 [27].

The study also highlighted a number of barriers to the realization of significant efficiency gains, including large initial outlays of capital required to improve infrastructure, the fragmentation of efficiency opportunities, societal apathy and simple lack of awareness. While the overall potential for energy-efficiency gains was vast, it was spread out across industrial, commercial and residential buildings, making widespread cooperation difficult. Additionally, the incentive and motivation of individuals and corporations to take responsibility for improvements by themselves were seen as being low [27].

Provision of Information can Enable Collective Impact

A green growth agenda requires policy makers to examine and influence behavior in a way that collectively impacts economic, social, and environmental outcomes on multiple scales [54]. Collective impact can be defined as the commitment of a group of actors from different sectors to a common agenda for solving a complex social problem [17]. As the prevailing characterization of human decision making in policy circles has until recently been a rational economic one, a wide range of factors that affect how people make decisions has been excluded from consideration and therefore needs to be considered in predictions of human reactions to environmental conditions or proposed policy initiatives [54].

Results from behavioral science have shown that providing high-energy consuming households with prescriptive normative information regarding the average home energy usage in their neighborhood constructively decreased energy consumption. For those that were doing better than the average, adding an injunctive component to the message (a smiley token) proved reconstructive by re-affirming their "good behavior" [36], [41]. The lesson is: People do not want to just save energy. They want to get information on how they are doing, and most importantly, to be acknowledged for their efforts.

---

[3]   http://www.epa.gov/ghgreporting/ghgdata/reported/index.html

Opower is an energy tech company with a mission: to motivate everyone on earth to save energy. Opower was founded on a simple premise: to engage the millions of people who are in the dark about their energy use. To do so, they provide people with information on their own energy consumption as compared to other similar households, thereby putting every customer's energy use in personal perspective. Opower merges and analyzes utility and open government data to create individual customer profiles, and subsequently uses these profiles to generate personalized insights that are delivered through various channels. In February 2014, the Opower home energy reports helped people around the world to save over 3.7 terawatt hours of energy and more than $417 million on their energy bills. We propose that policy makers, civil society and private companies can use different types of collaboration platforms to influence behavior. These platforms should provide people with relevant information as well as feedback mechanisms that enable them to respond to this information.

6.3   Challenge Number 3: Efficient Use of Public Resources

The importance of the efficient use of public resources for economic growth and stability, as well as for general well-being has been brought to the forefront by a number of developments over the past decades [1]. During the last 20 years, with the advent of the computer and the Internet as general technologies, a big portion of all processes in industrialized societies has become digitized. Research has shown that ICT has offered the capacity to reduce costs, increase the capability of machinery and increase flexibility in production planning and scheduling, thereby positively influencing productivity and efficiency.

During the initial stage of ICT adoption, many different systems were implemented, each with a specific purpose in mind, including payroll, human resources, production systems, resource planning, etc. This resulted in silos of disparate datasets in no way interconnected or integrated, causing various operational inefficiencies that included the same data being collected and hosted in different places, inability to automate processes across organizational boundaries and considerable overhead from trying to make sense of heterogeneous data sources. As an example, the costs incurred by recreating, verifying and transforming building information were estimated at $15.8 billion in the U.S. capital facilities supply chain for 2002 alone [8].

Efficient Use of Data Sets Resources Free

Increasing cross-boundary interactions and higher levels of information exchange between citizens and government due to digitization have increased the total amount of government data collected and stored. These trends call for more efficient processing of data in order to provide the expected services while still keeping costs under control [7]. Efficiency of public sector organizations can be gained by cutting processing costs, making strategic connections between and among government agencies, and creating empowerment [13]. This allows for better utilization of valuable resources, either by directing them from non-value adding to value adding tasks, or by reducing use in order to increase sustainability.

The Danish government has started an initiative where from 2012 to 2016 all basic government data will be improved in quality and context, and collection and dissemination of the data will be coordinated within the public sector. A national information infrastructure will be established for distribution of government data, with the aim of making the administration of the basic data registers easier and more efficient. Furthermore, as data will be freely available online, costs related to user support and billing are also expected to be reduced. The total yearly savings for the public sector are projected to be around $48 million[4].

The focus of the Danish authorities is on collective savings. The business case calculated would not have been positive for individual institutions or agencies due to the large initial costs incurred by making these big changes to the data model, data quality and data distribution channels. By ensuring a positive internal business case for this initiative, the Danish authorities have increased the likelihood of the initiative being economically sustainable. Moreover, the positive external effect from this project is that integrated government data of better quality will also benefit private industries, such as real estate dealers, insurance companies, the financial sector and the telecom industry, which previously had to spend resources on creating usable information from heterogeneous data-sources. The cost-savings for the private industry are estimated to be around $90 million per annum when the program is fully implemented.

6.4   Challenge Number 4: Urban Planning

Urbanization, the demographic transition from rural to urban, is associated with shifts from an agriculture-based economy to mass industry, technology and service. A hundred years ago, 20% of the global population lived in an urban area; by 1990, just under 40% of this population lived in cities; However, since 2010, for the first time ever, more than half of the world's population is living in urban areas. As this proportion continues to grow, by 2050, it is projected to have increased to seven out of 10 people.[5] With urban congestion on the rise, city planners are looking for new ways to improve transportation. According to the Texas Transportation Institute, the cost of congestion in the U.S. in 2012 was more than $120 billion, nearly $820 for every commuter.[6] Similar problems are endured by most of the world´s bigger cities.

Data-Driven Innovation to Ease Traffic Congestion
Following Schumpeter, we assume that innovation can have economy-wide effects. Innovation brings about novel combinations of resources, and new production methods which, in turn, can lead to the transformation of markets and industries, thus increasing value [42]. The traditional definition of innovation builds on the underlying motive to generate economic value. Numerous studies have confirmed that

---

[4] http://www.digst.dk/Servicemenu/English/Digitisation/~/
media/Files/English/Grunddata_UK_web_05102012_Publication.pdf
[5] http://www.who.int/gho/urban_health/situation_trends/
urban_population_growth_text/en/
[6] http://d2dtl5nnlpfr0r.cloudfront.net/tti.tamu.edu/documents/
tti-umr.pdf

innovative companies generate above-average returns and that innovative nations enjoy more economic growth.

Innovation, however, can also have clear social consequences. For instance, the computer has dramatically enhanced individual productivity, learning and creativity, and the World Wide Web has enabled the connectivity that has had disruptive effects on many societies, in some cases threatening dictatorship and corruption. In order to generate sustainable value, the innovation must at the very least not have negative social or environmental consequences, and optimally lead to the simultaneous generation of social, environmental and economic value. We use the term innovation to describe the mechanism that uses market forces to allocate resources in order to create a new method, product or service that generates sustainable value.

An increasing number of governments and cities in the world have started to publish open geospatial and traffic data. Many innovative solutions are currently being developed in addition to these data. One example is INRIX, a leading provider of traffic services with the goal of solving traffic worldwide. Their traffic intelligence platform analyzes data from public and private sources, including government road sensors, official accident and incident reports and data on real-time traffic speed, crowdsourced from a large community of local drivers. The company's analysis of crowdsourced data in combination with information from traditional sources provides drivers with insights that help them choose the best way to go, minimizing the amount of time spent.

As the app used to source traffic information from individuals is available for free, INRIX´s main source of income is from car-producers, GPS providers and media companies. Moreover, they have recently started to provide data and tools to public information services. In particular, the crowd-sourced data allow much faster congestion analysis than was previously possible.[7] This will allow public traffic engineers to measure and track congestion, thereby offering public decision makers better tools to analyze and manage transportation infrastructure for improved urban planning.

7   Conclusions

Our aim with this paper is to generate a theory that can explain the causal connections between use of open data and the consequent generation of sustainable value. We propose that the challenges faced by our societies urgently call for new forms of collective action between public and private stakeholders, and that we can move towards such collective action by actively sharing and re-using data across boundaries.

The first contribution of this paper is a new interpretation of the underlying behavioral assumptions. We propose that we are experiencing a paradigm shift in how people interact, enabled by the transformative power of information technology. This calls for a re-interpretation of some of the most prevalent behavioral assumptions underlying our current value theories. We propose that most people are driven not only by the wish to improve their own material situation, but also by the need for

---

[7] http://tti.tamu.edu/2010/01/11/
   texas-transportation-institute-teams-with-inrix/

subjective well-being and the wish to be a contributing member of society. While opportunism and corruption are certainly relevant behaviors, they can be influenced by social norms. Acknowledging [46], [55], [56]; we further propose that bounded rationality is a reasonable approximation of how people behave but that the boundaries of rationality can be affected, for instance, by providing people with information.

The second contribution is a framework that adds a new dimension to the well-established market-based mechanisms of efficiency and innovation (exploitation and exploration), containing two network-based mechanisms that generate value through information transparency and collective impact. We propose that all four mechanisms interact within an ecosystem we call the sharing society, and that these interactions are capable of generating synergies in value creation. All the mechanisms are dependent on the private and public sector, together providing the motivation, opportunity and ability to generate value from data.

The third and final contribution is the nomological network, where we visualize our theory and show the main antecedents that enable data to be transformed to sustainable value via the sharing society system of mechanisms. These antecedents are supposed to reflect the context within which value generation happens, a context that can differ a great deal between countries and initiatives. We propose that the motivation, opportunity and ability of individuals to use data for value generation are influenced by: the incentives provided; the level of technical and legal openness of data; the maturity of resource (data) governance; the general data-related capabilities in society; and the technological maturity and prevalence. The motivation, opportunity and ability of individuals positively influence the different mechanisms that eventually explain how use of data is transformed to sustainable value.

This paper is limited initially moving only towards theory development; the next step is to use empirical data to test the relationships proposed here. As both open data and the sharing society are emerging phenomena, there is still not much theory to build upon; however, we are able to borrow from established value generation theories and current research on open data and behavioral economics. Future developments and continuing research will have to testify whether or not the proposed relationships hold or not.

References

1. Afonso, A., Schuknecht, L., Tanzi, V.: Public sector efficiency: Evidence for new EU member states and emerging markets. Applied Economics 42(17), 2147–2164 (2010)
2. Benington, J.: From Private Choice to Public Value? In: Benington, J., Moore, M. (eds.) Public Value: Theory and Practice, pp. 31–52. Palgrave MacMillan, Basingstoke (2011)
3. Bellver, A., Kaufmann, D.: Transparenting Transparency: Initial Empirics and Policy Applications. World Bank Policy Research Working Paper (2005),
   http://tinyurl.com/k77rvlj
4. Bertot, J.C., Jaeger, P.T., Grimes, J.M.: Using ICTs to create a culture of transparency: E-government and social media as openness and anti-corruption tools for societies. Government Information Quarterly 27(2010), 264–271 (2010)

5. Blumberg, M., Pringle, C.D.: The missing opportunity in organizational research: Some implications for a theory of work performance. Academy of Management Review 7(4), 560–569 (1982)
6. Coleman, J.C.: Foundations of Social Theory. Harvard University Press, Boston (1990)
7. Cordella, A.: E-government: towards the e-bureaucratic form? Journal of Information Technology 22(2007), 265–274 (2007)
8. Curry, E., O'Donnell, J., Corry, E., Hasan, S., Keane, M., O'Riain, S.: Linking building data in the cloud: Integrating cross-domain building data using linked data. Advanced Engineering Informatics 27(2013), 206–219 (2013)
9. Daly, H.E., Cobb, J.B.: For the Common Good: Redirecting The Economy toward Community, The Environment and A Sustainable Future, 2nd edn. Beacon Press, Boston (1994)
10. Davies, T.: Open data, democracy and public sector reform: A look at OGD use from data.gov.uk (2010), http://tinyurl.com/7joks46
11. Davies, T.: Open Data Barometer: 2013 Global Report (2013), http://www.opendataresearch.org/dl/odb2013/Open-Data-Barometer-2013-Global-Report.pdf
12. Elster, J.: Explaining Social Behavior. Cambridge University Press, Cambridge (2007)
13. European Commission: eGovernment Economics Project (eGEP), Measurement Framework Final. DG Information Society and Media, European Commission (2006)
14. Goldberg, G.S.: Economic inequality and economic crisis: a challenge for social workers. Social Work 57(3), 211–224 (2012)
15. Hallahan, K.: Enhancing Motivation, Ability, and Opportunity to Process Public Relations Messages. Public Relations Review 26(4), 463–480 (2000)
16. Halonen, A.: Being Open about Data (2012), http://tinyurl.com/c8mz5vt
17. Hanleybrown, F., Kania, J., Kramer, M.: Channeling Change: Making Collective Impact Work. Stanford Social Innovation Review (2012)
18. Harrison, T.M., Pardo, T.A., Cook, M.: Creating Open Government Ecosystems: A Research and Development Agenda. The Future Internet 4(4), 900–928 (2012)
19. Hess, C., Ostrom, E.: Understanding Knowledge as a Commons – From Theory to Practice. MIT Press, Cambridge (2006)
20. Hujiboom, N., Van den Broek, T.: Open data: An international comparison of strategies. European Journal of e Practice n° 12 (2011)
21. Jansen, K.: The influence of the PSI directive on open government data: An overview of recent developments. Government Information Quarterly 28(4), 446–456 (2011)
22. Janssen, M., Charalabidis, Y., Zuiderwijk, A.: Benefits, Adoption Barriers and Myths of Open Data and Open Government. Information Systems Management 29(4), 258–268 (2012)
23. Jetzek, T., Avital, M., Bjørn-Andersen, N.: Generating Value from Open Government Data. In: Proceedings of the 34th International Conference on Information Systems, Milan, Italy (2013)
24. Kundra, V.: Digital Fuel of the 21st Century: Innovation through Open Data and the Network Effect. Joan Shorenstein Center on the Press, Politics and Public Policy, Harvard, Boston (January 2012)
25. Luna-Reyes, L.F., Bertot, J.C., Mellouli, S.: Open Government, Open Data and Digital Government. Government Information Quarterly 31(1), 4–5 (2013)
26. MacInnis, D.J., Moorman, C., Jaworski, B.J.: Enhancing Consumers' Motivation, Ability, and Opportunity to Process Brand Information from Ads: Conceptual Framework and Managerial Implications. Journal of Marketing 55(1991), 32–53 (1991)

27. McKinsey: Unlocking energy efficiency in the U.S. Economy. McKinsey Global Energy and Materials (July 2009)
28. McKinsey: Big data: The next frontier for innovation, competition, and productivity. McKinsey Global Institute (May 2011)
29. McKinsey: Open data: Unlocking innovation and performance with liquid information, McKinsey Global Institute, McKinsey Center for Government and McKinsey Business Technology Office (2013a)
30. McKinsey. Disruptive technologies: Advances that will transform life, business, and the global economy. McKinsey Global Institute (2013b)
31. Melville, N.: Information Systems Innovation for Environmental Sustainability. MIS Quarterly 34(1), 1–21 (2010)
32. Merton, T.: Social Theory and Social Structure. Free Press, New York (1949)
33. Moore, M.H.: Creating Public Value Strategic Management in Government. Harvard University Press, Boston (1995)
34. Murray, R., Caulier-Grice, J., Mulgan, G.: The Open Book of Social Innovation (2010), http://www.nesta.org.uk/publications/open-book-social-innovation
35. Nilsen, K.: Economic theory as it applies to Public Sector Information. Annual Review of Information Science and Technology 44(1), 419–489 (2010)
36. Nolan, J.M., Schultz, P.W., Cialdini, R.B., Goldstein, N.J., Griskevicius, V.: Normative social influence is underdetected. Personality and Social Psychology Bulletin 34, 913–923 (2008)
37. OECD: Fostering Innovation to Address Social Challenges. Workshop Proceedings (2011), http://www.oecd.org/sti/inno/47861327.pdf
38. Porter, M.E., Kramer, M.R.: Creating Shared Value. Harvard Business Review 89(1), 62–77 (2011)
39. Reinholt, M., Pedersen, T., Foss, N.J.: Why a Central Network Position isn´t Enough: The Role of Motivation and Ability for Knowledge Sharing in Employee Networks. Academy of Management Journal 54(6), 1277–1297 (2011)
40. Rothchild, M.L.: Carrots, Sticks, and Promises: A Conceptual Framework for the Management of Public Health and Social Issue Behaviors. Journal of Marketing 63(4), 24–37 (1999)
41. Schultz, P.W., Nolan, N.J., Cialdini, R.B., Goldstein, N.J., Griskevicius, V.: The Constructive, Destructive, and Reconstructive Power of Social Norms. Psychological Science 18(5), 429–435 (2007)
42. Schumpeter, J.A.: The Theory of Economic Development. Harvard University Press, Boston (1934)
43. Siemsen, E., Roth, A.V., Balasubramanian, S.: How motivation, opportunity, and ability drive knowledge sharing: The constraining-factor model. Journal of Operations Management 26(2008), 426–445 (2008)
44. Shapiro, C., Varian, H.R.: Information Rules: A Strategic Guide to the Network Economy. Harvard Business School Press, Boston (1999)
45. Shogren, J.: Behavioural Economics and Environmental Incentives. OECD Environment Working Papers 49. OECD Publishing (2012)
46. Simon, H.: A Behavioral Model of Rational Choice. Models of Man, Social and Rational: Mathematical Essays on Rational Human Behavior in a Social Setting. Wiley, New York (1957)
47. Stiglitz, J.E., Sen, A., Fitoussi, J.P.: Report by the Commission on the Measurement of Economic Performance and Social Progress, OECD (2009)

48. Tammisto, Y., Lindman, J.: Definition of open data services in software business. In: Cusumano, M.A., Iyer, B., Venkatraman, N. (eds.) ICSOB. LNBIP, vol. 114, pp. 297–303. Springer, Heidelberg (2011)

49. Tsang, E.W.K.: Behavioral assumptions and theory development: The case of transaction cost economics. Strategic Management Journal 27(11), 999–1011 (2006)

50. van Osch, W., Avital, M.: Generative Collectives. In: Proceedings of the International Conference on Information Systems (ICIS), Saint Louis, Missouri (2010)

51. van Veenstra, A.F., van den Broek, T.A.: Opening Moves – Drivers, Enablers and Barriers of Open Data in a Semi-public Organization. In: Wimmer, M.A., Janssen, M., Scholl, H.J. (eds.) EGOV 2013. LNCS, vol. 8074, pp. 50–61. Springer, Heidelberg (2013)

52. Vestergaard, J., Wade, R.: Establishing a new Global Economic Council: governance reform at the G20, the IMF and the World Bank. Global Policy 3(3), 57–69 (2012)

53. von Krogh, G., Haefliger, S., Spaeth, S., Wallin, M.W.: Carrots and Rainbows: Motivation and Social Practice in Open Source Software Development. MIS Quarterly 36(2), 649–676 (2012)

54. Weber, E.U., Johnson, E.J.: Psychology and Behavioral Economics Lessons for the Design of a Green Growth Strategy. White Paper for Green Growth Knowledge Platform, OECD, UNEP, World Bank (2012)

55. Williamson, O.E.: The Vertical Integration of Production: Market Failure Considerations. The American Economic Review 61(2), 112–123 (1971)

56. Williamson, O.E.: Transaction Cost Economics: The Process of Theory Development. In: Smith, K.G., Hitt, M.A. (eds.) Great Minds in Management: The Process of Theory Development, pp. 485–508. Oxford University Press, Oxford (2005)

57. Yu, H., Robinson, D.G.: The New Ambiguity of 'Open Government'. 59 UCLA Law Review (2012), http://ssrn.com/abstract=2012489

58. Zuiderwijk, A., Janssen, M., Choenni, S., Meijer, R., Alibaks, R.S.: Socio-technical Impediments of Open Data. Electronic Journal of e-Government 10(2), 156–172 (2012)

59. Zuiderwijk, A., Janssen, M.: Open Data Policies, Their Implementation and Impact: A Framework for Comparison. Government Information Quarterly 31(1), 17–29 (2014)

60. Ölander, F., Thøgersen, J.: Understanding of consumer behaviour as a prerequisite for environmental protection. Journal of Consumer Policy 18(4), 345–385 (1995)

The Interaction Effect of Complimentary Assets on Relationship between Information and Communication Technology and Public Health Outcomes

Supunmali Ahangama and Danny Chiang Choon Poo

Department of Information Systems, School of Computing, National University of Singapore,
13 Computing Drive, Singapore 117417
supunmali@comp.nus.edu.sg, dannypoo@nus.edu.sg

Abstract. This cross-national study evaluates the contingency of the relationship between ICT initiatives and public health outcomes on (1) education; (2) macro-economic stability and; (3) institutions. Resource Based View's resource complementary perspective and literature on Information and Communication Technology and delivery of public health are used as the guiding theoretical framework. Publicly accessible archived data from more than 150 nations are collected to comprehend the interaction effect. Delivery of public health outcomes is measured through mortality rate (adult), availability of sanitation facilities, incidence of TB and under nourishment. The results indicated that ICT initiatives interact with above three contingencies affecting public health outcomes. Education level positively moderated the relationship between ICT and public health outcomes. Institutions moderated the relationship of ICT and public health outcomes in a positive direction. The moderating effect is measured using PLS. Implications of the findings for theoretical discourse of the resource complimentary perspective and future research are discussed.

Keywords: public health, Information and communication technology (ICT), resource complementary perspective, country level, PLS.

1 Introduction

According to the definition of the World Health Organization (WHO), public health is "all organized measures to prevent disease, promote health, and prolong life among the population as a whole". Rather than concentrating on eradication of a single disease, public health focuses on the entire system, without limiting to individual patients or diseases. Improved public health outcomes and prevention of diseases can be achieved in low resource environments by investing in information and communication technology (ICT) tools. ICT applications would permit timely data collection, processing, storage and dissemination of health information to appropriate parties. Thus, public health policy makers and healthcare officials must invest in accessible, affordable applications focusing on entire community. ICT tools like health information systems, surveillance systems, m-health, and telemedicine could be used to monitor health concerns of the

B. Bergvall-Kåreborn and P.A. Nielsen (Eds.): TDIT 2014, IFIP AICT 429, pp. 83–95, 2014.
© IFIP International Federation for Information Processing 2014

population and promote healthy practices and behaviors. Moreover, the internet facilitates unparalleled access to important health information and it has become a common practice among patients and public (Heilman et al. 2011). For example, Wikipedia can be considered as a key tool for promoting public health and according to Pew Internet 2009 survey on health information, 53% of e-patients had used it (Jones and Fox 2009).

Introduction of ICT tools to healthcare services is extremely challenging due to numerous factors varying from limited availability of financial support to lack of proper framework for public health delivery. As per the World Bank, financial and other resource spending can be justified as improvement in public health leads to economic growth by reducing production losses caused by sick workers, by saving resources that would have been used for treating patients etc. (World Bank 1993). Thus, as supported by literature related to public health, it can be argued that a better public health system will lead to economic growth and poverty alleviation.

Most research has focused on demonstrating the contribution of ICT on improving healthcare services such as quality improvements and cost reductions (Jha et al. 2009; Khoumbati et al. 2006; Wu et al. 2006). Moreover, many studies have been restricted to evaluating the effectiveness of ICT solely for clinical services rather than on entire community (Jha et al. 2009; Wu et al. 2006) where, their main focus had been at micro level (specific healthcare organizations, regions or countries) and on specific aspects (e.g. clinical or personal) in implementation. As highlighted by Raghupathi and Wu (Raghupathi and Wu 2011), most of such research work are case studies of a specific country (Braa et al. 2007; Byrne and Sahay 2007; Jennett et al. 2004; Tomasi et al. 2004) or of a set of countries (Tomasi et al. 2004) or conceptual studies (Connell and Young 2007). Due to small sample sizes and failure of providing a complete cross-country level view, it is hard to generalize and apply such findings at different country levels. There is a dearth of country level studies carried out relevant to the contribution of ICT factors on better public health outcomes. Even in the limited cross-country research carried out, the moderating effect on the relationship of ICT on delivery of public health has not been considered. Thus, performing a cross-country level quantitative empirical study to assess the interaction effect on relationship between ICT factors and public health outcomes can be considered as a key research gap to be answered.

Using the resource complementarily perspective of Teece (Teece 1986), we propose that the relationship between ICT and public health outcomes is moderated by national environmental factors, namely, (1) education level; (2) macro-economic stability and; (3) institutional. These three factors will represent the political, economical and social factors of a nation. Delivery of public health outcomes are considered based on (1) mortality rate (adult); (2) availability of sanitation facilities; (3) incidence of TB and; (4) under nourishment. These complementary assets will be modeled using secondary data of 157 countries.

RQ: *How do a nation's complementary assets (education level, macro-economic stability and institutions) interact with national ICT initiatives in predicting its public health outcomes?*

The rest of the paper is organized as follows. First, the Theoretical Framework is briefly explained with role of ICT on public health delivery. Second, Descriptions on

Hypothesis Development and Research Design are dealt with. Third, we discuss the results and implication and finally, limitations and conclusions are discussed.

1.1 Theoretical Framework

According to WHO, two key roles of ICT on public health outcome are (1) organizing and distribution of health information to healthcare professionals and public and; (2) educating public on preventive measures. Various forms of ICT tools could be used in collection, analysis and communication of healthcare information. e-Health can be recognized as an essential tool in ensuring a safer, efficient and sustainable healthcare delivery around the world via wireless communication systems using computers and mobile phones. WHO program on e-health for healthcare delivery could be considered as an e-Health initiative where tele-consultations and tele-referrals are used to connect healthcare centres in remote areas (Raghupathi and Wu 2011). m-Health refers to the use of smart phones and other hand held computers for health care delivery and it encourages constantly to seek new health information from various media content and by participatory collaboration (Ahangama et al. 2014). Mobile applications allow tele-consultations between doctor and patient, wellness management, short message service (SMS) for behaviour change (Cole-Lewis and Kershaw 2010; Fjeldsoe et al. 2009). In addition, location based services enable community data collection and epidemiology and public health surveillance (Aanensen et al. 2009). Geographical Information Systems (GIS) allow mapping individual data using location reference data and it provides the opportunity to analyse the risk of disease spread, analyse environment hazards, carry out vaccination campaigns and locate healthcare services. . Even though, these technologies facilitate improvement in public health in general, the level of influence varies from nation to nation. The level of influence of these technologies on public health depends on other macro level factors in different countries.

Teece's (Teece 1986) concept of complementary assets describes that for commercializing a new product profitably, a firm needs access to complementary assets (manufacturing and distribution facilities) in a favourable manner (Teece 2006). Complementary assets are resources or capabilities used by firms to capture the profits associated with a strategy, technology or innovation (Shaw 1998). Competitor will not be able to gain a competitive advantage even if they copied and launched the same product as they do not have access to complementary assets possessed by the original producer. Complementary assets can be categorized into two different areas as resource co-presence view and resource channelling view based on the Resource Based View (RBV) (Barney et al. 2001). Resource co-presence view (interaction perspective) describes that a resource can be a complementary asset if its presence increases the value or outcome of another resource. Resource channelling view describes that complementary assets are formed when resource s are used in reciprocally reinforcing manner (Ravichandran and Lertwongsatien 2005). Even though, this was initially introduced to apply to organisational level, many studies have applied complementary asset perspective on country level too (Ahangama and Poo 2012; Krishnan and Teo 2011). Thus, former can be applied into our study to understand why certain nations have better public health outcomes compared to other nations (Mithas et al. 2009). Complementary assets will be helpful in achieving high delivery in public health outcomes from health care related ICT innovations. Rather than developing and deploying ICT tools itself, it is important to understand the complementary assets that could provide better utility. Moderating variables (macro-economic stability, education and institutions (Kauffman and Kumar 2008; Porter and Schwab 2009)) used in this study will be complementary assets that will enhance the relationship between ICT factors and public health outcomes.

2   Hypothesis Development

Through many prior studies it had been identified that ICT influences the delivery of public health (Jha et al. 2009; Khoumbati et al. 2006; Wu et al. 2006). The dearth of published literature on quantitative empirical research, studying the influence of national environmental factors (moderating variables) on ICT initiatives and delivery of public health outcomes in a country, persuaded us to develop our study aiming to fill that research gap. The research model (Fig. 1) was developed based on prior literature and theoretical frameworks mentioned above (section 1.1) and they will be tested using country level archived data.

2.1   Moderating Effect of Education Level

When the public become more educated they tend to care more about their own health and health of their family members and will follow health risk preventive practices. A high level of public health can be achieved with better educated and trained citizens (Ackerson and Viswanath 2009). Education level and knowledge of public is important for proper usage of healthcare applications for retrieval of trustworthy healthcare information, to communicate and to apply them correctly and in a timely fashion. When public is educated and computer literate, they tend to identify the use of web based and mobile based healthcare systems and they will continue to use such systems in an advanced manner (e.g. group support systems, online discussion forums, e-channelling) to manage their health and protect themselves from diseases while providing feedback to improve systems (Bagchi et al. 2005; Wu et al. 2006).

We recognize that the countries with educated community are in a better position to carry out and utilize ICT initiatives leading to low mortality rates (adult), high availability of sanitation facilities, low incidence of TB and low under nourishment. For example, highly educated community will use mobile applications to manage diseases like diabetes and they will look for new technology. We can hypothesize that when there is better education level among the community, higher benefits of ICT can be achieved to increase the public health outcomes.

H1: The relationship between ICT factors in a country and its public health outcome is moderated by education level. The relationship becomes stronger when education level is high and becomes weaker when education level is low.

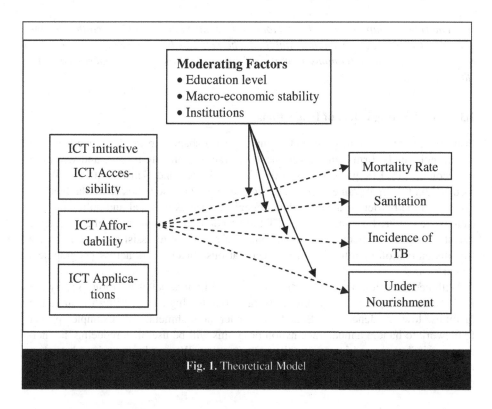

Fig. 1. Theoretical Model

2.2   Moderating Effect of Macro-economic Stability

A low inflation rate with declining budget deficits and trade deficits leads to the maintenance of macro-economic stability of a country. Stability of the macro-economic environment plays a central role in carrying out ICT initiatives in a country. With stable macro-economic conditions advanced countries in the world are more likely to carry out e-government development (Srivastava and Teo 2007), for healthcare too. When the macro-economy of a country is unstable, they may not be able to invest in ICT applications for healthcare. High inflation may lead governments to provide the people with only the essential services in the health sector rather than providing services like preventive care or healthcare education.

Relationship between ICT enabled applications and public health outcomes may be higher in countries with better macro-economic stability compared to unstable countries. We recognize that the wealthy countries are in a better position to carry out ICT initiatives leading to low mortality rates (adult), high availability of sanitation facilities, low incidence of TB and low under nourishment. For example, with better macro-economy, a nation is able to provide safer water and sanitation facilities to its community. Thus, following hypothesis was established in identifying the major role played by macro-economic stability of a country in developing and in implementing ICT relevant to healthcare.

H2: The relationship between ICT factors in a country and its public health outcome is moderated by macro-economic stability. The relationship becomes stronger when the stability of macro economy is high and becomes weaker when macro-economic stability is low.

2.3   Moderating Effect of Institutions

Institutional environment (both public and private) shapes up the framework within which individuals, firms, and governments interact to generate income and wealth in the economy (WEF- global competitive index (Porter and Schwab 2009)). While focusing on the legal framework, it also considers on how societies share the benefits and accept the burden of development strategies. Various political and policy modifications are required to amalgamate ICT tools to daily operations of public healthcare industry smoothly. There should be a suitable framework to assist secure and hassle free dissemination of information between various stakeholders across geographical boundaries.

With better institution framework, a nation will be in a better position to carry out ICT initiatives leading to low mortality rates (adult), high availability of sanitation facilities, low incidence of TB and low under nourishment. For example, proper framework to handle annual vaccination programs will be useful in reducing the incidence of infections and improving the immunization. We can hypothesize, that when there is better structure of institution, higher benefits of ICT can be achieved to increase the public health outcomes.

H3: The relationship between ICT factors in a country and its public health outcome is moderated by institutions. The relationship becomes stronger when the quality of institutions is high and becomes weaker when quality of institutions is low.

2.4   Control Variables

Three control variables that could explain the variance of predictor ICT are considered. We controlled physician (both generalists and specialists) density and nurse and midwife personnel density (proxy for quality of healthcare service) obtained for 2010 from World Development Indicator (WDI) Database at the World Bank website. It is the amount of health workforce per 10, 000 population (Mithas et al. 2009). Then we controlled the number of hospital beds per 10, 000 of the population as it is an indicator of quality of healthcare infrastructure of a country (Mithas et al. 2009). The number of hospital beds for 2010 is obtained from WDI database and are composed of beds available in public, private, general and specialized hospitals.

3   Research Design

For hypothesis testing, a cross sectional analysis of 157 countries is used. 2011 is used as the base year for dependent variable and values for all the other constructs are captured in previous years. Secondary data had to be used as it is not feasible to col-lect primary data within the time and resource constraints and also because secondary data will allow easy reproducibility and make the design generalizable (Kiecolt and Nathan 1985). Additionally, as the data is gathered from different sources, the com-mon method bias could also be avoided (Woszczynski and Whitman 2004). The main data sources are (1) World Bank ICT at-a-glance country database 2008 (World Health Organization 2011), (2) WDI database 2011 , (3) WEF Global competitiveness report 2008-2009 and (4) UNDP Human Development Report 2013 (Porter and Schwab 2009). These reports are considered to be reliable sources and many authors have used these data in their research. For example, WDI database is used by Raghupathi and Wu (Raghupathi and Wu 2011; Wu and Raghupathi 2012) to study the impact of four ICT factors on delivery of public health. These organizations follow rigorous procedures to maintain the reliability and validity of these data. To ensure quality of these data, for example, (1) data is collected only from CEOs or equivalent high ranked officials, (2) respondents can answer in their preferred language, (3) administration of survey in several modes (face-to-face, telephone and online interviews or surveys) and (4) performs a careful editing of data before aggregating to get country level data (Porter and Schwab 2009).

3.1   Operationalization of Constructs

We used four indicators of public health as dependent variables, namely, mortality rate (MR), sanitation, TB infection and under nourishment. Many prior studies (Mithas et al. 2009; Ngwenyama et al. 2006) had used life expectancy rate (LER) or MR to measure the quality of healthcare systems. However, the use of LER or MR will not be adequate to measure the quality of a public health system as it only con-siders the length of life (Robine et al. 1999). Thus, in this study we consider 4 indica-tors to represent different aspects of health to reveal the quality and performance of public health (OECD 2013). MR (adult) is measured using average of MR between ages 15 and 60 per 1,000 female adults and per 1,000 male adults. Average of im-proved sanitation facilities (% of population with access) and improved water source (% of population with access) are used to measure sanitation facility. Incidence of tuberculosis per 100,000 people is used as the indicator for TB infection. Degree of under nourishment will be indicated as the % of population getting incomplete or unbalanced nourishment. These dependent variables are obtained from WDI database for year 2011.

The high order construct for ICT is developed using (1) accessibility for ICT ser-vices, (2) affordability of ICT services and (3) adoption of ICT services in government and business. The data are obtained from World Bank ICT at-a-glance country database 2008 and average of these scores are used as the ICT index. Accessibility is composed of (1) telephone mainlines per 1,000 people; (2) international voice traffic minutes per person; (3) mobile phone subscriptions per 1,000 people, percentage of population covered by mobile telephony; (4) internet users per 1,000 people; (5) personal computers per 1,000 people; and (6) percentage of households with television. Af-fordability is composed of (1) price basket for residential fixed line (US$ per month);

(2) price basket for mobile (US$ per month); (3) price basket for internet (US$ per month) and (4) telephone average cost of call to US (US$ per three minutes). ICT applications are measured using (1) ICT expenditure (% of GDP); (2) secure internet servers per 1 million people; (3) percentage of schools connected to the internet and (4) e-government readiness index (scale 0-1).

Education index for 2010 obtained from UNDP Human Development Report 2013 is measured using (1) mean of years of schooling for adults aged 25 years and (2) expected years of schooling for children of school entering age. Macro-economic stability index is taken from WEF Global competitiveness report 2008-2009 (Porter and Schwab 2009). This is composed of (1) government surplus/ deficit, (2) national savings rate, (3) inflation, (4) interest rate spread and (5) government debt. Institutions index is obtained from the same report mentioned above and it is developed using (1) intellectual property rights, (2) ethics and corruption, (3) undue influence, (4) government inefficiency and (5) security. These three indices had been used in past studies to understand the e-government development (Srivastava and Teo 2007).

4   Analysis and Results

The model is represented with hierarchical constructs (high order construct) to allow theoretical parsimony and to reduce the complexity of the model. The dimensions for ICT were measured using formative constructs, such as accessibility and affordability and adoption of ICT is represented as first order constructs. Moreover, MR, sanitation, TB infection and under nourishment are formatively related to public health construct (second order construct). To treat missing data, we used 'mean value replacement' option as it is the recommended approach in PLS.

4.1   Hypothesis Testing

We used partial least squares (PLS) to test the interaction effects. PLS is appropriate when handling formative constructs and when testing theories in the initial stages of development (Keil et al. 2000). In this study to detect the interaction effect, we employed the product of sum (PS) approach of Goodhue et al. (Goodhue et al. 2007) instead of using product indicator approach of Chin et al. (Chin et al. 2003) as it provides less statistical power. Moreover, it is not possible to use the latter when the predictor variables are formative. Thus, we used two-stage approach, where in stage 1, the main-effect PLS path model is executed to get latent variable scores. In stage 2, the interaction term is computed as a product of latent score of the predictor and the moderator. The interaction term and the latent variable score of predictor and moderator could be used as independent variables in a multiple linear regression on public health construct (on latent score of it) (Henseler and Fassott 2010) or it could be implemented within the PLS. We implemented a PLS model using new interaction terms. Furthermore, it is important that all the interaction terms are entered simultaneously, thus, their effects can be assessed at the presence of other interactions.

As illustrated in Table 1, the relationship between ICT initiatives and public health is contingent on education level ($\beta=0.16$, $p<0.01$) and the direction of interaction pattern for ICT initiatives development and level of public health is consistent with the initial prediction. Thus, H1 is supported. The relationship between ICT initiatives and level of public health is contingent on institutions ($\beta=0.15$, $p<0.01$) and the direction of interaction pattern for ICT initiatives and public health is consistent with our prediction. Hence, we can conclude that H3 is supported. The relationship between ICT initiatives and public health is not contingent on macroeconomic stability ($\beta=0.05$, n.s.) indicating that H2 is not supported.

Table 1. Results

Factors	Dependent Indicator (public-health)	
	Stage 1	**Stage 2**
Physicians density	-0.17**	-0.13**
Nurses density	0.13**	0.03
Hospital beds	0.11**	0.08*
ICT	-.55***	-0.62***
Education	-0.35***	-0.17
Macro-Economic Stability	0.03	0.05
Institutions	-0.03	-0.15**
ICT* Education		0.16**
ICT* Macro-Economic Stability		0.05
ICT* Institutions		0.15**
R2	0.76	0.81
The table reports the path coefficients N= 157; *p < 0.05; **p <0.01; ***p<0.001 Note: See page 7 for description of variables		

A subsequent testing for effect sizes of the moderation effect where the effect size is computed as a proportion of variance explained by the determination coefficient R^2 of full model (with moderators) against the R^2 of the main-effect model (without moderators) the effect size of 0.26 ($f^2 > 0.15$) indicated that there is a moderate mediation effect.

5   Discussion

Through this research it was expected to understand and assess the environmental factors affecting the relationship between ICT initiatives and delivery of public health outcomes. Through the analysis carried out using country level data, it is identified that education level plays a significant role in improving public health as a result of ICT. Thus, we could depict that better education levels of the public will improve the public health status by adopting, transferring and diffusing ICT initiatives. Therefore, it is important to train and make the public knowledgeable about the benefits of ICT initiatives to achieve expected levels of public health improvements. Furthermore, as hypothesized, the interaction effect of the institutions is significant on the relationship between ICT delivery and public health. That is, the availability of a proper framework to transfer the technology to public and having regulations to ensure the quality of ICT will make public more confident of such systems, leading them to utilize ICT regularly in managing their health.

According to this analysis, there is no profound interaction effect of macroeconomic stability on the relationship between ICT and public health. Macro-economic stability indicates the economic growth of a country. However, the economic growth may not be reflected in the adoption of ICT, accessibility of ICT or affordability of ICT. With economic growth, nations tend to demonstrate high income disparity among the population and a major proportion of the income tends to be divided among a smaller segment of the population. Thus, even though high advanced systems are installed, still there may be groups who are disadvantaged and having no access to the latest ICT technologies to manage their health. Secondly, the nations with low macroeconomic stability may still be influencing ICT initiatives even though their economy is not so stable. These counties may introduce low tax rates for ICT goods and may provide ICT facilities at a low cost or at concessions to public with the aim of reducing the ever increasing healthcare expenditure by adopting ICT initiatives for efficient healthcare management and education (Chan et al. 2009).

6   Conclusion

6.1   Limitations

The use of archived data obtained from various sources can be considered as a limitation in carrying out this research. However, considering the budgetary and human resource constraints, it is not feasible to collect primary data from more than 150 countries. Since these data are retrieved from reputable organizations such as WHO, WEF, World Bank it can be ensured that these data are collected using stringent measures and statistical methods to ensure their validity and reliability. Moreover, many researchers have used similar data for their studies (Mithas et al. 2009; Raghupathi and Wu 2011; Srivastava and Teo 2007)

In this study, we have used 4 independent variables including the moderators. Therefore, the sample size of 40 is adequate to capture fairly small R^2 values at a significant level of 0.05 (Hair Jr 2006). Despite these limitations, the findings are useful in assessing the moderating effect of environment factors on the relationship of ICT factors and delivery of public health outcomes.

6.2   Implications and Future Research

As the theoretical implication of this study, we can identify; (1) Contribution made to theoretical discourse of RBV's resource complementary perspective. In previous studies, it is considered that ICT initiatives have direct effect on public health outcomes. However, our study maintains that having a specific resource can improve the outcome rather than having the predictors only (ICT). (2) Contribution made to the knowledge base of IT-healthcare standard in assessing the influence of environmental factors in national level on the relationship between ICT and delivery of public health. That is for better adoption, diffusion and transfer of ICT innovations to improve the level of public health in a nation, it is important to focus on the 3 environment variables we considered.

Capability of this study in assisting practitioners, policy makers and administrators to understand the reasons for various levels of health outcomes and usefulness of these findings in development of policy and in management of complementary assets can be considered as the practical implication of this study.

The findings of our research have implications for future research. First, while we show that macro-economic stability, education and institutions have interaction effect on ICT factors and public health delivery, new complementary assets like technological readiness, culture and gender equality too could be introduced into the model. Second, panel dataset could be used to examine the effect of leads and lags between predictors, moderators and dependent variables.

In conclusion, this study provides a new perspective to the relationship between ICT factors and delivery of public health outcomes by introducing complementary assets, namely, macro-economic stability, education and institutions. Through this study, we found the moderating effect of environmental factors on the relationship between ICT factors and public health outcomes. This will be helpful to understand how ICT should be managed and to understand how ICT initiatives influence the delivery of public health outcomes with reference to complementary assets.

References

Aanensen, D.M., Huntley, D.M., Feil, E.J., Spratt, B.G.: Epicollect: Linking Smartphones to Web Applications for Epidemiology, Ecology and Community Data Collection. PloS One 4(9), e6968 (2009)

Ackerson, L.K., Viswanath, K.: The Social Context of Interpersonal Communication and Health. Journal of Health Communication 14(S1), 5–17 (2009)

Ahangama, S., Lim, Y.S., Koh, S.Y., Poo, D.C.C.: Revolutionizing Mobile Healthcare Monitoring Technology: Analysis of Features through Task Model. In: International Conference on Human-Computer Interaction, Crete, Greece (2014)

Ahangama, S., Poo, D.C.C.: Moderating Effect of Environmental Factors on Ehealth Development and Health Outcomes: A Country-Level Analysis. In: Bhattacherjee, A., Fitzgerald, B. (eds.) Shaping the Future of ICT Research. IFIP AICT, vol. 389, pp. 143–159. Springer, Heidelberg (2012)

Bagchi, K., Udo, G., Kesh, M.: An Empirical Study Identifying the Factors That Impact Ehealth Infastructure and Ehealth Use (2005)

Barney, J., Wright, M., Ketchen, D.J.: The Resource-Based View of the Firm: Ten Years after 1991. Journal of Management 27(6), 625–641 (2001)

Braa, J., Hanseth, O., Heywood, A., Mohammed, W., Shaw, V.: Developing Health Information Systems in Developing Countries: The Flexible Standards Strategy. MIS Quarterly, 381–402 (2007)

Byrne, E., Sahay, S.: Participatory Design for Social Development: A South African Case Study on Community. Based Health Information Systems, Information Technology for Development 13(1), 71–94 (2007)

Chan, M., Campo, E., Estève, D., Fourniols, J.-Y.: Smart Homes—Current Features and Future Perspectives. Maturitas 64(2), 90–97 (2009)

Chin, W.W., Marcolin, B.L., Newsted, P.R.: A Partial Least Squares Latent Variable Modeling Approach for Measuring Interaction Effects: Results from a Monte Carlo Simulation Study and an Electronic-Mail Emotion/Adoption Study. Information Systems Research 14(2), 189–217 (2003)

Cole-Lewis, H., Kershaw, T.: Text Messaging as a Tool for Behavior Change in Disease Prevention and Management. Epidemiologic Reviews 32(1), 56–69 (2010)

Connell, N., Young, T.: Evaluating Healthcare Information Systems through an "Enterprise" Perspective. Information & Management 44(4), 433–440 (2007)

Fjeldsoe, B.S., Marshall, A.L., Miller, Y.D.: Behavior Change Interventions Delivered by Mobile Telephone Short-Message Service. American Journal of Preventive Medicine 36(2), 165–173 (2009)

Goodhue, D., Lewis, W., Thompson, R.: Research Note-Statistical Power in Analyzing Interaction Effects: Questioning the Advantage of Pls with Product Indicators. Information Systems Research 18(2), 211–227 (2007)

Hair Jr, J.F., Black, W.C., Babin, B.J., Anderson, R.E., Tatham, R.L.: Multivariate data analysis (2006)

Heilman, J.M., Kemmann, E., Bonert, M., Chatterjee, A., Ragar, B., Beards, G.M., Iberri, D.J., Harvey, M., Thomas, B., Stomp, W.: Wikipedia: A Key Tool for Global Public Health Promotion. Journal of Medical Internet Research 13(1) (2011)

Henseler, J., Fassott, G.: Testing Moderating Effects in Pls Path Models: An Illustration of Available Procedures. In: Handbook of Partial Least Squares, pp. 713–735. Springer (2010)

Jennett, P., Scott, R., Affleck Hall, L., Hailey, D., Ohinmaa, A., Anderson, C., Thomas, R., Young, B., Lorenzetti, D.: Policy Implications Associated with the Socioeconomic and Health System Impact of Telehealth: A Case Study from Canada. Telemedicine Journal and e-Health 10(1), 77–83 (2004)

Jha, A.K., DesRoches, C.M., Campbell, E.G., Donelan, K., Rao, S.R., Ferris, T.G., Shields, A., Rosenbaum, S., Blumenthal, D.: Use of Electronic Health Records in Us Hospitals. New England Journal of Medicine 360(16), 1628–1638 (2009)

Jones, S., Fox, S.: Generations Online in 2009. Pew Internet and American Life Project, Washington, Dc (2009)

Kauffman, R.J., Kumar, A.: Impact of Information and Communication Technologies on Country Development: Accounting for Area Interrelationships. International Journal of Electronic Commerce 13(1), 11–58 (2008)

Keil, M., Tan, B.C., Wei, K.-K., Saarinen, T., Tuunainen, V., Wassenaar, A.: A Cross-Cultural Study on Escalation of Commitment Behavior in Software Projects. MIS Quarterly, 299–325 (2000)

Khoumbati, K., Themistocleous, M., Irani, Z.: Evaluating the Adoption of Enterprise Application Integration in Health-Care Organizations. Journal of Management Information Systems 22(4), 69–108 (2006)

Kiecolt, K.J., Nathan, L.E.: Secondary Analysis of Survey Data. Sage Publications, Inc. (1985)

Krishnan, S., Teo, T.: Moderating Effects of Environmental Factors on E-Government, E-Business, and Environmental Sustainability (2011)

Mithas, S., Khuntia, J., Agarwal, R.: Information Technology and Life Expectancy: A Country-Level Analysis (2009)

Ngwenyama, O., Andoh-Baidoo, F.K., Bollou, F., Morawczynski, O.: Is There a Relationship between Ict, Health, Education and Development? An Empirical Analysis of Five West African Countries from 1997-2003. The Electronic Journal of Information Systems in Developing Countries 23 (2006)

OECD, Better Life Index (2013),
      http://www.oecdbetterlifeindex.org/topics/health/

Porter, M.E., Schwab, K.: The Global Competitiveness Report 2008-2009 (2009)

Raghupathi, W., Wu, S.J.: The Relationship between Information and Communication Technologies and the Delivery of Public Health: A Country Level Study. Communications of the Association for Information Systems 28(1), 99–116 (2011)

Ravichandran, T., Lertwongsatien, C.: Effect of Information Systems Resources and Capabilities on Firm Performance: A Resource-Based Perspective. Journal of Management Information Systems 21(4), 237–276 (2005)

Robine, J.-M., Romieu, I., Cambois, E.: Health Expectancy Indicators. Bulletin-World Health Organization (77), 181–185 (1999)

Shaw, B.: Innovation and New Product Development in the Uk Medical Equipment Industry. International Journal of Technology Management 15(3), 433–445 (1998)

Srivastava, S.C., Teo, T.S.H.: What Facilitates E-Government Development? A Cross-Country Analysis. Electronic Government, An International Journal 4(4), 365–378 (2007)

Teece, D.J.: Profiting from Technological Innovation: Implications for Integration, Collaboration, Licensing and Public Policy. Research Policy 15(6), 285–305 (1986)

Teece, D.J.: The Strategic Management of. In: The Oxford Handbook of Strategy, p. 138 (2006)

Tomasi, E., Facchini, L.A., Maia, M.d.F.S.: Health Information Technology in Primary Health Care in Developing Countries: A Literature Review. Bulletin of the World Health Organization 82(11), 867–874 (2004)

World Bank, World Development Report 1993: Investing in Health,The International Bank of Reconstruction and Development/The World Bank (1993)

World Health Organization, World Health Statistics. WHO Press, Geneva (2011)

Woszczynski, A.B., Whitman, M.E.: The Problem of Common Method Variance in Is Research. In: The Handbook of Information Systems Research, pp. 66–77 (2004)

Wu, S., Chaudhry, B., Wang, J., Maglione, M., Mojica, W., Roth, E., Morton, S.C., Shekelle, P.G.: Systematic Review: Impact of Health Information Technology on Quality, Efficiency, and Costs of Medical Care. Annals of Internal Medicine 144(10), 742–752 (2006)

Wu, S.J., Raghupathi, W.: A Panel Analysis of the Strategic Association between Information and Communication Technology and Public Health Delivery. Journal of Medical Internet Research 14(5) (2012)

We All Know How, Don't We? On the Role of Scrum in IT-Offshoring

Christian Koch, Claus Jørgensen, Martin Olsen, and Torben Tambo

Aarhus University, Denmark
christian.koch@chalmers.se

Abstract. Offshoring in the IT-industry involves dual interactions between a mother company and an external supplier, often viewed with an implicit perspective from the mother company. This article review general off shoring and IT offshoring literature, focusing on the proliferation of a globally available set of routines; Scrum and Agile. Two cases are studied; a small company and short process and a large mother company with a long process. The interactions of the set ups shows that global concepts like Scrum and Agile are far from a common platform. The "well known" concepts are locally shaped and the enterprises have mixed experiences.

Keywords: Offshoring, Scrum, Agile, Routines.

1   Introduction

The global IT industry has for quite some time used offshoring of activities as part of a costcutting strategy, however as transaction approaches dominates, the results remain ambiguous [1,2]. It can hardly be claimed to be underilluminated what the challenges of offshoring are, as the general literature on offshoring [3,4], as well as the IT literature is ripe with studies [5,6,7,8,9,10]. Across these there are common understandings pointing at the importance of transfer of routines and knowledge between the mother company and the supplier [11,12].

The focus on routines and knowledge, "incidently" overlap with another approach to innovative organisational change, that of management innovation [13,14]. This stream of literature studies how concepts take the role of globally spreading fashions including their proposal for changed routines and their inbuilt knowledge. Such a globally spreading concept is "Scrum" [15,16], usually accompanied with "Agile" [17,18]. Scrum is argued to be producing high productivity software development through incremental delivery of working code and is adopted by a number of international players and researched in extenso [19]. Agile principles value collaboration and communication over processes, tools and contracts as well as working software (artefacts) over comprehensive documentation [17,20,21]. Together Scrum and Agile represents, a global available concept, a bundling of recommended routines and know how on carrying out the management of software development. The process of using a global concept in the offshoring interaction between mother company and supplier could be perceived as a provision of a common known approach [22].

B. Bergvall-Kåreborn and P.A. Nielsen (Eds.): TDIT 2014, IFIP AICT 429, pp. 96–112, 2014.

As transfer of routines and knowledge are claimed to be crucial to offshoring, this article aims at an empirical analysis of two cases using the same routine and knowledge (Scrum and Agile). The two empirical cases enable a cross case comparison of offshoring types: the small enterprise with a short- medium term and complex project, versus the large enterprise with large volume, long term and simple cooperation.

The article contributes to the understanding of the use of Scrum and Agile in distributed software development as well as innovative models and approaches for managing complexity and multiplicity, by investigating the role of the standardized routine and knowledge in global concepts engaged in local contexts, and it underlines the difficulties of cultural exchange, mutual iterative learning, and issues tackling distance across boundaries.

The structure of the article is the following: An opening introduction and a subsequent theoretical review and frame, method discussion, two cases, discussion and analysis.

2   Theory Frame

The theoretical frame is developed in three steps. First a general discussion on offshoring studies. Second a review of IT-offshoring studies and third a presentation of Scrum and Agile as a global concept for managing standardized routines and knowledge.

General studies of offshoring is dominated by various types of business economics such as transaction cost theory [3], agency theory [23], the knowledge based theory of the firm [24] and the resource based view [25]. Further studies introduce sociological and psychological explanations [26,27,28,29]. In early empirical studies of Danish companies [30,31] it appears to show that cost reduction was a key motive in those year whereas [32,33,34] provide examples of more profound long term business transformation of Danish service and manufacturing companies. Internationally studies of offshoring are split in a similar manner [1,2,3]. A German study by Westner and Strahringer [36] thus exhibit focus on cost reduction. Whereas [37,38,39] indicate resource-based dimensions also occur as motives for sourcing decisions, partly including knowledge integration.

In this article our focus is in line with Nelson & Winter's [40] notion of the importance of routines and knowledge in the development of firms. Accordingly the knowledge-based theory of the firm maintains that "the primary role of the firm, and the essence of organizational capability, is the integration of knowledge" [24]. Knowledge integration occurs through two primary mechanisms, identified by [41]: direction of Demsetz [42] and organizational routines of Nelson and Winter [40]. Direction occurs, through management, when "firms convert sophisticated knowledge into directives, rules and operating procedures that can be imposed by authority based relationships" while organizational routines "are complex patterns of co-ordination that permit different specialists to integrate their knowledge into the production of goods and services while preserving the efficiencies of knowledge specialization" [76,77]. Both mechanisms become more complex when IT-firms offshore their product development operations since specialists may be separated by time, space and sociocultural settings outside the usual organisational routines. Authority-based relationships tend to rupture when product development is not only offshored, but also outsourced. New directions and new organisational routines have to be established to manage the new relations created through the offshoring. In the focal firm, heavier demands on coordination capabilities regarding knowledge integration intra- and interorganisationally arise due to increased complexity when handling the sociocultural, physical and time distances. In a global offshore context "performativity struggles between competing agencements lead to their mutual adjustment involving (temporary) predominance of a strong programme, or the emergence of a new programme from the coexistence/assemblage of different ones" [27]. In the cases to follow such a development and adjustment of a strong programme (the agile and scrum methods) will be identified in both cases due to the challenges regarding mainly geographical and sociocultural differences between the actors, and being mainly initiated by the focal company and at least in one of the cases finishing as indicated by D'Adderio (resulting stability) [27] and Nelson and Winter (truce) [40].

According to Carlile [43], knowledge integration can be divided into three increasingly complex processes: transfer, translation and transformation. As part of the initial transfer of technologies, codified or codifiable knowledge is transferred. In the second phase, the goal is to make the tacit knowledge of the sender explicit through translation and integration of the knowledge at the receiving end. This process builds capabilities at the receiving end for exploiting knowledge originally generated by the sender. The last step augments knowledge, where the sender's original knowledge is transformed into new products and processes at the receiving end. The demands on the organizational routines and direction of the organizations in the process of integrating knowledge increase when companies begin the translation and transformation processes. In the cases to follow, we find at least a move to local translation of the global concepts of Agile and Scrum during the offshoring process.

Finally it should be noted, that a majority of the studies of offshoring assume a mother company perspective [44][78,79,80]. It is thus the offshoring company which possesses the knowledge and routines needed for the establishment of the offshoring activity.

3   IT-Offshoring

When IT companies offshore their product development, their challenges follows broadly the same patterns as discussed above. Also IT-offshoring studies are spread over a number of positions [74,75]. Here we choose to organise the literature into two streams according to their view on transfer of knowledge and routines. One position, the rational technical approach represented by Lacity et al. [6], claims that routines and knowledge should be transferable, as they are well described and formalised [6]. Another position argue that the development of routines in setting which is not co-located anymore should be seen through the community of practice lenses and therefore in a situated manner [9,27].

Lacity et al [6] adopt a realist position equalising a number of features including routines and practices acrosss settings. This review counts 191 articles on IT-offshoring from 1991 to 2009. The factorial splitting, enable them to count and measure experiences of offshoring in terms of for example firm size, degree of outsourcing, the role of IS technical/methodological capability as well as business process outsourcing. These aspects are however not transcended much further. Similar results occur in contributions like [45]. In a parallel publication Willcocks & Lacity [10] argue for two significantly different periods of outsourcing in the IT sector, one from the 1990s and another from 2000 and on. In the last period offshoring has become prevalent. In this volume (and elsewhere) the authors advocate the notion of "configuration" to help describe and manage offshoring [10]. Offshoring components in the configuration include the scope of IT, supplier grouping, financial aspects, duration and commercial relationships.

Vaast and Walsham [9] take a different position adopting an interpretive case-based position. They argue that distributed interactions should be viewed through practice-based learning theory [46]. As point of departure they acknowledge that situated learning is impaired by the lack of collocation. However Vaast & Walsham [9] propose a concept of transsituated learning, and thereby arrive relatively close to Carlile's understanding [43] discussed above. Vaast and Walsham [9] emphasise that the translation and transformation of knowledge does not "just occur", but has to emerge. In prolongation of this D'Adderio [27] in her discussion of transfer of routines, point at the performativity of (standard) routines, as the mutual adaption between the routines and actual performing of processes and practices both converge and diverge in interactive processes. A discussion of the standard routine is as we shall see prevalent in studies of Scrum and Agile in distributed environments [47].

4   Scrum and Agile

In this section we describe the global variant of Scrum and Agile. The primary objective for agile methods is to be able to cope with uncertainty as an alternative to traditional plan-driven methods [19]. Agile software development methods [18] share the principles in the agile manifesto written by 17 experienced practitioners in 2001 (http://agilemanifesto.org). The principles emphasize collaboration and communication between individuals more than processes, tools and contracts, and they focus on working software over comprehensive documentation [21][20][22][9].

One of the most popular agile methods is Scrum [15] where a key element is incremental delivery of working code. A prioritized product backlog with high-level descriptions of potential features of the system to be developed is maintained throughout the Scrum process. The process is iterative and organized in so called sprints (typically a few weeks) where the objective of a sprint is to develop the feature currently at the top of the product backlog. The outcome of a sprint is an increment of the system to be developed – this increment is evaluated with the stakeholders and the product backlog might be changed at this phase. A so called product owner represents the customer throughout the process and a Scrum master facilitates the process in order to keep it on the right track. As for all agile methods the system to be developed becomes the key object for the communication among the parties involved [20,21]. The Scrum method also sets up a framework for how meetings are organized and it may be combined with ingredients and practices from other agile methods such as XP [48].

4.1   Scrum and Agile in Distributed Settings

We now turn to related work on the use of agile methods in a distributed setting with respect to geography and culture [47]. Iivari & Iivari [49] have proposed suggestions for deployment of agile methods in cross cultural environments. Duan et al. [50] looks into the required trans-national knowledge transfer. Uy and Ioannou [51] describe how their company Kelley Blue Book uses "The Five Dysfunctions of a Team"-model by Patrick Lencioni to help set up offshore Scrum development teams in India and China. Sutherland et al. [52] show that distributed Scrum teams can obtain "... the same velocity and quality as a colocated team ..." and Kussmaul et al. [53] report "lessons learned" on a case of a development project with a distributed Scrum team. The findings in these papers [47, 51,52,53] indicate that it is possible and beneficial to use agile methods in an onshore/offshore distributed setting, although [54] summarizes various concerns. Discussing global software development (GSD) [55,73] claim that "... the more common view is that agile methods are not applicable " in a context of global development (GSD), but nevertheless arrive at a more positive conclusion suggesting among other things that "... agile methods may be more amenable to GSD than has been previously reported".

Offshoring of services particularly digital, professional services in the IT sector has become increasingly popular. Virtual development teams are largely regarded to increase organizational development capability [56,57]. Lampel and Bhalla [2,35,72] discuss various pitfalls and models for IT offshoring, and [2] provide a longitudinal study of IT project offshoring with a continual low cost focus; [58] contribute with the aspect of risk management in IT offshoring. Culture and geography is widely recognized as an influencing factor on software engineering [59,60,61]. Deng & Zhao [62] describe a shift from informal to formal control to improve delivery quality.

It derives from the above presentation that studies of Scrum and Agile in offshoring and similar constellation are rich with discussions on the use of the globally presented concept. However the understanding of the concepts varies significantly, probably because specific contextual interpretations of Agile principles, Scrum methods and even XP programming occur. Moreover the challenges regarding the concepts of Scrum and Agile as being mainly promoted by consultants, professional press and education institutions, and thereby often more loosely coupled to the enterprises are not discussed.

5   Method

The article places itself within the multidisciplinary IS-research with an overarching interpretive approach [63]. The review and theoretical frame encompasses contributions from IS-research focusing on offshoring [6] as well as on Agile and Scrum [15], business economics [37], and sociological approaches such as [43][27][9]. These approaches are used in mutually complementary manner, using a soft multidisciplinary synthesis [64].

The cases were selected due to the author group's insight in the two companies based on two authors being employed in each of the companies respectively. The experiences from the two companies as presented by two of the authors seemed at the outset to provide an interesting tension of difference. The clear limitation of selecting and developing the cases in this manner leads to a need to lend support from the method literature on autoethnography [65,66]. It should moreover be noted that both cases build on ex post reflections on the offshoring processes, and not on ex ante decisions to research on offshoring. In the development of the case analysis, given the two authors close ties to the cases with regular participation in the companies, two approaches were used; a strong element of, first securing a distinction between the 'information insider' and the 'analyst outsider' [65], and second an intercollegial challenging of the work experiences in the broader author group was carried out[66]. It has been chosen in the description and analysis not to enter more detailed references to the sources used by the authors directly involved in the cases. Their memory and point of view is therefore thoroughgoing and counterbalanced by the author teams external perspective. As a final limitation, the ideal research approach given our emphasis on the emergent character of implementing routines and knowledge, spanning the mother company and the supplier, would probably be "global ethnography" as suggested by [67], lending equal voice to the two settings investigated, rather as it is done here, with point of departure in the (Western) mother company. It can be noted however, that in one case the author employed has visited the receiving organisation, and in the other the author employed has been closely following the offshoring process.

6   Cases

6.1   Case A: HouseCo Offshoring to Ukraine

HouseCo is a Danish company running a web site offering users the possibility to book a holiday home in Europe. The company employs 11 people and the web site contains roughly 100.000 European holiday homes. In Q2 2009 HouseCo decided to upgrade the search infrastructure of their web site in order to meet future demands for search efficiency and flexibility. The project is a relatively complex development task and the initial estimate on manpower needed for the project was 2 man-years assuming the project was to be handled in-house, but due to other projects HouseCo could not allocate the man power in-house so extra man power was needed. In 2009 the demand of local and qualified IT developers was high so HouseCo decided to contact a Danish company SourceCo. Through the company SourceCo, a Ukrainian development team dedicated to the project, was set up in Kiev. Following one of the agile principles, it was decided not to base the work on a contract specifying the software to be developed, and the Ukrainian team - consisting of approximately 6 people on average - was paid by the hour instead.

According to HouseCo the Ukrainian educational system does not seem to have "matured" with respect to teaching system development. Almost all of the members of the Ukrainian development team have university degrees at the master level but not necessarily IT related degrees – and if the degree is in IT the degrees have a narrow technical perspective. Two HouseCo employees, including the scrum-master, made regular visits to Kiev and two visits to Denmark for members of the Ukrainian team were organized as well. Scrum has been used to manage the development process.

HouseCo neither consider the project as a "success" nor a "failure" with the HouseCo Scrum master leaning more towards "failure" and the CEO estimating the outcome somewhere in between. The cost of Ukrainian man power is roughly 60 % in average (including the share of the broker company SourceCo) compared to the cost of manpower in HouseCo. The development time exceeds the initial estimate. The initial estimate is also characterized as "very optimistic". The agile approach with extensive involvement and regular visits by the HouseCo employees is characterized as "absolutely crucial" by HouseCo. According to the Scrum master HouseCo was not mature using agile methods internally when diving into the onshore/offshore variant. As an example the very important processes of specifying the features to implement in the sprints and evaluating the resulting increments were improved a lot as the development process went along. In the beginning the communication was oriented towards the technical architecture and written code. A more user-oriented perspective replaced the technical perspective later where the feature(s) to be implemented in a sprint were specified by scenarios telling exactly how the system should react on specific inputs. In other words, the brokering of the information should be done upfront, as needed information had to be conveyed in the beginning of the development process. The Scrum frame was too unclear and thin at the beginning of the process but all in all the development process resembled the Scrum model. The distributed setting made it necessary to focus more on written as opposed to verbal communication compared to the non-distributed setting.

The HouseCo people sometimes had the impression that the members of the offshore development team had a fine understanding of what was to be developed for the next sprint but later it turned out not to be the case. Besides the initial unclear Scrum frame, communication difficulties also have triggered the problems. As an example video-conferences did not work nearly as well as the face-to-face meetings. According to HouseCo there appears to be a "yes-sir"-culture offshore where the members of the development team are not persistent enough in trying to reach an understanding of the goals of a sprint so the sociocultural distance also constituted a problem. The offshore team tried to "impress" the HouseCo people in some of the sprints leading to increments failing the tests – the HouseCo people were disappointed and the communication suffered.

HouseCo succeeded to hire local man power and decided to finish the project in-house finishing the offshore activities primo 2010. There have been many obstacles along the way but by using an agile approach a reasonable result has been obtained that forms the basis of the ongoing work in-house. The flexibility of the man power allocation is seen as the major advantage of the approach used and HouseCo questions that the project could have been solved fully in-house since the demand of qualified and local IT personnel was very high at the time the project was launched. HouseCo will be very careful, if the company should offshore software development in the future, but if the company decides to do so, HouseCo is convinced an agile approach will be chosen again. The lessons learned from the project presented above have led to an increased maturity inhouse regarding conducting the Scrum process that would help to avoid at least some of the problems discussed above. On the other hand, the lessons learned have improved the agile skills of the HouseCo developers so they now produce high quality code efficiently according to their Scrum master.

6.2   Case B: TexCo Offshoring to India

TexCo is a Danish trading company within the consumer goods sector with a turn-over of 2 billion EUR, and 14,000 customers in 45 countries. The IT Department at the local TexCo headquarter consisted of 150 employees in 2005, but was facing an increased requirement for further IT resources within development, maintenance and operations activities. An increase in internal staffing was considered, as well as vari-ous options for relying upon existing relationships to local consultancies to fulfill the need for further resources. Based on traditions for buying physical products in India, the CEO asked the IT management to start using Indian offshoring to access further IT-resources. Captive offshoring (a fully owned subsidiary) was considered, but dis-regarded in favor of an independent company. As a result of a former relationship, SoftCo in Maharashtra, India was chosen. SoftCo had at this time approximately 2000 employees, representation offices in several European and US cities, and had expe-rienced 25% annual growth rates.

The relationship was initiated with a startup meeting at TexCo's premises in Den-mark, where SoftCo presented the expected trading/legal documents, and suggested a competitive pricing scheme. SoftCo explicitly defined themselves as a service com-pany delivering resources to the customers opposed to a traditional software devel-opment company. An agreement to establish a team of Full Time Equivalent (FTE) resources was reached. FTE means that the employees from SoftCo were allocated to TexCo for all working hours reasonably billable; SoftCo contributed with internal time registration systems and a detailed planning system, whereas TexCo was ex-pected to formally allocate resources and track project progress using regular project management tools.

Mid-2005 two employees from SoftCo started at TexCo's headquarter to gather in-formation for tasks to come: Development of reports (database queries, graphical formatting) was chosen as the first initiative. From two employees the relationship grew to 80 employees over the next 24 months. The dominant background of the SoftCo employees was 3 to 18 months of working experience as B.Sc.´s in Computer Science. Managers were promoted from this group further including 3 – 4 more expe-rienced project managers for the overall engagement. Activities were during the growth aligned with the organization of employee activities within TexCo's IT Department, and mutual teams were grouped within the areas of Java development,

Reports development, Integration Services development and operation, Standard ERP maintenance and operations, and IT Operations – mainly database server monitoring and problem resolution. The development activities are further discussed below.

The development oriented assignment accounted for around 60 of the team members. After 30 months of growth TexCo's functional and technical project managers were questioning the outcome and cost of the cooperation. Deadlines from SoftCo were repeatedly delayed. There were severe quality issues with delivered software. Training given by TexCo staff at SoftCo's premises did not seem to help. Guidelines and requirement specifications were not followed in detail. A number of "proof of concept" projects yielded no results only further cost. Relationships decayed with the supplier of standard ERP, development tools, and server technologies, and SoftCo failed to maintain relationships with their suppliers during this conflict as well as failing to include experiences from other clients. A review on staff experience showed that SoftCo largely exaggerated working experience of the associates. Something needed to be done within Texco's IT department, otherwise the situation would become a subject for the top level management requiring their intervention.

The project management team of TexCo had over time followed professional discussions on governance and management of IT development projects. The team decided to receive training in and implement Scrum on internal and external delivery processes. Five project managers obtained Scrum Master Certification. For some months Scrum was tested only on internal project deliverables with whiteboards and physical meetings in TexCo's offices. It was very well received by developers and project managers. Emphasis was given on micro-planning (day-to-day and sprint), issue resolution – with users or other technical staff, and self estimation.

TexCo made a plan for SoftCo that required most development activities to switch to Scrum. It was initially assumed, that a number of the learnings from the internal use of Scrum could not be transferred identically due to the time difference of 4.5 hours between Denmark and India. It was ideally expected, that Scrum would speed up the delivery pace from SoftCo and satisfy TexCo's project managers on cost and delivery issues. TexCo's Scrum Masters undertook the training of SoftCo's staff in SoftCo's offices.

In moving from and internal use of Scrum to Scrum in offshoring, a number of issues were created. The micro-planning aspect shifted face-to-face contact among developers, projects managers and product owners, to daily Scrum meetings at the offices of the offshoring company, where product owner and teams with in-depth knowledge could not play the same role. In issue resolution, internal Scrum projects had immediate access to product owners, and deep insight in technology and business, and therefore excellent opportunities for making high precision sprint estimation. In the offshoring case, interaction inevitably became secondary causing lost transparency, again creating confusion and tensions. Furthermore mis-estimations were mostly the case. The Scrum routines developed by the internal Scrum activities resembled strongly the culture and behaviour normally utilized at Texco, and the offshoring teams abroad had difficulties in mimicking this. The loyalty of internal teams to "play the game" was based on the project managers and immediate users; loyalty and readiness. In the offshored scrum activities on the other hand this turned more towards satisfying local managers and customer managers compared to accomplishing the requirements of the customer.

TexCo's project managers started to use sprint time estimation between internal and Indian developers in allocation of assignments, and proforma business cost quotations. Changes in development policy at the same time meant less development assignments. The FTE agreement was loosened, so TexCo no longer had to pay for under-utilized resources at SoftCo. The business between the two parties continued at a lower, but more transparent level.

TexCo saw Scrum as one of several methods for creating agile development projects as it was also supported by formalised training. TexCo sought to use an agile approach to improve the business' acceptance of proposed software, and to 1) improve the overall project management's insight into business requirements and other constraints – and 2) improve adaption to the former by having shorter and more standardised cycles introduced in the development process. Furthermore, the offshore team's progressive understanding was expected to improve concerning the basic technology, the business requirements, and the solution design. Scrum should thus balance between (1) necessary breaks to adjust to the understanding of the required outcome, (2) the control of resources spend by the self-estimation and the explanations given in case of wrong self-estimation.

It never became clear to Texco actors if SoftCo had actual past experience with Scrum. Despite TexCo's open-mindedness regarding purchasing in Asia, the quality lens for software was far different from garment, the core business of TexCo. The business relationship both during the ramp-up and the stable phases had an element of crisis management to it. Constantly new "incidents" were brought up. Scrum was a mediation toole in the mutual conflicts over blame/success. TexCo's main successes with software consultancies were mainly achieved with smaller teams of highly dedicated and skilled people, i.e. directly resembling and reflecting TexCo's own organization and culture, and making tools like Scrum superficial. This constitutes a pattern of routines within TexCo hard to transfer to offshore collaboration partner. SoftCo had much less issues with other customers, and has sustained its growth with by end of 2013 more than 8.800 employees.

7   Discussion

The cases are addressing the issue of agile and scrum as a target of distributed organizational learning [46][9] as both hosting organization were unexperienced in agile and scrum prior to the described development process cases. The cases suggest a general issue of agile and scrum as colloquialisms rather than institutionalized routines [5]. The process of the cases assumed a fast track to routinisation of agile and scrum mechanisms that proved more problematic than expected by the involved parties. Furthermore both cases seem to focus on, but generally fail to reach, a dualism of organizational learning involving both the onshore and the offshoring organization [68][69][59]. In Texco previous methods were rather haphazard and Agile and scrum offers itself in by articulating the existence of a development method [62] and transferring sporadic and unstructured communication and collaboration [21][20] into routines although aspects of learning and "mental" embedding of routines seem over-looked in the cases.

Scrum and Agile have been around as a global standardised routine "offer" for around ten years. Nevertheless our cases show that the assumption that this might act as a common denominator, a common know how, in an offshoring process seems to be overestimated. Scrum and Agile unfolds in the case in ways, where these principles fail to perform as common understanding [27], neither as brokerage nor as boundary objects [43]. Failure of both the sending and receiving organization to comply with the demands within the standardized routine are mainly due to barriers at both ends to translate tacit knowledge during the development process [12] directed by the chosen standardized routine as well as managing the identified roles (i.e. the scrum master and more) supporting the interorganisational coordination part supplementing the standardized routine. The concepts turn out to be too general and unprecise. In the HouseCo case this occurred as difficulties when specifying the early sprints, and in the TexCo Scrum routines became dependent of intraorganisational tacit knowledge, developed as TexCo felt they need more routines than the described. This is a result paralleled by [55], which witness a "filling out" by XP methods [48,55]. Moreover it remains unclear in the processes of Houseco and Texco to what extent the suppliers actually master Scrum and Agile and what type or variant they embraced. Scrum and agile methods act as primarily a intraorganisational coordination tool, through micro planning, delivery of sprints and the like, and missing an interorganisational coordina-tion part. In the internal processes Scrum perform the distribution of roles and devel-opment of the actors' capability to fulfil the identified roles. In the interorganisational coordination we witness a mutual adaption/adjustment towards the other party in the Houseco, where expectation to sprints (the short term artefacts) has to be mutually bended [69]. In the Texco case however it appears that, scrum masters from Texco are willing to establish authoritative relations and subjugate actors from the supplier to insist in exercising the scrum estimations, which illustrate the role of direction [42]. Furthermore the role played by the mother company's knowledge base is a finding parallel to [52], which maintains that it is the mother organisations understanding of Scrum that makes the difference.

The routine perspective adds an issue of control and expectancy of work. The routine is whether tacit or explicit supporting the inter-relational communication in inter- and intra-organisational contexts alike [20]. Using Carlile's [43] context of knowledge integration in the state of transformation, the cases suggest is takes more than some months of transition to actually move to a state of internalisation. Finally, considering [62][71][45][28] agile and scrum contain attractive aspects of control of performance, developers perception, ability to deliver, and cost. Routines provide a certain degree of control as performativity is relatively direct recognisable; this proves more complex in offshoring although scrum is providing parts of this given necessary learning and internationalisation.

At the outset the two cases are rather different. One HouseCo is a small to small and a single project, whereas the other Texco is a large to large longitudinal collabora-tion. They can be characterised as Win-Loose (HouseCo) versus Loose-Loose (Texco).

As a result both case companies return to a captive set up, which along with the general offshoring literature [6,7,8], is probably merely a temporal choice until another occasion will stimulate the companies to use offshoring again. At least in the HouseCo case management is prepared for this future turn.

On this background it appear that other differences between the cases, such as informal versus formal contractual relations have mattered less as both dyads, mother companies and suppliers struggle with making acceptable results out of the scrum processes. Issues of quality and time are occurring. They both experience that direct collocated interaction are superior to IT-mediated communication [20]. Texco and Softco invest heavily for some time in the collaboration (up to 80 employees involved, with 60 involved in software development) and it continue to be a likely future alliance.

Finally it could be interesting to consider alternatives to agile and scrum. In the HouseCo case it could have been a classical waterfall requirement specification that would have proven difficult given the small size of both organisations and the complexity of the project [70][51]. In TexCo agile and scrum was sought for as a replacement for a highly ad-hoc based development methodology characterized by a very low degree of experience from all sides [18][36]. Requirement specifications were rarely more than 15 pages and did more set the framework of the project, and TexCo's prior methodology could thus be seen as "haphazard prototyping" [11]. Therefore TexCo can be viewed as potential terrain for getting into trouble using almost any method.

8   Conclusion

In establishing offshoring relations we have discussed the role of globally accessible standardised routines and methods, Scrum and Agile. It was chosen by the case companies as a direction to enable the integration of knowledge and to establish routines between a mother company and a supplier. We saw how this partly failed as it appears that the involved companies have not succeeded in practicing Scrum and Agile in a collaborative manner even if managerial direction were in place. However our results underline that Scrum and Agile also act as an independent reference point for the receiving organization, even if it turns out to be an imprecise reference.

Failure of both the mother and supplier organization to comply with the demands within the standardized routine was interpreted as due to barriers at both ends to translate and/or externalize tacit knowledge during the development process. Both failures relate to the chosen standardized routine as well as managing the identified roles as the interorganisational part supplementing the standardized routine. Scrum and Agile functions primarily as an intra-organisational coordination tool whereas the interorganisational coordination part fails, leading to a captive backshoring of the activities in both cases. Routines are not like tin cans. The trajectories of the two cases reveals the performativity of routines especially within the interorganizational area and partly also within the organizations.

References

1. Lacity, M., Willcocks, L.P.: Outsourcing business processes for innovation. MIT Sloan Management Review 54(3), 63–69 (2013)
2. Lampel, J., Bhalla, A.: Living with offshoring: The impact of offshoring on the evolution of organizational configurations. Journal of World Business 46(3), 346–358 (2011)
3. Bunyaratavej, K., Doh, J., Hahn, E.D., Lewin, A.Y., Massini, S.: Conceptual Issues in Services Offshoring Research: A Multidisciplinary Review. Group & Organization Management 36(1), 70–102 (2011)
4. Pedersen, T., Bals, L., Jensen, P.Ø. (eds.): The Offshoring Challenge: Strategic Design and Innovation for Tomorrow's Organization, pp. 141–154. Springer, London (2013)
5. Jayatilaka, B., Hirschheim, R.: Changes in IT-sourcing arrangements – an interpretive field study of technical and institutional influences. Strategic Outsourcing: An International Journal 2(2), 84–122 (2009)
6. Lacity, M.C., Khan, S., Willcocks, L.P.: A review of the IT outsourcing literature: insights for practice. Journal of Strategic Information Systems 18(3), 130–146 (2009)
7. Lacity, M.C., Khan, S., Yan, A., Willcocks, L.P.: A review of the IT outsourcing empirical literature and future research directions. Journal of Information Technology 25, 395–433 (2010)
8. Lacity, M.C., Solomon, S., Yan, A., Willcocks, L.P.: Business process outsourcing studies: a critical review and research directions. Journal of Information Technology 26, 221–258 (2011)
9. Vaast, E., Walsham, G.: Trans-situated learning: supporting a network of practice with an information infrastructure. Information Systems Research 20(4), 547–564 (2009)
10. Willcocks, L.P., Lacity, M.: The practice of outsourcing: from information systems to BPO and offshoring. Palgrave, London (2009)
11. D'Adderio, L.: Crafting the virtual prototype: how firms integrate knowledge and capabilities across organisational boundaries. Research Policy 30, 1409–1424 (2001)
12. Jørgensen, C.: Offshore supplier relations: knowledge integration among small businesses. Strategic Outsourcing: An International Journal 3(3), 192–210 (2010)
13. Birkinshaw, J., Hamel, G., Mol, M.J.: Management Innovation. Academy of Management Review 33(4), 825–845 (2008)
14. Knights, D., McCabe, D.: Organization and innovation: guru schemes and American dreams. Open University Press, Maidenhead (2003)
15. Schwaber, K., Beedle, M.: Agile Software Development with Scrum. Prentice Hall, Upper Saddle River (2001)
16. Sutherland, J., Schwaber, K.: The Scrum Papers: Nuts, Bolts, and Origins of an Agile Method. Scrum, Inc., Boston (2007)
17. Conboy, K.: Agility from first principles: Reconstructing the concept of agility in Information Systems Development. Information Systems Research 20(3), 329–354 (2009)
18. Misra, S.C., Kumar, V., Kumar, U.: Identifying some important success factors in adopting agile software development practices. The Journal of Systems and Software 82, 1869–1890 (2009)
19. Dingsøyr, T., Nerur, S., Balijepally, V., Moe, N.: A decade of agile methodologies: Towards explaining agile software development. The Journal of Systems and Software 85, 1213–1221 (2012)
20. Hummel, M., Rosenkranz, C., Holten, R.: The Role of Communication in Agile Systems Development. Business & Information Systems Engineering 5(5), 343–355 (2013)

21. Sahar, F., Raza, S.T., Nasir, M.N.: Communication Tools in Offshore Development with Scrum. IACSIT International Journal of Engineering and Technology 5(4) (2013)

22. Gupta, A., Crk, I., Bondade, R.: Leveraging temporal and spatial separations with the 24-hour knowledge factory paradigm. Information Systems Frontiers 13(3), 397–405 (2011)

23. Aubert, B.A., Patry, M., Rivard, S.: A Framework for Information Technology Outsourcing Risk Management. SIGMIS Database 36(4), 9–28 (2005)

24. Grant, R.M.: Prospering in dynamically-competitive environments: organizational capability as knowledge integration. Organization Science 7(4), 375–387 (1996)

25. Hätönen, J., Eriksson, T.: 30+ years of research and practice of outsourcing – Exploring the past and anticipating the future. Journal of International Management 15(2), 142–155 (2009)

26. Abbott, P., Zheng, Y., Duc, R., Willcocks, L.: From boundary spanning to creolization: A study of Chinese software and services outsourcing vendors. The Journal of Strategic Information Systems 22(2), 121–136 (2013)

27. D'Adderio, L.: The performativity of routines: Theorising the influence of artefacts and distributed agencies on routines dynamics. Research Policy 37(5), 769–789 (2008)

28. Heiskanen, A., Newman, M., Eklin, M.: Control, trust, power, and the dynamics of information system outsourcing relationships: a process study of contractual software development. Journal of Strategic Information Systems 17(4), 268–286 (2008)

29. Ågerfalk, P., Fitzgerald, B., Slaughter, S.: Flexible and Distributed Information Systems Development: State of the Art and Research Challenges. Information Systems Research 20(3), 317–328 (2009)

30. Maskell, P., Pedersen, T., Petersen, B., Dick-Nielsen, J.: Learning paths to offshore outsourcing: from cost reduction to knowledge seeking. Industry and Innovation 14(3), 239–257 (2007)

31. Præst Knudsen, M., Cederquist, N.: Outsourcing i mindre danske virksomheder. Syddansk Universitet, Tuborgfondet og Danmarks Erhvervsforskningsakademi (2007)

32. Jensen, P.Ø.: A learning perspective on the offshoring of advanced services. Journal of International Management 15(2), 181–193 (2009)

33. Jensen, P.Ø.: A passage to India: A dual case study of activities, processes and resources in offshore outsourcing of advanced services. Journal of World Business 47(2), 311–326 (2012)

34. Koch, C., Jørgensen, C., Mathiesen, J.B.: Strategic Sourcing Development–Emerging Resource Combination and Knowledge Interaction. IMP Journal 7(1), 12–23 (2013)

35. Lampel, J., Bhalla, A.: Embracing realism and recognizing choice in IT offshoring initiatives. Business Horizons 51, 429–440 (2008)

36. Westner, M., Strahringer, S.: Determinants of success in IS offshoring projects: Results from an empirical study of German companies. Information & Management 47, 291–299 (2010)

37. McIvor, R.: How the transaction cost and resource-based theories of the firm inform outsourcing evaluation. Journal of Operations Management 27, 45–63 (2009)

38. Bengtsson, L., Berggren, C.: The integrator's new advantage – the reassessment of outsourcing and production competences in a global telecom firm. European Management Journal 26, 314–324 (2008)

39. Lewin, A.Y., Massini, S., Peeters, C.: Why are companies offshoring innovation? The emerging global race for talent. Journal of International Business Studies 40, 901–925 (2009)

40. Nelson, R.R., Winter, S.G.: An Evolutionary Theory of Economic Change. Belknap Press, Cambridge (1982)
41. Grant, R.M., Baden-Fuller, C.: A knowledge assessing theory of strategic alliances. Journal of Management Studies 41(1), 61–84 (2004)
42. Demsetz, H.: The theory of the firm revised. In: Williamson, O.E., Winter, S.G. (eds.) The Nature of the Firm, pp. 159–178. Oxford University Press, New York (1991)
43. Carlile, P.R.: Transferring, translating, and transforming: an integrative framework for managing knowledge across boundaries. Organization Science 15(5), 555–568 (2004)
44. Pagano, A.: The role of relational capabilities in the organization of international sourcing activities: A literature review. Industrial Marketing Management 38(8), 903–913 (2009)
45. Straub, D., Weill, P., Schwaig, K.: Strategic dependence on the IT resource and outsourcing: a test of the strategic control model. Information Systems Frontiers 10(2), 195–211 (2008)
46. Brown, J.S., Duguid, P.: Organizational Learning and Communities-of-Practice: Toward a Unified View of Working, Learning, and Innovation. Organization Science 2(1), 40–57 (1991)
47. Lee, S., Yong, H.-S.: Distributed agile: project management in a global environment. Empirical Software Engineering 15(2), 204–217 (2010)
48. Beck, K.: Extreme Programming Explained: Embrace Change. Addison-Wesley, Harlow (1999)
49. Iivari, J., Iivari, N.: The relationship between organizational culture and the deployment of agile methods. Information and Software Technology 53(5), 509–520 (2010)
50. Duan, Y., Nie, W., Coakes, E.: Identifying key factors affecting transnational knowledge transfer. Information & Management 47(7), 356–363 (2010)
51. Uy, E., Ioannou, N.: Growing and Sustaining an Offshore Scrum Engagement. In: Proceedings of Agile Conference 2008 (2008)
52. Sutherland, J., Schoonheim, G., Rijk, M.: Fully Distributed Scrum: Replicating Local Productivity and Quality with Offshore Teams. In: Proceedings of the 42nd Hawaii International Conference on System Sciences, pp. 1–8 (2009)
53. Kussmaul, C., Jack, R., Sponsler, B.: Outsourcing and Offshoring with Agility: A Case Study. In: Zannier, C., Erdogmus, H., Lindstrom, L. (eds.) XP/Agile Universe 2004. LNCS, vol. 3134, pp. 147–154. Springer, Heidelberg (2004)
54. Ionel, N.: Critical Analysis of the Scrum Project Management Methodology. In: Proceedings of the 4th International Economic Conference on European Integration - New Challenges for the Romanian Economy, Oradea, pp. 435–441 (2008)
55. Holmström, H., Fitzgerald, B., Ågerfalk, P., Conchúir, E.O.: Agile Practices Reduce Distance In Global Software Development. Information Systems Management 23(3), 7–18 (2006)
56. Vaccaro, A., Veloso, F., Brusoni, S.: The impact of virtual technologies on knowledge-based processes: An empirical study. Research Policy 38, 1278–1287 (2009)
57. Sakthivel, S.: Virtual Workgroups in Offshore Systems Development. Journal of Software & Information Technology 47, 305–318 (2005)
58. Chatfield, A.T., Wanninayaka, P.: IT Offshoring Risks and Governance Capabilities. In: Proceedings of the 41st Hawaii International Conference on System Sciences (2008)
59. Jaakkola, H., Heimbürger, A., Linna, P.: Knowledge-oriented software engineering process in a multi-cultural context. Software Quality Journal 18, 299–319 (2010)
60. Niederman, F., Kundu, S., Salas, S.: IT Software Development Offshoring: A Multi-Level Theoretical Framework and Research Agenda. Journal of Global Information Management 14(2), 52–74 (2006)

61. Gregory, R.W.: Review of the IS Offshoring Literature: The Role of Cross-Cultural Differences and Management Practices. In: Proceedings of 18th European Conference on Information Systems (2010)
62. Deng, C., Zhao, S.: Control, Affect and Cognition Trust in Determining IT Offshoring Outsourcing Service Quality. In: Proceedings of the International Conference on Management and Service Science, MASS (2010)
63. Walsham, G.: Doing interpretive research. European Journal of Information Systems 15(3), 320–330 (2006)
64. Gioa, D., Pitre, E.: Multiparadigm Perspectives on Theory Building. The Academy of Management Review 15(4), 584–602 (1990)
65. Cunningham, S.J., Jones, M.: Autoethnography: A tool for practice and education. In: CHINZ; Proceedings of the 6th ACM SIGCHI New Zealand Chapter's International Conference on Computer-human Interaction: Making CHI Natural, vol. 94 (2005)
66. Lapadat, J.C.: Writing our way into shared understanding: Collaborative Autobiographical Writing in the Qualitative Methods Class. Qualitative Inquiry 15(6), 955–979 (2009)
67. Burawoy, M., Blum, J.A., George, S., Gille, Z., Gowan, T., Haney, L., Klawiter, M., Lopez, S.H., Riain, S., Thayer, M.: Global Ethnography: Forces, Connections, and Imaginations in a Postmodern World. University of California Press, Berkeley (2000)
68. Jørgensen, M.T.N., Hovmøller, H., Nielsen, J.R., Tambo, T.: Improving offshoring of low-budget agile software development using the dual-shore approach: An autoethnographic study. In: Proceedings of 36th Information Systems Research in Scandinavia (IRIS) Seminar, pp. 2–17. Oslo (2013)
69. Kornstädt, A., Sauer, J.: Mastering dual-shore Development–The tools and materials approach adapted to agile offshoring. In: Meyer, B., Joseph, M. (eds.) SEAFOOD 2007. LNCS, vol. 4716, pp. 83–95. Springer, Heidelberg (2007)
70. D'Adderio, L.: Inside the Virtual Product: How Organisations Create Knowledge Through Software. Edward Elgar, Cheltenham (2004)
71. Maruping, L.M., Venkatesh, V., Agarwal, R.: A Control Theory Perspective on Agile Methodology Use and Changing User Requirements. Information Systems Research 20(3), 377–399 (2009)
72. Bhalla, A., Sodhi, M.S., Son, B.-K.: Is more IT offshoring better? An exploratory study of western companies offshoring to South East Asia. Journal of Operations Management 26, 322–335 (2008)
73. Ågerfalk, P., Fitzgerald, B.: Outsourcing to an Unknown Workforce: Exploring Opensourcing as a Global Sourcing Strategy. MIS Quarterly 32(2), 385–409 (2008)
74. Cummings, J.N., Espinosa, J.A., Pickering, C.K.: Crossing Spatial and Temporal Barriers in Globally Distributed Projects: A Relation Model of Coordination Delay. Information Systems Research 20(3), 420–439 (2009)
75. Contractor, F.K., Kumar, V., Kundu, S.K., Pedersen, T.: Reconceptualizing the Firm in a World of Outsourcing and Offshoring: The Organizational and Geographical Relocation of High-Value Company Functions. Journal of Management Studies 47(8), 1417–1433 (2010)
76. Pollock, N., Williams, R., D'Adderio, L., Grimm, C.: Post local forms of repair: The (extended) situation of virtualised technical support. Information and Organization 19, 253–276 (2009)
77. Roberts, R.: Offshoring: Individual short-term gain versus collective long-term loss? IT Professional 7(5), 25–30 (2005)

78. Kedia, B.L., Mukherjee, D.: Understanding offshoring: A research framework based on disintegration, location and externalization advantages. Journal of World Business 44, 250–261 (2009)
79. Tambo, T., Olsen, M.: Offshoring - the new dilemma of IS research. In: Proceedings of the First Scandinavian Conference of IS & The 33rd IRIS Seminar, Denmark, pp. 1–12 (2010)
80. Khan, S.U., Niazi, M., Ahmad, R.: Barriers in the selection of offshore software development outsourcing vendors: An exploratory study using a systematic literature review. Information and Software Technology 53(7), 693–706 (2010)

Designing Project Management for Global Software Development
Informality through Formality

Gitte Tjørnehøj[1], Maria B. Balogh[2], Cathrine Iversen[2], and Stine Sørensen[2]

[1] Department of Economics, Politics and Public Administration, Aalborg University
gtj@dps.aau.dk
[2] Master of Science in Information Technology from Aalborg University Denmark
{mariabbalogh,iversen.cathrine,stiness}@gmail.com

Abstract. Software development in distributed teams remains challenging despite rapid technical improvement in tools for communication and collaboration across distance. The challenges stem from geographical, temporal and sociocultural distance and manifest themselves in a variety of difficulties in the development projects. This study has identified a range of difficulties described in the literature of global software development, lacking sufficient solutions. In particular, advice for project managers is lacking. Design science research has been applied to design a model to guide project managers of distributed software teams, based on a practice study and informed by well-known theories. Our work pinpoints the difficulties of handling the vital informal processes in distributed collaboration that are so vulnerable because the distances risk detaining their growth and increasing their decay rate. The research suggest to support and securing these informal processes through explicit and formal means and to ensure management's continuous focus on this effort to succeed.

Keywords: Global Software Development, Project Management, Informal Processes, Formal Processes, Distributed Teams, Communication, Coordination, Control, Trust.

1   Introduction

Global software development (GSD) remains challenging despite rapid technical improvement in media and tools for collaboration over distance [1, 2]. Numerous studies report difficulties when distributing software development across geographical, temporal and sociocultural distances [3]. The challenges manifest themselves in a variety of difficulties on all collaborating levels of the involved organizations. This paper, however, focuses on the level of distributed development projects and thus on the special challenges for the project manager of geographically (and often also temporally and socioculturally) distributed teams.

The literature describes many challenges for GSD projects (see section 2) and also some advice on how to handle these challenges. The common project management

B. Bergvall-Kåreborn and P.A. Nielsen (Eds.): TDIT 2014, IFIP AICT 429, pp. 113–132, 2014.

literature, however, provides little advice for project managers on distributed projects. Project managers can find advice in parallel fields, for example on managing cultural differences in organizations [4,5], managing and building teams (both virtual [6] and co-located [7]), and knowledge management [8]. However, the integration and adaption of this knowledge in(to) the practice of project managers of GSD teams is less widely explored.

This research aims to develop knowledge on how these project managers can cope with the numerous, complex and interwoven challenges that are dominant in their practice. To focus the paper we will present our findings in order to answer the following research question: How do project managers cope with the challenges of GSD, and in particular, how do they establish and sustain the crucial informal processes and interactions in their projects?

We have applied design science to develop a model for distributed global project management. Through the design work we have extracted challenges and design criteria that should apply to the development of models for this purpose. Here we present the most important generic design elements of the proposed solution. We end up suggesting that continuously supporting and securing the informal processes of the distributed team through explicit and formal means is crucial for project success.

The paper is structured as follows. In section 2, GSD challenges are presented and in section 3 the design science approach is described. In section 4 design criteria are formulated and in section 5 the proposed model is sketched and the design elements are described. Section 6 discusses how informality can be supported by formality and section 7 concludes by answering the research question and suggesting further research.

2   Challenges of Global Software Development Projects

The rapid technical improvement in media and tools for communication and collaboration over distance ease some of the early reported problems in GSD, but not all [1]. In this overview we have thus focused on described problems that are less likely to diminish through technical means. The challenges of GSD tend to congregate around the processes of communication, coordination and control [3] in projects. Communication is a key issue for GSD. Being dislocated influences all three processes directly, but insufficient and low-quality communication in turn influences control and coordination negatively since good communication and thus good working relations are cornerstones for these two processes [9]. We here present the most commonly reported challenges for GSD in these processes.

The basic problems in communication across distances include language problems and misunderstandings [10], less or no overlap in working hours hindering communication [3], [9], lack of natural communication channels [11] despite the technological progress, fewer or no face-to-face meetings due to the travel costs [3], [12], and delay of communication feedback and increased risk of misunderstandings on the often utilized asynchronous channels [3], [13]. All this makes all communication more demanding for the participants [14] and thus leads to less communication [15] and especially less informal communication [16,17]. If (when) sociocultural differences between the on- and offshore organizations exist, the lack of communication (and face-to-face meetings) will hinder the development of personal relations [12], [18], shared knowledge [10], [19,20] and common practice [21] that could have helped overcome the problems. Likewise, the development of mutual understanding and common working culture [9,10], [15], [22] that could have eased difficulties such as misunderstandings [3], conflicts [3] and lack of trust [21], [23] stalls. All in all, the personal relations between team members are weaker than when the team is co-located [24].

Coordinating the work in a project involves both formal and informal processes. The formal processes are often supported by various tools that provide needed insight into products and processes. Distance demands much from these technical tools, which often lack the needed functionality and are often less accessible for offshore employees [3], [25]. For the formal coordination processes to be effective and efficient, informal processes based on substantial shared knowledge, "team awareness" and trust are needed. However, all of these are likely to be weaker or even missing when team members are geographically dispersed because of less and maybe even low-quality communication [3], [14,15,16], [26]. The special challenges of GSD often relate to establishing these fragile informal processes, which is overly difficult when the team is dislocated [27].

Controlling is obviously more difficult when project managers are not located with the entire team. It is difficult to have enough insights into the work of the other location(s) to ensure adherence to goals, policies, standards or quality level [3]. Even the more technical task of configuration and version management of artifacts can be difficult across time zones when based on time stamps. When team members do not share working culture, differences in, for example, understanding of the state of completion of work artifacts [28] and procedures can complicate or even prohibit control. The control process can also be hampered by sociocultural differences in the perception of authority and organizational hierarchies [3], [21]. Kirsch [29] suggests supplementing formal control with an informal control mechanism in complex development work, but the connectedness, shared work culture and social relations it takes for the team to exercise informal control are difficult to build when working in distributed teams [9].

To meet these challenges many different approaches are suggested, from tactics to avoid [9] and reduce the distances [30] to suggestions for tools [31] and methods (for example agile methods [32,33]). Many of these suggestions are useful but often they target only one or a few specific challenges and do not address how mangers of GSD can cope with the complex of interwoven numerous challenges that they face in their everyday work.

3   Research Approach

In order to provide help for project managers to face the challenges of GSD projects the research was designed and took place in accordance with Hevner et al.'s [34] model for design science research. The research process is depicted in figure 1 below.

First the problem area (environment) was investigated in order to grasp and understand more deeply the challenges that practitioners face and ensure the relevance of the research. The exemplary practice was one middle-sized organization in the financial sector with experiences of from 5 to 10 years of offshoring. Six semi-structured interviews with four project managers from three different departments, one project member and one system manager were conducted. The interviews were guided by a literature review on the challenges of GSD that congregates around communication, coordination and control. Most interviews were transcribed and citations from all interviews were organized in data displays structured by the framework of Ågerfalk et al. [3] to support the elucidation of challenges experienced in practice and criteria that could guide the design. Their main challenges were generally found to be in accordance with the theoretically described challenges.

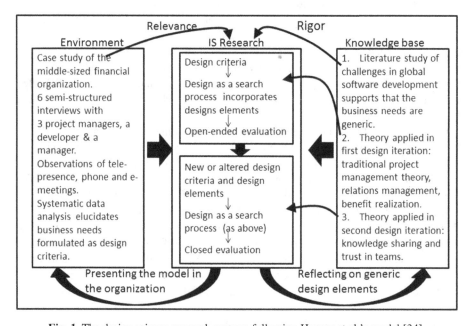

Fig. 1. The design science research process following Hevner et al.'s model [34]

The design criteria (see section 4) were compiled to guide the following two design and evaluation iterations, each resembling the design process described in Hevner & Chatterjee [35] including problem definition, searching for solutions supported by existing knowledge, artifact development and evaluation that feed new knowledge into the next iteration. Rigor was instilled by taking outset in the knowledge base and by the formulation of generic design elements based on the concrete design.

In practice, the researchers in each design iteration listed the design criteria and the challenges from both practice and literature that lurked behind them and carried out a creative process fluctuating between digging deeper into the problems, searching for theoretical input and coming up with new solution suggestions that they could incorporate into the model under design. Activities included literature search and study and available innovative techniques or tools such as mappings, brainstorming, boards, stories etc.

Since evaluation is a significant issue in design science research [36], evaluation strategies in the two iterations were chosen carefully. The model draft resulting from the first iteration was evaluated through open-ended interviews with employees not unlike prototype sessions. The aim was to confirm (or not) the incorporated design elements, but also to gather new ideas for the further development of the model. By opening up for inputs of all kinds including new problems and solutions the practice relevance of the model was enhanced. Figure 2 left shows the visual result from one of those sessions that were also documented through notes and recordings. The confirmations, rejections, comments and new ideas from all the sessions were systematically analyzed and synthesized into new or altered design criteria and design elements (see figure 2 right).

Including the conclusions from the first iteration a second design iteration was carried out. The evaluation of the second model draft and the incorporated design elements were aimed at "testing" the model through an *ex ante* evaluation. Time constraints limited the effort to an artificial evaluation based on realistic scenarios [36]. The participants (the same as in the first iteration) were asked to evaluate the model using one of their current projects as the test scenario. Again all feedback was synthesized into new or altered design elements, based on which the resulting model for distributed global project management was designed (presented in section 5). Later the model was presented and discussed at a project manager experience meeting in the case organization, where it sparked an interest in and a discussion about how to establish and sustain the informal processes of a globally distributed software development project. This discussion inspired the focus of this paper.

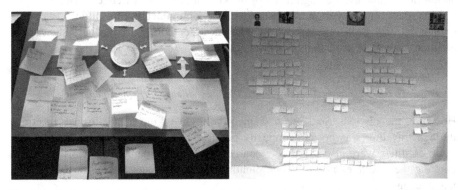

Fig. 2. Left: The visual result from one of the first iteration evaluation sessions. Right: The working area (a board full of post-its) used in the systematic analysis of the results from evaluation during the first design iteration.

Based on the model and its concrete design elements, generic design elements have been formulated trying to pinpoint the learnings from the design work. The most important result of this design science research effort is thus the elucidated design criteria and the generic design elements expressing the challenges of globally distributed software development projects and their possible management solutions, while the model in itself has not proven its value in practice – yet.

Another interesting insight is how this design science research process enabled the development of deeper knowledge about the actual practice than an ordinary case study could. Through participating in the iterative design process the practitioners pushed their understanding of their own practice and of possible solutions, and thus provided increasingly deeper insights from the environment. So even though the most important result is the researchers reflections on design criteria and elements, the process also offers an opportunity for the involved organizations to reflect on their own practice and its possible improvements. This effect is not unlike the effect of action research.

4   The Design Criteria

4.1   The Concrete Challenges of the Case Organization

The investments in outsourcing (time and money) by the case company were beginning to pay back. They had found a fundamentally useful and efficient practice across the global distance, but still saw great possibilities for improvements and their reporting is thus not only beginners struggling. The firm has more domestic development sites and the global practices vary both across these locations and across the different business domains and projects, but all felt a need to improve the management of the projects. The horror stories of cultural misunderstandings, nondelivery and hostile or unwilling attitudes both on- and offshore, so well-known from the literature, were absent in the data, even though many of the known difficulties were enduring.

First, they often experienced obstacles from communicating too little, from being unfamiliar with each other and from unclear expectations across the distances. In addition there were some language problems.

> *"The geographical distance means that when you work, informal communication is limited. To me the geographical distance is the key challenge." (Project manager)*

However, the obvious (and much wanted) solution of more face-to-face meetings through traveling was not economically possible and tele-presence or video conference facilities were also a scarce resource. The project managers spent much time booking the resources needed, underpinning the need to "get closer" in these distributed teams.

Second, bothersome technical problems especially offshore still hindered coordination. Also the important team awareness forming the basis of efficient and effective coordination was feeble because insufficient communication gave weak insights into available skills, the business and the work tasks.

"it is the classic one when not knowing each other that well; if you give a task to an offshore developer and you do explain it and ask: 'Can you do this task?' the answer is 'yes, I can.' If you give it to an onshore developer they say 'yes, but I'll do it this way and not do this and that and so on...' So I'll get a complete picture of how it will be done, so that I know I can expect it to be done within the scope we agree on and on schedule." (Project manager)

The adoption of agile approaches had in some projects alleviated the problems somewhat, by imposing formal structures to the division of work and coordination of responsibilities, task progress, and task-related knowledge sharing. Still project managers found it challenging to support the necessary informal communication and achieve the necessary personal relations and trust in their teams for dealing with unforeseen situations not accounted for in the formal structures.

"I am not sure if you have heard that we work in agile, where there is nobody who is asking you or ordering you. So the tasks are there, and we have what is known as a rational tool, which we share during the e-meeting where everybody can see that same screen. So when there is a task that is not taken by anybody we just take it. And that is how we share the work. And if I take up a task which I don't know and I would like to learn, then I would take it up and speak to somebody who knows it. Either call them up, or chat with them, send them an email. That's how we pretty much do it." (Developer)

Third, some project managers felt a need for closer control of the performances of their offshore team members.

"But, ehm – it may be something cultural, but the offshore developers tend to need a bit more strict control and firmer management than the onshore developers, because if not you do not know what will be delivered." (Project manager)

All in all, the formal means for control were in place except for a few problems with different perceptions of hierarchy and commitment. However, the projects lacked the informal communications needed to take advantage of the strength of informal control between the members of the teams.

"Informal communication is much easier when you have met face to face, just as it is much easier to trust people you have met." (Project manager)

Most of the challenges described in the literature were present in the organization – or had been present. The organization had, during their first years in offshoring, managed to find solutions for some of the challenges, at least in some of the most advanced projects. Three solutions that the interviewees pointed to were the use of agile methods, their high-tech tele-presence rooms and the visiting training program for offshore employees. These solutions were allowed to inspire the design work.

4.2   Five Design Criteria

Based on the challenges found in the data and described in the literature, five design criteria that are presented here were elucidated.

To communicate within, coordinate and control projects in order to succeed, both formal and informal processes are important [16], [29], [37]. Most project management literature suggests formality in order to secure control and coordination in projects. In the case organization agile approaches provided structure and formality to both coordination and control, but still it was difficult to establish and sustain sufficiently supporting informal processes. The project managers dealing with the distributed teams all found their projects short of team awareness, mutual and affective trust [6], shared working practices, good and adequate communication and knowledge sharing, probably due to the limited face-to-face meetings. Also Gupta and Govindarajan emphasize the importance of informal processes and interaction: "having the right organizational structure but inappropriate informal processes and behavior is more problematic than having an inappropriate organizational structure but the right informal processes and behavior" [38]. Thus the first design criteria for the model for distributed global project management focus on informal processes as the key component.

1. It is important that the model can support project managers in establishing informal processes and interactions within GSD project teams.

Good communication is the foundation for effective informal processes as well as for informal coordination and control. In the case organization, managers felt unsure whether the informal control worked across distance in their projects and they experienced coordination problems that would be handled informally if co-located.

2. Thus the model needs to support informal processes and interactions for coordination and control, but most importantly for communication as successful communication provides a necessary basis for the others.

Relations will develop in any collaboration through the interactions that take place. Poor interactions risk resulting in poor relations and can turn into mistrust, hostility and withdrawal. Redressing bad relations and mistrust is very hard, so establishing a good trusting relationship from the start and sustaining it actively and continuously is crucial [6]. Distance gives rise to many misunderstandings that can even be difficult to realize, so good relations are under pressure throughout the project.

3. Any such model should emphasize the sustainment of the trust and personal relations needed for continued successful informal processes and interactions.

In the case organization, formal processes as described in traditional project management literature formed the backbone of the projects. Many authors recommend these tools and methods while stressing that these are not sufficient and may not even be addressing the biggest challenges [39]. To be successful, both formal and informal processes are needed [16].

4. While accentuating the informality above, the model needs to embrace the formal processes and interactions that are so well described in the literature already to allow project managers to integrate formal and informal processes into an effective and efficient management practice.

The above criteria are at a rather abstract level of description. From the interviews it was clear that project managers needed both this kind of deeper understanding of their complex challenges and concrete advice that they could integrate and test in their own practice. They were looking for more tools to add to their already existing toolbox. In particular, explicit and concrete models would be very helpful for new project managers or project managers new to GSD projects.

5. Such a model must both support understanding of the complex practice of managing GSD projects and provide concrete advice that (new) managers can utilize.

These abstract design criteria were elucidated from the challenges of GSD described in the literature and the empirical findings. They express the priority and focus that, it is argued, any tool for GSD project management should have, though the formal processes described in design criterion 4 are well described in more general project management models also used in co-located projects.

5   The Design Elements

The seven design elements are based on the learning from the concrete design solution. The proposed model is presented in section 5.1 followed by an overview of how the model satisfies the criteria in 5.2. Finally, the design elements are formulated and argued in 5.3.

5.1   The Proposed Model for Distributed Global Project Management

The proposed model consists of four focus areas: *clarifying project conditions, project establishment, execution of the project* (which is repetitive) and *post-project evaluation*. The focus areas have no resemblance with project phases, but express important concerns for the project manager throughout the project. At any time, change and unexpected events can demand the project manager to refocus between the focus areas. However, *clarifying project conditions* and *project establishment* will probably need most management attention initially, while *post-project evaluation* is likely to take place late in the project.

This model may seem to accentuate the traditional start-up activities of clarifying project conditions and establishing the project in comparison with the actual systems development activities. The scope of the model is activities necessary for handling the special challenges of GSD, while activities that are parallel to the ones in co-located projects have been left out. The focus area of *project execution* holds the execution-integrated activities sustaining the well-functioning team, while breakdowns often demands project managers to reclarify conditions or re-establish the project.

The focus area of *clarifying project conditions* aims to provide a solid foundation for successful GSD project execution. Traditional tasks aimed at understanding the work, goals, risks and stakeholders of the project and grounding the choice of formal structures, organization and methods for the project are carried out, but with special considerations of the challenges of GSD. Project managers should explicitly strive for formal structures that allow for, support or even demand informal processes. An example is the agile approaches that are well-known in the case organizations for demanding and supporting frequent, direct and rather informal contact across the distances between the on- and offshore team members.

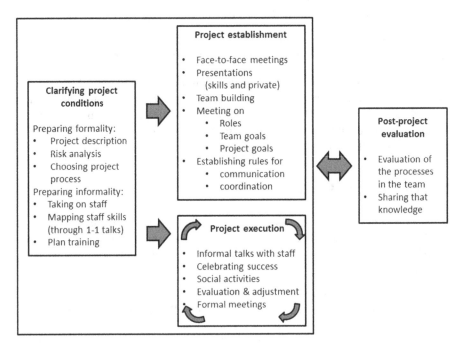

Fig. 3. The four focus areas of the model for distributed global project management. For each focus area recommended activities are listed.

Just as important are activities to create the bedrock for developing trust and good personal relations in the team [1], [13], [24]. The literature confirms that management attention before and during staffing is crucial [6], [27]. Managers need to understand the goals and tasks of the project in order to staff properly, taking into account both professional skills and personal skills in communication, bonding and cross-distance work. They need explicitly to plan for staffing and mapping of skills [40] in order to arrange for necessary pre-project or project-start-up training. Often training on culture, communication and business knowledge is appropriate [13], [26]. The skill-mapping is recommended to take place through one-to-one talks between the project manager and every team member. Through these conversations the manager can display leadership and start to build a trusting relationship with the team members.

During *project establishment* the project team should establish themselves as a team, while the project manager provides the needed settings and support. In order to commit themselves, the team members must get to know each other both professionally and personally to build trust and relations and to reach a common understanding on the tasks, goals and working approaches of the project [41]. This is a very complex process and is best done through face-to-face meetings that can involve employees' personal presentations, team-building activities, discussions of roles, team and project goals and establishing norms for communication and coordination tasks in the project [42]. This is the key focus area for establishing the informal processes of the GSD project and is only rarely given enough attention, even in the case organization. Since these kinds of relations, common understandings and agreements are usually renegotiated continuously in co-located projects, the project manager instead must continuously refocus on this area and make sure that the team re-establishes if required.

Sustaining the informal processes is the key goal of the *project execution* focus area. Also the formal processes need to be sustained, but these are often sustained through the mere systems development and management activities of the organization that are well described in the existing literature, and even though distance does matter for these too, the progress in support tools has reduced the impact. Examples of activities of this focus area that can sustain personal relations, trust and commitment towards the team are informal talks between the project manager and team members, frequent celebrations of successes or other social activities throughout the project and continuous explicit evaluation and adjustment of the agreed-on processes as part of a planned line of formal meetings.

Through the focus area of *post-project evaluation*, learning at individual, project and organizational level is stressed because knowledge sharing by the case organization was mentioned as being crucial for successful project management in GSD. The project managers must evaluate the activities targeting the needed informal and formal processes to contribute to shared knowledge in the organization. For individual team members the one-to-one talks with the project manager will help to turn experiences into valuable knowledge for the next projects.

5.2   Satisfying the Design Criteria

This section provides an overview of how the model design satisfies the design criteria by listing the elements that contribute to the satisfactory solution. For each design criterion the basic assumptions that the design elements rest on is articulated.

Table 1. How the design criteria are satisfied by the model design

Design criterion 1	Support establishment of informal processes.
Basic assumption	The foundation for informal processes is the team members' mutual relations and trust, team awareness and shared work practice and understandings.

Table 1. (*Continued*)

This design criterion is mainly satisfied through the two early focus areas and their activities: •*Clarifying project conditions* pinpoints a need for preparatory management activities and puts emphasis on staffing, personal skills, pre-project training targeting the GSD challenges and early exercising of leadership and initial trust building. •The key for *Project establishment* is to ensure that the team establishes itself as a team, which happens best through face-to-face meetings, team-building activities, and discussions on roles and goals. Norms for communication and coordination must be explicitly agreed on.	

Design criterion 2	Ensure informal processes within all of communication, coordination and control.
Basic assumption	Good communication and personal relations and trust are both important for and result from informal processes. Good teamness and communication allow for better informal coordination and control. The opposite hinders informal coordination and control.

The model provides advice for all these areas: •The activities of the two early focus areas provide the conditions for close personal relations and trust to develop and thus for informal communication to happen. In particular, the explication of communication norms and the staffing with communication skills and culture awareness in mind is very important. •Norms for coordination are explicitly discussed and an appropriate choice of systems development approaches that support informal coordination is encouraged. Also continuous exercising, evaluation and adjusting of informal coordination during project execution is important. •The choice of formal structures, for example an appropriate system development approach, is important to enhance informal control. For example, the agile practice of stand-up meetings and burn down charts provides the basic information for informal control in the project to develop. The team awareness and teamness accomplished in the above-mentioned activities will lay the grounding for informal control within the team.	

Design criterion 3	Support sustaining of informal processes.
Basic assumption	Since conditions in GSD projects change continuously and distances continuously create (new) threats towards teamness the informal processes need to be sustained continuously.

The concept of focus areas rather than phases mirrors this basic assumption. The focus area of *project execution* explicitly designed to sustain the team relations and provide opportunities for team building and re-establishments by integrating activities such as celebrations, evaluations and renegotiations of informal norms and work practices as part of the formal agenda of the project. The focus area of *post-project evaluation* enables "sustaining" across projects by knowledge sharing.	

Table 1. (*Continued*)

Design criterion 4	Support establishing of appropriate formal processes.
Basic assumption	The formal processes are the easiest to establish and sustain as they are visible in procedures and documents and "speak" of projects and many tools for distributed collaboration focus on these processes. Thus it is important to establish these and it could be convenient for informal processes to piggyback on them if possible.
The focus area of *clarifying project conditions* is intertwined with the traditional start-up activities of understanding the tasks and goals of the project, establishing the formal organization, and evaluating risks and stakeholder interests. All this provides the basis for the formal processes of the project. But the attention of the manager is here drawn to choosing formal processes that can benefit the informal processes.	
Design criterion 5	Provide concrete advice.
Basic assumption	Each project manager has to adapt his practice all the time as the professional practitioner [43] he or she is. Concrete and detailed advice eases the process of integrating new practices into the exciting practices of these professionals.
This criterion was met in the model presented to the organization, but is unfortunately not reported in these details here.	

5.3   Seven Design Elements

The learning from the concrete design solution is summarized in seven generic design elements that are important aspects of the solution found important for all project management practices in GSD.

Management models tend to focus on either formal or informal processes, only rarely including both equally in their prescribed solutions. An important design element in this model is that the two are equally important for successful management of GSD projects. Not only are both kinds of processes needed, but the project manager can take advantage of formality in order to strengthen the more vulnerable informal processes so badly affected by distance, if they choose the ordinary formal structures with that in mind, and add formality to traditionally purely informal processes. This gives rise to the following three design elements:

1. Include both formal and informal processes.
2. Choose formal structures conscious of the need for informal processes.
3. Formalize informality.

The team, their relations and commitment are, as described clearly above, the key for informal processes to contribute to successful GSD projects. So explicit activities to establish and sustain the team and their teamness are an important design element.

4. Explicit activities to establish and sustain the team.

The role and timing of project management are also important for the solution suggested here. First it is important to display leadership early in order to increase the likelihood of trust building and commitment in the team. Getting a good start is not enough. This model suggests the elements of focus areas in opposition to phases, to underpin the constant need for monitoring and adjusting with respect to the informal and formal processes throughout the life span of the project.

6. Early leadership through staffing and considerate planning.
7. Focus areas, not phases, are needed.

Eventually knowledge sharing between projects over time will help project managers to adapt their practice to the ever-changing conditions.

8. Learning from the past will ease the future projects.

In this paper the design elements of the relationship between formal and informal processes are regarded as the most important results, and how project managers by combining them wisely can take full advantage of both is reckoned to be an important discussion.

6   Discussion

The core of distributed work is the dislocation [30], although other distances are mentioned as providing equal challenges. Even if successful in diminishing sociocultural and temporal distance, the dislocation will still naturally lower the interaction between team members [2]. The negative effects start occurring when workplace distance is more than 30 meters [37], [44], thus being an inherent challenge for project managers of GSD.

For newcomers to offshoring, establishing the necessary formal processes will probably be the first challenge, but since these processes are well described in the literature, visible in the organization and the target of many tools for distributed collaboration, they may be relatively easy to establish and sustain. If an appropriate choice of formal processes is in place, they can form the backbone of the collaboration through explicit procedures, formal roles and responsibilities and allow essential information about tasks and progress to flow. However, formal processes tend to be rather static, bureaucratic and conservative, which makes them less suited to complex, fast-changing and unpredictable environments.

In such environments human agency is suitable and informal processes bear the capacity of rapid change, adaptive and improvisational behavior to meet the complex and unexpected. If successful, the informal processes ensure a greater visibility in the project, by allowing for much richer information and knowledge sharing than by only formal means [45]. This broadcast of knowledge and information allows the team members to develop trust and team awareness and thus (re)commit themselves to the task and the team, allowing for effective informal control and coordination. Because of the increased informationflow project managers can realize unexpected situations timely and the robust informal processes let the team rise to the challenges.

These informal processes are just as difficult to establish and sustain in GSD as they are vital. Good personal relations and trust between team members are both the root of and stem from informal processes and interactions. They form a kind of snowball effect that naturally gathers speed when interacting face to face and results in a feeling of teamness. However, face-to-face communication only happens rarely in distributed teams because of travel costs; even though to some extent it is substitutable by high-tech tele-presence media, these are still rather costly and thus rare resources. Despite technological development, it is still reported that face-to-face settings do work better for building trust and awareness. So until saved by technology, other means will have to do and the vital informal processes often never develop [2] or diminish quickly.

Personal relations, trust and informal processes will be negotiated continuously, build and decay through experiences in the project. Being distributed, the risk of decay is greater because of more potential misunderstandings and difficulties of settlements due to more effort-demanding communication. At the same time, the building of trust and relationships is not supported through natural settings or structures of the project (as it is in co-located settings). Examples of very important structures in co-located projects are the coffee machine or printer or corridors that allow people to meet informally and discuss and even settle important matters.

This vulnerability of the informal processes incites focused and careful management, employing the more sturdy formal processes as a support and stabilizing the informal processes by introducing and insisting on formality in and around these processes. Examples of this drawn from the proposed model above will be discussed in the following.

Managers can add formality through procedures. Project managers can support their meticulous preparation for project start-up by describing it in project procedures along with, for example, risk assessment or stakeholder analysis. They will carefully have to map the GSD challenges of the project as a backdrop for describing staff requirements, interviewing employees, careful staffing and planning needed training – activities that, if done in close communication, preferably face to face with employees, can spark trust building and commitment. The formality of the actual inquiry and interviews helps provide the needed resources and make room for the activity in crowded calendars. Still the content and the tone of the inquiry and the interviews need to be informal to allow for sufficient information to flow and for trust to start building. This formal "hiring" process provides the best conditions for swift trust between team members from the start, since they know that all have been evaluated and approved [6].

Formality with regard to meetings, in agendas, chairing, preparation and documentation, can support informal meetings by ensuring they actually happen and by allowing the necessary time to be taken. For example, project managers need to support team establishment, even if the full team does not meet in person. It may be difficult to find time to meet for the vital social team-building activities,[1] but formal notice, agendas and memos for start-up meetings mixing "professional" topics and activities to lay the ground for informal processes will signal the importance and create participation. Participants are more likely to prepare decently for both personal presentations and professional topics such as understanding the task, roles, goals etc. When chairing the establishment events, the project manager should insist on spending enough time "with each other" online (if face to face is not possible) in order to explicitly discuss informal processes as well such as roles and norms for communication and coordination.

---

[1] http://www.infiniteams.com/ is an example of an online team-building game.

Whatever is negotiated and decided should be documented semi-formally, for example in a project charter, to stabilize the agreements, but also to allow for easy change.

Exploiting the already installed formal structures is an obvious possibility. Piggybacking on the formal processes of the systems development can be done by adding informal routines to the formal ones For example, tele-presence meetings could start with a coffee together for ten minutes, celebrations of successes could be shared across the distance through appropriate media and the built-in evaluations of the progress can include explicit evaluations (and adjustments) of not only the formal but also the informal processes. This way the project manager can nurse the connectedness of the team and the informal processes throughout the project without special arrangements.

All routines can strengthen the informal processes. For example, the project manager can keep in close contact with the individual team member to ensure that information flows by frequent regular phone calls that allow for informal communication. Because the calls are routine the team member gets the opportunity to air concerns and is likely to speak freely.

Finally, explicit inheritance of practice from well-performed finished projects will ease the establishment of the new projects. This can be done through knowledge sharing, planning for and insisting on post-project evaluations and learning. However, experience shows that post-mortem analysis is likely to fail, so maybe the evaluations could start in the last iterations of the project execution. It may be easier to keep (parts of) successful teams when staffing new projects bringing a practice to start from. Of course, the risk is that old habits and too much teamness will prevent the team from taking on new tasks, including newcomers and improving work approaches. Even though the problem of knowledge sharing is not special for GSD, the investment needed to establish and sustain teams as the basis for the crucial informal processes is higher here, and thus finding a solution is more important.

Through the design work and the reflection presented here it has become evident that the informal processes in GSD project work are crucial yet very difficult to establish and sustain. The described design elements and this discussion suggest that project managers should choose formal processes not only for their own means but also for supporting the establishment and sustaining of informal processes and they should add formality even to processes that do not need formality when the team is co-located. Even if this is done, project management must still monitor and insist on informal processes to sustain an appropriate level of connecting, trusting and sharing knowledge across work locations in distributed teams. All this effort can, of course, fail, just as if the team was co-located. In both cases conflict resolutions, training or even new team members may help, but that is not particular to GSD.

7   Conclusions

The research was carried out in order to provide project managers with advice on how to cope with the challenges of GSD. Design science was applied to develop a draft of a project management model that could be helpful. Through the study of the research environment, GSD challenges were mapped and confirmed as generic through literature studies. Five design criteria were formulated to guide the development of project management models for this purpose and seven generic design elements were formulated based on the proposed model. Finally, how to support informal processes through formality was discussed, answering the research question by concluding that project managers will cope with the challenges of GSD by:

— Finding a viable balance between formal and informal processes in the project to exploit both the stability, visibility and order of the formal and the flexibility, engagement and agility that the informal provide.

And that they establish and sustain the crucial informal processes by:

— Choosing formal processes conscious of the need for informal processes.
— Supporting informality by formal means as discussed above.
— Investing a great deal of effort early in the project in order to establish the good conditions that eventually can lead to good informal processes.
— Supporting team establishment, creation of personal relations, building of trust and teamness as a foundation for informal processes.
— Explicitly and continuously managing well-functioning informal processes.
— Working towards knowledge sharing across instances of GSD projects.

All in all, the research suggests that supporting and securing the informal processes of the distributed team through explicit and formal means and continuously keeping the foundation for and the informal processes in management's focus are crucial for project success. Project managers are advised to do exactly that, and to find inspiration in the design elements presented above. Organizations that rely on GSD are advised to provide the formal means and allow for the apparently extra work of grounding the informal processes at project initiation and later [41].

However, this research gives only examples of means that could work. Since the proposed model as such has not been evaluated on a full scale, evidence of actual effect is NOT reported here. Testing out the tenet of supporting informality through formality in GSD projects to increase their success rates could be an interesting way forward for future research, where perhaps the ideas from second-order project management [46] could be inspirational.

References

1. Kotlarsky, J., Oshri, I.: Social Ties, Knowledge Sharing and Successful Collaboration in Globally Distributed System Development Projects. European Journal of Information Systems 14, 37–48 (2005)
2. Sarker, S., Sahay, S.: Implications of Space and Time for Distributed Work: An Interpretive Study of US–Norwegian Systems Development Teams. European Journal of Information Systems 13, 3–20 (2004)
3. Ågerfalk, P., Fitzgerald, B., Holmström, H., Lings, B., Lundell, B., Conchúir, E.: A Framework for Considering Opportunities and Threats in Distributed Software Development. In: Proceedings of the International Workshop on Distributed Software Development, pp. 47–61 (2005)

4. Hofstede, G.: Culture and Organizations. International Studies of Management & Organization 10, 15–41 (1980)
5. Schein, E.H.: Organizational Culture and Leadership, 3rd edn. John Wiley and Sons, Inc., San Francisco (2006)
6. Greenberg, P.S., Greenberg, R.H., Antonucci, Y.L.: Creating and Sustaining Trust in Virtual Teams. Business Horizons 50, 325–333 (2007)
7. Wenger, E.: Communities of Practice: Learning, Meaning, and Identity. Cambridge University Press, Cambridge (1998)
8. Sambamurthy, V., Subramani, M.: Special Issue on Information Technologies and Knowledge Management. MIS Quarterly 29, 193–195 (2005)
9. Carmel, E., Agarwal, R.: Tactical Approaches for Alleviating Distance in Global Software Development. IEEE Software 18, 22–29 (2001)
10. Ai, S., Du, R., Abbott, P., Zheng, Y.: Internal and Contextual Factors, Knowledge Processes and Performance: From the Chinese Provider's Perspective. Expert Systems with Applications 39, 4464–4472 (2012)
11. Kock, N.: Compensatory Adaptation to Media Obstacles: An Experimental Study of Process Redesign Dyads. Information Resources Management Journal 18, 41–67 (2005)
12. Šmite, D., Borzovs, J.: A Framework for Overcoming Supplier Related Threats in Global Projects. In: Richardson, I., Runeson, P., Messnarz, R. (eds.) EuroSPI 2006. LNCS, vol. 4257, pp. 50–61. Springer, Heidelberg (2006)
13. Verburg, R.M., Bosch-Sijtsema, P., Vartiainen, M.: Getting it Done: Critical Success Factors for Project Managers in Virtual Work Settings. International Journal of Project Management 31, 68–79 (2013)
14. Daim, T.U., Ha, A., Reutiman, S., Hughes, B., Pathak, U., Bynum, W., Bhatla, A.: Exploring the Communication Breakdown in Global Virtual Teams. International Journal of Project Management 30, 199–212 (2012)
15. Herbsleb, J.D.: Global Software Engineering: The Future of Socio-Technical Coordination. In: Future of Software Engineering (FOSE 2007), pp. 188–198 (2007)
16. Espinosa, J.A., Slaughter, S.A., Kraut, R.E., Herbsleb, J.D.: Team Knowledge and Coordination in Geographically Distributed Software Development. Journal of Management Information Systems 24, 135–169 (2007)
17. García Guzmán, J., Saldaña Ramos, J., Amescua Seco, A., Sanz Esteban, A.: How to Get Mature Global Virtual Teams: A Framework to Improve Team Process Management in Distributed Software Teams. Software Quality Journal 18, 409–435 (2010)
18. Qureshi, S., Liu, M., Vogel, D.: The Effects of Electronic Collaboration in Distributed Project Management. Group Decision and Negotiation 15, 55–75 (2005)
19. David, G.C., Chand, D., Newell, S., Resende-Santos, J.: Integrated Collaboration Across Distributed Sites: The Perils of Process and the Promise of Practice. Journal of Information Technology 23, 44–54 (2008)
20. Kotlarsky, J., van Fenema, P.C., Willcocks, L.P.: Developing a Knowledge-Based Perspective on Coordination: The Case of Global Software Projects. Information & Management 45, 96–108 (2008)
21. Levina, N., Vaast, E.: Innovating or Doing as Told? Status Differences and Overlapping Boundaries in Offshore Collaboration. MIS Quarterly 32, 307–332 (2008)
22. Kumar, K., van Fenema, P.C., von Glinow, M.A.: Offshoring and the Global Distribution of Work: Implications for Task Interdependence Theory and Practice. Journal of International Business Studies 40, 642–667 (2008)
23. Lanubile, F., Calefato, F., Ebert, C.: Group Awareness in Global Software Engineering. IEEE Software 30, 18–23 (2013)

24. Lin, C., Standing, C., Liu, Y.: A Model to Develop Effective Virtual Teams. Decision Support Systems 45, 1031–1045 (2008)
25. Tunkelo, T., Hameri, A., Pigneur, Y.: Improving Globally Distributed Software Development and Support Processes – A Workflow View. Journal of Software: Evolution and Process 25, 1305–1324 (2013)
26. Søderberg, A., Krishna, S., Bjørn, P.: Global Software Development: Commitment, Trust and Cultural Sensitivity in Strategic Partnerships. Journal of International Management 19, 347–361 (2013)
27. Pauleen, D.J.: An Inductively Derived Model of Leader-Initiated Relationship Building with Virtual Team Members. Journal of Management Information Systems 20, 227–256 (2003)
28. Sutherland, J., Viktorov, A., Blount, J., Puntikov, N.: Distributed Scrum: Agile Project Management with Outsourced Development Teams. In: HICSS 2007 the 40th Annual Hawaii International Conference on System Sciences, p. 274a (2007)
29. Kirsch, L.S.: Portfolios of Control Modes and IS Project Management. Information Systems Research 8, 215–239 (1997)
30. Carmel, E., Abbott, P.: Why 'Nearshore' Means that Distance Matters. Communications of the ACM 50, 40–46 (2007)
31. Lanubile, F., Ebert, C., Prikladnicki, R., Vizcaino, A.: Collaboration Tools for Global Software Engineering. IEEE Software 27, 52–55 (2010)
32. Holmström, H., Fitzgerald, B., Ågerfalk, P.J., Conchúir, E.Ó.: Agile Practices Reduce Distance in Global Software Development. Information Systems Management 23, 7–18 (2006)
33. Ramesh, B., Cao, L., Mohan, K., Peng, X.U.: Can Distributed Software Development be Agile? Communications of the ACM 49, 41–46 (2006)
34. Hevner, A.R., March, S.T., Park, J., Ram, S.: Design Science in Information Systems Research. MIS QQuarterly 28, 75–105 (2004)
35. Hevner, A., Chatterjee, S.: Design and Creativity. In: Design and Creativity Design Research in Information Systems, pp. 145–156. Springer (2010)
36. Pries-Heje, J., Baskerville, R., Venable, J.R.: Strategies for Design Science Research Evaluation. In: Proceedings of the 16th European Conference on Information Systems, ECIS 2008 (2008)
37. Herbsleb, J.D., Mockus, A.: An Empirical Study of Speed and Communication in Globally Distributed Software Development. IEEE Transactions on Software Engineering 29, 481–494 (2003)
38. Gupta, A.K., Govindarajan, V.: Global Strategy and Organization. John Wiley, Danvers (2004)
39. DeMarco, T.: The Deadline: A Novel AboutProject Management. Dorset House Pub., New York (1997)
40. Whitener, E., Stahl, G.K.: Creating and Building Trust. In: Lane, H.W., Masnevski, M.L., Mendenhall, M.E., et al. (eds.) The Blackwell Handbook of Global Management: A Guide to Managing Complexity, pp. 109–120. Blackwell Publishing Ltd., Oxford (2004)
41. Gluesing, J.C., Gibson, C.B.: Designing and Forming Global Teams. In: Lane, H.W., Masnevski, M.L., Mendenhall, M.E., et al. (eds.) The Blackwell Handbook of Global Management: A Guide to Managing Complexity, pp. 199–226. Blackwell Publishing Ltd., Oxford (2004)
42. Pries-Heje, J., Pries-Heje, L.: Designing Virtual Team Building with a Focus on Social Capital. In: Hertzum, M., Jørgensen, C. (eds.) SourceIT: Balancing Sourcing and Innovation in Information Systems Development, pp. 123–144. TAPIR Akademisk Forlag (2011)

43. Schön, D.A.: The Reflective Practitioner: How Professionals Think in Action. Basic Books, Inc. (1983)
44. Allen, T.B.: Managing the Flow of Technology: Technology Transfer and the Dissemination of Technological Information within the R&D Organization. MIT Press, Cambridge (1977)
45. Oshri, I., van Fenema, P.C., Kotlarsky, J.: Knowledge Transfer in Globally Distributed Teams: The Role of Transactive Memory. Information Systems Journal 18, 593–616 (2008)
46. Saynisch, M.: Mastering Complexity and Changes in Projects, Economy, and Society Via Project Management Second Order (PM-2). Project Management Journal 41, 4–20 (2010)

Pragmatic Software Innovation

Ivan Aaen and Rikke Hagensby Jensen

Department of Computer Science, Aalborg University, Denmark
{ivan,rjens}@cs.aau.dk

Abstract. We understand software innovation as concerned with introducing innovation into the development of *software intensive systems*, i.e. systems in which software development and/or integration are dominant considerations. Innovation is key in almost any strategy for competitiveness in existing markets, for creating new markets, or for curbing rising public expenses, and software intensive systems are core elements in most such strategies. Software innovation therefore is vital for about every sector of the economy. Changes in software technologies over the last decades have opened up for experimentation, learning, and flexibility in ongoing software projects, but how can this change be used to facilitate software innovation? How can a team systematically identify and pursue opportunities to create added value in ongoing projects? In this paper, we describe Deweyan pragmatism as the philosophical foundation for *Essence* – a software innovation methodology – where unknown options and needs emerge as part of the development process itself. The foundation is illustrated via a simple example.

Keywords: Software innovation, software development, pragmatic philosophy, Deweyan pragmatism, Essence.

1   Introduction

Innovation has been a recurring theme in public as well as academic debate for decades. Despite the widespread interest, there seems to be little advice on how to make innovation more likely to happen in software development – at least at the team or project level.

The classic commitment for software development is to ensure quality and efficiency [9]. Therefore, software engineering – whether traditional or agile – focus on delivering quality solutions in a predictable and effective way. But today we need more than just meeting requirements effectively. To stay competitive, we must create high value solutions.

Software innovation addresses a number of challenges including the development of innovative software products, designing software support for innovative business processes, transforming known solutions to innovative uses in new contexts, and stimulating paradigmatic changes among developers and customers concerning the framing of problem domain and the discovery of potential game changers on the market [45].

B. Bergvall-Kåreborn and P.A. Nielsen (Eds.): TDIT 2014, IFIP AICT 429, pp. 133–149, 2014.
© IFIP International Federation for Information Processing 2014

In a global world where ICT increasingly becomes commoditized to provide a shared and standardized infrastructure [11], there is a need to move from mainly operational considerations towards more strategic ones: Software development in high-cost countries is under pressure to deliver more valuable results than development overseas [4].

To remain competitive in this environment there is a need for software development to move beyond the traditional efficiency and quality focus: How can software teams deliver high value solutions?

Essence evolves as part of an ongoing effort to develop a software development methodology that facilitates a team in producing high value software solutions [1-3]. Essence sees software innovation as a reflective practice [38-40] where options and needs emerge as part of ongoing team-based efforts. At any given time, the team may work towards a goal and employ the means deemed relevant to attain it, but while working on a problem and on solutions to it, the team and other stakeholders discover needs and options that were unknown at the start.

The purpose of this paper is to outline a philosophical foundation for Essence – and team-based software innovation – based on Dewey's pragmatic philosophy [17-20]. The aim is to investigate core concepts of pragmatic philosophy, to find ways to help a software team develop, mature, and implement ideas.

The paper starts out by outlining software innovation as a concept and surveys contributions within the field (Section 2). Section 3 presents main ideas and concepts in Deweyan pragmatism. Section 4 is a simple illustration of reflective practices in incremental software innovation. Section 5 describes how this illustration was facilitated by key concepts in Essence and how these concepts reflect core ideas in Deweyan pragmatism. Section 6 concludes the paper.

2   Software Innovation Concepts and Contributions

Software innovation is not an established term yet, and contributions to the field are scattered over organizational levels and project stages. Some contributions are generic and have little focus on either organizational level or particular stages [35]; some focus on the company level [33]; some on picking and improving promising ideas [22]; some on ideation in the requirements stage [28, 29]; and some on innovation as part of an ongoing project [1-3, 10, 12].

This paper is aimed at the methodology level. It is part of building a foundation to help software teams increase the value of what they build as they go about building it. There are numerous techniques and tools for creativity, and many insights on how to stimulate creative thinking and innovative work, but very little work has been done on methodology for software teams.

We focus on innovation as part of the software development project. We see software innovation as part of everyday life in a team, and thereby as part of what designers, users, and stakeholders in the project do. We focus less on what happens before a project is decided and more on what takes place from the decision to start a project until the end of it. We assume that modern development techniques are used to allow for iteration and experimentation within reasonable levels of risk. In other words, we see software innovation as a reflective process where experiences and insights during a project may change its course.

We understand software innovation as concerned with introducing innovation into the development of *software intensive systems*; i.e. systems in which software development and/or integration are dominant considerations. Our focus is on innovations that offer something new to known users or customers, or something known to new users or customers. Specifically, software innovation here refers to the contribution of innovation to the user or customer side only. Therefore, we do not include changes in the software development process itself into our understanding of software innovation in this context.

Innovation usually extends creativity in the sense that ideas are developed and matured in the context of implementation. Basically ideation is concerned with the generation of socially acceptable ideas [42], whereas innovation by definition implies change in the real world [45].

While the interest in software innovation is fairly recent, there has been some interest in ideation and creativity since the early and mid 90ies. J. Daniel Couger worked on creative problem solving [14] and creativity techniques [15, 16] for information systems development, and Ben Shneiderman worked on creativity support in the same field [41]. Within software engineering, Neil Maiden has worked on creativity workshops [30] and stakeholder collaboration [29].

Contributions with a direct bearing on software innovation are still relatively few. Within information systems development, innovation research tends to focus on the business context and adoption of innovations. For example Burton Swanson [43] advocate mindfulness when innovating with IT. Within software development, there is some interest in innovation as a goal for software development. Jim Highsmith and Alistair Cockburn point to the potential for agile development to support innovation [25], but as Conboy et al. observe based on a number of studies on the relationship between agility and innovation or improvisation: *These have tended to focus more on the agile practices themselves as the innovation and not the extent to which the practices facilitate agility and innovation* [13].

In the last few years a growing number of writers have published very varied work on software innovation.

Jeremy Rose [35] proposes eight work-style heuristics for software developers, and Pikkarainen et al [33] offer eight fundamental practice areas for innovation with software, each containing a number of activities at the company level to master that particular practice.

Misra [32] presents a goal-driven measurement framework for software innovation processes linking these metrics to business goals. The processes per se are not part of this framework. Also at the business level, Gorschek [22] suggests Star Search, an innovation process using face-to-face screening and idea refinement for software-intensive product development. This process has particular focus on ideation and selection prior to actual development.

Focusing on the team level, Aaen discusses ways to facilitate software innovation [1-3]. At a similar level, Conboy and Morgan [12] discuss the applicability and implications of open innovation in agile environments, and Mahaux and Maiden [28] suggest using improvisational theater as part of requirements elicitation.

These contributions generally focus on methods and normative principles, whereas work on philosophical foundations for software innovation still seems to be missing in the field.

Based on pragmatic philosophy, Donald A. Schön discussed reflective practices in design. In many ways, Schön's work can serve as inspiration for software innovation at the level of the individual or the team. To Schön, design is a reflective inquiry into a problem, what it is about, and possible ways to address it.

Schön completed his doctoral thesis at Harvard University in the 1950's, which dealt with John Dewey's theory of inquiry [39]. Schön's most notable work depicted in *The Reflective Practitioner* [38] and *Designing as reflective conversation with the materials of a design situation* [37] reworks Dewey's *theory of inquiry* into *reflective practice* [39].

Schön gives an insightful perspective on how to understand the design process, by illustrating the reciprocal interplay between the designer and the design situation. Schön describes this process in three steps: *Seeing-moving-seeing*. These steps are small iterations, where the designer with actions and the materials at hand allows the situation to talk back and thereby sees the design situation anew [40]. Schön compares this reflective conversation with a Deweyan inquiry, where human actors inquire into a problematic situation [37].

Lim et al. brings Schön's reflective conversations into the world of interaction design of information systems. In their article *The Anatomy of Prototypes* [27], the authors discuss the nature of prototyping and how the production of prototypes can induce reflection. They formulate a framework to help designers frame and refine design ideas by means of prototypes.

Biskjaer & Dalsgaard instigate a connection between design creativity and Deweyan pragmatism [8], while Goldkuhl discusses the philosophy of pragmatism in relation to information system design research in *Design Research in Search for a Paradigm: Pragmatism Is the Answer* [21] . By examining different pragmatic epistemic types of design research and relating these to four aspects of pragmatism, the author proposes pragmatism as an appropriate paradigm for information system design research.

Having presented some examples on how Dewey has inspired work on information systems design, we will present his original ideas in more detail.

3   Deweyan Pragmatism

Pragmatism originates from the United States. The philosophy emerged in the last decades of the 19th century as a response to experiences acquired by migrants settling the American frontier in search of the American Dream [36]. To cultivate and survive in this rogue and demanding environment, the migrants were constantly exposed to practical problems necessitating creative solutions. To choose among alternatives these choices had to somehow be judged. This judgment was based on the practical consequences each choice induced.

One of the main contributors to the pragmatic philosophy tradition is John Dewey (1859-1952). His work covers a vast variety of topics including logic, ethics, education, politics and technology. In his lifetime, Dewey saw many innovations come to life: Power plants, automobiles, airplanes, the telephone, radio, AI and the first robot only to mention a few [24]. Dewey was an active part of this society and the innovation of technological artifacts was a catalyst to his work. His philosophic views are a reaction to the opportunities and problems that occur in a technological society [24].

One of Dewey's points of interests was how technological tools and instruments come to be, how they change the way we experience the world, and how they become part of shaping and building our own future [24]. One of Dewey's core ideas is that the problem solving process of producing of artifacts - physical (technology) as well as mental (theories/ideas) - are occurrences of the same creative process [36].

Dewey's critique of technology is a central topic in his work and becomes synonymous with his *theory of inquiry* [24]. The theory of inquiry is pivotal in Dewey's perspective on pragmatism, most noticeable depicted in *Logic: The Theory of Inquiry* [17]. This particular subject is central to this article, as we see software innovation as a recurring process of inquiry among team members and stakeholders.

We will discuss four core concepts of Deweyan pragmatism: *Problematic situation, inquiry, means, and ends (ends-in-view)*. These highly interconnected concepts are all presented in Dewey's *theory of inquiry*. To illustrate the social implications of inquiry in teams, we also present a fifth concept: *Community of inquiry*.

3.1   Problematic Situation

A situation can be seen as an environment wherein we live, experience, and most importantly act, reason, and reflect. The subjects, the environment, means, artifacts, and social constructs, and the relations among them, determine how we experience and understand a situation [17]. This means that our thoughts and actions can only be understood in the context of the unique situation we find ourselves in.

We may experience a situation as stable and determinate where we fully comprehend the implications of our actions. However, when encountering something uncertain and doubtful, an *indeterminate situation* supervenes. At this stage, the situation will appear *problematic,* and to actively engage in its resolution entails venturing into a process of inquiry [17].

Dewey describes the problematic situation as *open* [17]. The openness has two dimensions: The situation is open, as the elements that constitute the situation are in imbalance and dissociated. Therefore, the situation is also open for new actions and interpretations as we examine what caused it to become unsettled.

3.2   Inquiry

Inquiry means to make an investigation into matters of interest or problems in search of knowledge. Dewey sees inquiry as a process throughout life and in all aspects of living. To live means facing daily challenges. Meeting these challenges requires intelligent *inquiry*. In Deweyan pragmatism, this entails examining matters, inferring conclusions, and evaluating and reflecting upon these conclusions. The evaluation follows from the practical consequences the inquiry induces.

For Dewey, inquiry starts with the problematic situation. The objective is to intelligently transform the problematic situation into a stable and determinate one:

Inquiry is the controlled or directed transformation of an indeterminate situation into one that is so determinate in its constituent distinctions and relations as to convert the elements of the original situation into a unified whole [17].

To transform the problematic situation implies not only to understand what caused the situation to become doubtful in the first place, but also – through exploration and experimentation – to actively seek means *in* the situation for settling it [19]. Dewey describes the inquiry process as a sequence of iterative and intertwined states [17]:

A) The Indeterminate Situation: An inquiry is initiated by an indeterminate situation – an uncertain, unsettled, and disturbed situation. Doubt may arise from the confusing, obscuring, or conflicting in the situation.

B) Institution of a Problem: By doubting, the problematic in the situation becomes the focal point of the investigation. Framing the problem entails identification and examination into the subject matters that causes the situation to become problematic. This knowledge will also direct the transformation of the situation to its resolution.

C) The Determination of a Problem-Solution: In the process of framing the problem, observations are made concerning the facts affecting the situation. Based on these observations a possible solution is drawn, represented as one or more ideas. An idea forecasts the consequences to be expected from the employed activity. Thereby the idea instigates a course of direction. The more facts are observed, the more enhanced the perception of the idea and possible solution becomes.

D) Reasoning: The idea is developed and matured through experimentation and exploration. In the experiment, facts and ideas are tested against the problem at hand. The employed activity is maneuvered in the direction that makes the most common sense. Hence, inquiry combines both action and mental reasoning to make the situation determinate.

An inquiry should be understood as *transactional.* Dewey sees human activity as a transaction between an actor and the environment [20]. Here actors are not bare observers from the outside but an active part of resolving the situation, as they act and reason *within* the situation [19].

However, inquiry does not only resolve doubt found in the situation. The outcome of the inquiry is likely to bring on new surprises and doubts, as the actor will create new environmental conditions, producing a new unique situation. This reciprocal relation will continue in a highly iterative manner. While transforming the problematic situation, the process will bring on new situations with new problems, *because every settlement introduces the conditions of some degree of a new unsettling* [17].

3.3   Means

Confronted with a problematic situation we face choices among actions. To evaluate the consequences of our actions, we need valuation criteria to determine if our actions are successful in transforming the problematic situation into a stable and determinate one. Dewey sees criteria as something that arises from inquiry. Dewey forms this something in the concepts of means and ends and the inseparable relation between these [17].

Means are tools waiting to be employed in an activity. Tools can be external materials or bodily and mental organs. However, they only become means when they are employed. One way to understand the concept is to look at the distinction between materials, tools/techniques, and means according to Dewey [18].

Materials are objects an actor utilize to produce an artifact. Tools/techniques are instrumentals that have the potential of becoming means. When these are not employed in an activity they are just passive tools/techniques. They become means only when they are employed in conjunction with our bodily or mental organs. As means they become an active part of the actual situation and context, the actors find themselves in.

Where means can be seen as intermediates – a series of acts with an end – *ends* help to elaborate on what acts to perform and look at the next act in perspective of the context [18]. Ends give a clear direction of the course of action an actor should take to solve a problem. Hence, means and ends are inseparable. They coexist and one cannot be defined without taking the other into consideration - they are two names of the same reality [18].

3.4 Ends and Ends-in-View

Ends provide an activity – an adapted human action – with a purpose that suits the current situation. If an action has no meaning or purpose, the action becomes blind and disorderly. Having an aim for an activity is what Dewey calls ends or ends-in-view [18].

To Dewey, an *end-in-view* is conceived and tested in a process of inquiry. For this reason, it also indicates the aim of an activity is framed and bound within the problematic situation. The end-in-view thus establishes a course of direction for our activities to produce the solution we are committed to in the given situation. Ends-in-view define and deepen the meaning of activities, as they trigger evaluation and reflection. When we evaluate and reflect upon the results of our activities, we also learn new things about the end and the experiences we gained to get here.

Ends-in-view are dynamic and alive entities in the process of inquiry. Therefore they can change the course of activity to suit the current situation in connection to resolving the problem [17]. Inquiry elucidates both ends to be achieved and necessary means to achieving them.

3.5 Community of Inquiry

Dewey saw a *community of inquiry* as a group of individuals inquiring into problematic situations together [39].

A problematic situation causes the community to form and undertake inquiry. Any inquiry is socially contingent and has cultural and social consequences [17] as humans live in communities and take pleasure in the culture the association with others brings [17].

Knowledge emerges and exists within a social context and therefore requires agreement among those involved in the inquiry for legitimacy. *An inquirer in a given special field appeals to the experiences of the community of his fellow workers for confirmation and correction of his results* [17].

The social and cultural aspects of the environment will influence the perception of the problematic, means, and ends, utilized to transform idea into solution. If an idea and its meaning cannot be communicated and understood, the idea is nothing else but fantastic beyond imagination [17]. As a social activity, inquiry depends not only on the physical environment, but also on the traditions, organizations, customs and common practice embedded in the situation [17].

4   Illustration: Telerehab

Software innovation is about the exploration of problem domain needs and possible software-based ways to approach them. For this, we need not only to focus on how to develop solutions, but more importantly inquire into why we develop them and what we want to achieve.

We will illustrate our pragmatic approach via a very simplified example. The example is partly based on a thesis project where software engineering students worked on a system to support rehabilitative physiotherapy for post-surgery patients in their own home [26]. The idea was to improve rehabilitation effects while spending fewer resources on transportation at the same time.

Could a system be designed to help patients and therapists collaborate virtually? A system where patients exercise in their home under therapist supervision using an Internet connection?

We will use this case to illustrate how innovative solutions emerge as technological expertise is combined with problem domain insights. The gradual development is described in a series of prototypes, where each prototype reflects a deeper understanding of problems, means, and ends.

The project team consists of three people: Charlie, Ralph and Alex. Charlie is a physiotherapist and she represents the customer-side and flow of resources into the project. Charlie has agreed with Pat, a patient recovering from shoulder surgery, to discuss and try out various ideas, scenarios, and prototypes aiming to facilitate therapeutic sessions with Charlie in her office and Pat in his home.

The two other team members, Ralph and Alex, are software developers. Both of them are experts in software technologies whereas their a priori knowledge of the problem domain is limited. Being the senior, Alex is responsible for facilitating and enacting an agile and iterative development process, and she is also the interface between the team, management, and external stakeholders.

We will describe the first iteration in the project, which results in the first prototype and ideas for a second prototype.

4.1   1ˢᵗ Iteration: X-ray

Physiotherapeutic rehabilitation requires the patient to do prescribed exercises correctly. Performed incorrectly, these exercises might be less effective or even worsen the condition. Furthermore, problems with doing an exercise correctly might indicate sideeffects from surgery, or recovery complications such as joint, tendon, and muscle problems related to fatigue and stress.

Based on such concerns the team could start out discussing how a system could support Charlie in instructing Pat on the movements of an exercise and deciding whether these steps are performed correctly.

Charlie knows of existing telerehab systems using web cameras and two-way video links. She suggests building a similar system where Pat will see her demonstrate the individual movements of an exercise, while she can see how he follows her lead. The audio would be used to explain and discuss issues.

The team agrees that this might work but Ralph asks Charlie if a two-dimensional image on her screen will be enough for her to evaluate Pat's moves. Charlie replies that it might for example be hard to see how much a limb twists in the joint during a particular movement. It might also prove difficult to see if Pat uses compensation movements to make the exercise easier.

After some discussion Ralph suggests using a Microsoft Kinect camera. A Kinect would compensate for some of the limitations of an ordinary video-feed by highlighting bones, joints, and movements of the patient. This would help the therapist to see how the exercise is performed and give precise instructions to the patient.

Alex and Ralph research the Kinect SDK and decide that the platform offers some interesting possibilities. The API provides easy access to the Kinect's sensors and supplies enhanced features such as skeleton tracking and gesture recognition. Also, as it integrates nicely with the .Net platform, it would be easy to interface with external software components. Building a system for a Kinect-based platform therefore seems to be viable design.

The team agrees to base a first prototype on the Kinect and they nickname this first prototype *X-ray* to reflect the primary motive for using a Kinect: To compensate for limitations in patient-therapist interaction based on a conventional video feed via human pose estimation. The Kinect is used to enhance those parts of the feed that are most important for a therapist in order to assess the movements of an exercise.

4.2 Testing and Further Development

Having built the prototype, the team invites Pat to test-drive it from his rural home. Charlie successfully instructs Pat, and she is able to monitor and correct his movements with sufficient precision.

Charlie asks Pat to carry on with the exercise to see if the movements change over time as Pat tires or simply forgets exactly how to do the exercise. Unfortunately, this part of the session suffers from a series of communication breakdowns ranging from bandwidth reductions and time lags to complete disruptions. Although the connection is reestablished after 5-15 seconds or less, these recurring disruptions make it impossible for Charlie to monitor Pat let alone offer him meaningful feedback.

After the test, the team and Pat discuss the prototype with mixed feelings.

Charlie is not enthusiastic about the system, although it does what she asked for – except for the connection problem. Obviously, the system allows the therapist to instruct the patient, but longitudinal monitoring of the patient requires stable high-quality connections. If breakdowns were frequent she could not see much use of the system.

Ralph and Alex are disappointed. The system does what it should but the connection problems are ISP-related and clearly out of scope for this project. Moreover, the system is merely a medium between the therapist and the patient, and seen as a tool it offers little support to the users compared to its potential. The platform is seriously underutilized and could offer much more. Ralph wonders if the system could be more stand-alone.

Pat jokingly regrets that Charlie could not be automated. Before the surgery, he used to play table tennis on his son's Kinect and enjoyed the thrill of competing against the machine. If Charlie were 'inside the box' somehow, he would be able to carry on exercising even if connections broke down. It could even be more fun compared to just being controlled by Charlie like a puppet on a string.

Alex replies that building a Charlie-avatar for the system would probably be out of scope for the project, but perhaps they could use some of the unused resources in the platform to copy parts of what Charlie would do. Ralph agrees and says that it should be fairly simple to have the system monitor Pat's movements and compare them to previously registered 'ideal' movements. After all, the skeleton data points from the Kinect could easily be converted to vectors and used in calculations where actual movement vectors are compared with 'ideal' vectors.

They decide to start working on a new prototype extending the first one. This time the system should autonomously monitor Pat's exercises and show on his screen how his movements compare with how they are supposed to be performed. Reflecting the addition of such features, they nickname the second prototype *Biofeedback*.

After a similar second iteration the team decides to continue on a third prototype – *Trend Analyst* comparing Pat's progress with other patients' data – and then a fourth one – *Timestretch* aggregating data to save time for Charlie. We will not describe these iterations in detail, but in the next section we will discuss how this work was facilitated by Essence – a methodology for software innovation – and how this methodology stands on pragmatic ideas.

5   Essence: Pragmatic Software Innovation

The pragmatic ideas presented in this paper can be linked to an ongoing effort to develop *Essence* – a methodology for software innovation [1-3].

In Essence, software innovation is a recurring process of inquiry in software teams. Essence therefore is aimed at facilitating such inquiry among team members. A basic assumption in Essence is that an innovative software team integrates software expertise and problem domain expertise. This combination requires experts from different domains to combine their knowledge in constructive ways.

Essence is based on three types of elements: Values, views, and roles. There are four values, four views, and four roles (see Table 1).

Table 1. Essence elements

Value	View	Role
Reflection over requirements – working on ends gives a deeper understanding than found in requirements	*Paradigm* – underlying mental models of the problematic situation shared in the team	The *Child* is the main idea-developer for the problematic situation – not bounded by convention
Affordance over solution – every solution affords new options and potentials to be discovered via inquiry into the problem domain	*Product* – means and ends seen from the 'inside' with a focus on architectures, data, components, etc.	The *Responder* sees the problematic situation from a developer perspective, creates solutions and explores options
Vision over assignments – it is more important to share the end-in-view under conditions of learning and change than listing tasks	*Project* – plans, status, and priorities in the project based on a project vision that represents the end-in-view for the team	The *Challenger* prioritizes ends and approves the end-in-view in the problematic situation from a customer perspective
Facilitation over structuration – it is more important to facilitate inquiry and valuation of means and ends than following standard procedures	*Process* – facilitating idea generation and indeed idea evaluation and maturation via identifying potentials and supporting decision-making	The *Anchor* is liaison with outside stakeholders, and facilitates inquiry and valuation in the team

Values are normative statements encouraging the team to focus on valuable choices at all times. The values in Essence seek to push the values in the agile manifesto [5] explicitly towards software innovation [2].

Views are analytical perspectives encouraging the team to view problems and possible solutions from several perspectives. The inspiration to use analytical perspectives comes from 3 directions: (1) the more than two thousand year old philosophical tradition of portraying all worldly structures as made from four elements thereby offering a generic totality consisting of mutually exclusive elements; (2) the four perspectives on Software Engineering [7, 34]; and (3) Tidd et al.'s [45] distinction between four categories of innovations.

Roles are personal and seek to install a sense of personal responsibility for creating innovative solutions. Every team member has a permanent role, but they may temporarily take the only fleeting role in Essence: Child. The Child role is for creating new ideas even if the new ideas conflict with ideas and doctrines previously agreed upon in the project.

Usually a particular role is closely related to a particular view and value. The rows in Table 1 represent such triads. The following four sections therefore describe these triads with illustrations from the Telerehab case.

5.1   Reflection, Paradigm View, and the Child

The *Child* role is fleeting. Any team member has a permanent role but may temporarily take this role. Even people outside the team – for example the patient Pat – may act as Child on occasion and bring new insights and ideas to the team.

This role encourages anyone to propose new ideas even if in direct conflict with the principal shared understanding in the team about the problematic situation faced by the project. The Child role is one way to overcome indeterminate situations and suggest means and ends that may restore a situation to be determinate and thereby manageable for the team.

The *Paradigm* view is where the Child works. This View is used to inquire into the problematic situation, i.e. the challenges that brought the project into existence in the first place. The view is used to share insights from the problem domain, for example by describing users, needs, situations, scenarios, etc. When the first iteration started, Charlie – using the Child role – saw the paradigm as centered on instruction: How could Charlie show Pat the right way to do an exercise? The problem domain was explored at the Paradigm view and centered on how to exchange factual information between two people in different locations using a software-based system.

Such insights typically reflect determinate situations where the team feels confident in the problems to solve and how. Yet inquiry at this and the other views might bring about indeterminate situations. This was what happened when the test of the first prototype was obstructed by connection problems and Pat –as Child – pointed to an alternative paradigm for the project: *Learning*.

The Child role and the Paradigm view are both for *Reflection*. Reflection mirrors the inquiry into the problematic situation where insights regarding problems and needs emerge and bring about new ideas. The connection problems and Ralph's dissatisfaction with unused potential in the platform were two indeterminate situations that caused the team to inquire deeper into the situation.

As a value, Reflection encourages the team to consider who the users are, what to expect from them, how to scope the project, what value a solution could bring to customers and users, etc. The problems faced in this case could be understood from different paradigms: *Instruction* (showing how), *learning* (user empowerment), *coaching* (comparing with other patients), or *quality time* (spending less time observing and more time talking with the patient). Each paradigm reflects fundamentally different notions of the situation at hand and which ends would be called for, and each paradigm is a product of our inquiries.

5.2   Affordance, Product View, and the Responder

The *Responder* role is permanent. This role is for developers and their main responsibility is to respond and design solutions to the challenges that the project confronts. In the case, both Ralph and Alex were responders, although Alex had extra responsibilities being the Anchor as well.

Responders work primarily at the *Product* view. This view is for designing architectures, deciding on components, algorithms, and data – always with a view to create and pursue potential wherever possible.

Their work is driven by *Affordance* – the aspiration to always ask if any component, algorithm, database, etc. could bring more to the situation than originally anticipated. A design at a given time might afford more potential later than was recognized when the design actually took place.

Ralph suggested using a Kinect to enable Charlie to see Pat's movements better. When the connection problems emerged, he suggested using the unused potential of the platform to make Pat's side of the system more stand-alone. This technically motivated move led to a change in the paradigm for the project to focus on learning and empowering Pat.

At a later time, Charlie might mention that she wants data from the system to be exported to the hospital database for research on treatments and complications. Alex might suggest using data from the database to compare Pat's progress with similar records in the database.

Alex and Ralph's continuous inquiry into the problematic situation entails hands-on experience with the means at their disposal. This experience leads to a deeper understanding of the technology and what the technology affords of new possibilities in the situation they find themselves in. Affordance thereby might lead to a new paradigm for the next prototype: *Trend Analyst*. This way, the data requested by Charlie turns from ends (deliverables) wanted from the system into means used in the system to service Charlie and Pat better.

5.3   Vision, Project View, and the Challenger

The *Challenger* role is a permanent role for a person representing the problem domain. Charlie is the Challenger in our case. Acting on behalf of the customer she not only contributes with knowledge and resources, but also with the challenge as well as acceptance of solutions as they emerge.

The challenge is the problematic situation the team is thrown into by the Challenger. Charlie started out by asking for support for collaboration between therapist and patient in separate locations. As the team inquired into this challenge in iterations, the vision and the project scope developed into more and more valuable solutions.

The Challenger works at the *Project* view where features are prioritized and the project vision is represented, maintained, and shared within the team as well as with external stakeholders. The vision represents the *end-in-view* for the project at a given time. In the case described here, each prototype name represents end-in-views as they change over time from X-ray over BioFeedback and Trend Analyst to TimeStretch.

The value for the Project view and the Challenger is *Vision*. It is important to share the end-in-view among the members of the team. A list of requirements can hardly reflect the overall idea of the project let alone help the team spot subtle changes in project goals as problems and solutions emerge from inquiry. Visions – perhaps expressed as metaphors – are well-known ways to share this overview [6, 44].

5.4   Facilitation, Process View, and the Anchor

The *Process* view is for *facilitating* the team itself in making the best out of the work at the three other views. It is used for idea generation and in particular for evaluations.

Criteria for acceptance, for determining the qualities sought for in a solution are examples of contributions to this view.

Evaluations are when visions are tested in the process of inquiry. Core elements in evaluations include the choice of criteria and how they are used. Developing criteria is as much a reflective activity as is the design of solutions.

The *Anchor* is liaison between the team and outside stakeholders and responsible for facilitating productive working in the team. As such, the Anchor insists on fair and sober discussions in the team to ensure sensible decisions and choices.

Alex was Anchor and helped the team evaluate strengths, weaknesses, opportunities, and threats for each prototype. Ralph pointed to unused potential in the first prototype and this helped inspire an answer to the communication problems. Later, when Charlie required that data about Pat's progress be registered in a hospital database, Alex suggested using this opportunity to improve the system itself for analyzing Pat's progress compared to similar patients. A proposal that lead to the *Trend Analyst* prototype.

6   Conclusion – Essence and Pragmatic Software Innovation

This paper suggests a pragmatic approach to software innovation. Using Essence as methodological foundation – based on agile principles and in particular incremental development – Essence was used to illustrate inquiry into a problem domain identifying technological options.

In incremental projects, sprint deliverables serve as prototypes. A prototype reflects the perceived scope of and needs in a problem domain and also a vision for how to answer these needs. The prototype can be evaluated in connection with a sprint review meeting, and scope, needs, vision, and configuration may change as the team inquires deeper.

Our illustration started out with a plain problematic situation and a team of technology and problem domain experts. The problematic situation offered a challenge with known scenarios and needs, but after testing the first prototype, new scenarios and needs were discovered. The inquiry changed the problematic situation.

The values, views, and roles in Essence highlight key characteristics of pragmatic software innovation.

Values encourage the team to inquire into the problematic situation and study the problem domain and its needs (reflection); to consider if there is untapped potential in the technological answers (affordance); to establish an end-in-view allowing the team to work determined under uncertainty (vision); and to constantly evaluate the fit between the problems and the answers under conditions of constraints (facilitation).

Views focus on artifacts – shared representations offering common ground for inquiry. Are problems well represented, consistent, and meaningfully scoped on the Paradigm view? Are design options represented on the Product view in a way where they can be assessed, and does the design offer flexibility to embrace such options? Is the vision on the Project view represented in a format easy to understand and maintain? Are tools and techniques for idea development available on the Project view and are evaluation criteria visible and representative for the current end-in-view?

Roles focus on the personal reflection and responsibility. The Challenger represents problem domain knowledge in the team and maintains the project vision. Responders represent technological insight and suggest answers for the problematic situation. The Anchor is responsible for the process and for ensuring fair evaluations and timely criteria. Finally, the Child – the fleeting role at the Paradigm view – is key for inquiring with a free hand.

Inquiry in Essence is both theoretical – using the expertise of the team members – and experimental – using every artifact to reflect and learn. Evaluation in Essence therefore is an important way to improve the design, and serve as a stimulus to creativity in software design [31]. Evaluations and judgments may be according to predefined or ad hoc criteria, and they may even be tacit and intuitive [40].

In Essence any design forms the basis for a new beginning. A prototype is a transaction with the problematic situation [37]. Testing the prototype in the illustration necessitated the system to be stand-alone. This new design created opportunities – new ends – that were not anticipated when the project started. As the vision develops, it will usually grow increasingly stable as the product is tested with customers and users. Still, the vision remains changeable and allows the project to adapt to changes by guiding without excessive detail [23].

In this paper we have tried to show how Essence facilitate a pragmatic approach to software innovation – an approach characterized with learning across knowledge domains and with incremental development of not only ideas – but also solutions – throughout the span of the project. We believe that pragmatic software innovation offers a way to opportunistically pursue innovation in everyday projects.

References

1. Aaen, I.: Essence: Facilitating Software Innovation. European Journal of Information Systems 17, 543–553 (2008)
2. Aaen, I.: Software Innovation - Values for a Methodology. In: Aanestad, M., Bratteteig, T. (eds.) SCIS 2013. LNBIP, vol. 156, pp. 72–86. Springer, Heidelberg (2013)
3. Aaen, I.: Roles in Innovative Software Teams – A Design Experiment. In: Human Benefit through the Diffusion of IS Design Science Research, IFIP WG 8.2 + 8.6 International Working Conference, Perth, Australia, pp. 73–88 (2010)
4. Aspray, W., Mayadas, F., Vardi, M.Y.: Globalization and Offshoring of Software. Association for Computing Machinery, Job Migration Task Force (2006)
5. Beck, K., Beedle, M., van Bennekum, A., Cockburn, A., Cunningham, W., Fowler, M., Grenning, J., Highsmith, J., Hunt, A., Jeffries, R., Kern, J., Marick, B., Martin, R., Mellor, S., Schwaber, K., Sutherland, J., Thomas, D.: Manifesto for Agile Software Development (2001)
6. Beck, K.: Extreme Programming Explained: Embrace change. Addison-Wesley, Reading (2000)
7. Bernstein, L., Yuhas, C.M.: People, Process, Product, Project - The Big Four. In: Bernstein, L., Yuhas, C.M. (eds.) Trustworthy Systems Through Quantitative Software Engineering, pp. 39–71. John Wiley & Sons, Inc., New York (2005)
8. Biskjaer, M.M., Dalsgaard, P.: Toward A Constraing Oriented Pragmatism Understanding of Design Creativity. In: The 2nd International Conference on Design Creativity (ICDC 2012), pp. 65–74 (2012)

9. Bourque, P., Fairley, R.E. (eds.): SWEBOK v3.0 – Guide to the Software Engineering Body of Knowledge. IEEE Computer Society, Washington (2014)

10. Campos, P.: Promoting innovation in agile methods: Two case studies in interactive installation's development. International Journal of Agile and Extreme Software Development 1, 38 (2012)

11. Carr, N.G.: IT Doesn't Matter. Harvard Business Review 81, 41–49 (2003)

12. Conboy, K., Morgan, L.: Beyond the customer: Opening the agile systems development process. Information and Software Technology 53 (2011)

13. Conboy, K., Wang, X., Fitzgerald, B.: Creativity in Agile Systems Development: A Literature Review. In: Dhillon, G., Stahl, B.C., Baskerville, R. (eds.) CreativeSME 2009. IFIP AICT, vol. 301, pp. 122–134. Springer, Heidelberg (2009)

14. Couger, J.D.: Creative problem solving and opportunity finding. Decision making in operations management series. Boyd & Fraser Pub. Co., Hinsdale (1994)

15. Couger, J.D., Dengate, G.: Measurement of Creativity of I.S. Products. In: Proceedings of the Twenty-Fifth Hawaii International Conference on System Sciences, vol. 4, pp. 288–298 (1992)

16. Couger, J.D., Higgins, L.F., McIntyre, S.C. (Un)Structured Creativity in Information Systems Organizations. MIS Quarterly 17, 375–397 (1993)

17. Dewey, J.: Logic: The Theory of Inquiry. Henry Holt and Company, New York (1938)

18. Dewey, J.: Human nature and conduct: An introduction to social psychology. The Modern Library, New York (1957)

19. Dewey, J.: Essays in experimental logic. SIU Press (2007)

20. Dewey, J., Bentley, A.F.: Knowing and the known. 111. Beacon Press Boston, MA (1960)

21. Goldkuhl, G.: Design research in search for a paradigm: Pragmatism is the answer. In: Helfert, M., Donnellan, B. (eds.) EDSS 2011. CCIS, vol. 286, pp. 84–95. Springer, Heidelberg (2012)

22. Gorschek, T., Fricker, S., Palm, K., Kunsman, S.A.: A Lightweight Innovation Process for Software-Intensive Product Development. IEEE Software 27, 37–45 (2010)

23. Hey, J.H.G.: Framing innovation: Negotiating shared frames during early design phases. Journal of Design Research 6, 79–99 (2007)

24. Hickman, L.A.: John Dewey's pragmatic technology. The Indiana series in the philosophy of technology. Indiana University Press, Bloomington (1990)

25. Highsmith, J., Cockburn, A.: Agile software development: the business of innovation. Computer 34, 120–127 (2001)

26. Jensen, R.H., Brodersen, K.H.: Responder's Inquiry - Spikes. Department of Computer Science Master Thesis, 83 (2013)

27. Lim, Y.-K., Stolterman, E., Tenenberg, J.: The anatomy of prototypes: Prototypes as filters, prototypes as manifestations of design ideas. ACM Trans. Comput.-Hum. Interact. 15, 1–27 (2008)

28. Mahaux, M., Maiden, N.: Theater Improvisers Know the Requirements Game. IEEE Software 25, 68–69 (2008)

29. Maiden, N., Ncube, C., Robertson, S.: Can Requirements Be Creative? Experiences with an Enhanced Air Space Management System. In: 29th International Conference on Software Engineering, ICSE 2007, pp. 632–641 (2007)

30. Maiden, N., Robertson, S.: Integrating Creativity into Requirements Processes: Experiences with an Air Traffic Management System. In: Proceedings of the 2005 13th IEEE International Conference on Requirements Engineering (RE 2005), pp. 105–114 (2005)

31. McCall, R.: Critical Conversations: Feedback as a Stimulus to Creativity in Software Design. Human Technology 6, 11–37 (2010)
32. Misra, S.C., Kumar, V., Kumar, U., Mishra, R.: Goal-Driven Measurement Framework for Software Innovation Process. Journal of Information Technology Management XVI, 30–42 (2005)
33. Pikkarainen, M., Codenie, W., Boucart, N., Alvaro, J.A.H. (eds.): The Art of Software Innovation - Eight Practice Areas to Inspire your Business. Springer, Heidelberg (2011)
34. Pressman, R.S.: Software engineering: A practitioner's approach. McGraw-Hill Higher Education, Boston (2005)
35. Rose, J.: Software Innovation: Eight work-style heuristics for creative system developers. Software Innovation, Aalborg University, Department of Computer Science (2010)
36. Samuelsen, R.: A Pragmatist Contribution to Science. Technology and Innovation (STI) Studies (2013)
37. Schön, D.A.: Designing as reflective conversation with the materials of a design situation. Knowledge-Based Systems 5, 3–14 (1992)
38. Schön, D.A.: The Reflective Practitioner: How professionals think in action. Basic books (1983)
39. Schön, D.A.: The Theory of Inquiry: Dewey's Legacy to Education. Curriculum Inquiry 22, 119–139 (1992)
40. Schön, D.A., Wiggins, G.: Kinds of seeing and their functions in designing. Design Studies 13, 135–156 (1992)
41. Shneiderman, B.: Creativity support tools: Accelerating discovery and innovation. Communications of the ACM 50, 20–32 (2007)
42. Sternberg, R.J., Lubart, T.I.: The concept of creativity: Prospects and paradigms. In: Handbook of Creativity, pp. 3–15. Cambridge University Press, Cambridge (1999)
43. Swanson, E.B., Ramiller, N.C.: Innovating Mindfully with Information Technology. MIS Quarterly 28, 553–583 (2004)
44. Takeuchi, H., Nonaka, I.: The new new product development game. Harvard Business Review 64, 137–146 (1986)
45. Tidd, J., Bessant, J.R., Pavitt, K.: Managing innovation: Integrating technological, market and organization change. Wiley, Hoboken (2005)

Creating Business Value through Agile Project Management and Information Systems Development: The Perceived Impact of Scrum

Karlheinz Kautz[1], Thomas Heide Johansen[2], and Andreas Uldahl[3]

[1] Faculty of Business, University of Wollongong, Wollongong NSW 2522, Australia
kautz@uow.edu.au
[2] Progressive AS, DK-2730 Herlev
thj@progressive.dk
[3] Ernst & Young Denmark, DK-2860 Søborg
Andreas.Uldahl@dk.ey.com

Abstract. Value creation through information systems (IS) and information technology (IT) is a major IS research topic. However there still exists an ambiguity and fuzziness of the 'IS business value' concept and a lack of clarity surrounding the value creation process. This also true for organizations that develop IS/IT and for development technologies like information systems development and project management methods that are applied in the production of IS/IT. The agile method Scrum is one such technology. In the research presented here we studied productivity, quality and employee satisfaction as supported by Scrum as value creating measures. Our positive assessment is built upon subjective perceptions and goes beyond hard measures and indicators. It provides insights into individual and organisational impacts and sheds light on the value generation process. The measures we present thus deal with some of the deficiencies in current IS business value research and contribute to filling existing gaps in an IS business value research agenda.

1 Introduction

Value creation through information systems (IS) and information technology (IT) is one of the major research topics for IS/IT researchers. In a recent literature review of IS business value research Schryen [1] however laments the ongoing ambiguity and fuzziness of the 'IS business value' concept and the lack of clarity surrounding the value creation process. He proposes that to develop a consistent and comprehensive understanding of the complex phenomenon research should account for linkages between different types of performance depending on varying contexts, for different capabilities that go beyond hard indicators and measures, and for perceived impacts and benefits that are dependent on the respective stakeholders. Schryen [1] focuses on business value of IS in general, but his conclusions are also true for business organizations that develop IS and IT and for development technologies like information systems and software development and project management methods that are applied in the production of IS and IT.

B. Bergvall-Kåreborn and P.A. Nielsen (Eds.): TDIT 2014, IFIP AICT 429, pp. 150–165, 2014.

The agile development and project management method Scrum is one such technology. While numerous publications claim a positive impact of Scrum on information systems and software development, only little empirical work exists to verify these claims. To further contribute to the body of knowledge on IS value creation and the impact of Scrum we set out to answer the following research question: What kind of value is created and which impact has the introduction of the agile development and project management method Scrum on information systems and software development? We apply Schryen's [1] taxonomy of IS business value types consisting of internal value, external value, tangible and intangible values. Here we focus at the outset on internal value provided by Scrum throughout the development process. The results we present in the following are part of a larger project where we developed a framework for investigating value creation and the impact of Scrum (see [2]). In this paper however we concentrate on three of these concepts, namely productivity, quality, and employee satisfaction. In the remainder of the paper we first briefly introduce Scrum. Then we describe our theoretical background and the research setting and method. Subsequently we present and discuss our findings against the existing literature on Scrum and relate them in our conclusions to the literature on IS business value research.

2 SCRUM – An Agile Development and Project Management Method

Scrum is an agile information systems and software development method with a strong focus on project management, which was formalized and tested by Schwaber and Sutherland in the mid 1990ties [3, 4]. Scrum focuses on an iterative and nimble development process, on transparency, visibility and on cooperation in and between the development team and the customers. In Scrum the development team is called the Scrum team. Unlike traditional development projects where analysts, developers and testers are typically separated, Scrum teams are built on an interdisciplinary basis and comprise all these roles in one team preferably in one physical location. This structure, as well as Scrum's focus on self-organization aims at creating team dynamics and a better understanding of the tasks to be performed jointly. In this context the role of the Product owner has the responsibility to represent the project and product externally to other stakeholders and customers and to handle and manage the tasks that appear in the product and release backlogs (see below) [3]. Internally, the role of the Scrum master will provide leadership, motivate and facilitate the team in line with the Scrum values, practices and development process.

A Scrum development process is structured through a product backlog, which is a prioritized list of required business and technical functions of the envisioned product. It might change in line with new customer needs. A release backlog is a prioritized subset of the total product backlog and defines the functions to be included in a release. A Scrum, performed in so-called sprints, is a set of development tasks and processes which a Scrum team carries out to achieve a given sprint goal. The length of a sprint is predefined. It typically lasts between 5 and 30 calendar days [3]. What needs to be done during a sprint is determined by a prioritized sprint backlog, which is determined together with a sprint goal before the start of each sprint by the team and Scrum master and others, if necessary, at a planning meeting. Throughout a project a burn down chart shows the amount of work left to do versus time over a given period [4]). In short daily Scrum meetings project members briefly present what they have done during the preceding day, which tasks they take on that day, as well as any challenges and obstacles that might have prevented them from carrying out their work without any solution being discussed. Scrums of Scrums are additional short meetings by the Scrum masters of projects, which consist of several Scrum teams. At the end of a sprint a sprint review meeting takes place where the Scrum team, the Product owner, other management, and one or more representatives from the customer [3] assess the team's development process and progress in relation to the predefined sprint goal. Finally the Scrum team, the Scrum master and possibly the Product owner hold a meeting, called a retrospective, to secure learning and further improvement in the team where both the process and the product are assessed and discussed by each individual team member.

3   Literature Review and Theoretical Background

With the IS business value literature as examined by Schryen [1] as a point of departure in our study we were interested in the impact of a specific method, namely Scrum on information systems and software development. Our literature review was therefore focused on that particular approach and not in general on project management methods' or agile methods' impact on information systems and software development. This limited our sources to writings which take their starting point in agile software development. We combined a concept-centric with an author-based approach [5] and approximated the value concept through the concept of impact, either by focussing on economic impact [6] or on organizational and/or individual impact [7, 8]. On this background our original search with keywords such as 'impact of Scrum', 'effect of Scrum', 'impact of Scrum implementation', and 'effect of Scrum implementation' primarily in Google, Google Scholar and IEEE sources lead to about 90 sources, of which 8 dealt more precisely with our research problem. An additional 8 sources were identified through backwards referencing. From that literature we derived a number of concepts and for these concepts indicators for the impact of Scrum on information systems and software development processes and projects. The resulting framework consisted of the identified, interrelated concepts productivity, quality, employee satisfaction, team leadership, as well as process transparency, and a total of 28 indicators, which defined the concepts on a more detailed level. Here we are focusing on Scrum's impact on the first three.

Productivity is a prominent concept in the IS business value literature (see f.ex. [9]; for a detailed discussion [1]); in the agile development literature it is an expression of the development team's productivity [10]. There are a number of interrelated indicators that are linked to different areas that may impact on productivity. Dybå and Dingsøyr [11] describe the results of a comparative case study where productivity was measured in projects driven by traditional and agile development methods based on the number of lines of code (LOC) per hour, month or employee. Guang-Yong [12] describes the measurement of productivity in the number of lines of code, and demonstrates how productivity increases gradually as a team becomes more self-organized and manages to review its development processes to avoid the repetition of mistakes.

Appelo [13] has a different view how productivity can be measured. He highlights the increased functionality to the final product as a direct indicator of improved productivity. The way he measures the functionality is the number of story points that have been completed within a given period. A story point is a number that reflects the severity of a given task. Mahnic and Vrana [14] and Mahnic and Zabkar [15] define the assessment of productivity as a ratio of the added value versus the associated financial costs as well as costs associated with bug fixes. We use these sources to investigate the indicators employee performance, the time associated with fixing bugs, and repetition of the same mistakes. Sutherland and Altman [16] use the term "perfect hours" as a label for a project participant's undisturbed and uninterrupted work. They emphasize that a project's progress and productivity should be measured by taking perfect hours combined with other indicators into account. The number of interruptions and the number of uninterrupted development hours were the two indicators we descended from these authors. Moore et al. [17] argue that increased productivity through the use of Scrum is grounded on its focus on delivering functional software in short time intervals with fixed deadlines where developers do not end up in endless development cycles in an attempt to provide perfect solutions with a product that can handle everything at one time. The avoidance of continuous development cycles and compliance with deadlines are the last two indicators we derived from these authors.

Quality is another important concept in the IS business value literature, in the form of product quality [18, 19] or system and information quality [7, 8]. In the agile development literature a strong focus is on measures that can be applied during the development process. In their comparative study Dybå and Dingsøyr [11] identify various quality measures that were applied across a wide range of projects. In line with their findings Mahnic and Vrana [14]) and Mahnic and Zabkar [15] put forward two different indicators for measuring quality both related to error density: the number of errors as detected during the development process by the development team itself, and those reported by the customers over a fixed period of time, in both cases the measurement unit is defects or errors per 1000 lines of code (KLOC), which we adopt for our study. Dybå and Dingsøyr [11] emphasize that the 'seriousness' of the errors might have an impact on the perception of quality; we follow their suggestion and also use number of bugs or minor errors as a quality indicator. As another important measure for quality to be taken into account during the development process Appelo [13] highlights that the number of errors identified by testers during the integration of software modules is an essential metric as well. Another undisputed indicator for quality is of course the overall useability of the final product [11]. Thus, although we in our study did not have access to customers directly (see below) we collect, to the extent possible, data about this indicator.

Customer and user satisfaction [7, 8, 20] as well as consumer welfare [18, 19] are significant performance measures for IS business value; in our context we identified employee satisfaction of the different team members in the development teams that perform a development task, as an important concept. These team members have the roles of project managers, analysts, developers, and testers. As such we do not focus on staff in general or those who maintain the final product. In the reviewed agile development literature there are significant differences in the perceptions of the various authors concerning employee satisfaction. Mann and Maurer [21], Manhic and Vrana [14] as well as Manhic and Zabkar [15] argue that a reduction of overtime hours raises the overall satisfaction among team members. Mann and Maurer [21], Manhic and Vrana [14] Moore et al. [17], and Manhic and Zabkar [15] also argue that improving the lines and channels of communication within the team, as well as externally, with other organizational units and with the customer increases employee satisfaction. In particular better information about project progress and more direct feedback about the work in progress are emphasised as influential indicators for employee satisfaction. Finally, a general agreement among most of the above authors, supported also by Moe and Dingsøyr [10] and Green [22], was that Scrum provides general working conditions and a working environment that have a bearing on a positive social life at the workplace as well as on work pleasure, also described as job satisfaction, that increase overall employee satisfaction. We therefore included these two indicators also into our framework.

4   Research Setting and Method

We chose a case study approach to research the impact of Scrum on information systems and software development processes and projects. The chosen case organization has approximately 40 years of experience in solving complex IT tasks. Some years ago it changed from being publically owned to private company. It has about 3,000 employees, who are involved in the development of administrative and statutory software solutions. The investigated case department falls into the latter category and has 45 employees. Its sole product is a case management system for municipal job centers, which gives administrators the opportunity to work across different platforms. For the development of the case management system, the department previously followed the traditional waterfall model. In 2011 it launched the implementation of Scrum as the preferred development model. At the time of our investigation, the department had completed three full releases with the use of Scrum. As such the department had the profile of the unit of analysis which we were looking for: an organization that had recently, within the past year, chosen to implement Scrum, and that had previously used the traditional waterfall model. With the former model still in their minds we expected the employees to make candid assessments of the impact of Scrum as compared to the past.

As we were not able to make direct measurements nor had direct access to data, such as number of interruptions, uninterrupted development hours, number of overall, integration or minor errors, over time registrations, etc., we chose to directly ask respondents about their perceptions of the given concepts. The indicators, which we had derived from the literature review, were therefore transformed into direct questions for our interviews, which we validated with 2 employees in a small pilot study before putting them to the 11 interview partners, who were available for the study. We developed 3 largely overlapping interview guides for the three stakeholder groups, with 6 developers as respondents, 4 respondents in leadership roles such as Scrum master, Product owner or unit managers and one representative from the service department, which is responsible for external liaisons. All interviews were recorded, transcribed and handed over to the respondents for approval. The results of our analysis were also presented to the participants of this study and the case organization at large.

The data collection with standardized interviews allowed both collections of qualitative and quantitative data. We first asked the respondents to numerically assess, on a scale from -5 to + 5, for each indicator its individual change, improvement or decline, as compared to the situation before the implementation of Scrum and then to evaluate its impact on the concept in question. After that quantitative judgment we asked into the reasons for these assessments, which provided rich qualitative data. This combination of data allowed for data and method triangulation to improve the validity of our findings [23]. The subsequent analysis was based on mean values for the quantitative data within each indicator; these were interpreted on the basis of the qualitative opinions. The results were then compared and discussed with regard to published Scrum guidelines and findings from the literature. It is worth pointing out that the numerical element of the collected data should be considered secondary. The interviews were intended as the primary source to collect qualitative data with a statistical element - and not vice versa. The quantitative data was exclusively used to create an indication and an overview over any specific area.

5   Finding and Results

The investigation of Scrum's value creation through and impact on productivity, quality and employee satisfaction in information systems and software development was part of a larger study, which both developed and applied a comprehensive framework consisting of a further two concepts. Although a presentation of the overall result would give a more comprehensive portrait of the method's value and impact we have here focused on three concepts mostly due to length limitations. This still provides some valuable insights and where necessary we will relate to the other two concepts. As a background for our subsequent discussion in the following we summarize the results of our analysis concerning Scrum's value and impact on productivity, quality and employee satisfaction in the case unit.

5.1   Scrum's Impact on Productivity

Table1 summarizes the respondents' assessment of Scrum's impact on productivity. Despite some individual variations the respondents' mostly positive scores indicate their favourable assessment and an improvement in productivity after the implementation of Scrum.

We found that the decrease in the number of interruptions was limited, but it had led to a significant, perceived impact on productivity. In addition, in the changed process interruptions now came from an authorized person and were thus being less perceived as disturbances. The perception of the number of uninterrupted, continuous development hours had only seen a very modest increase. The respondents reasoned that the use of Scrum had led to more meetings than in the past which led to interruptions in the continuity of their work. The frequent meetings resulted, however, in a better understanding of the tasks. This was appreciated by the respondents as having a positive impact on their productivity as they thought they now both worked more efficiently and tackled unforeseen challenges much better.

Prioritizing new functionality higher than error-free deliveries had been the organization's strategy to avoid endless development cycles. Nevertheless these were experienced by the majority of the respondents. The increased focus on delivering functional software in defined, short iterations has prevented endless development and has resulted in more productivity, however not on the expense of product quality as described in the next subsection.

Table 1. Scrum's impact on productivity

Productivity	Improvement	Impact on productivity	Score Range
No of interruptions	1.4	2.0	0 - 4
No of uninterrupted development hours	0.8	1.3	0 - 3
Endless development cycles	2.8	2.8	1 - 5
Compliance with deadlines	2.9	2.1	0 - 5
Repetition of mistakes	1.1	1.4	-1 - 3
Bug fixing time	0.5	1.7	-2 - 3
Employee performance	3.5	4	3 - 4

The respondents felt that Scrum's decomposition and prioritization of tasks had positively changed the compliance to deadlines and had had a positive impact on productivity in general. With regard to the repetition of mistakes there was also positive development. Primarily the respondents' explained this progress with Scrum's focus on self-organization and not that much with the practice of retrospectives, which are the method's explicit mechanism for the identification of weaknesses and subsequent process and product improvements.

Bug fixing time was the area with the least perceived improvement compared to the other indicators. Despite low average ratings, respondents expressed that although the actual time spent had not decreased, bug fixing now happened at a much better and appropriate time in the process. Thus, its impact on productivity was assessed significantly higher.

The managers among the respondents assessed that the employees' performance had increased significantly. They provided two different arguments for this. First Scrum's emphasis on process clarity resulting in visibility and transparency which we had identified as a separate concept for investigating Scrum's impact on information systems and software development, made it compulsory for developers to publically present their work and take a position with regard to any challenges they had encountered. As a consequence they put more focus on the execution of their tasks. The other reason was related to the avoidance of project overruns. In the past overruns had always been passed through the chain of development tasks, with the results that the developers or even more so the testers became time-pressured and could not do their job properly. The shorter iterations carried out by a multidisciplinary team avoided this effect and resulted in overall better performance.

5.2   Scrum's Impact on Quality

Table 2 summarizes the respondents' assessment of Scrum's impact on quality. There were two indicators, where the respondents had perceived improvements and a positive change. These were the number of defects per KLOC and the number of minor errors. The two parameters were interdependent, as we from the responses could conclude that the reduction of the number of defects per KLOC had mostly come from the reduction of the number of minor errors; there had been little change in the number of serious errors, especially no change in the number of integration errors, which were usually categorised as serious defects. The reason that there had been an improvement in this area, was that with the implementation of Scrum, also unit testing as part of the Scrum team's tasks jointly performed by specific testers and the developers was introduced. This rationale was spelled out explicitly in the responses to our questions concerning the number of defects per KLOC and the number of minor errors in specified development units and modules. In view of this, we conclude that the noteworthy improvement in this area had come about through the interplay between the introduction of unit and iterative testing as featured and emphasised by Scrum.

Table 2. Scrum's impact on quality

Quality	Improvement	Impact on quality	Score Range
Defects per KLOC	2.7	3.2	1 - 4
No of integration errors	0	0.6	-2 - 2
No of minor errors	1.9	1.9	0 - 4
End product usability	0	0	0 - 0

The respondents had not perceived any improvement with regard to the number of integration errors. The minimal increase of the impact on quality, according to respondents, was an outcome of the participation of staff from different professional areas and different sub-projects in the sprint meetings and their resulting increased understanding of the product under development. In addition, individual respondents believed that although the level of complexity and the number of interfaces between modules had increased, the constant number of integration errors indicated that quality had not been impaired; on the contrary, they saw this as a positive effect on the resulting quality. No change was perceived concerning the overall useability of the end product. However, in the absence of the possibility to access customers and end users, questions relating to this indicator were posed to employees in leadership roles, who admitted that the organisation in the future, beyond representatives from the service department, had to include customers directly into the development process to both improve useability and to make informed judgements about it.

5.3   Scrum's Impact on Employee Satisfaction

Table 3 summarizes the respondents' assessment of Scrum's impact on employee satisfaction. The examination of the concept shows both areas where respondents had experienced positive changes, but also areas where the situation was largely unchanged.

The latter proved to be the case in the assessment of overtime. Some respondents felt that this area had improved for two reasons. First of all, there had been a relief that Scrum had not led to the amount of overtime work that the individual respondents had feared. In addition, Scrum had made it more fun to work, which diverted attention from overtime. Common to most respondents concerning this indicator was, however, that the reorganization of work processes had a neutralizing effect on the negative perception of overtime.

Table 3. Scrum's impact on employee satisfaction

Employee satisfaction	Improvement	Impact on employee satisfaction	Score Range
Overtime	0.4	0.9	0 - 5
Project progress	2.2	2.0	0 - 4
Communication	1.7	1.3	-3 - 4
Feedback	0.8	1.3	0 - 3
Social life	1.9	2.1	0 - 4
Work pleasure	2.8	3	-2 - 5

With regard to the possibilities to track, monitor, and follow a project's progress the respondents perceived a clear improvement. With the exception of a few, most respondents highlighted the role of product backlogs in their responses. The majority of the respondents felt that using backlogs was rewarding, but at the same time, they found them cumbersome to work with because of a, at times, paucity of clarity and transparency which were explained with a lack of experience with this tool and expected to disappear in the future.

In relation to the assessment of lines of communication, the respondents were divided into two factions. Those in leadership roles felt there had been a deterioration since the transparency of who at management level was associated with the various Scrum teams had become blurred and elusive. In contrast, respondents in developer roles had the perception that the communication paths had clearly improved. The reason for this was that as part of the Scrum implementation clearer guidelines had been put in place about the ways any communication should take in case of problems; in addition the introduction of Scrum of Scrums had improved communication across the different teams. Concerning the amount of feedback there had not been a notable change. One respondent however put strongly forward that the amount of feedback had indeed increased, which explains the positive mean value of both the perceived improvement and its impact on the indicator.

When respondents were asked to assess the social life in the Scrum teams, most of them responded that they saw an improvement in this respect. The improvement had been achieved because professional and disciplinary boundaries between the different roles had been broken down and because staff were now sitting together in an open office landscape. Finally, pleasure of work or job satisfaction was the indicator which by far received the most top scorings of all indicators – the largest number of '5 scores'. All but one respondent felt that Scrum had supported the elevation of job satisfaction. Breaking tasks down in smaller bites, cross disciplinary collaboration and increased process clarity and transparency of the development process and the product under development had all together contributed to this perceived improvement.

6   Discussion

On this background, in the following we contrast our empirical data with the literature on agile information systems and software development and in particular the identified writings about Scrum.

6.1   Empirical Findings on Productivity and the Agile Development Literature

There are a number of areas that impact on productivity; according to the Scrum and agile development literature, which we reviewed for this research, these are: sprints, a focus on functional software, retrospectives, self-organization, the product backlog and the daily scrum meetings.

The iterative sprint development process [3] plays a central role in the use of Scrum. In the case unit, sprints had made it easier to comply to deadlines as tasks were now decomposed in smaller manageable items with clear definitions, which allowed for their easier handling and execution. These results are confirmed in empirical work reported by among others Augstine et al. [24], Vidgen and Wang [25] as well as Wang and Vidgen [26]. Scrum's increased focus on iterative delivery of functional software should according to the literature increase productivity while avoiding falling into endless development cycles in an attempt to develop the 'perfect piece' of software [17]. This was the effect Scrum had on the case unit, which thus was an area where the method lived up to the expectation.

Retrospectives are intended to increase the productivity among others as a result of the project participants' learning from their own and others' mistakes, so that errors and faults are not repeated in the next sprint or iteration. Retrospectives should address both, the overall application of the method, its processes and practices, but also the more specific experience in the daily development work and its relation to the resulting product [4]. The latter turned out to be an area the case unit did not focus on and thus did not benefit from in their daily work. This prioritization of topics discussed during retrospectives can be explained with the case unit's early stage of utilizing Scrum and their lack of experience with regular retrospectives. In the case organization this area should therefore get further attention with an increased focus on Scrum's practices to support learning. Self-organization in a Scrum team has among others the objective to protect and relieve individual team members from certain tasks and create an environment where they are not constantly disturbed in their work. In a successfully self-organized team, everyone has insights into the other team members' tasks, while at the same time a Scrum master is clearly identified and appointed [3]. This means that when there is a need for input from a specific team member, the other team members are not unnecessarily disturbed, as the tasks have been clearly defined, broken down and distributed. If in doubt, the Scrum master is available to facilitate or solve the problem. At the case unit this had not yet been fully achieved, which meant that employees were still interrupted and disturbed in their work and further efforts will be needed to progress. However, one of the benefits of the Scrum master role had been achieved already: the respondents expressed that the interruptions now came from the right person.

In the literature the avoidance of repeating errors is ascribed to retrospectives. As discussed above in the case unit retrospectives had not yet been applied to their full potential, yet the perception of the respondents had been that the repetition of errors had drastically decreased. This was attributed to the influence that self-organization had. As a consequence of the increased individual developer's responsibility now, team members had become more mindful not to repeat the same mistakes. Individual and collective mindfulness have been reported as characteristics of agile development independently of a particular method or agile practice [27]. This supports that the lack of exploiting retrospectives in the case organization has been compensated by self-organization and mindfulness to lead to a positive outcome with regard to avoiding the repetition of mistakes.

In the case organization the introduction of a product backlog had primarily an effect on compliance with deadlines. As the work was now broken down to single items, there were ongoing opportunities to check whether the agreed schedule was met. Additionally, there was now the possibility to prioritize and plan the order of executing the items in an appropriate manner, which according to the literature (see e.g. [3]) further increases the overall productivity. The introduction of a product backlog at the case unit had affected both of these areas positively, and thus the overall productivity. Product backlogs can also be used to plan a specific test, debugging and error correction period in form of a dedicated item for these tasks [4]. In the case unit this did not lead directly to a reduction of the time spent on bug fixing, but it had resulted in bug fixing happening at a more appropriate point in time, which ultimately had had an impact on productivity.

Finally, daily Scrum meetings, have among others the objective to create visibility in a Scrum team. This helps that everyone in a team gains insight into what the others are working on and at the same time it makes it difficult for employees to conceal modest work efforts, since they publically have to communicate and document their results [3]. The latter had a substantial impact on employee performance in the case unit. It affected productivity positively as openly explaining why as task took longer than expected had the psychological effect that it deprived the employees of the opportunity to hide behind a task longer than necessary. In addition, the meetings had both a positive and negative impact on the number of uninterrupted development hours. The increased number of meetings had reduced the amount of uninterrupted development hours. This was outweighed, however, by the fact that the meetings created better visibility, oversight and knowledge. This allowed employees to tackle unforeseen challenges better, which had a positive effect on productivity as waste time was avoided.

6.2   Empirical Findings on Quality and the Agile Development Literature

The Scrum measures, which have an influence on quality, are according to the reviewed literature: the Scrum team, the Scrum team's maturity, the sprints and the sprint reviews.

A well-functioning Scrum team raises the quality of the end product through its interdisciplinary cooperation, its team dynamics and its utilization of self-organization [3]. Based on the respondents' assessments we can conclude that case unit had managed to exploit these areas as there had been a noticeable improvement in the decrease of the number of defects per KLOC and of the number of minor errors. A Scrum team's maturity also contributes to the improvement of quality; it affects quality through increasing the mutual understanding within the team and by raising the level of self-organization [12]. Scrum was a relatively new initiative of the case unit, and our results showed that the Scrum team had so far only achieved a limited degree of maturity, especially with regard to reaching out beyond the team boundaries. This was probably one of the main reasons that there had been no significant improvements in either the number of integration errors and end product usability.

A change of the development process to sprints can affect quality in several areas [3]. The largest impact on quality happens through a change to a process where analysis, design, programming and testing activities are not performed separately, but in parallel during defined periods of time. The case unit had performed its first iterative development cycles with Scrum as classic 30-day sprints. After a period, learning from their own practice concerning a sustainable rhythm of work, the unit decided to run 14-day sprints. This led to a further refinement and decomposition of the tasks the team and its individual members were working on, and an even greater focus on the delivery of functional software. Both actions, according to respondents, helped to reduce the number of defects per KLOC and the number of minor errors, which had a positive impact on the product quality as a whole.

According to the literature [3] a sprint review meeting should be held at the end of each sprint. At this meeting customers have the opportunity to interact directly with the development team. Quality can be raised as customers at these meetings have the opportunity to provide input, feedback, but also objections and change requests. The latter may be the case if, according to the customer there has been too big a discrepancy between the agreed sprint goal and the developed software. Before the meeting ends any disagreements should be discussed and resolved [3]. The case unit had in this area not utilized customer and user involvement as intended by the method. One possible explanation for not involving customers to a larger extent could be that the case organization was concerned that individual incoming requests would be too diverse to be fully integrated in the standard information system under development. Another reason could simply be a lack of experience with customer involvement, a deficiency the organisation intends to resolve in the future. The lack of user involvement was one of the main reasons that the perception of end product usability remained unchanged despite the implementation of Scrum. The case unit might experience better results in terms of final product usability, as the Scrum team becomes more mature in the use of the method and thus learns which actions, processes and tools, likely including active and direct customer participation, are best suited for them. In any case the case unit has to consider a change of practice in the way customers will be involved in the development process to make the most of Scrum.

6.3   Empirical Findings on Employee Satisfaction and the Agile Development Literature

According to the reviewed literature the measures that have an impact on employee satisfaction are: sprints, Scrum master, Scrum teams, Scrum of Scrums, product backlog, and burn down charts.

The change to a defined development process, in the form of 14-day sprints, had an influence on employee satisfaction in the case unit. Schwaber and Beedle [3] put forward that at the end of each sprint there should be a defined piece of developed and tested functional software. They highlight that it is up to the team itself to judge and decide how much work needs to be performed in a sprint to reach the agreed sprint goal. In the case unit the short and iterative development cycles had the effect that the employees found their work more satisfying and enjoyable. They therefore did not consider overtime as something necessarily negative. We can conclude although the case unit with regard to functional software - not every sprint ended with such a result yet - did not fully follow Schwaber and Beedle's [3] advice, this had no negative consequences, on the contrary the case unit actually experienced progress with regard to employee satisfaction, specifically increased job satisfaction and pleasure of work, due to the utilisation of sprints and the reorganization of the development processes. This effect corresponded well with what the literature suggests as potential improvement.

According to Schwaber and Beedle [3], the introduction of sprints also alleviates the social life and communal atmosphere in the teams as employees encounter progress and success due to the frequent delivery of a functional product at the end of each sprint. The case unit had commenced to celebrate milestones and started to experience these effects, however thus far not to the extent predicted by Schwaber and Beedle [3].

The Scrum master also plays a significant role in employee satisfaction. Schwaber and Beedle [3] emphasize that clearer guidelines concerning the lines of communication involving the Scrum master, as well as an active protection of the Scrum team through this role from unnecessary disturbances, both are actions that contribute to increasing employee satisfaction. The case unit had followed the recommendation from the literature and established Scrum masters and communication guidelines, which resulted in a positive outcome evidenced by the respondents' answers concerning the lines of communication. It is however important to emphasize that the improvement of communication links were only perceived at the Scrum team level and not at a senior level beyond the Scrum masters. As the case organization becomes more familiar and accustomed to the use of Scrum, Schwaber and Beedle [3] argue that management will also experience these improvements.

Concerning team structures the respondents repeatedly mentioned that the destruction of disciplinary boundaries and the gathering of team members in the Scrum teams with different professional background had contributed positively to their perceptions of employee satisfaction. This is an intended effect of interdisciplinary Scrum teams [3]. Self-organization as part of Scrum teams' governance contributed to the respondents' favourable assessment. On this background we can conclude that the case unit has been able to benefit from the composition of their Scrum teams. This is also manifested through the respondents' positive statements regarding the indicators social life and work pleasure.

Scrum of Scrums should be used in large, complex development projects where several Scrum teams are associated [4]. The idea behind the Scrum of Scrums is to ensure the sharing and exploitation of the potential knowledge that exists between different Scrum teams. The responses we received document that the way the case unit had chosen to use Scrum of Scrums had affected the lines of communication between the teams in a positive direction despite the fact that no clear guidelines for this particular communication activity had been developed by the case unit.

Although it remained unclear whether the case unit used Scrum of Scrums, as the literature recommended it, the use of Scrum of Scrums did not only contribute to improve communication lines in general, but also had a positive influence on the ability to monitor project progress. The interaction between the Scrum teams raised the common understanding of the individual Scrum team's status, where they positioned themselves as compared to the other teams and with regard to the development process of the overall product.

Schwaber [4] argues that the product backlog is one of the most important tools in Scrum as breaking down the development tasks to more tangible and manageable size and to increase their visibility is essential for a well functioning product backlog. The case unit has had difficulties with the utilisation and exploitation of the product backlog: the employees felt that the product backlog was unmanageable and cumbersome to work with. This indicates that they did not use the product backlog as proposed by f. ex. Schwaber and Beedle [3]. Nevertheless, they also felt that the product backlog had helped to improve their ability to monitor project progress as there had been no monitoring tool for this before the Scrum implementation. In the context of product backlogs, another tool, namely a burn down chart is intended to provide information about the development work. Depending on the status of the burn down chart it is the Scrum master's responsibility to adjust the number of hours available for the unfinished development tasks, so that the team can reach the sprint goal on time [4]. Although the case unit used burn down charts, it was surprising that no respondents mentioned that this had contributed to any improvement with regard to monitoring and following project progress. A possible explanation could be that the respondents were not yet fully aware of the difference and the different roles the product backlog and the burn down charts play in a Scrum managed development process. This did however not have negative effects on the respondents' overall positive perception of employee satisfaction.

7   Conclusion and Contribution

We have applied Schryen's [1] taxonomy of IS business value as an analytical and structuring device and demonstrate its overall viability. We identified and studied different types of performance measurements in particular productivity, quality and employee satisfaction as value creating measures and provide a useful operationalization of the concepts through 17 indicators. Our positive assessment of Scrum through these measures for the value and impact of information systems and software development confirms empirically the expectations and claims, which are made in many of the conceptual and non-academic writings we had identified in our literature review. It also fills a gap in the area of empirical studies of the value and impact of agile software development [11].

Our study is built upon subjective perceptions; as with all qualitative studies of this kind we of course have to take the danger of positive bias and a respondents' tendency of reporting future expectations rather than stating actual perceptions into account. However, the fact that the respondents reported no or only minimal impact on some of the indicators gives confidence that the reported efforts were genuine rather than showing a general positive bias. In doing so, we however follow Schryen's [1] call and go beyond hard measures and indicators. While it might be argued that our results lack the objective strength of economic value measured in monetary revenue, they provide insights about individual and organisational impact, benefits and values as perceived by the different stakeholders. We take into account internal capabilities which are usually out of scope of the value considerations, and regard the normally disregarded subjective preferences of stakeholders. We investigate an IS business value generation process within its context and environment, in our case agile development, which usually is ignored.

While not making up for a lack of a theory of IS business value our discussion sheds light on the value generation process and the measures we present deal with some of the deficiencies in current IS business value research and contribute to filling gaps in the research agenda as put forward by Schryen [1]. His distinction of internal and external value was helpful, the distinction of tangible and intangible is however not that easy to apply. While productivity is overly linked to tangible value and employee satisfaction is clearly linked to intangible value, elements of quality are both tangible and intangible. The work presented here is a first contribution to solving the identified challenges, however further research is needed to understand the IS business value and IS value in general.

References

1. Schryen, G.: Revisiting IS business value research: What we already know, what we still need to know, and how we can get there. EJIS 22(2), 139–169 (2013)
2. Johansen, T., Uldahl, A.: Measuring the Impact of the Implementation of the Project Management Method Scrum. MSc Thesis. Copenhagen Business School, Denmark (2012) (in Danish)
3. Schwaber, K., Beedle, M.: Agile Software Development with Scrum. Prentice Hall, Upper Saddle River (2002)
4. Schwaber, K.: Agile Project Management with Scrum. Microsoft Press, Redmond (2004)
5. Webster, J., Watson, R.T.: Analyzing the Past to Prepare for the Future: Writing a Literature Review. MISQ 26(2), 13–23 (2002)
6. Kohli, R.: Business value of IT: An essay on expanding research directions to keep up with the times. J. AIS 9(1), 23–39 (2008)
7. DeLone, W.H., McLean, E.R.: Information systems success: The quest for the dependent variable. ISR 3(1), 60–95 (1992)
8. DeLone, W.H., McLean, E.R.: The DeLone and McLean model of information systems success: A ten-year update. J. of MIS 19(4), 9–30 (2003)
9. Brynjolfsson, E., Hitt, L.: Paradox lost? Firm-level evidence on the returns to information systems spending. Mgt Science 42(4), 541–558 (1996)
10. Moe, N.B, Dingsøyr, T.: Scrum and Team Effectiveness: Theory and Practice. In: Abrahamsson, P., Baskerville, R., Conboy, K., Fitzgerald, B., Morgan, L., Wang, X. (eds.) XP 2008. LNBIP, vol. 9, pp. 11–20. Springer, Heidelberg (2008)
11. Dybå, T., Dingsøyr, T.: Empirical studies of agile software development: A systematic review. Inf. & Soft. Tech. 50(9-10), 833–859 (2008)
12. Guang-Yong, H.: Study and Practice of Import Scrum Agile Software Development. In: Int. IEEE Conf. on Communication Software and Networks, Nanjing, China. IEEE Press, New York (2011)

13. Appelo, J.: Management 3.0 - Leading agile Developers, Developing agile Leaders. Addison-Wesley, Crawfordsville (2010)

14. Mahnic, V., Vrana, I.: Using stakeholder-driven process performance measurement for monitoring the performance of a Scrum-based software development process. El.-Tech. Rev. 74(5), 241–247 (2007)

15. Mahnic, V., Zabkar, N.: Using COBIT Indicators for Measuring Scrum-based Software Development. WSEAS Trans. on Comp. 7(10), 1605–1617 (2008)

16. Sutherland, J., Altman, I.: Organizational Transformation with Scrum: How a Venture Capital Group Gets Twice as Much Done with Half the Work. In: 43rd HICCS. Kauai (2010)

17. Moore, R., Reff, K., Graham, J., Hackerson, B.: Scrum at a Fortune 500 Manufacturing Company. In: Agile Conference. St. Paul (2007)

18. Thatcher, M.E., Pingry, D.E.: An economic model of product quality and IT value. ISR 15(3), 268–286 (2004)

19. Thatcher, M.E., Pingry, D.E.: Understanding the business value of information technology investments: Theoretical evidence from alternative market and cost structures. J. of MIS 21(2), 61–85 (2004)

20. Devaraj, S., Kohli, R.: Information technology payoff in the health-care industry: A longitudinal study. J. of MIS 16(4), 41–67 (2000)

21. Mann, C., Maurer, F.: A Case Study on the Impact of Scrum on Overtime and Customer Satisfaction. In: Agile Development Conference, pp. 70–79. IEEE Computer Society (2005)

22. Green, P.: Measuring the Impact of Scrum on Product Development at Adobe Systems. In: 44th HICSS. Kauai (2011)

23. Andersen, I.: The apparent Reality (in Danish). Samfundslitteratur Publisher, Frederiksberg (2006)

24. Augustine, S., Payne, B., Sencindiver, F., Woodcock, S.: Agile project management: Steering from the edges. Comm. of the ACM 48(12), 85–89 (2005)

25. Vidgen, R., Wang, X.: Organizing for Agility: A Complex Adaptive Systems Perspective on Agile Software Development Process. In: Ljunberg, J., Andersson, M. (eds.) 14th ECIS, pp. 1316–1327. Gothenburg (2006)

26. Wang, X., Vidgen, R.: Order and Chaos in Software Development: A comparison of two software development teams in a major IT company. In: Winter, R., et al. (eds.) 16th ECIS, pp. 807–818. St. Gallen (2007)

27. Matook, S., Kautz, K.: Mindfulness and Agile Software Development. In: 19th ACIS, pp. 638–647. Christchurch (2008)

A Creative and Useful Tension?
Large Companies Using "Bring Your Own Device"

Don Kerr[1] and Christian Koch[2]

[1] University of the Sunshine Coast, Maroochydore, Queensland, Australia
dkerr@usc.edu.au
[2] Chalmers University of Technology, Göteborg, Sweden
christian.koch@chalmers.se

Abstract. This paper looks at processes of embedding of computer systems in four organisational case studies in three different countries. A selective literature study of implementation of computer systems leads the authors to suggest that seen from a top down managerial perspective employees may be assumed to accept and use new computer systems, for example an ERP system but what happens deep down in the organisation are a reshaping, domestication or appropriation of the software for example through developing workarounds. The authors further suggest that traditional implementation models may incorrectly assume that the computer systems has been embedded in the organisation because things appear to be running smoothly when in fact software and/or processes have been reshaped by employees to suit their local needs. These social shapings appear to be done for a multitude of reasons. However, from the qualitative case studies it appears that most workarounds are done to make work easier and/or to overcome perceived inflexibilities in existing enterprise mandated systems. The ubiquitous access to cloud technologies and an increasing workforce of tech savy "digital natives" using their own devices (BYOD) has exacerbated the situation.

Keywords: Domestication, Adoption, Bring your own device (BYOD), Management of IT.

1 Introduction

There are strong indications from the literature [1], [2] that employees are developing IT artefacts or just software elements outside the accepted ICT infrastructure of their organization, usually as a workaround to existing systems. In the past, this has been controlled to some extent, as these developments have been confined to corporately condoned software applications. While these artefacts or software functionalities have caused some concern to centralized IT departments, they have been able to be accessed from time to time and this has usually resulted in a purge of these systems. In this paper we are referring to these workarounds as feral information systems (FIS), based on the work of [2]. These audits of FIS have resulted in a better understanding of what people have developed and why they were developed it and

B. Bergvall-Kåreborn and P.A. Nielsen (Eds.): TDIT 2014, IFIP AICT 429, pp. 166–178, 2014.

why decisions are made whether to keep the system or remove them. However, we contend that given the greater access to the internet and cloud computing and the increasing number apps available for use by anyone as well as the large number of employees who now have their own devices, the game is changing and IT departments are finding it harder to exercise the same amount of control over FIS applications as they have in the past.

We suggest that this represents a major paradigm shift for corporate computer technology in both usage and how these 'innovations' affect corporate IT governance and systems security. The large-scale adoption of devices such as iPads and smartphones for example, has shown that individuals from Generation Y are very quick to digest new computer technologies and systems. In many cases these "digital natives" are very "techno-savvy" and not only want to use the technology they want to "create with it" [3], page 41. They are continually customising how they gather and share information [3] and in many cases are able to adapt software they know about to their own work situation. However, whether this adaptation is in the best interests of the organization can be debated. There may well be advantages with respect to greater agility for the organization and this could lead to innovation, however there could also be problematic situations with unbridled use without proper controls leading to errors in software outputs and subsequent reporting. Examples of this can be shown in work by [4] who showed that user developed Excel spreadsheets had many errors.

The title of this paper infers differentiation between characteristic manners/ways of implementing of software and in this context, domestication [5, 6] is defined as a process in which actors shape technology, even when supposed to merely consume it. Here we use domestication as term for employees shaping software in a way that allows them to do their task on their own device, at their own place and in their own time (home, on the road, or at work). Domestication appears as an unstructured customization of software at the level of tasks relevant to the employee or his/her workgroup and limited to an individual's IT expertise. Managerial controlled implementation on the other hand is a structured customization at the process level of an organization and is related to the IT expertise of the organization's implementation group [7] [8]. Therefore we contend that the domesticated computer technology to fit the task is in contrast to the managed implementation models presented in the past and this may require a re-think on how effective the managed implementation models are in today's ever changing, cloud based world. Therefore the research questions we pose in this paper are:

1. How comprehensive are managed implementation models examined in the light of the new environment of internet based applications and cloud computing?

2. How does this new trend influence IT management in organizations?

This paper is divided into the following sections. The next section is a selective literature review looking at domestication and how it relates to this research. The next section identifies inconsistencies in the managed implementation models predictive capabilities, this followed by an analysis of the domestication process couched in terms of a paradigm shift to BYOD.

2   Literature Review

The reshaping of software through newer technologies such as cloud computing and ubiquitous access was not considered when the various variants of technology implementation models were first devised and subsequently modified. The traditional view has been that the adoption of technology has been an important aspect of enterprise wide systems implementation with information systems being considered to be effective and efficient tools to gain organizational competitiveness [7, 8]. However for quite some time and continually reactualized an important question has been "why have sufficient results not been achieved in spite of the fact that the organization has made huge investments in information technology?" [9, 10, 11, 12].

This has opened an avenue of research which seeks to evaluate the information systems from different perspectives. [13] suggest that the way computers have been used has changed substantially over time and a much broader range of people are using computers. This extends to knowledge workers who now have the ability to work from home using increasingly sophisticated computing equipment that enables them to modify and/or develop applications to help them with their work. One such perspective on this is the concept of Domestication [5, 6, 14], domestication involves "taking technologies and objects home, and in making, or not making, them acceptable and familiar." [14], page 45.

However [14] also suggest that the term not be limited to the home and that domestication should have a wider relevance and this is further expanded upon by [6, 15] with an up dated definition, namely "Domestication is defined as processes whereby people encounter the technologies and deal with them, either rejecting the technologies or fitting them into their everyday routines" [6, 15]. It is this wider relevance, namely the development of new artefacts or the modification of or even complete rejection of corporately condoned IT artefacts that we discuss in this paper. These developments or modifications can be done equally at home or at the workplace, however we suggest that the increasing use of bring your own devices (BYOD) and cloud computing has given employees more flexibility to undertake these projects.

[13] have also provided another perspective that fits within our research propositions, namely the thoughts and actions of the end user. Silverstone and Haddon suggest that "Users are not just technical users" [13], page 45 and that manufacturers refuse to accept that the user is not a impassionate user of the technology but in many cases an enthusiastic, engaged individual who wants to do the job effectively using the tools provided in a way that suits their own unique style. However the ability to engage with the technology in other, more diverse ways is denied due to the inflexibility of the IT system. We contend that it is this lack of flexibility that leads end users to develop new artefacts or modify existing systems.

The concept of domestication has also been used in other areas such as with students on a wireless network using laptop computers [14]. In this case aspects of how students domesticated their personal laptop computers on a wireless campus were investigated. It was found that it was important that students were able to configure the computer to be compatible with their own individual learning experience and that the computer needs to be more than a tool for learning but an integral part of the student's digital environment. The authors suggested that the best test of successful domestication was how comfortable the student was with their use of IT. In summary, [14] concluded that domestication of individual personal laptops was an important consideration to ensure student's felt comfortable with IT and enhanced their learning experience. We therefore suggest that there is a natural inclination for people (students and employees) to want to modify inflexible IT artefacts to suit their own personalized requirements.

2.1 Evidence of Domestication Rather than Managed Implementation of Software in the Workplace

Several case studies have been conducted in the area of understanding why end users develop workarounds (in this context called Feral Information systems – see [16] in order to shape their work with the workplace information systems rather than completely adopting the system as intended by the corporation at the time of implementation. We suggest that this is a form of domestication in that it provides end users with enough flexibility to allow them to use the system (apparent adoption) yet only use components they are comfortable with or to circumvent components they do not understand or are uncomfortable with.

3   Method of Analysis

In order to test the level of domestication in a business setting, four case studies designed to investigate workarounds are reported in this paper. The objective was to provide insights into the social aspects of ICT usage in a mandated ICT environment. The case study approach [17], [18] was selected and qualitative methods were used as the investigation centred on exploring how stakeholders accommodated their ICT usage to "get the job done". As we were concerned with organizational rather than technical issues, the case method [17] was considered highly appropriate for our purposes. All four case studies took an explorative approach since the adaptation of the mandated ICT was considered to be local and emergent rather than a priori. Therefore the approach to understanding is primarily abductive, looking to existing theories to provide plausible explanations but not aiming to build or test theory. The cases were all qualitative in nature and included Australian, United Kingdom and Danish organizations and business. Table 1 shows the details of research undertaken.

Table 1. Overview of the case studies

Case Pseudonym	Location	Type of Enterprise	Interviews
TRANS	Australia	Transport company	15
UNI	Australia	Tertiary Education	4
DOT	United Kingdom	A UK training organisation associated with a UK University	13
SUP	Denmark	A large supermarket	5

With all these cases, the research approach was the same; namely an interpretative case study approach [19], [20]. Interviews were conducted with key decision makers in each of the 4 cases described (see table 1). The interview transcripts were analysed for relevant themes using the software package Leximancer.

Transcripts from research conducted on all four research locations have been used to gain some insights to the domestication of existing information systems from a variety of perspectives and cultures. The following extracts from transcripts demonstrate the various examples of how end users attempt to shape technology to suit their own work needs rather than attempt to adopt the technology as expected by the organization.

4   Case 1 – TRANS

This case is about the domestication of existing technology in a heavily industrialized (transport corporation) setting. It describes workarounds or FIS and how employees have used domestication of ICT to make changes to existing systems to suit their own needs.

There were many examples of the potential to develop workarounds through the domestication of various technologies in this organization. For example; there appeared to be extensive work around of technology through the use of applications other than the mandated system (in this case the enterprise system, SAP). This is confirmed through statements by workers (in this case an engineer) such as "… we've got a diary that tracks all material usage on a daily basis so it will have on there [the IT system] how [much product] we unloaded today so Bruce will come in write in the diary in that section, how many items of [product] he does. That diary then goes into a database internally within here and onto a spreadsheet…" These databases and spreadsheets were developed internally and away from the SAP system. They were examples of domestication of technology to either supplement the SAP system or replace it. This domestication uses traditional technology (Spreadsheets on workplace computers), however the expectation is that more technology aware employees will accommodate the speadsheet to a cloud based application in the future to enable more remote applications of the technology.

In another example an employee expanded on a common theme throughout this research, namely the perceived need for a complete analysis of SAP and its role within the organization, for example the quote "Better metrics needed – that is better ways to apply models of analysis etc." indicate a degree of discontent with the organisation and the ERP implementation and a possible lead into software domestication further down the track. Other cases included the entry of data into a spreadsheet before it was entered into SAP. This quote is from a manager in TRANS "So the new approach is to vet the data first in an Excel spreadsheet and only load into SAP what is valid catalogued material and I see that as a good process because we are not putting rubbish into SAP. Everything that gets put in has been vetted and approved." This process may be a valid approach but it still involves the development of another system (a spreadsheet) to effectively use the mandated SAP system. There is not the same level of quality control in user developed spreadsheets as there is in the SAP system and this could end up being a data quality problem further down the track.

5   Case 2 – UNI

This case is about the concerns management have about the domestication of technology in an academic setting. It describes the concerns management have about these processes and the security issues they have to contend with.

The university case was based on questioning security issues and how employee computer usage (access to the cloud and software) affected the governance and security of the organization. The transcripts reflected the views of the information technology manager's perspective on security and cloud computing and three people were interviewed at the same time. They were the Director of information technology services, the manager of Information Technology Services (ITS) and the ICT Infrastructure Team Leader and data security manager.

The director of security for ITS considered security to be very important for the university with the introductory statement suggesting that "The most fundamental aspect of security is accountability through the audit function of the institution, we are held responsible for the custodianship of financial data" and …"ICT security at the most fundamental level in terms of being audited as an organisation". The Director further asserts that "The place that the auditors will go is IT to determine how secure the financial data is…. This is extended to all assets associated with the university's core business" She then posed the question "Does increased use of non-corporate cloud based applications affect the organization's ability to provide auditable secure financial data?"

The Data manager suggested that a major challenge for the University was maintaining information security in a mobile world and this is not so much the technology but the behaviour pattern of staff and students. He went on to ask the question "How do we know if the person accessing the information is the person they claim to be?

The director went on to suggest that cloud computing is the next threat because although systems can be locked down within your own environment, the problem is the accountability the University has when a service that is not housed on the campus. IT staff have no capability to control over what is done "in the cloud" by academic staff and students. The director was concerned that nothing is done about "the cloud" until there is a security problem and then it is fixed but the industry is always in catch-up mode.

This case example demonstrates the concern the centralized IT function has with respect to employees and students adapting technology to suit their own requirements. The industry appears to be always in "catch up mode".

6   Case 3 – DOT

This case provides an example of how a lack of feedback and potential misunderstandings leads to employees want to undertake domestication of an ICT artefact (namely an Excel spreadsheet). The end user is in a difficult situation as he wants to make changes (domestication) but could find even more difficulty and misunderstandings if he did. In this case the end user needs to accept the existing situation and not change things despite the flaws in the software that he has identified.

The accommodation of technology to "fit" within the existing system was prevalent in this organization. For example, the deputy director of DOT had concerns about the financial system and how the lack of feedback was particularly problematic for him. He stated that "Financial systems are an example where the financial information is entered and stored and managed by a separate finance department ...... They give us a printout which is designed to suit their purposes and not necessarily designed to suit our purposes in managing the team ....The finance department have produced an outline spreadsheet which is very course in the way that the data is presented so we have short courses that we budget so much – then they ask us "does that look OK?" and we don't know what assumptions underpin that particular number {and] what courses are included [and] what the associated risk of these courses. Does it include courses that are 100% certain to run or does it include aspirations and to what level so our interpretation of that can be difficult – it could also mean that other department's interpretations can be different to ours which means that they're not getting a good picture of what our financial situation is and as a result we are not getting the right information in which to manage our activities to best effect to deliver the financial performance targets of [DOT]". [Deputy Director of DOT]

This is an example of the frustration expressed about systems lacking in feedback capability and how the continued use of the existing system is more acceptable solution rather than the adoption of a flawed system (at least perceived to be flawed by the respondent).

7   Case 4 – SUP

This case study is an example of a generation Y employee simply downloading an application that can do a job that his employer did not provide software for. This is an example of creating new software through domestication; in this case an understanding of what software could do the job and make his work a little easier.

The e-business manager of a large supermarket chain in Denmark provided an excellent example of his domestication of existing software. His example involved the downloading of software from the Internet. He elaborated "...downloaded from the Internet as you could say public software available on the Internet that we download and integrate with our own systems in order to have an easier day. An example of that, we have our Notes calendar and email. So, calendar, as today my meetings are wall to wall, all morning. So, I'm very dependent on knowing where to go next and at this point of time the business or the organisation doesn't offer [an] electronic calendar that you could carry around. We only have the calendar here. But in 2012 it's pretty convenient to have the calendar on your mobile phone. So, when the organisation doesn't offer that, what do we do? It's only top management who has this feature. So, middle management like me and a lot of my colleagues, we find [a] work-around. It's not authorised, but we do it anyway. So, I downloaded this application here called AweSync. It's a product that can take my Notes ID Calendar here and put it into my Google account. Okay? So, when it's on Google Calendar, I can set up my smartphone and that I can hook up with Google. So, now I have an updated calendar on my phone with business information."

This demonstrates a situation where a prevalence of Internet based software makes it easy for end users to extend and thereby domesticate their corporate system to suit their own needs.

8   Lessons Learnt from the Cases

The TRANS case showed examples of domestication of software to fit individual tasks in order to make their work easier (in this case the development of an Excel spreadsheet application). There appeared to be a clear case of SAP not being able to emulate the material usage process within this work group effectively or the task associated with the process was not aligned with the standard approach developed during the implementation and adoption of the SAP software (see table 2). In addition, the statements about looking for "better ways to apply models of analysis" appeared to be a further indication that the SAP system did not fit the requirements of the workgroup. The lessons learnt from this case relate to the people directly involved with specific tasks and how well those tasks reflect the enterprise wide process that the ERP was supposed to cater for (see table 2).

The UNI case provided an example of how IT management were concerned about the domestication process with employees' computer usage possibly effecting governance, security and risk management profiles of the University. The director of IT services considered the IT infrastructure to be a vital component of the University's governance structure and suggested that any audit of any aspect of the University will start at the IT services level and that the university executive needs the system to be accurate and accountable. Therefore the concern about adaptation of software and cloud computing is that there may be some inadvertent or even deliberate attempts to alter the integrity of the IT systems in place. Naturally there are safeguards in place and the technology is very good, however the IT director was more concerned about the behaviour pattern of staff and she posed the question "How do we know if the person accessing the information is the person they claim to be? ". The lessons learnt from this case are related to domestication causing possible concerns about governance, security, privacy, liability and risk management (see table 2).

The DOT case provided an example of the problems with inter-organizational information systems and how an inter-organizational IT application did not provide the required level of detail. This resulted in a temptation to reshape the application to suit the specific requirements of the case study department. Lessons learnt from this case relate to the IT abilities of the individuals concerned. In this particular case the individuals have very limited knowledge and expertise in spreadsheet development and this situation could have led to a risk of inaccurate calculations, inadequate privacy and problematic security (see table 2).

The SUP case provided us with an example of domestication from a true BYOD perspective. In this case the person actually downloaded an app to allow him more flexibility in his appointment scheduler. The lesson learnt from this case is in relation to a requirement for flexibility in tasks and a need for the BYOD ideal of access to his diary and scheduler at any time, any place and on any device. In this particular case it was his smartphone. The implications to security and privacy are unknown at this point in time, however there were no security checks on the software for malware or keyloggers etc.

While the first three case examples may have been related to the workplace environment, they could have equally been achieved under a BYOD environment. For example Excel spreadsheet can be easily developed and/or edited on any device, at any time and at any place. It is entirely possible that these domestications were done at home (!) on an ipad, smartphone or a personally owned notebook computer. In fact it would seem more likely that it was done in a BYOD environment thus allowing for more flexibility and freedom from the pressures of work in a home setting.

9   Domestication: A Paradigm Shift towards Bring Your Own Device (BYOD)

Although domestication has been around for quite some time, we suggest that the concept of BYOD will help accelerate domestication of ICT in businesses. The recent advances in ubiquitous technologies have brought the attention of some businesses into the concept of anywhere, anytime and any device, as a possible promise to reduce cost and seek more efficiency by asking employees to use their own devices and in a time and place they feel most comfortable in with respect to the given task. On the other hand many other businesses are struggling with the BYOD concept due to many factors, associated with the old model of a centralised IT department and the perceived need to have tight IT controls to ensure proper governance structures and to ensure the network is secure. Regardless of how conservative the organization is with respect to governance and security issues, employees from all walks of life and industries are embracing the concept of BYOD because it provides them with benefits such as work satisfaction, and a flexible working environment. This has led to a growing trend among employees looking to gain access to their workplace networks on their own devices, in their own place and at their own time to get their tasks done.

Table 2. Domestication versus Managed implementation

		Domestication	Managed Implementation
School of thought		BYOD: Characteristics - Any time - Any place - Any device	Enterprise software Characteristics: - During working hours - At the place of work - On a work station
Definition of Customization	Who	Individuals or local work groups	Enterprise wide
	What	Tasks	Processes
	How	- unstructured - kept secret	- highly structured - corporately deployed
	IT abilities	IT expertise of employees	IT expertise of implementation group
Implications	Governance	No support of governance processes	Governance processes are strategically supported
	Security	Low level of security	Highly secured (relevant security software and policies are in place etc.)
	Privacy	Determined by individuals	Determined by enterprise policies
	Liability	Individuals' responsibility	Supported by the legal infrastructure of the enterprise
	Risk management	- handled by individuals - reactive	- handled by enterprise - proactive
	Ownership	Who owns the work?	Enterprise wide ownership
	Efficiency	Highly related to the context of development	Highly related to the context of development

Employees, having brought their own devices, may no longer seek corporately purchased technologies, rather they may look for reshaping the given task with the technology that they are already familiar with and use regularly. According to the above described cases and the lessons learned from them, Table 2 provides a comparison between domestication and managed implementations.

10 Discussion

The discussion addresses the two research questions posed. First are managed implementation models comprensive seen in light of BYOD and second what does it mean for IT management. Above the paper has provided examples of how employees use domestication approaches to existing, adopted and usually mandated software to suit their own requirements or download Internet based applications to support their own work related tasks. This trend appears to be much more prevalent over the past few years and we argue that this is possibly due to employers wishing to continue with the implementation of enterprise wide systems that some employees consider inflexible systems. An external factor could be the loose labour market after the global financial crises leading to people needing to stay with existing employment. Whatever the reason, the net effect is that users could be developing workarounds in order to make their job easier and this workaround approach is further facilitated by greater access to cloud computing and other Internet services. In this research we have described the customization process in terms of domestication. We suggest that domestication is becoming more prevalent with increased knowledge of the technology and the BYOD phenomena. We also suggest that managed implementation is related to enterprise wide applications and is mostly done in the work environment by trained IT professionals. On the other hand the domestication process is much less controlled with developments being undertaken by people who may not be professionally trained but have adequate knowledge. This domestication process is likely to occur at home or some other non-work related location.

We suggest that the managed implementation models mentioned in the literature review may have inherent problems as they are not able to cater for this domestication process. In the situations we outlined in our case studies, employees did not actively reject the technology but on the other hand they did not actively adopt it either. The managed implementation model may indicate acceptance and adoption of a certain technology but in fact end users are happily using workarounds, reshaped or alternative technologies in order to get their work done and due to the clandestine nature of many of these systems, they may not be detected by the centralized IT department at all. This domestication rather than managed implementation could in part explain the negative results with respect to technology adoption reported by Legris et al. [21]. However we also suggest that when users do appear to have adopted the technology they might in fact have only reshaped and domesticated it and other technologies to suit their specific job requirements or tasks. It may also be that actors are taking up and shaping technology in order to more fully understand and complete their tasks because of other external factors such as: fears of job security, shifts in global markets, increases in layoffs adversarial relations between employees and management and between employees and the IT-department and other related issues.

In answer to our second question about change in IT management, we suggest that this new world of Techno-savvy, digital natives [3] and their ability to domesticate software to their own requirements needs to be accounted for by managers, IT managers, IT departments and IS researchers. Managers need to be aware of and either stamp out the resultant software domestications or cater for the new approach. There are obvious risks with catering for domesticated technologies (although there may be no other option), for example the domesticated software is only as good as the IT abilities of their author and they may contain errors. Research by McGill [4] demonstrated that spreadsheets in particular can be problematic with respect to end user errors [4]. On the other hand, the domestication of software can bring agility and innovation for the organization and can lead to new ideas and ways of doing business. From an IS research perspective, there appears to be a need to reconsider the domestication of technology to cater for digital natives and their natural affinity to actively shape rather than passively accept the technology. From an organizational perspective, this phenomenon could be particularly problematic if the board and upper management is expecting reports and forecasts to be obtained from the "a single point of truth", namely the implemented ERP system.

The domestication of mandated enterprise systems may also be of concern to centralized IT departments with rigid command and control structures. However if a less rigid structure is adopted, a more flexible workforce could lead to greater agility and innovation for the organization. Companies such as Intel have demonstrated an awareness of this phenomenon through their acknowledgement of a BYOD workplace [22]. Intel has suggested that this is the future of IT and that, by our inference, the domestication of corporate software is here to stay.

10.1 Contribution to Theory and Practice

This paper contributes to domestication theory by providing examples of how employees become unsettled with existing corporately condoned software and develop their own versions through the process of domestication. It also provides a practical link between workarounds, Feral Information systems and domestication of ICT systems in a business environment.

11 Conclusions

The paper set out to answer two questions:

1. How comprehensive are managed implementation models examined in the light of the new environment of internet based applications and cloud computing?
2. How does this new trend influence IT management in organizations?

Although this research is looking at emergent behaviours, we suggest that it does provide enough evidence to suggest that the present implementation models may be lacking in providing an explanation for the domestication process and that this phenomena may be subsumed within the model and simply assumed to be genuine adoption of the technology under study. In this research we are suggesting therefore that the Managed implementation type models be modified to allow for adaptation or domestication of software as another factor in the adoption process.

We suggest, re the first question, that the domestication process should be catered for as mentioned above, the existing technology implementation models may be reporting complete adoption by employees yet many employees may be adapting technology to suit their purposes and giving researchers and management the impression that they have adopted the system completely. This could be a flaw in the model with quite serious repercussions for both the company and the end users if the non-recognized software purchases and/or modifications cause problems further down the track. This is apart from our obvious position of requiring models that can accurately predict outcomes and allow for as many contingencies as appropriate. In this research we are suggesting that an understanding of the nature of software domestication is an important consideration when applying managed implementation models in the real world.

With respect to the second question regarding the influence on IT management, the domestication of corporate software could lead to innovation for the organization, or it could lead to erroneous reporting due to spreadsheet errors or problems with downloaded software (for example). Whatever the case, the domestication of software is here to stay and both managers, IT managers and IS researchers need to be aware of the phenomena and any implications it may have on the organization. In relation to potential errors, it is important that consideration be given to the quality of work that may come from domestication of software by people who do not have a deep understanding of software development processes. Although digital natives may be very familiar with the technology, it does not mean that they are necessarily very good at the process. It may be that they have knowledge a mile wide but only an inch deep and end up developing inappropriate of flawed software. This is an area that could warrant further research.

In concluding our analysis of we argue that there is a need to study the phenomena of technology domestication further. In particular, more research is needed to understand how modern software platforms increase the problems of risk, software adaptation and FIS creation. This research leads to the question, what are the implications of these issues on the modern enterprise? We have argued here that these systems are a natural response given that technology to facilitate these actions is increasingly available through the internet and that the new generation of employee is much more technologically aware of possible digital solutions. However, more research needs to be conducted so we can understand the phenomena of technological domestication better.

References

1. Kerr, D.V., Houghton, L.: Just in time or Just in case: A Case study on the impact of context in ERP implementations. Australian Journal of Information Systems 16(2), 5–16 (2010)
2. Spierings, A., Kerr, D., Houghton, L.: What drives the end user to build a feral information system? In: Proc. of the 23rd Australasian Conference on Information Systems, ACIS, Geelong, Vic., pp. 1–10 (2012)

3. Martin, C.A.: From high maintenance to high productivity: What managers need to know about Generation Y. Industrail and Commercial Training 37(1), 39–44 (2005)

4. McGill, T.: The role of spreadsheet knowledge in user-developed application success. Decision Support Systems 39(3), 355–369 (2005)

5. Lie, M., Sørensen, K. (eds.): Making technology our own? Domesticating technology into everyday life. Scandinavian University Press, Oslo (1996)

6. Haddon, L.: Domestication Analysis, Objects of Study, and the Centrality of Technologies in Everyday Life. Canadian Journal of Communication 36(2), 311–323 (2011)

7. Kale, V.: Implementing Sap R/3: The Guide for Business and Technology Managers. Sams, Indianapolis (2000)

8. Harwood, S.: ERP the implementation cycle. Butterworth Heinemann Oxford (2003)

9. Brynjolfsson, E., Hitt, L.: Beyond the Productivity Paradox: Computers Are The Catalyst For Bigger Changes. Communications of the ACM 41(8), 49–55 (1998)

10. Davenport, T.: Mission Critical: Realizing the promise of Enterprise Systems. Harvard Business School Press, Boston (2000)

11. Flyvbjerg, B., Budzier, A.: Why Your IT Project May Be Riskier Than You Think. Harvard Business Review, 23–25 (September 2011)

12. Sauer, C., Willcocks, L.: Unreasonable expectations - NHS IT, Greek choruses and the games institutions play around mega-programmes. Journal of Information Technology 22(3), 195–201 (2007)

13. Cummings, J.N., Kraut, R.: Domesticating Computers and the Internet. Human-Computer Interaction Institute. Paper 94 (2001), http://repository.cmu.edu/hcii/94 (accessed February 9, 2014)

14. Silverstone, R., Haddon, L.: Design and the Domestication of ICTs: Technical Change and Everyday Life. In: Silverstone, R., Mansell, R. (eds.) Communication by Design: The Politics of Information and Communication Technologies. Oxford University Press, Oxford (1996)

15. Haddon: The Contribution of Domestication Research to In-Home Computing and Media Consumption in The Information Society: An International Journal 22(4) (2006); Special Issue: ICT in Everyday Life: Home and Personal Environments Guest Editor: Alladi Venkatesh

16. Kerr, D., Houghton, L., Burgess, K.: Power relationships that lead to the development of feral systems. Australasian Journal of Information Systems 14(2), 141–152 (2007)

17. Stake, R.: The art of case research. Sage Publications, Thousand Oaks (1995)

18. Yin, R.K.: Case Study Research: Design and Methods. Sage Publications, London (1994)

19. Klein, H.K., Myers, M.D.: A set of principles for conducting and evaluating interpretive field studies in information systems. MIS Quarterly 23(1), 67–94 (1999)

20. Walsham, G.: Interpreting Information Systems in Organizations. John Wiley, Chichester (1993)

21. Legris, P., Ingham, J., Collerette, P.: Why Do People Use Information Technology? A Critical Review of the Technology Acceptance Model. Information & Management 40(3), 191–204 (2003)

22. Intel. Insights into the current state of BYOD Intel's IT manager survey (2012), http://www.intel.com.au/content/www/au/en/mobile-computing/consumerization-enterprise-byod-peer-research-paper.html (accessed April 13, 2013)

What Drives Fitness Apps Usage?
An Empirical Evaluation

Duwaraka Yoganathan and Sangaralingam Kajanan

School of Computing, National University of Singapore, Singapore
{duwaraka,skajanan}@comp.nus.edu.sg

Abstract. The increased health problems associated with lack of physical activity is of great concern around the world. Mobile phone based fitness applications appear to be a cost effective promising solution for this problem. The aim of this study is to develop a research model that can broaden understanding of the factors that influence the user acceptance of mobile fitness apps. Drawing from Unified Theory of Acceptance and Use of Technology (UTAUT) and Elaboration Likelihood Model (ELM), we conceptualize the antecedents and moderating factors of fitness app use. We validate our model using field survey. Implications for research and practice are discussed.

Keywords: Fitness apps, mobile apps, physical activity.

1   Introduction

Increasing sedentary lifestyle has resulted in obesity and overweight. According to World Health Organization, worldwide obesity has more than doubled since 1980 and 3 million deaths from heart disease, diabetes and certain cancers are caused by obesity and overweight. However obesity is preventable.

The current healthcare system does not have sufficient resources to prevent and manage these preventable health risks. Therefore, individual effort is paramount in disease prevention, i.e., managing the risks before they develop into more serious health problems. Regular physical activity can not only help individuals to prevent these health risks, but also would enable them to lead a healthy lifestyle.

Mobile phone based interventions hold promise for healthy behavioral change. As immediacy of consequences to a target behavior is important for behavior modification (Skinner, 1969), using mobile phones for promoting healthy behaviors is more effective. The mobile phones will be in the users' vicinity almost all the time and enable immediate feedback to users' behavior. Smartphones and mobile apps are the latest mobile interventions. Smartphone apps are embedded with sophisticated sensors that could monitor the user's behavior. Therefore mobile apps are a viable cost effective solution for self-health management.

While having recognized the advantages and demands to employ mobile apps in healthcare, healthcare apps have a high dropout rate with 26% of apps being used only once and 74% of apps being discontinued by the tenth use (McLean, 2011). The high churn rate with healthcare apps is concerning to the healthcare practitioners and researchers as Smartphone apps are beginning to play an important role in healthcare.

B. Bergvall-Kåreborn and P.A. Nielsen (Eds.): TDIT 2014, IFIP AICT 429, pp. 179–196, 2014.

Studies related on healthcare apps are still in its infancy. A handful of existing studies provides some insides on mobile apps that can be used to blood glucose control, and smoke cessation programs (Valdivieso-López et al 2013). However, research related to adoption of fitness apps is limited.

Realizing importance of smartphone apps in healthcare, the purpose of this study is to deepen our understanding of the factors that influence tendencies to use fitness apps, which in turn will improve physical activity behavior of users. Drawing from Unified Theory of Acceptance and Use of Technology (UTAUT) and Elaboration Likelihood Model (ELM) we conceptualize our model. A filed survey was conducted to validate our conceptual model.

This paper is organized into six sections including this introduction. The next section surveys the salient literature, from which we draw our constructs for user acceptance of mobile fitness apps. The third section presents the research model and develops the research hypotheses characterizing the relationships depicted in the model. The fourth section describes our research methods, while the fifth discusses the results and their implications for research and practice. The last section summarizes the study's contributions.

2   Theoretical Background

We review literature on IS acceptance, usage, and persuasion to understand the factors of fitness app acceptance and integrate them into a model.

2.1   Unified Theory of Acceptance and Use of Technology (UTAUT)

Venkatesh, et al (2003), developed a unified technology acceptance model by synthesizing the elements of eight different theories. This model conceptualizes that performance expectancy, effort expectancy, social influences, and facilitating conditions as important antecedents for the intention to use and subsequently the IT usage behavior. We have chosen UTAUT as theoretical lens for our study, because it a unified theory that includes concepts from various technology acceptance theories such as theory of reasoned action, technology acceptance model, motivational model, theory of planned behavior, a combined theory of planed behavior/technology acceptance model. Thus UTAUT can better explain the adoption of fitness apps.

In addition to the factors that influence the intention to use fitness app, certain persuasive factors can moderate the influence. We use Elaboration Likelihood Model (ELM) to explain the moderating effect on the factors that influence the intension to use fitness app.

3   Elaboration Likelihood Model (ELM)

ELM is a dual process theory about how attitudes are formed and changed. The model has two routes of persuasion namely the central route and peripheral route (Petty and Cacioppo 1986). Central path is used when the individual is motivated and think about the message. When the individual is motivated, cares about the issue then he/she will elaborate on the message and lasting persuasion likely. In contract if the person has unfavorable attitude towards the issue, persuasion is unlikely. If the person has neutral attitude about the issue and not motivated to listen to the message, then he/she would look for peripheral cues. Usually expert judgment and message credibility are considered as peripheral cues (O'Keefe, 1990). If the peripheral cue association is accepted then the individual may develop a temporarily attitude change for persuasion. If peripheral cue is not accepted, or not present, then person will not be persuaded with the message.

4   Research Model and Hypothesis

We have conceptualized that individuals use different paths in adopting fitness apps to do physical activity. When individual choose a central path UTAUT factors (such as performance expectancy of fitness app, effort expectancy of fitness app, social influence to use fitness app and facilitating conditions) strongly predict fitness app adoption. However, when individuals choose peripheral path UTAUT factors become less significant predictors of fitness app adoption (Refer fig1).

4.1   Intention to Use Fitness App (BI)

Behavioral intention to use fitness app can be defined as a measure of the strength of one's intention to use a mobile fitness app (Fishbein & Ajzen, 1975, p. 288). According to technology acceptance literature behavioral intension is an accurate predictor of actual use (Davis, 1989). In this study we use behavioral intention to use fitness app as a proxy to user acceptance of fitness app. Thus, we use Behavioral intention to use fitness app as the DV in our study.

4.2   Intrinsic Motivation to Physical Activity

Intrinsic motivation toward physical activity refers the degree to which an individual feel pleasure or satisfaction while engaging in physical activity. Researchers have suggested that regardless of one's initial motive for exercising (such losing weight and attractive appearance), intrinsic motivation is critical for exercise adherence and maintaining physical activity behavior (Brawley and Vallerand 1984). Extrinsic reasons for participation may lead to poor exercise adherence rates, since extrinsically focused individuals may derive less enjoyment from the activity itself. Studies have found that lack of enjoyment to be a primary reason for withdrawing from physical activity programs (Boothby, et al 1981). Therefore to the extent that one exercises for intrinsic reasons, he/she is more likely to feel energized, confident, and satisfied and continue physical activity for a longer duration (Frederick ad Ryan (1993). Thus intrinsic motivation is a key factor for exercise adherence.

4.3   Credibility of Information in Fitness App

Credibility of Information in fitness app refers the truthfulness, trustworthiness and reliability of the information in a fitness app. Credibility of information in fitness app is decided by the reputation of the source from which, the information is taken. Evidence based information and information with scientific basis are perceived to be highly credible. According to Patrick Wilson's cognitive authority theory (1983), individuals trust the source, based on the cognitive authority of the source i.e. the source should be trustworthy or is of high reputation. For example information from US department of Health & human services could be highly credible. Due to the indispensability of source credibility in health care, trusting the provider is critical in usage intention (Lanseng and Andreason , 2007; Pavlou, 2003).

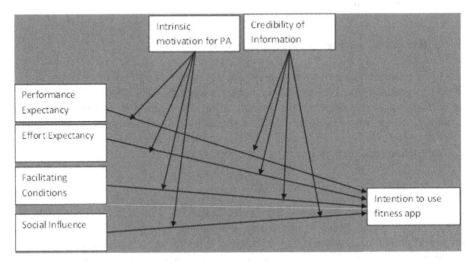

Fig. 1. User Acceptance model for fitness apps

4.4   Performance Expectancy of Fitness App

Performance Expectancy of fitness app is defined as the degree to which an individual believes that using the fitness app will help him/her to attain gains in physical activity performance or achieve physical activity goals. A user can speculate that by using a fitness app he/she could be at relative advantage of being more physically active, adhere to scheduled exercise programs, quickly loose weight within a short period /become more attractive and achieve physical activity goals. Thus, an individual believes that using the fitness app he/she would improve his/ her ability to enhance the effectiveness in managing the health and fitness. Several previous studies have indicated that performance expectancy or perceived usefulness of a technology is associated with the acceptance of the technology (Jimison et al, 2008; Boberg et al, 1995; Lai et al, 2008; Wilson and Lankton, 2004; Venkatesh et al, 2003; Davis et al, 1989). Therefore, users will be more likely to adopt the fitness app, or intend to use it if they expect higher exercise performance by using the fitness app. However, from theoretical point of view, it is reasonable to expect that performance expectancy and intention to use fitness app will be moderated by intrinsic motivation to physical activity, and credibility information in fitness app.

Drawing from ELM, when individuals are intrinsically motivated they are likely to choose central path (Petty and Cacioppo 1986) in the adoption of fitness app. Intrinsically motivated individuals will be regularly exercising, due to their fitness enthusiasm

(Brawley and Vallerand 1984). Therefore they would use the fitness app only if they expect greater performance out of the fitness app. Thus, we can expect a stronger the relationship between performance expectancy and intention to use fitness app among individuals who are intrinsically motivated to exercise.

However, when individuals are not fitness enthusiast and if the app provides credible information, peripheral path will be chosen in adopting fitness app. When peripheral cues such as credibility of the source is demonstrated, the trustworthiness of the app is increased (Lanseng and Andreason, 2007; Pavlou, 2003). If users highly trust the app, then it is less likely they expect greater performance out of the fitness app in order to use it. Thus, we can expect a weaker the relationship between performance expectancy and intention to use when the app provides credible information. Thus we hypothesize:

H1: The influence of performance expectancy on behavioral intention to use fitness app will be moderated by individual's intrinsic motivation for exercise and credibility of information provided by fitness app. Such that the relationship will be stronger when the user is intrinsically motivated to exercise and the relationship will be weaker when the app provides credible information.

4.5 Effort Expectancy of Fitness App

Effort expectancy of fitness app is defined as the degree of ease associated with using the fitness app. When user perceive ease or less effort in using the app its highly likely that they accept the fitness app. Using short cuts and user friendly interface designs can enable users to expend less effort from user side in order to carry out the task. Previous studies on technology acceptance indicate that perceived ease of use positively predict acceptance (Kerr et al, 2002; Kleijnen et al, 2004; Lee et al, 2002). Thus individuals are more likely to accept a fitness app if they feel that the app is easy to use.

As intrinsically motivated individuals are regular exercisers (Brawley and Vallerand 1984) they would choose a central path in adopting fitness app (Petty and Cacioppo 1986). In that sense they are likely to use the fitness app only if the app extremely easy to use. Thus, we can expect a stronger the relationship between performance expectancy and intention to use fitness app among individuals who are intrinsically motivated to exercise.

However, when the individuals are not fitness enthusiast and if the app provides credible information, the user will be choosing a peripheral path in using the fitness app. When peripheral cues such as credibility of the source is established, the trustworthiness of the app is demonstrated (Lanseng and Andreason , 2007; Pavlou, 2003). Hence perceived ease of use would less is likely to be significant factor in adopting the fitness. Thus, we can expect a weaker the relationship between performance expectancy and intention to use when the app provides credible information. Thus we hypothesize

H2: The influence of effort expectancy on behavioral intention to use fitness app will be moderated by individual's intrinsic motivation for exercise and credibility of information provided by fitness app. Such that the relationship will be stronger when the user is intrinsically motivated to exercise and the relationship will be weaker when the app provides credible information.

4.6   Social Influence

Social Influence in fitness app is defined as the degree to which an individual perceives that important others believe he/she should use the fitness app. Social support has been speculated to promote general health, wellbeing and healthy lifestyle modifications including smoke cessation (Deelstra, M. C. Peeters, et al. 2003, Dormann, and Zapf, 1999). Social influences act as an environmental stimulus for a person to take positive actions in maintaining good health (Fredrickson, 2000; Sloan and Gruman, 1988). In addition, previous studies have found that the perceived relationship strength of an individual with their colleagues has a positive effect on participation in offline health programs (Cohen and Syme, 1985; Prochaska et al, 1985). Extending the similar logic to the mobile heath apps, when a conducive social environment exist with supportive social ties encouraging exercise and usage of fitness app it reinforces user's positive beliefs about fitness app. Hence an individual is more likely to have a higher intention to use fitness app.

Drawing from ELM, when individuals are intrinsically motivated they are likely to adopt central path for using fitness app (Petty and Cacioppo 1986). Since intrinsically motivated individuals are enthusiastic about exercising they are likely to perform exercises with variety of methods (Brawley and Vallerand 1984). Hence they are more likely to adopt a fitness app only if peers strongly influence using the app. Thus, we can expect a stronger the relationship between social influence and intention to use fitness app among individuals who are intrinsically motivated to exercise.

However, when individuals are not enthusiast about exercise and if when fitness app provides credible information, peripheral path will be chosen in fitness app adoption. If the app demonstrate credibility of the source, it is highly likely the app is trusted by the users (Lanseng and Andreason , 2007; Pavlou, 2003). When the app is trustworthy, influence of others (e.g peers, colleagues, family, friends) is less likely to impact fitness app adoption. Thus, we can expect a weaker the relationship between social influence and intention to use when the app provides credible information. Therefore we hypothesize:

H3: The impact of social influence on behavioral intention to use fitness app will be moderated by individual's intrinsic motivation for exercise and credibility of information provided by fitness app. Such that the relationship will be stronger when the user is intrinsically motivated to exercise and the relationship will be weaker when the app provides credible information.

4.7   Facilitating Conditions

Facilitating conditions in fitness app is defined as an individuals' perceptions of internal (i.e. familiarity, knowledge and self-confidence in his/her ability of using apps) and external conditions (i.e, the compatibility of the fitness app platform with the mobile phone: iOs, Android) on using the fitness app. Studies of healthcare literature and studies outside healthcare have shown that facilitating conditions significantly predict acceptance and use of information technology. (Ajzen 1991; Taylor S, Todd , 1995; Venketesh et al, 2003, Moore and Benbasat, 1991, Thompson et al. 1991). Prior studies on technology acceptance by healthcare professionals found that when the mobile heath system (MHS) is well matched with clinical and patient care working practices, then the MHS will be highly accepted(Fitch, 2004; Haron et al, 2004). Using the same logic regular mobile apps users have greater tendency to download, install and use a fitness apps.

Drawing from ELM, when individuals are intrinsically motivated to exercise they use the central path in adopting a fitness app (Petty and Cacioppo 1986). Exercise enthusiastic would be doing exercise regularly with enthusiasm, therefore if facilitating conditions are also conducive, (for example if the individual is familiar with using mobile apps), they will have a stronger tendency to use fitness apps, in order to try different types of physical activities to satisfy their intrinsic needs (Ryan and Deci 2000). Thus, we can expect a stronger the relationship between facilitating conditions and intention to use fitness app among individuals who are intrinsically motivated to exercise.

In contrast, when the individuals are not fitness enthusiast and if the fitness app provides credible information, the users would choose the peripheral path in adopting the fitness app. This is because when the peripheral cues such as credibility of the source is provided user's trust in the app would be increased (Lanseng and Andreason , 2007; Pavlou, 2003) and it is less likely for the facilitating conditions (such familiarity with apps) to have a significant   impact in adopting the fitness app. Thus, we can expect a weaker the relationship between facilitating condition and intention to use. Therefore we hypothesize:

H4: The influence of facilitating condition on behavioral intention to use fitness app will be moderated by individual's intrinsic motivation for exercise and credibility of information provided by fitness app. Such that the relationship will be stronger when the user is intrinsically motivated to exercise and the relationship will be weaker when the app provides credible information.

Table 1. Formal Definitions of Constructs

Construct	Definition
Intention to use fitness app (INT)	The measure of the strength of one's intention to use fitness app (Adopted from Fishbein & Ajzen, 1975, p. 288);
Performance Expectancy(PE)	The degree to which an individual believes that using fitness app will help him/her to attain gains in physical activity performance. (Venkatesh et al 2003)
Intrinsic motivation to Physical Activity(IM)	The degree to which an individual feel pleasure or satisfaction while engaging in physical activity.
Effort Expectancy(EE)	The degree of ease associated with the use of the fitness app.(Venkatesh et al 2003)
Social Influence(SI)	The degree to which an individual perceives that important others believe he/ she should use the fitness app (Venketesh et al 2003)
Facilitating Conditions(FC)	The perceptions of internal (i.e. familiarity of using mobile apps, and self-confidence in his or her ability to of using fitness app) and external constraints (i.e., the compatibility of the fitness app platform with the mobile phone) on using fitness app (Ajzen, 1991, p. 188).
Credibility of Information in fitness app (CRED)	The truthfulness, trustworthiness and reliability of the information provided in the fitness app

5   Research Methodology

Survey methodology was used to collect data for testing the research hypothesis. Survey methodology was chosen because it enhances generalizability of results.

5.1   Instrument Development

Table 1 illustrates the definition of constructs. Constructs were measured using questions adapted from prior studies to enhance validity and new constructs were developed based on the review of Healthcare and Mobile Technologies literature. All items were anchored on a 7-point Likert scale (1= Strongly Disagree; 7 = Strongly Agree). Additionally, data was collected for several control variables that may influence our findings. i.e Gender, Age, Education Level, Prior Experience with Smartphones and mobile apps. Face and content validity of all items were assessed. First, items were examined by 3 colleagues with expertise in methodology and subject area to identify problems in framing and wordings of the questions. Second, conceptual validity of the instrument was tested by conducting label sorting with four judges (Moore and Benbasat, 1991). Minor modifications were made based on the sorting results. Two academics were asked to review the survey questionnaire for clarity, content validity, and semantic consistency before a pilot study was conducted.

5.2   Pilot Study

Pilot study involved convenient sample of 10 graduate students who were familiar with mobile health apps were given the initial questionnaire. Based on the feedback from pilot study, minor revisions were made to the instrument. Particularly, some participants commented on the difficulty in interpreting the negatively worded item "Source information in the fitness app is not important to me in order to use it". To reduce the confusion the item was rephrased as "Source information in the fitness app is important to me in order to use it". Marsh (1996) indicate that "the potential advantages of including negatively worded items seemed to be offset by associated problems in the present investigation, and these results may generalize to other applications" (p. 817).".

Further, some similarly phrased items were deleted as long as the deletion would not affect the content validity of the scales. This was done to save the time consumed to respond the questionnaire and to reduce the redundancy. The resultant survey instrument was used in the fiend survey.

5.3   Survey Administration

The field study was conducted among undergraduate and post graduate students, over a period of 2 weeks in October, 2011. All of the respondents possessed Smartphones. Among the 120 undergraduate and post graduate students recruited for the study, 103 responses were returned (86 percent response rate). Out of the 103 collected responses, 20 responses with incomplete data were eliminated from further analysis. The responses were discarded since the missing data could not be recovered due to the anonymous nature of our survey. The remaining 83 responses were used in the data analysis.

Most of the respondents were in the age group of 21-30 years (87.95%) and males (55.4%). A majority of respondents were post graduates (67.47%) with the rest undergraduates. Most of the respondents had smartphones (92.67%) and out of which majority of them used mobile apps (90%). Majority of respondents had used Smartphone for a period of 1.5 years.

Nonresponse bias was assessed by verifying that (1) respondents' demographics were similar to that of other undergraduate and graduate students, and (2) early and late respondents were not significantly different. The first set of tests compared gender, age, education, and smartphone usage. The second set of tests compared these characteristics, plus all principle constructs for the two groups. All possible t-test comparisons between the means of the two groups in both sets of tests showed insignificant differences ($p< 0.1$ level).

5.4 Data Analysis and Results

Partial Least Squares (PLS)(Chin 1998), a Structured Equation Modeling (SEM), was used for testing the conceptual model and hypothesis. PLS analysis concurrently test the psychometric properties of each scale used to measure the construct in the model and analyze the strength and directions of the relationships among the constructs. Thus, PLS handle both formative and reflective measures that occur jointly in a model. In our study, the constructs Performance Expectancy (PE), Effort Expectancy (EE), intention to use (INT), Social Influence (SI), and Intrinsic Motivation for Physical Activity(IM) were reflective because these constructs were uni-dimensional and exclusion of an item did not alter the meaning of construct. The constructs Credibility of Information in fitness app (CRED) and facilitating conditions (FC) were considered formative because each item jointly determined the meaning of a construct and exclusion of an item could alter its meaning.

PLS is also less stringent about the distribution assumption and sample size to validate the model compared to alternative structural equation modeling techniques. SmartPLS2 bootstrap (BT) methods were used to assess the measurement model and structural model. In addition, the data was standardized according the PLS requirements, before testing.

5.5 Test of Measurement Model

Recommended two-stage analytical procedures (Anderson and Gerbing 1988; Hair et al, 1998) were carried out. Confirmatory factor analysis was first conducted to assess measurement mode, then structural relationships were examined. Assessment of measurement model includes evaluation of internal consistency, convergent validity and discriminant validity of the instrument items. Reflective and formative constructs were treated differently during validation because, unlike reflective constructs, different dimensions of formative constructs are not expected to demonstrate internal consistency and correlations. To assess the relevance and level of contribution of each item to the formative constructs, we examined the items weights instead.

For reflective constructs, internal consistency was assessed using Cronbach's alpha reliability coefficients. All reflective constructs in our model had Cronbach's alpha scores that exceeded the criterion of 0.7 (Nunnally 1978). Convergent Validity was asses through item reliability, composite reliability and Average Variance Extracted (AVE) for each construct. Convergent validity reflects the extent to which the items of the constructs are similar. All items t-value of loadings were significant. All reliabilities, item composite reliability (CR) were well above the recommended threshold of 0.7 and all AVE were well above the threshold of 0.5(Hair et al, 1998).

Discriminant validity reflects the extent to which the items of each constructs are distinctly different from items of other constructs. This is generally assessed by factor analysis, in which items of each construct load more highly on their intended construct than on other constructs (Thompson et al. 1991; Cook and Campbell 1979). In addition, Discriminant validity can also be assessed by ensuring each item should correlate more highly with other items that measure the same construct than with the items measuring other constructs. For this study, both factor analysis using principal component analysis and verimax rotation and item correlations (i.e squared correlation between constructs compared with AVE of the construct) were carried out.

In addition to validity assessment, we also checked for multicollinearity among variables due to high correlations. VIF and tolerance of all construct variables were within the acceptable thresholds.

5.6   Test of Structural Model

With adequate measurement model and acceptable level of multicollinearity PLS Structural model (Chin 1998) was assessed to determine the explanatory power (i.e variance explained) and the significance of the hypothesized paths. The explanatory power of the structural model was determined by the amount of variance in the dependent variable (intension to use fitness app that) is explained by the model. Our model can explain 60.2% of the variance in the DV. The explanatory power above 10 % is adequate (Falk and Miller, 1992). Each hypothesis corresponds to path in Structural model. Bootstrapping procedure was used to estimate the significance (T-value and the corresponding p-value) of the path coefficients. All statistical tests were assessed at 5% significance. The results of the analysis are summarized below.

Table 2. Results of Hypothesis testing

Hypothesis		Path coefficient	t-value	Results
H1	IM*PE	0.262	0.812	Not supported
	CR*PE	-0.859	3.538 ***	Supported
H2	IM*EE	0.801	3.328 ***	Supported
	CR*EE	-0.243	0.826	Not supported
H3	IM*SI	0.463	1.695*	Supported
	CR*SI	-0.233	1.040	Not supported
H4	IM*FC	0.251	0.940	Not supported
	CR*FC	-0.194	0.797	Not supported

Based on the results three hypothesis are partially supported.

6   Discussion, Implications and Limitations

Based on our estimation results, hypothesis 1 is partially supported. I.e. the moderating effect of intrinsic motivation on the relationship between performance expectancy and intention to use fitness app is not supported. This result emphasizes the fact that exercise enthusiastic who are intrinsically motivated to exercise, primarily exercise for enjoyment, interest and satisfaction gained in the physical activity itself (Ryan and Deci 2000). Therefore greater performance expectation out of fitness app is not a major concern for using the app. However the hypothesis on the moderating effect of credibility information is supported. This indicates that when credibility information is provided in fitness app, trustworthiness of the app increased (Lanseng and Andreason , 2007) and users are less likely to look for greater performance expectation in order to use the fitness app.

As hypothesized the moderating effect of intrinsic motivation to exercise on the relationship between effort expectancy and intention to use is supported. This finding indicate that since exercise enthusiast are intrinsically motivated and perform exercise for the enjoyment and satisfaction (Ryan and Deci 2000), they are likely to use fitness app if it is extremely easy to use. The hypothesis on the moderating effect of credible information on relationship between effort expectancy and intention to use is not supported. This shows that is even if the app provides credible information, if the app is not easy to use it is less likely that the user adopt the app for exercising. Thus consistent with the previous findings ease of use is an (Kerr et al, 2002; Kleijnen et al, 2004) important factor in fitness app adoption.

Hypothesis 3 is also partially supported. The moderating effect of intrinsic motivation on the relationship between social influence and intention to use is supported but the moderating effect of credible information is not supported. This shows that since intrinsically motivated individuals are enthusiastic about exercising (Brawley and Vallerand 1984) they are likely to adopt fitness app if their peers strongly recommend using the fitness app. The hypothesis on the moderating effect of credible information is not supported. This shows that credibility of the information does not influence users, when important others prefer him/her using the app. This finding is also consistent with previous finding that colleagues' influence can have a significant impact on an individual's adoption (Prochaska et al, 1985).

Finally, the hypothesis 4 is not supported. The moderating effect of intrinsic motivation to exercise and credibility of information in fitness app doesn't impact the relationship between facilitating condition and intention to use fitness app. This indicates that since intrinsically motivated individuals are regular exercisers they use variety of exercise methods (Brawley and Vallerand 1984) therefore they do not consider mere facilitating condition (such as familiarity with mobile apps) as an important antecedent to use fitness app. Similarly, the finding on the moderating effect of credibility information shows that even if fitness app provides credibility information and facilitating conditions (such as familiarity with mobile apps) are conducive individuals are not likely opt to use fitness app for exercising. This indicates that favorable facilitating condition itself is not sufficient for individuals to adopt fitness apps for exercise. However, fitness app features such as keeping track of goals, measuring progress and health can more important for users (Yoganathan and Kajanan 2013).

6.1   Limitations and Future Work

While interpreting the findings of this study, several limitations need to be recognized. First, the application studied was described to the respondents - they did not actually use it. This makes the results less general than if the system actually had been used by the respondents. For instance, it is hard to see how the respondents could have a good understanding of the system's ease of use from a short description. While this limits this study's generality, it does not invalidate the findings. A number of studies of technology acceptance are done in this way and further, the actual adoption process resembles this when users have to buy the goods before they are able to try them. However, future studies, can design a mobile app with stipulated features, let them actually use the application and increase the study's generality.

Secondly, there may be response bias in our measurement. Our respondents are mainly from students sample and are well conversant with new mobile technologies than those who are deprived of such mobile technologies. Future studies may strive to obtain responses from other populations such as working class, senior citizens and professionals.

Third due to the scale of the survey and the process of eliciting unqualified participants, the size of the sample for the final analysis is limited. Although the sample size is acceptable for PLS analysis, a larger and more heterogeneous sample would bring more statistical power and allow more rigorous testing. Thus, caution needs to be exercised in generalizing our results to other setting, since our study targeted student population.

Fourth, our study did not measure actual use. It is well known that the link between Intention to use and actual use is not perfect. Knowing the respondents' intention does not mean that we know what they will do. The actual behavior of fitness app usage can be measured in future studies. However, with considerable support on intention as a significant predictor of actual usage (Taylor and Todd 1995; Venkatesh and Morris 2000; Venkatesh et al, 2003), this issue may be less critical.

Lastly, we investigated one specific (i.e., health and fitness) mobile behavior change application. Investigating one of a kind is a poor background for generalizing to the whole class. Future studies may be designed to study other type of mobile health apps such as smoking cessation, health and nutrition, and chronic disease control apps. Taken together these caveats suggest that the results are interpreted with care. Moreover, quantitative study can also be conducted in future and provide more insight to this study. Further, future studies can also refine the measures and constructs to get a deeper understanding of the study.

6.2   Theoretical Contributions

In a preliminary effort to understand the factors that influence smartphone users' tendencies to use fitness apps, this study attempts to synthesize relevant work from IS technology acceptance, Health care IT, mobile technologies and provides a comprehensive view. In addition, this study explores the various the psychological, technical and social perception of an individual that influence a person's decision making in using a mobile technology that is related to health.

Moreover, the results shows that UTAUT model (Venkatesh et al, 2003) and ELM can be combinedly used to predict fitness app adoption. While UTAUT could be used to explain the main antecedent of fitness app use, ELM could be used to explain the moderating factors of fitness app use.

In comparison with most previous IS acceptance studies conducted in workplace settings (Venkatesh et al, 2003; Thompson et al, 1991), this study highlights some of the difference in terms of antecedent for individuals in non-work place situations. Particularly the facilitating conditions in work place setting such as organizational and technical infrastructure that exist to support the system use, do not apply in the context of this study. They are replaced by internal factors such as self-confidence/ individual's ability to use fitness app and external constrains such as compatibility of the operating system, previous experience of using mobile apps.

Apart from the theoretical implications with reference to technology acceptance, this study also contributes to the emerging mobile health technologies.

In terms of methodology, the study suggests insights into how survey instruments can be designed to cater to the reduced cognitive capabilities of the respondents. Thus while designing a survey reverse phrased items may be confusing for respondents and should probably be avoided, and length of the survey questionnaire must be kept manageable.

6.3   Practical Implications

Lack of physical activity is a huge problem around the globe. Our literature review suggests that this problem in part can be controlled by mobile interventions. Several practical implications from this study may assist m-health app developers in designing tailored motivational applications.

The present study results indicate that individuals who are more intrinsically motivated to do physical activity may expect greater ease of use and strong social influence in order to use fitness app. Thus, fitness app designers should consider these factors when designing fitness apps.

In addition the findings suggest the significance of credibility of information that in fitness apps. When credible information is provided users may not have greater concerns of performance expectancy. This is an important indication for designers of fitness app to provide reliable, evidence based scientifically proven information in the fitness apps. For example it would be useful to incorporate information such as "Recommended amount of physical activity", by "World Health Organization", "UK physical activity guidelines, "U.S. Dept of Health and Human Services" and "British Heart Foundation" guidelines. Incorporating such information into the fitness apps might increase an individual's trust in fitness app and encourage using fitness app.

Future studies will need to shed more light on the target population relative to system design requirements and marketing, as well as document increases in physical activity due to fitness app usage.

6.4   Conclusions

The current research represents a first step in understanding the acceptance of fitness apps. For this reason we choose to apply well known theories and models from theories of technology acceptance, and models of persuasion to test their associations with logically related individual characteristics. By providing empirical evidence regarding the antecedents and moderating factors of fitness app, we feel that we have contributed to the development of a richer understanding for fitness app acceptance. Further, by following a rigorous process in defining the constructs and rigorous validation process, the model and finding will be a beneficial contribution for theory and practice.

Given the importance of cost effective mobile healthcare technologies we hope that our findings will be useful in designing effective mobile apps that can improve the health and wellbeing of the public at large. From these finding it is important to expand the research mobile health apps. Research in the area of mobile health technologies is likely to provide deeper insights in the process of creating healthy communities in a cost effective way.

References

1. Agarwal, R., Karahanna, E.: Time flies when you're having fun: Cognitive Absorption and beliefs about information technology usage. MIS Quarterly 24, 665–694 (2000)
2. Ajzen, I.: The Theory of Planned Behavior. Organizational Behavior and Human Decision Processes 50(2), 179–211 (1991)
3. Atkinson, M.A., Kydd, C.: Individual characteristics associated with World Wide Web use: An empirical study of playfulness and motivation. The DATA BASE for Advancement in Information Systems 28, 53–62 (1997)
4. Anderson, J.C., Gerbing, D.W.: Structural Equation Modeling in Practice; A Review and Recommended Two-Step Approach. Psychological Bulletin 103(3), 41–423 (1988)
5. Becker, M.H., Maiman, L.A., Kirscht, J.P., Haefner, D.P., Drachman, R.H.: The health belief model and prediction of dietary compliance: A field experiment. Journal of Health and Social Behaviour 18, 348–366 (1977)
6. Brawley, L.R., Vallerand, R.J.: Enhancing intrinsic motivation for fitness activities: Its systematic increase in fitness environment (Unpublished manuscript, University of Waterloo) (1984)
7. Boberg, E.W., Gustafson, D.H., Hawkins, R.P., et al.: Development, acceptance, and use patterns of a computer-based education and social support system for people living with AIDS HIV infection. Comput Human Behav. 11, 289–311 (1995)
8. Boothby, J., Tungatt, M.F., Townsend, A.R.: Ceasing participation in sports activity: Reported reasons and their implications. Journal of Leisure Research 12, 1–14 (1981)
9. Chen, C., Czerwinski, M., Macredie, R.: Individual differences in virtual environments - introduction and overview. Journal of the American Society for Information Science 51(6) (2000)
10. Chin, W.W.: The Partial Least Squares Approach to Structural Equation Modeling. In: Marcoulides, G.A. (ed.) Modern Methods for Business Research, pp. 295–336. Lawrence Eribaum Associates, Mahwah (1998)
11. Chau, P.Y.K., Hu, P.J.-H.: Investigating healthcare professionals' decision to accept telemedicine technology: An empirical test of competing theories. Information and Management 39, 297–311 (2002)
12. Cohen, S., Syme, S.L.: Social support and health. Academic Press, San Diego (1985)
13. Csikszentmihalyi, M., Rathunde, K.: The measurement of flow in everyday life: Toward a theory of emergent motivation. In: Jacobs, J. (ed.) Nebraska Symposium on Motivation, 8th edn., pp. 57–97. University of Nebraska Press, Lincoln (1992)

14. Davis, F.D.: Perceived Usefulness, Perceived Ease of Use, and User Acceptance of Information Technology. MIS Quarterly 13, 319–340 (1989)
15. Davis, F.D., Bagozzi, R.P., Warshaw, P.P.: Extrinsic and intrinsic motivation to use computers in the workplace. Journal of Applied Social Psychology 22, 1111–1132 (1992)
16. Davis, F.D., Bagozzi, R.P., Warshaw, P.R.: User acceptance of computer technology: A comparison of two theoretical models. Management Science 35, 982–1003 (1989)
17. Deci, E.L., Ryan, R. M.: Intrinsic Motivation and Self Determination in Human Behavior. Plenum Press, New York (1985)
18. Deelstra, J.T., Peeters, M.C., et al.: Receiving Instrumental Support at Work: When Help Is Not Welcome. Journal of Applied Psychology 88(2), 324–331 (2003)
19. Dickinger, A., Arami, M., Meyer, D.: The role of perceived enjoyment and social norm in the adoption of technology with network externalities. European Journal of Information Systems 17, 4–11 (2008)
20. Dormann, C., Zapf, D.: Social Support, Social Stressors at Work, and Depressive Symptoms: Testing for Main and Moderating Effects with Structural Equations in a Three-Wave Longitudinal Study. Journal of Applied Psychology 84(6), 874–884 (1999)
21. Lanseng, E.J., Andreassen, T.W.: Electronic healthcare: A study of people's readiness and attitude toward performing self-diagnosis. International Journal of Service Industry Management 18(4), 394–417 (2007)
22. Falk, R.F., Miller, N.B.: A primer for soft modeling. The University of Akron Press, Akron (1992)
23. Fredrickson, B.L.: Cultivating positive emotions to optimize health and well-being. Prevention and Treatment 3(1), 1 (2000)
24. Frederick, C.M., Ryan, R.M.: Differences in motivation for sport and exercise and their relationships with participation and mental health. Journal of Sport Behavior 16, 125–145 (1993)
25. Fitch, C.J.: Information systems in healthcare: Mind the gap. In: Proceeding of the 37th Hawaii International Conference on System Sciences (2004)
26. Foa, E., Rothbaum, B., Furr, J.: Augmenting exposure therapy with other CBT procedures. Psychiatric Annals 33(1), 47–56 (2011)
27. Grise, M., Gallupe, B.: Information overload: Addressing the productivity paradox in face-to-face electronic meeting. Journal of Management Information Systems 16(3), 157–185 (1999–2000)
28. Grime, P.R.: Computerized cognitive behavioural therapy at work: A randomized controlled trial in employees with recent stress-related absenteeism. Occup. Med. 54, 353–359 (2004)
29. Gould, S.J.: Consumer attitudes toward health and health care: A differential perspective. The Journal of Consumer Affairs 22(1), 96–118 (1988)
30. Heijden, H.: User acceptance of hedonic information systems. MIS Quarterly 28, 695–704 (2004)
31. Hu, P., Chau, P., Tam, K.: Examining the technology acceptance model using physician acceptance of telemedicine technology. Journal of Management Information Systems 16(2), 91–112 (1999)
32. Jansson, M., Linton, S.J.: Cognitive-behavioral group therapy as an early intervention for insomnia: A randomized controlled trial. J. Occup. Rehabil. 15, 177–190 (2005)

33. Jayasuriya, R.: Determinants of microcomputer technology use: Implications for education and training of health staff. International Journal of Medical Informatics 50, 187–194 (1998)
34. Kerr, J.H., Fujiyama, H., Campano, J.: Emotion and Stress in Serious and Hedonistic Leisure Sport Activities. Journal of Leisure Research 34, 272–289 (2002)
35. Kraft, F.B., Goodell, P.W.: Identifying the health conscious consumer. Journal of Health Care Marketing 13(3), 18–25 (1993)
36. Kleijnen, M., Wetzels, M., de Ruyter, K.: Consumer acceptance of wireless finance. Journal of Financial Services Marketing 8, 206–217 (2004)
37. Koestner, R., McClelland, D.C.: Perspectives on competence motivation. In: Pervin, L.A. (ed.) Handbook of Personality: Theory and Research, pp. 527–548. Guilford Press, New York (1990)
38. Koh. C.: Ezyhealth & Beauty (2011)
39. Lai, T.Y., Larson, E.L., Rockoff, M.L.: User acceptance of HIV TIDES-Tailored interventions for management of depressive symptoms in persons living with HIV/ AIDS. J. Am. Med. Inform. Assoc. 15, 217–226 (2008)
40. Lamminmäki, E., Pärkkä, J., Hermersdorf, M., Kaasinen, J., Samposalo, K., Vainio, J., Kolari, J., Kulju, M., Lappalainen, R., Korhonen, I.: Wellness Diary for Mobile Phones. In: EMBEC (2005)
41. Lee, Y., Kim, J., Lee, I., Kim, H.: A crosscultural study on the value structure of mobile internet usage: Comparison between Korea and Japan. Journal of Electronic Commerce Research 3, 227–239 (2002)
42. Lee, G., Tsai, C., Griswold, W.G., Raab, F., Patrick, K.: PmEB: A Mobile Phone Application for Monitoring Caloric Balance. CHI, Work-in-Progress, 1013–1018 (2006)
43. McLean, Motivating Patients to Use Smartphone Health Apps, Consumer Health Information Corporation (April 25, 2011)
44. Marsh, H.S.: Positive and Negative Global Self-Esteem: A Substantively Meaningful Distinction or Artifactors? Journal of Personality and Social Psychology 70(4), 810–819 (1996)
45. Moore, G., Benbasat, I.: Development of an Instrument to Measure the Perceptions of Adopting an Information Technology Innovation. Information Systems Research 2(3), 192–222 (1991)
46. Newsom, J.T., McFarland, B.H., Kaplan, M.S., Huguet, N., Zani, B.: The health consciousness myth: Implications of the near independence of major health behaviours in the North American population. Social Science & Medicine 60, 433–437 (2005)
47. Nunnally, J.C.: Psychometric Theory. Mcgraw-Hill Book Company, New York (1978)
48. Pavlou, P.A.: Consumer Acceptance of Electronic Commerce: Integrating Trust and Risk with the Technology Acceptance Model. International Journal of Electronic Commerce 7(3), 69–103 (2003)
49. Plank, R.E., Gould, S.J.: Health consciousness, scientific orientation and wellness; An examination of the determinants of wellness attitudes and behaviors. Health Marketing Quarterly 7(3-4), 65–83 (1990)
50. Pelletier, L.G., Fortier, M.S., Vallerand, R.J., Tuston, K.M., Blais, M.R.: Toward a new measure of intrinsic motivation, extrinsic motivation and amotivation in sports: The Sport Motivation Scale (SMS). Journal of Sports &- Exercise Psychology 17, 35–53 (1995)
51. Prochaska, T.R., Leventhal, E.A., et al.: Health practices and illness cognition in young, middle aged and elderly adults. Journal of Gerontology 40(5), 569–578 (1985)

52. Reeve, J., Deci, E.L.: Elements of the competitive situation that affect intrinsic motivation. Personality and Social Psychology Bulletin 22(14), 33 (1996)
53. Scheier, M., Carver, C.S.: Effects of optimism on psychological and physical well-being: Theoretical overview and empirical update. Cognitive Therapy and Research 16(2), 201–228 (1992)
54. Sheppard, B.H., Hartwick, J., Warshaw, P.R.: The theory of reasoned action: A meta-analysis of past research with recommendations for modifications and future research. J Consumer Res. 15, 325–343 (1988)
55. Skinner, B.F.: Contingencies of reinforcement: A theoretical analysis. Prentice-Hall, Englewood Cliffs (1969)
56. Sloan, R.P., Gruman, J.C.: Participation in Workplace Health Promotion Programs - The Contribution of Health and Organizational-Factors. Health Education Quarterly 15(3), 269–288 (1988)
57. Taylor, S., Todd, P.: Understanding information technology usage: A test of competing models. Information Systems Research 6, 144–176 (1995)
58. Thompson, R.L., Higgins, C.A., Howell, J.M.: Personal Computing: Toward a Conceptual Model of Utilization. MIS Quarterly 15(1), 124–143 (1991)
59. Venkatesh, V., Morris, M.G., Davis, G.B.: User acceptance of information technology: Toward a unified view. MIS Quarterly 27, 425–478 (2003)
60. Venkatesh, V., Morris, M.G., Ackerman, P.L.: A longitudinal field investigation of gender differences in individual technology adoption decision-making processes. Organizational Behavior and Human Decision Processes 83(1), 33–60 (2000)
61. Valdivieso-López, E., et al.: Efficacy of a mobile application for smoking cessation in young people: Study protocol for a clustered, randomized trial. BMC Public Health 13(1), 1–6 (2013)
62. Yoganathan, D., Kajanan, S.: Persuasive Technology for Smartphone Fitness Apps (2013)

Appendix A

Table 3. Results of Confirmatory Factor Analysis

Construct	Cronbch's alpha	AVE	CR
INT	0.907	0.7973	0.9401
PE	0.869	0.7137	0.9087
SI	0.943	0.7712	0.9818
EE	0.956	0.7905	0.9378
IM	0.902	0.8971	0.9721

Table 4. Item Weights for Formative Constructs

Construct and Items	Item Weights
Credibility	
CRED1	0.2540
CRED2	0.5607 *
CRED3	0.6248 **
CRED4	0.9587 ***
Facilitating Condition	
FC1	0.7074 **
FC2	0.7120 ***
FC3	0.7982 ***
FC4	0.8834 ***
*p<0.05 ;**p < 0.01 level; ***p < 0.001 level	

Table 5. AVE Against Square Correlations among Formative Contructs

Constructs	INT	PE	SI	EE	IM
INT	**0.7973**				
PE	0.169778	**0.7137**			
SI	0.193226	0.029653	**0.7712**		
EE	0.177918	0.275099	0.159509	**0.7905**	
IM	0.304056	0.169778	0.029653	0.407450	**0.8971**

Motivation and Knowledge Sharing through Social Media within Danish Organizations

Pia Nielsen and Liana Razmerita

Department of International Business Communication,
Copenhagen Business School, Denmark
{pn.ibc,lr.ibc}@cbs.dk

Abstract. Based on an empirical quantitative study, this article investigates employee motivation in Danish companies and aims at determining which factors affect employees' knowledge sharing through social media in a working environment. Our findings pinpoint towards the potential social media have for enhancing internal communication, knowledge sharing and collaboration in organizations, but the adoption is low, at this point, due to mainly organizational and individual factors. Technological factors do not seem to affect employees' motivation for knowledge sharing as much as previous research has found, but it is the influence from the combination of individual and organizational factors, which affect the adoption of the platforms. A key finding in the study is that knowledge sharing is not a 'social dilemma' as previous studies have found. The study shows a positive development in employees' willingness to share knowledge, because knowledge sharing is considered more beneficial than to hoard it.

Keywords: Knowledge sharing, Motivation, Social Media, Social Business, Internal Communication, Enterprise Social Networks, Enterprise 2.0.

1 Introduction

In a digitalized world, organizations face increasingly competitive environments and many companies are forced to downsize in order to cut costs and adapt to a changing marketplace. This can lead to loss of valuable knowledge unless it has been captured and stored in the organization. Knowledge is a key source of competitive advantage, and knowledge has become the most important resource and strategic asset for organizations [1,2,3]. Managing knowledge and knowledge sharing have, consequently, gained increased attention in organizations.

Social media is slowly reshaping the concept of knowledge management in organizations and more and more companies adopt 'social business' [4,5] communication strategies in order to enhance the internal communication and collaboration to become more productive and competitive.

Social media provide new opportunities for knowledge sharing through collaborative platforms [6] such as social networks, blogs and wikis, which allow employees to share knowledge easier across departmental and geographic boundaries [7]. The platforms

B. Bergvall-Kåreborn and P.A. Nielsen (Eds.): TDIT 2014, IFIP AICT 429, pp. 197–213, 2014.
© IFIP International Federation for Information Processing 2014

Chatter, Yammer and Podio are examples of social media, which are used in an organizational context for internal communication and collaboration. Salesforce Chatter is an enterprise social network as well as a collaborative application based on cloud-computing apps. Podio is also an enterprise social network and an online work platform. Podio users can create workspaces to collaborate with specific groups of people, and use an employee network for company-wide communication across departments and get their work done using apps. Yammer is a secure, private social network, which enables employees to collaborate easily. These platforms are also referred to as 'Enterprise 2.0' [8] or enterprise social networks, because they are deployed in a business environment for internal communication. The platforms provide new opportunities for organizations to benefit from the human resources and valuable knowledge that resides in the organization, which, potentially, can enhance work routines, business practices and knowledge sharing.

According to studies conducted by the consultancy firm McKinsey & Company, companies, which deploy social media, have gained measurable business benefits such as: better access to knowledge, lower cost of doing business, higher revenues and more innovative products and services [9,10]. A more recent study conducted by McKinsey & Company from 2012, shows that social technologies within an enterprise can raise the productivity of the employees by 20-25 percent [11]. According to this study, the average employee spends an estimated 28 percent of the workweek managing e-mails and nearly 20 percent looking for internal information or tracking down colleagues, who can help with specific tasks. But when companies use social media internally, messages become content; a searchable record of knowledge, which can reduce, by as much as 35 percent, the time employees spend searching for company information.

Social media provide new opportunities to manage knowledge at both personal and organizational levels through social-collaboration and networking opportunities provided by such platforms [12,13]. Personal knowledge could be synergized into collective knowledge through social collaborative processes that may facilitate externalization of knowledge, fostering creativity and innovation [14,15]. All these processes may have the potential to increase companies' competitiveness. However engaging employees to adopt and use these platforms on regular basis seems to be the main challenge organizations are facing nowadays owing to both organizational and individual factors [13]. According to a recent report conducted by Gartner, the vast majority of social collaboration initiatives fail due to lack of purpose and a 'provide and pray' approach, which only leads to a 10 percent success rate [16].

Despite the potential social media have for enhancing organizations' internal communication [6], [3], [17,18] only few studies exist related to which factors affect employees' knowledge sharing through social media, and how organizations can deploy social media in order to increase their competitive advantage. Due to the recognition of knowledge as a source of competitive advantage and the growing significance of knowledge sharing in organizations, the purpose of this article is to contribute to a better understanding of how knowledge workers can be motivated to share knowledge using social media [19, 20]. The article draws on human psychology motivation theory [21]. The following research question: Which factors affect employees' knowledge sharing behavior through social media? was investigated using empirical data collected using a questionnaire distributed to several Danish organizations.

The article is structured as follows: Section 2 provides a literature review. In section 3, we introduce our research methodology. The findings from our study are presented in section 4. The main findings are discussed in section 5. Our conclusions are outlined in section 6.

2 Literature Review

Previous studies emphasize that many companies already reap benefits from the collaborative nature of social media, which improve collaboration and knowledge sharing within and between organizations due to faster and more efficient communication [11], [22]. And Von Krogh [23] argues that drawing increasingly on social software, knowledge management is "becoming less costly, more cloud-based, ubiquitous, standardized, and mobile, but also more personalized and more effective in meeting individual needs". Companies such as IBM, Siemens AG and Royal Dutch/shell (KPMG) have successfully adopted social media as part of their knowledge management strategy and are already gaining measurable business benefits [24], [22].

Central to this study is the potential social media have for enhancing internal communication, knowledge sharing and collaboration in organizations. For many companies the organization's employees are an unused source of knowledge, which could improve the organization's competitive advantage, if their knowledge is shared and distributed in more effective ways through social media platforms [22].

According to recent work conducted by Von Krogh [25] social practices do not only evolve and refine employees' tacit and explicit knowledge. Under certain conditions, such as a history of interaction, their members also pursue higher collective standards of excellence related to their work. The platforms Chatter, Yammer and Podio, are examples of social media that are used in an organizational context for internal communication, collaboration and knowledge sharing.

Recent studies and literature from the beginning of the 2000s till now, have identified several factors, which affect employees' knowledge sharing behavior through social media, as well as, identified three main categories they fit into. These categories are: individual, organizational and technological factors. The following literature and studies have identified a number of factors, which affect employees' knowledge sharing through social media: [3], [6], [26], [27] virtual communities [8], [29], knowledge sharing in multinational corporations with focus on managerial support [30]. Furthermore, factors such as: organizational culture [31], [32], cultural influences on knowledge sharing [33], and critical barriers to effective knowledge management [26], have also been identified as significant factors to affect employees' knowledge sharing.

Companies need to get an understanding of their employees, their needs and their motivation to share knowledge if they want to stay competitive. The reason for this is that the traditional approach to doing business is a top-down approach, but social media bring power back to people and employees. This reality challenges the existing business model in many companies, because the implementation of social platforms is all about the employees, which demands a more employee centric and bottom-up approach. This means that it is crucial to focus on the employees and understand their needs in order for management and managers to facilitate the right kind of motivation to promote use and adoption of the social platforms.

As mentioned earlier, previous research has identified several factors that affect the individual employees' willingness to share knowledge using different theories. In particular understanding knowledge sharing in virtual communities has been investigated using social capital and social cognitive theories [34], social exchange theory [35, 36] or theory of planned behavior [37]. In the this study, in order to understand which factors affect employees' knowledge sharing, we attempt to understand the human psychology behind employees' motivation to share knowledge.

The concept of motivation has been discussed frequently by using Deci and Ryan's framework [21] and original separation of intrinsic and extrinsic motivation, which is applied to explain some of the factors that drive people to action. This motivational theory framework was chosen for this study to explain why employees share or do not share knowledge due to the simplistic and employee centric nature of the theory of only two determinants; the two basic human needs: intrinsic and extrinsic motivation.

Deci and Ryan's framework of motivation [21] can be divided into two categories based on the different reasons and goals, which drive a person to action: intrinsic motivation (internal) and extrinsic motivation (external). The two types of motivation influence individual employees' intentions regarding an activity as well as their behaviors.

Intrinsic motivation refers to motivation that is driven by an interest or enjoyment in the task itself or enjoyment in helping others, and exists within the individual rather than relying on any external pressure or reward. People who are intrinsically motivated are more likely to engage in the task willingly, as well as, work to improve their skills, which will increase their capabilities as well as the organization's productivity [21].

Extrinsic motivation refers to the performance of an activity, which leads to a desirable outcome. Extrinsic motivation focuses on goal-driven reasons, such as monetary rewards and career advancement [21]. Extrinsic motivation is typically based on the perception of the cost (effort) and benefit (reward) associated with sharing knowledge. If the perceived benefits exceed or equals the cost, then knowledge sharing will happen. Many organizations have reward systems, which can be useful for motivating the employees to share knowledge.

Furthermore, the concept of 'social dilemma' is also relevant to consider, since some scholars [38, 39] argue that knowledge sharing can be considered a social dilemma, because organizational interests conflict with employees' individual interests. Taking a social dilemma perspective, organizations have an interest in making knowledge available for all employees, but from an employee's point-of-view it is a rational choice to hoard knowledge in order to save time, conserve power and thereby remain valuable for organization and reduce the risk of getting fired [38, 39, 40,41].

3   Research Method

Based on the above presented literature review, the studies conducted by Paroutis and Al Saleh [3], Kirchner, Razmerita and Sudzina [6] and Lin [27] were selected for this study, because they provide the most systematic framework of analysis of individual, organizational and technological factors, which affect employees' knowledge sharing through social media.

In order to provide a systematic understanding of the possible factors, which affect employees' knowledge sharing, the identified individual, organizational and technological factors are proposed as a framework, which is illustrated in Fig. 1.

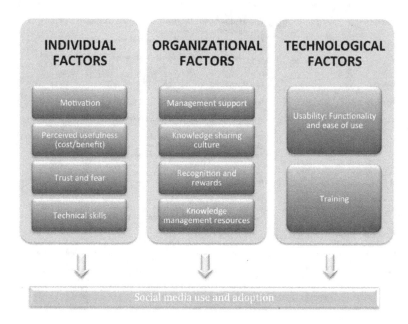

Fig. 1. Factors that affect employees' knowledge sharing behavior

Each category has several sub-categories of the identified factors, which are further described in Table 1. The identified factors can be considered as both drivers and barriers, depending on the point of view.   For instance, if managers take on a supportive role, the factor can increase the employees' use of social media. And if managers take on a passive role, it becomes a barrier for the employees' knowledge sharing behavior. The factors are described in Table 1 as barriers.

Based on the framework illustrated in Fig. 1 an online questionnaire was developed for data collection. The questionnaire was distributed to a number of Danish companies from different industry sectors, which are using one of the social media platforms.

Table 1. Knowledge sharing barriers

Knowledge sharing barriers	
Factors	Description
Individual factors	
Motivation	Lack of motivation and commitment
	Unwillingness to do extra work
	Lack of time
	Lack of participation and contribution from colleagues
	Lack of recognition from colleagues
	Lack of content quality and relevance
	Information overload
	Lack of understanding of social media and its benefits
Perceived usefulness (cost/benefit)	The benefits of using the platform to share knowledge should outweigh the costs
Trust and fear	Lack of trust in collegaues and fear of misuse of shared knowledge
	Fear of giving up expert power, authority
	Fear of becoming replaceable if too valuable knowledge is shared
	Fear of reducing job security
	Fear and uncertainty of providing faulty information
Technical skills	Lack of technical skills
Organizational factors	
Managment support	Lack of management support and commitment to promote knowledge sharing
Knowledge sharing culture	Hierarchical organizational structure, that does not foster a knowledge sharing culture
	Lack of participation and contribution from colleagues
	Knowledge sharing is not promoted or expected
Recognition and rewards	Lack of monetary reward system (extrinsic motivation) and recognition (social reward) from colleagues
Knowledge management resources	Lack of knowledge management strategy
	Lack of money and time for knowledge management
	Lack of staff with knowledge management skills
Technological factors	
Usability: Functionality and ease of use	Low level of usability and ease of use, which makes the tools too complicated to use
Functionality	To what extent do the tools fit to the user's needs and tasks that they need to fulfill
Training	Lack of training and sharing of best practices of how to use and work with the social media platforms as part of the current work routines

Chatter, Yammer or Podio for internal communication and knowledge sharing. The majority of the companies are from different industry sectors such as telecommunications, media and marketing, banking and financial services and shipping and logistics.

The survey questionnaire consists of 15 questions. The questions are constructed in a restricted manner in order to get answers, which are specific and related to our research question: Which factors affect employees' knowledge sharing behavior through social media?

The questions relate to employees knowledge sharing behavior and their use and adoption level of social media platforms during work. The first part of the questionnaire focuses on how frequent employees share knowledge, which type of knowledge they share, and which platforms they share it on. Traditional communication channels have also been included as part of the answer options in order to determine the adoption level of the new social media platforms. The second part and the majority of the questionnaire, entails questions, which focus on employee motivation and the drivers and barriers to knowledge sharing. Demographic questions are included in the last part of the questionnaire in order to provide a profile of the participants.

4   Survey Results

4.1   Adoption and Use of Social Media Platforms

Employees play a central role in knowledge sharing and social media can be a facilitator for more effective knowledge sharing to unlock valuable knowledge in organizations. The use and adoption of Chatter, Yammer and Podio was investigated in a number of Danish companies from different industry sectors based on an online questionnaire. In total 114 responses were collected. The majority of the employees, who participated in the survey (63%), are relatively young (between 20-39 years) and only few senior respondents have participated. A profile of the respondents is illustrated in Fig. 2.

The participation of female and male respondents is almost 50/50, with only 8% more male respondents. The majority of the respondents (69%) have worked from 1-5 years in their organization, which, most likely, correlates to the majority of the respondents' relatively younger age. All levels of positions are represented in the survey, but it is noteworthy that almost 50% of the respondents are specialists. Specialists are employees, who possess a high level of expert knowledge within a field, which they often are hired for.

The survey results show that 95% of the employees share knowledge with their colleagues. Only 5% are passive and never share their knowledge. Over half of the employees share

RESPONDENT PROFILE		
		In total: 114
POSITION		
Manager	24	21%
Specialist	53	46%
Office worker	23	20%
Trainee	5	5%
Other	9	8%
AGE		
20-29 years	24	21%
30-39 years	48	42%
40-49 years	33	29%
50-59 years	6	5%
60+ years	2	2%
Other	1	1%
GENDER		
Female	48	42%
Male	66	58%
WORKING YEARS		
< 1 year	2	2%
1-5 years	79	69%
5-10 years	18	15%
10-15 years	9	8%
20-30 years	3	3%
30+ years	3	3%

Fig. 2. Respondent profile

knowledge frequently: 55% of the employees share knowledge daily and some several times daily. 25% only share knowledge occasionally (weekly) and 15% rarely (monthly), which is illustrated in Table 2.

Table 2. Knowledge sharing frequency

SURVEY RESULTS		Responses in total : 114
How often do you contribute and share your knowledge with your colleagues?		
1. Very frequently (several times a day)	35	31%
2. Frequently (daily)	27	24%
3. Occasionally (weekly)	28	25%
4. Rarely (monthly)	17	15%
5. Never	5	5%

The survey results show that the adoption of social media platforms is limited, at this point. The fact that 95% of the employees actively share knowledge is very positive, but the employees, primarily, share knowledge through email (91%) and face-to-face meetings (79%), as illustrated in Table 2. Chat (41%), intranet (27%) and Google Docs (24%) are other frequently used ways to share knowledge in organizations.

The social media platforms: Yammer (14%), Podio (13%) and Chatter (14%), still score low compared to traditional communication channels. The usage of wikis also scores 14% and blogs scores as low as 4%, which is illustrated in Table 3.[1]

Table 3. Use of traditional communication channels and social media

TRADITIONAL COMMUNICATION CHANNELS			SOCIAL MEDIA PLATFORMS	
EMAIL	91%		SOCIAL NETWORKS	
			❖ YAMMER	14%
			❖ CHATTER	14%
FACE-TO-FACE MEETINGS	79%	VS	❖ PODIO	14%
			WIKIS	14%
CHAT	41%			
			BLOGS	4%
INTRANET	27%		GOOGLE DOCS	24%

---

[1] The percentages in Table 3 do not sum up to 100% due to a multiple choice question in the questionnaire.

4.2   Social Media: The Benefits

The survey shows that the social media platforms are providing benefits and business value, and in particular improve the internal communication (41%), increase knowledge sharing (37%) decrease the amount of emails (35%). Other identified benefits are it is easier: reaching colleagues in other departments (34%), employees get faster response to work related problems (34%) and it is easier to collaborate on projects (30%). The key benefits are presented in Fig. 3.[2]

These findings are similar to previous research [27] that found that technological tools positively affect employees to share knowledge, because it enables faster communication and knowledge sharing.

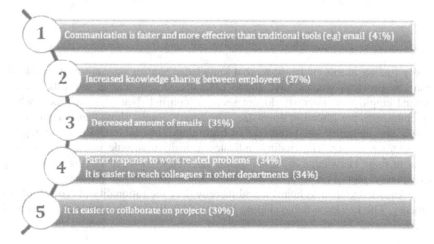

Fig. 3. Key benefits from the adoption of social media platforms

4.3   Knowledge Sharing Drivers and Barriers

The analysis and discussion of the factors, which affect employees' knowledge sharing is based on the framework developed for this study, which was introduced earlier in Figure 1.

The survey shows that the majority of the employees are motivated by intrinsic motivation [21], which means they are motivated to share knowledge out of altruistic and unselfish reasons, simply, because they feel it is important to help colleagues and provide value to the organization. This is consistent with previous studies [27], [42], which identified similar findings. Only few employees are motivated by extrinsic motivation and monetary rewards, such as a higher salary, a bonus or a promotion. The key knowledge sharing drivers identified in this survey are presented in Fig. 4.[3]

---

[2] The percentages in Fig. 3 do not sum up to 100% due to a multiple choice question in the questionnaire.

[3] The percentages in Fig. 4 do not sum up to 100% due to a multiple choice question in the questionnaire.

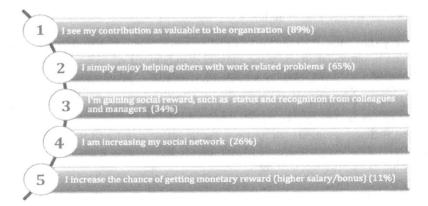

Fig. 4. Knowledge sharing drivers

A key finding in this study shows that knowledge sharing may not be a 'social dilemma', as previous studies have found [38, 39]. Organizational interests and the individual employees' interests do not seem to conflict. Not even in times, where many companies are forced to downsize. The survey results show that fear of giving up power and authority (4%) and fear of becoming replaceable (5%) are among the lowest scoring factors. The finding indicates a positive attitude in employees' willingness to share knowledge in organizations and that knowledge sharing is becoming a more integral part of employee's work life. Employees find that it is more beneficial to share knowledge than to hoard it and thereby defy the rationality of 'social dilemma' theory. The key knowledge sharing barriers identified in this study are presented in Fig. 5. [4]

Fig. 5. Knowledge sharing barriers

---

[4] The percentages in Fig. 5 do not sum up to 100% due to a multiple choice question in the questionnaire.

This study identifies lack of employees' participation (38%) and lack of management commitment and motivation (34%) as the top two key factors, which affect employees' willingness to share knowledge negatively. The finding emphasizes that motivation and encouragement from management and managers to get employees to adopt social media and share knowledge is closely related. Previous studies have also emphasized the need for management and managers to get actively involved, since the deployment of social media alone does not promote adoption of the platforms and knowledge sharing [3], [6], [43], [44].

In general, employees urge management and managers to explain the value and benefits of the social media platforms and to get more involved to motivate and encourage knowledge sharing and adoption of the platforms. This emphasizes the lack of a strategic approach to knowledge management, and the deployment of a 'provide and pray' approach, which according to a recent study conducted by Gartner, is the reason why the majority of social collaboration initiatives fail and only leads to a 10% success rate [16].

5   Discussion

Social media platforms can be a facilitator for more effective knowledge sharing and collaboration within organizations and thereby make organizations more productive and competitive. Due to the recognition of knowledge as a source of competitive advantage, the purpose of this study is to identify which factors affects employees' knowledge sharing on social media platforms within organizations.

A key finding in the study is that knowledge sharing is not a 'social dilemma' as previous studies [38, 39] have found. The organizational interest in making knowledge available to all employees do not seem to conflict with the employees' individual interest in hoarding knowledge in order to stay valuable and reduce the risk of getting fired. The study shows a positive trend in employees' willingness to share knowledge, because they consider sharing knowledge to be more beneficial than to hoard it, which defies the rationality of 'social dilemma' theory. The study, however, shows that only few employees have adopted social media for knowledge sharing and that employees, primarily, share knowledge through traditional communication channels such as: email and face-to-face meetings. A reason for this seem to be that employees are creatures of habits and prefer their current work routines due to convenience, why it takes time to adopt a new platform in their work routine. Even though the adoption of the platforms is limited, the organizations are still reaping benefits and business value. Overall, social media have enhanced the organizations internal communication, collaboration and knowledge sharing.

5.1   Factors Affecting Knowledge Sharing

The survey results show that employees are motivated to contribute and share knowledge by a number of different factors. In general employees feel that knowledge sharing is an integral part of their work and it is important to share knowledge with colleagues and provide value to the organization. The survey shows that the majority of the employees are motivated by so-called 'intrinsic motivation' [21], which means they are motivated to share knowledge out of altruistic and selfless reasons, because they believe it is important to help colleagues and create value to the organization. This is consistent with previous studies [27], [42], which also identified that recognition from colleagues and managers is a key motivating factor. Only few employees are motivated by so-called 'extrinsic motivation' [21], which entails monetary rewards, such as a higher salary, bonus or promotion.

This study also identifies a number of factors, which affect employees' knowledge sharing negatively. Lack of other employees' participation (38%) and lack of management commitment and motivation (34%) are identified as the top two barriers to affect employees' knowledge sharing negatively. The finding emphasizes the need for management and managers to get actively involved to motivate and encourage knowledge sharing. In general, employees urge management and managers to explain the value and benefits of social media platforms, which 19% of the employees see as a barrier to knowledge sharing, as well as to get more involved to motivate and encourage knowledge sharing. To some employees the active participation of management and managers on the social media platform does not seem to be a particularly motivating factor. This, however, seem to be correlated to the fact that knowledge sharing is a part of some of the employee's job description, why this may not be the case for other employees.

Recent reports by Gartner emphasize that lack of a strategy is not the road to become a social business. The vast majority of social collaboration initiatives fail due to lack of purpose and a 'provide and pray' approach, which only leads to a 10 percent success rate [16]. It is crucial that the individual organization get an understanding of their employees and how they work and what their needs are in order for them to opt into a technological and cultural change. In order to become a social business, organizations need to focus on the employees, make a cultural change within the company and make sure management and managers are actively involved [45].

Among the key factors to affect knowledge sharing negatively, the study identified the following factors: lack of content quality and relevance (26%), information overload (26%), lack of time (24%) and lack of understanding of social media and the benefits it provides (19%) (Fig. 5). It is noteworthy, that lack of content quality and information overload are factors that have been rated as barriers to knowledge sharing on the same level as lack of time.

Lack of content quality (26%) is among the key factors, which concern employees when they share knowledge, since the essence of social media is to share relevant content with colleagues and provide value to the organization. Some employees find it hard to determine, which kind of content they should share and whether it is relevant for their colleagues, which may prevent them from sharing knowledge. On the other hand it prevents some employees from using the platform, due to the irrelevant content. Lack of need, simply, keeps some employees from using the platform, which could be part of the reason for the limited adoption of the social media platforms. This could be correlated to the fact that almost 50% of the respondents are hired as specialists (Fig. 2), who primarily, use other systems, where they find the majority of the content they need during work. This indicates that there is a correlation between the limited adoption of the social media platforms and the type of position and the specific knowledge employees have. This sort of issue could be addressed by a set of social media guidelines, which could help employees by defining what is relevant, which would ensure a higher level of relevance and content quality.

Information overload (26%) is also identified among the key factors, which prevent employees from sharing knowledge. However, Paroutis and Al Saleh [3] argue if, for instance, all relevant content is on the platform, and the 'perceived usefulness' and the benefits of using the platform outweigh the costs, then employees, eventually, will start using it.

Contrary to the findings in a study conducted by Paroutis and Al Saleh [3], this study identifies lack of technical skills (15%) and training (18%) among the lowest scoring barriers to knowledge sharing. Lack of time (24%), however, is a key factor that prevents employees from getting familiar with the platforms. Lack of time seems to be a key factor, which affects participation from management, managers as well as employees negatively. These findings seem to be correlated to the fact that majority of the employees (63%), who participated in this survey, are relatively young (between 20-39 years) and only few senior respondents have participated, why lack of technical skills and training do not seem to be factors, which affect knowledge sharing in this specific case study (Fig. 2). This could, very likely, be linked to the younger generation is more technically skilled due to more frequent use of social media in their private lives.

Another noteworthy finding in this study is that lack of trust does not seem to be a factor, which affects employees' knowledge sharing negatively. Even though many previous studies have identified lack of trust as a key barrier to knowledge sharing, only 6% of the employees find that lack of trust is a barrier. The finding indicates that the employees in the participating companies, simply, know and trust each other relatively well, why trust is not a barrier associated with knowledge sharing in this specific study.

5.2   Towards a Research Model

Our research results can be summarized based on the discussion and analysis of the individual, organizational and technological factors, which are presented in the framework we have proposed in Fig. 1 in this study. The findings identified in this study are presented in a modified framework, which is illustrated in Fig. 6 below.

The original framework, illustrated in Fig. 1, is based on the findings of previous studies, which identified a number of individual, organizational and technological factors, which affect employees' knowledge sharing through social media. The results of this survey have identified a number of key findings, which differ from the previous studies, which means that some of the factors no longer are considered to affect employees' knowledge sharing as much as previously.

The initial framework in Fig. 1 includes 11 factors, which are, almost equally, divided among the individual, organizational and technological factors. The updated framework is slightly modified from the original version and consists only of 7 key factors that impact the adoption and use of social media. The original framework highlights that individual, organizational and technological factors, almost equally, affect employees' knowledge sharing through social media.

Based on the findings in this study, fewer factors seem to affect employees' knowledge sharing. The organizational factors: management support, knowledge sharing culture, recognition and rewards, and knowledge management resources have the strongest influence on employees' knowledge sharing followed by the individual factors: Motivation and perceived usefulness (cost/benefit). The technological factors do not seem to affect employees' knowledge sharing as much as previous research has found, but it is the influence from a combination of the individual and organizational factors, which determine whether an employee adopts social media for knowledge sharing.

The fact that technological factors do not seem to affect the employees' knowledge sharing in this particular study is most likely very case specific. These findings are very likely correlated to the fact that the majority of the employees (63%), who participated in this survey, are relatively young (between 20-39 years) and only few senior respondents have participated as illustrated in Fig. 2. Why lack of technical skills and training, consequently, do not seem to be factors, which affect knowledge sharing in this specific case. This could, very likely, be linked to the younger generation is more technically skilled due to more frequent use of social media in their private lives.

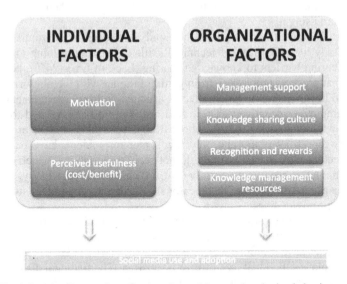

Fig. 6. Results: Factors that affect employees' knowledge sharing behavior

6   Conclusion

This study investigates employee's motivation and has attempted to determine which factors affect employees' knowledge sharing through social media in their working environment. The study identifies a number of factors that differ from previous studies, which shows a positive development in employees' knowledge sharing through social media within organizations.

The study shows that organizational factors such as: management support, knowledge sharing culture, recognition and rewards, and knowledge management resources have the strongest influence on employees' knowledge sharing. Furthermore, individual factors and in particular motivation and perceived usefulness (cost/benefit) seem to play an important role. Technological factors including usability (ease of use) functionality and training do not seem to affect employees' knowledge sharing as previous research has found, but it is the influence from the combination of the individual and organizational factors, which determine whether an employee adopts social media platforms for knowledge sharing.

A key finding of this study is that knowledge sharing is not a 'social dilemma' and that employees do not hoard knowledge as much as previously found due to the fact that it is more beneficial to share knowledge than to hoard it. The majority of the employees are motivated by intrinsic motivation, which means they are motivated to share knowledge out of altruistic and unselfish reasons, simply, because they feel it is important to help colleagues and provide value to the organization. Only few employees are motivated by extrinsic motivation and monetary rewards, such as a higher salary, a bonus or a promotion. Employees are more concerned with providing valuable content, since the essence of knowledge sharing trough social media is to provide value to colleagues and the organization.

The survey shows that the social media platforms have improved the companies' internal communication, collaboration and knowledge sharing among the limited group of employees, who have adopted the platforms. The biggest challenge for the organizations seems to be to promote and foster continued adoption of the platforms in order to become a social business and reap more benefits from social media. So far, none of the case companies can be considered to be social businesses, which means integrating social media into all of the organization's business practices and processes in order to build stronger relationships among employees, customers and business partners.

The findings of this study emphasize that a number of factors determine an organization's success of social media adoption. Each organization is unique and has a different structure, culture, number of employees, industry sector and so on. The combination of these factors affects the organization's approach to knowledge management, which will have an influence on whether the adoption of a social media platform will be a success among employees or not.

Acknowledgment. This research is partally supported by CBS Competitiveness Platform.

References

1. Nonaka, I.: The Knowledge Creating Company. Harvard Business Review, 162–171 (July-August, 2007)
2. Davenport, T.H.: Thinking for a Living: How to Get Better Performance and Results from Knowledge Workers. Harvard Business School Publishing, Boston (2005)
3. Paroutis, S., Al Saleh, A.: Determinants of Knowledge Sharing Using Web 2.0 Technologies. Journal of Knowledge Management 13(4), 52–63 (2009)
4. Kiron, D., Palmer, D., Phillips, A.N., Berkman, R.: Social Business: Shifting Out of First Gear. MIT Sloan Management Review Research Report (2013), retrieved from http://sloanreview.mit.edu/reports/shifting-social-business/
5. Rennie, A.: More Than Facebook: The Time Is Right For Social Business. Forbes (2011), retrieved from http://www.forbes.com/sites/ciocentral/2011/10/31/more-than-facebook-the-time-is-right-for-social-business/
6. Kirchner, K., Razmerita, L., Sudzina, F.: New Forms of Interaction and Knowledge Sharing on Web 2.0. In: Lytras, M.D., Damiani, E., Patricia, O.D.P. (eds.) Web 2.0: The Business Model, pp. 21–36. Springer Science and Business Media, New York (2008)

7. Andriole Stephen, J.: Business Impact of Web 2.0 Technologies. Communications of the ACM 53(12), 67–79 (2010)
8. McAfee, A.P.: Enterprise 2.0: The Dawn of Emergent Collaboration. MITSloan Management Review 47(3), 21–28 (2006)
9. McKinsey & Company: How Companies Are Benefiting from Web 2.0: McKinsey Global Survey Results. McKinsey Quarterly (2009)
10. Bughin, J., Chui, M.: The Rise of the Networked Enterprise: Web 2.0 Finds Its Payday. McKinsey & Company. McKinsey Quarterly (2010)
11. Chui, M., Manyika, J., Bughin, J., Dobbs, R., Roxburgh, C., Sarrazin, H., Sands, G., Westergren, M.: The Social Economy: Unlocking Value and Productivity through Social Technologies. McKinsey Global Institute Research Report (2012)
12. Razmerita, L., Kirchner, K., Sudzina, F.: Personal Knowledge Management: The Role of Web 2.0 tools for Managing Knowledge at Individual and Organisational levels. Online Information Review 33(6), 1021–1039 (2009)
13. Razmerita, L., Kirchner, K., et al.: Social Media In Organizations: Leveraging Personal And Collective Knowledge Processes. Journal of Organizational Computing and Electronic Commerce 24(1), 74–93 (2014)
14. Razmerita, L.: Collaboration using Social Media: The Case of Podio in a Voluntary Organization. In: Antunes, P., Gerosa, M.A., Sylvester, A., Vassileva, J., de Vreede, G.-J. (eds.) CRIWG 2013. LNCS, vol. 8224, pp. 1–9. Springer, Heidelberg (2013)
15. Popadiuk, S., Choo, C.W.: Innovation and knowledge creation: How are these concepts related? International Journal of Information Management 26(4), 302–312 (2006)
16. Gartner: Gartner Says the Vast Majority of Social Collaboration Initiatives Fail Due to Lack of Purpose (2013), http://www.gartner.com/newsroom/id/2402115
17. Harvard Business Review: The New Conversation: Taking Social Media from Talk to Action. Harvard Business Review Analytic Services (2010)
18. Social Semantic: Social Media Factbook. Denmark (2011), retrieved from http://blog.socialsemantic.eu/factbook/
19. Denyer, D., Parry, E., Flowers, P.: Social, Open and Participative? Exploring Personal Experiences and Organizational Effects of Enterprise 2.0 Use. Long Range Planning 44, 375–396 (2011)
20. Danis, C., Singer, D.: A Wiki Instance In the Enterprise: Opportunities, Concerns and Reality. In: Proceedings of the 2008 ACM Conference on Computer Supported Cooperative Work. ACM, New York (2008)
21. Deci, E., Ryan, R.: Intrinsic and Extrinsic Motivations: Classic Definitions and New Directions. Contemporary Educational Psychology 25, 54–67 (2000)
22. O'Dell, C., Hubert, C.: The New Edge In Knowledge: How Knowledge Management is Changing the Way We Do Business. John Wiley & Sons Inc., New York (2011)
23. Von Krogh, G.: How does social software change knowledge management? Toward a strategic research agenda. The Journal of Strategic Information Systems, 154–164 (2012)
24. Bernal, J.: Web 2.0 and Social Networking for the Enterprise: Guidelines and Examples for Implementation and Management within Your Organization. IBM Press, USA (2010)
25. Von Krogh, G., Haefliger, S., Spaeth, S., Wallin, M.W.: Carrots and Rainbows: Motivation and Social practice in Open Source Software Development. MIS Quarterly 36(2), 649–676 (2012)
26. Sajeva, S.: An Investigation of Critical Barriers to Effective Knowledge Management. Social Sciences/Socialiniai Mokslai 58(4), 20–27 (2007)
27. Lin, H.-F.: Knowledge Sharing and Firm Innovation Capability: An Empirical Study. International Journal of Manpower 28(3/4), 315–332 (2007)

28. Hsu, M.H., Ju, T.L., Yen, C.H., Chang, C.M.: Knowledge Sharing Behavior In Virtual Communities: The Relationship Between Trust, Self-efficacy and Outcome Expectations. International Journal of Human-Computer Studies 65(2), 153–169 (2007)

29. Ardichvili, A., Page, V., Wentling, T.: Motivation and Barriers to Participate in Virtual Knowledge-sharing Communities of Practice. Journal of Knowledge Management 7(1), 64–77 (2003)

30. Riege, A.: Actions to Overcome Knowledge Transfer Barriers in MNCs. Journal of Knowledge Management 11(1), 48–67 (2007)

31. De Long, D.W., Fahey, L.: Diagnosing Cultural Barriers to Knowledge Management. The Academy of Management Executive 14(4), 113–127 (2000)

32. Alawi, A.I., Al Marzooqi, N.Y., Mohammed, Y.F.: Organizational Culture and Knowledge Sharing: Critical Success Factors. Journal of Knowledge Management 11(2), 22–42 (2007)

33. Ardichvili, A., Maurer, M., Li, W., Wentling, T., Stuedemann, R.: Cultural influences on Knowledge Sharing through Online Communities of Practice. Journal of Knowledge Management 10(1), 94–107 (2006)

34. Chiu, C.M., Hsu, M.H., Wang, E.T.: Understanding Knowledge Sharing in Virtual Communities: An Integration of Social Capital and Social Cognitive Theories. Decision Support Systems 42, 1872–1888 (2006)

35. Zhang, X., Ordóñez de Pablosc, P., Zhoud, Z.: Effect of Knowledge Sharing Visibility on Incentive-based Relationship in Electronic Knowledge Management Systems: An empirical investigation. Computers in Human Behavior 29, 307–313 (2013)

36. Chen, C.J., Hung, S.W.: To give or to receive? Factors Influencing Members' Knowledge Sharing and Community Promotion in Professional Virtual Communities. Information and Management 47, 226–236 (2010)

37. Tohidinia, Z., Mosakhani, M.: Knowledge Sharing Behaviour and Its Predictors. Industrial Management & Data Systems 110(4), 611–631 (2010)

38. Cabrera, A., Cabrera, E.F.: Knowledge-sharing Dilemmas. Organisation Studies 23(5), 687–710 (2002)

39. Kimmerle, J., Wodzicki, K., Cress, U.: The Social Psychology of Knowledge Management. Team Performance Management 14(7), 381–401 (2008)

40. Casimir, G., Lee, K., Loon, M.: Knowledge Sharing: Influences of Trust, Commitment and Cost. Journal of Knowledge Management 16(5), 740–753 (2012)

41. Gammelgaard, J.: Why Are We So Hostile to Sharing Knowledge? European Business Forum 18, 80–81 (2004)

42. Wasko, M., Faraj, S.: Why Should I Share? Examining Social Capital and Knowledge Contribution In Electronic Networks of Practice. MIS Quarterly 29(1), 35–57 (2005)

43. McAfee, A.P.: Enterprise 2.0: New Collaborative Tools For Your Organization's Toughest Challenges. Harvard Business School Publishing, Boston (2009)

44. Stenmark, D.: Web 2.0 in the Business Environment: The New Intranet or a Passing Hype? In: Proceedings of the 16th European Conference on Information Systems, Ireland (2008)

45. Gartner: Gartner Says 80 Percent of Social Business Efforts Will Not Achieve Intended Benefits Through 2015 (2013), retrieved from
http://www.gartner.com/newsroom/id/2319215

A Literature Review on Cloud Computing Adoption Issues in Enterprises

Rania Fahim El-Gazzar

Department of Information Systems, University of Agder, Kristiansand, Norway
`rania.f.el-gazzar@uia.no`

Abstract. Cloud computing has received increasing interest from enterprises since its inception. With its innovative information technology (IT) services delivery model, cloud computing could add technical and strategic business value to enterprises. However, cloud computing poses highly concerning internal (e.g., Top management and experience) and external issues (e.g., regulations and standards). This paper presents a systematic literature review to explore the current key issues related to cloud computing adoption. This is achieved by reviewing 51 articles published about cloud computing adoption. Using the grounded theory approach, articles are classified into eight main categories: internal, external, evaluation, proof of concept, adoption decision, implementation and integration, IT governance, and confirmation. Then, the eight categories are divided into two abstract categories: cloud computing adoption factors and processes, where the former affects the latter. The results of this review indicate that enterprises face serious issues before they decide to adopt cloud computing. Based on the findings, the paper provides a future information systems (IS) research agenda to explore the previously under-investigated areas regarding cloud computing adoption factors and processes. This paper calls for further theoretical, methodological, and empirical contributions to the research area of cloud computing adoption by enterprises.

Keywords: Cloud computing, adoption, enterprise.

1 Introduction

Over the past decade, there has been a heightened interest in the adoption of cloud computing by enterprises. Cloud computing promises the potential to reshape the way enterprises acquire and manage their needs for computing resources efficiently and cost-effectively [1]. In line with the notion of shared services, cloud computing is considered an innovative model for IT service sourcing that generates value for the adopting enterprises [2]. Cloud computing enables enterprises to focus on their core business activities, and, thus, productivity is increased [3]. The adoption of cloud computing is growing rapidly due to the scalability, flexibility, agility, and simplicity it offers to enterprises [3–6]. A recent cross-sectional survey by [7] on the adoption rates of cloud computing by enterprises reported that 77% of large enterprises are adopting the cloud, whereas 73% of small and medium-sized enterprises (SMEs) are adopting the cloud.

B. Bergvall-Kåreborn and P.A. Nielsen (Eds.): TDIT 2014, IFIP AICT 429, pp. 214–242, 2014.

Cloud computing is "an old idea whose time has (finally) come" [8]. The term cloud is old since it was drawn in network diagrams as a metaphor representing the Internet [9]. Cloud computing is generally referred to as providing "Internet-based computing service" [10]; however, the technical meaning is richer, as cloud computing builds on already-existing computing technologies, such as grid computing and virtualization, which are forms of distributed computing technology [9]. Virtualization involves masking the physical characteristics of computing resources to hide the complexity when systems, applications, or end users interact with them [9]. Grid computing is "a model of distributed computing that uses geographically and administratively distant resources, and, thus, users can access computers and data transparently without concern about location, operating system, and account administration" [11]. With the advent of cloud computing, the merits of virtualization and grid computing have been combined and further improved. Cloud computing shares some characteristics with virtualization and grid computing; however, it still has its own distinguishing characteristics as well as associated risks [12–15].

Cloud computing has been given numerous definitions since its advent. Basically, definitions started with the notion of an application service provision (ASP) that is an IT sourcing model for renting business applications over the Internet [16]. This definition became wider as Internet-based IT service offerings comprised storage, hosting infrastructure, and network; thus, it is given the name net sourcing, to fit the variety of IT service offerings [17]. HP defines cloud computing as "Everything as a Service" [18], while Microsoft perceives the value of cloud computing as "Cloud + Client," emphasizing the importance of the end user [19]. T-Systems define cloud computing as "the renting of infrastructure and software, as well as bandwidths, under defined service conditions. These components should be able to be adjusted daily to the needs of the customer and offered with the utmost availability and security. Included in cloud computing are end-2-end service level agreements (SLAs) and use-dependent service invoices" [20].

T-Systems' definition conveys the idea of cloud computing as being a utility computing or 5th utility, because enterprises are able to consume computing resources on a pay-as-you-go basis just like the four public utilities (water, electricity, gas, and telephone). The widely known definition of cloud computing is by the National Institute of Standards and Technology (NIST). The NIST defines cloud computing as "a model for enabling convenient, on-demand network access to a shared pool of configurable computing resources (e.g., networks, servers, storage, applications, and services) that can be rapidly provisioned and released with minimal management effort or service provider interaction" [21]. According to the NIST definition, the basic actors in the cloud computing context are the cloud service provider (CSP) and the cloud service consumer (CSC), despite that there might be service brokers involved [22].

CSPs offer various service models depending on the enterprise's requirements, whereas the basic service models are [21]: (1) Software-as-a-Service (SaaS), the capability of the consumer to use the provider's applications running on a cloud infrastructure; (2) Platform-as-a-Service (PaaS), the capability of the consumer to deploy onto the cloud infrastructure consumer-created or acquired applications created using programming languages, libraries, services, and tools supported by the provider; and (3) Infrastructure-as-a-Service (IaaS), the capability of the consumer to provision processing, storage, networks, and other fundamental computing resources, where the consumer is able to deploy and run arbitrary software, which can include operating systems and applications. It has been reported that 32% of large enterprises are testing the concept of cloud computing; 37% are already running applications on the cloud; and 17% are using cloud infrastructure [7]. Contrarily, 19% of SMEs are testing the concept; 29% are running applications on the cloud; and 41% are using cloud infrastructure [7].

Cloud computing service models share five common essential characteristics that distinguish cloud computing from other computing technologies [21]:

1. On-demand self-service, where the consumer can unilaterally provision computing capabilities, such as server time and network storage, as needed automatically without requiring human interaction with each service provider;
2. Broad network access, where the capabilities are available over the network and accessed through standard mechanisms that promote use by heterogeneous thin or thick client platforms (e.g., mobile phones, tablets, laptops, and workstations);
3. Resource pooling, where the provider's computing resources are pooled to serve multiple consumers using a multitenant model, with different physical and virtual resources dynamically assigned and reassigned according to consumer demand;
4. Rapid elasticity, where capabilities can be elastically provisioned and released, in some cases automatically, to scale rapidly outward and inward commensurate with demand; and
5. Measured service, where cloud systems automatically control and optimize resource use by leveraging a metering capability at some level of abstraction appropriate to the type of service (e.g., storage, processing, bandwidth, and active user accounts).

Cloud service models can be deployed in one of the four deployment models [21]: (1) private cloud, where the cloud infrastructure is provisioned for exclusive use by a single organization comprising multiple consumers (e.g., business units), and it may be owned, managed, and operated by the organization, a third party, or some combination of them, and it may exist on or off premises; (2) community cloud, where the cloud infrastructure is provisioned for exclusive use by a specific community of consumers from organizations that have shared concerns (e.g., mission, security requirements, policy, and compliance considerations), and it may be owned, managed, and operated by one or more of the organizations in the community, a third party, or some combination of them, and it may exist on or off premises; (3) public cloud, where the cloud infrastructure is provisioned for open use by the general public. It may be owned, managed, and operated by a business, academic, or government organization, or some combination of them, and it exists on the premises of the cloud provider; (4) hybrid cloud, where the cloud infrastructure is a composition of two or more distinct cloud infrastructures (private, community, or public) that remain unique entities but are bound together by standardized or proprietary technology that enables data and application portability (e.g., cloud bursting for load balancing between clouds). It has been reported recently that 61% of enterprises are currently using public clouds; 38% are using private clouds; and 29% are using hybrid clouds [7].

At the enterprise level, cloud computing adoption takes place in three contexts. Large enterprises have slack resources, both financial and technical, to afford deploying private IaaS, PaaS, and SaaS clouds on a pay-as-you-go basis [4, 23]. Whereas, SMEs tend to deploy public SaaS clouds, which are appropriate for their start-up due to their limited financial and IT capabilities, which impede their deploying and maintaining private clouds [4, 24–26]. For governments, deployment of private IaaS clouds is favorable [4].

In spite of its appealing benefits for enterprises, cloud computing raises serious technical, economic, ethical, legal, and managerial issues [6, 27]. The extant literature is focused more on the technical issues of cloud computing, with less attention paid to business issues regarding the adoption of cloud computing [10]. Further, there is a lack of in-depth studies about issues related to the cloud computing adoption process in the context of enterprise users [10, 28]. The purpose of this study is to review systematically the extant literature regarding cloud computing adoption to identify the key issues that have been researched. In addition, the quality of the extant research will be assessed. Then, the under-researched areas will be identified, and a future IS research agenda will be proposed accordingly. The remainder of this study is organized as follows: Section 2 presents the methodology of the systematic literature search process and the classification schemes adopted. Section 3 presents the findings from the review. Implications for future IS research are discussed in Section 4. Conclusions of this review are presented in Section 5.

2   Research Method

Reviewing the literature is an essential process that creates a firm foundation for advancing knowledge; it facilitates uncovering areas where research is needed [29]. This paper aims at systematically reviewing the literature to represent the current state of IS research regarding cloud computing adoption issues. This review process followed the fundamental guidelines for conducting an effective literature review by [29–31], and it is done within boundaries [29]. The contextual boundary for this review is the enterprise users, not individuals, as there are significant issues that need to be addressed before enterprises start using clouds [27, 32]. The temporal boundary of this review covers the published articles in all previous years until February 2014.

2.1   Literature Search Process

The literature search process of this review involved querying seven quality scholarly literature databases (AISeL, IEEE Xplore, ScienceDirect, EBSCOhost, ProQuest, Wiley online library, and ACM digital library). These databases provide access to leading IS journals and high-quality peer-reviewed IS conference publications [31]. Further, online databases are appropriate and practical sources for reviewing the literature about a contemporary phenomenon such as cloud computing [10]. The search criterion was limited to the article's title to ensure the relevance of the articles. The terms used for searching all seven databases are 'cloud computing' in combination with 'adopt*' and other related terms, such as 'accept*' and 'diffus*'. This initially resulted in 94 articles in total including recurrences. An overview of the search process is provided in Table 1.

Table 1. Literature search overview

Literature data-bases	Search query	Search results
AISeL	title:"cloud computing" AND title:adopt*	15
	title:"cloud computing" AND title:accept*	2
	title:"cloud computing" AND title:diffus*	0
IEEE Xplore	(("Document Title":"cloud computing") AND "Document Title":"adopt*")	22
	(("Document Title":"cloud computing") AND "Document Title":"accept*")	2
	(("Document Title":"cloud computing") AND "Document Title":"diffus*")	1
ScienceDirect	TITLE("cloud computing") and TITLE(adopt*)	6
	TITLE("cloud computing") and TITLE(accept*)	0
	TITLE("cloud computing") and TITLE(diffus*)	0
EBSCOhost	TI "cloud computing" AND TI "adopt*"	30
	TI "cloud computing" AND TI "accept*"	0
	TI "cloud computing" AND TI "diffus*"	1
ProQuest	ti("cloud computing") AND ti(adopt*)	6
	ti("cloud computing") AND ti(accept*)	1
	ti("cloud computing") AND ti(diffus*)	0
Wiley (Online Library)	"cloud computing" in Article Titles AND "adopt*" in Article Titles	1
	"cloud computing" in Article Titles AND accept* in Article Titles	1
	"cloud computing" in Article Titles AND diffus* in Article Titles	0
ACM (Digital Library)	(Title:"cloud computing" and Title:"adopt*")	5
	(Title:"cloud computing" and Title:"accept*")	1
	(Title:"cloud computing" and Title:"diffus*")	0
Total		94

The practical screen involved reading the abstract of the articles to decide their relevance to the focus of this review [30, 33]. Further, the filtering criteria involved the exclusion of recurring articles, research-in-progress articles, articles that were not written in English, articles with a focus on individuals, periodical articles published by news websites, trade journals, and magazines. These exclusion criteria delimit the sample of articles so that the literature review becomes practically manageable [33]. Eventually, this resulted in 51 articles for the classification.

2.2 Classification Scheme

The reviewed articles are classified according to the research methods employed in each study to identify how adequately the adoption of cloud computing is researched [34–36]. The research methods used in the reviewed articles are lab experiments, field studies, Delphi study, interviews, literature reviews, case studies, and surveys. Some articles do not have a methodology section and reflect on some concepts in relation to cloud computing (i.e., cost, security, performance, etc.) or they adopt theories without empirical testing. This group of articles is labeled as "conceptual papers."

Cloud computing adoption issues are discussed diversely in the literature; thus, this review sought to develop a classification scheme to better gain insights from the preceding academic contributions to the area of cloud computing adoption. The classification of the 51 articles involved using a bottom-up grounded theory (GT) approach [37]. The GT approach is said to be valuable for conducting a rigorous literature review [38], "instead of force-fitting the data to an a priori theory" [39]. The 51 reviewed articles are classified according to a GT approach for reviewing the literature recommended by [38]. Using a GT approach in reviewing the literature helps "reach a thorough and theoretically relevant analysis of a topic" [38].

The classification process involved a close reading of the articles. Then, the open coding was utilized to generate codes from analyzing each article's text to capture the themes that appear in each article. This resulted in 30 concepts, which were labeled. Next, the axial coding was applied to develop the relations between the concepts identified in the open coding [38]. This resulted in a grouping of the 30 subcategories identified from the open coding into eight corresponding categories (i.e., internal, external, evaluation, proof of concept, adoption decision, implementation and integration, IT governance, and confirmation).

Finally, the selective coding technique was applied to integrate and refine the eight main categories and to develop relations between them [38]. This resulted in two abstract categories: cloud adoption factors (i.e., internal and external) and cloud adoption processes (i.e., evaluation, proof of concept, adoption decision, implementation and integration, IT governance, and confirmation), where the former influenced the latter (see Table 2).

Table 2. Classification scheme

Selective coding	Axial coding	Open coding
1. Cloud computing adoption factors	1. External	1. Government regulations
		2. IT industry standards institutes
		3. Cloud providers
		4. Business partners
		5. Competitors
		6. Cloud service broker
	2. Internal	7. Willingness to invest
		8. Top management
		9. Firm size
		10. Organizational culture
		11. Employees' IT skills
		12. Prior experience
2. Cloud computing adoption processes	3. Evaluation	13. Cost and benefits
		14. Impact on people and work practices
		15. Internal readiness
		16. Cloud provider selection
	4. Proof of concept	17. Trialability
		18. Perceived benefits and risks
	5. Adoption decision	19. Business needs identification
		20. Criticality determination
		21. Strategic value evaluation
		22. Implementation planning
		23. Service model selection
		24. Deployment model selection
		25. Contract and SLA negotiation

Table 2. (*Continued*)

6.	Implementation and integration	26. 27.	Complexity Compatibility
7.	IT governance	28. 29.	Auditability and traceability Risk management
8.	Confirmation	30.	Usage continuance

3   Findings

The findings from reviewing 51 articles are presented in light of six dimensions: distribution of articles over years, outlets in which articles were published, theories/frameworks used, research methods used, and cloud computing adoption factors and processes. Fig. 1 illustrates that interest in researching the topic of cloud computing adoption has grown exponentially from 2009 until 2013, denoting that cloud computing adoption is remarkable. However, the three articles published in 2014 do not present a full picture of research endeavors of the whole year 2014.

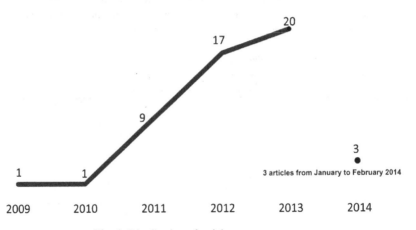

Fig. 1. Distribution of articles over years

The outlets in which the articles were published and the number of articles (N) in each are presented in Table 3; the outlets are categorized as IS and non-IS journals and conferences. The IS journals and conferences are identified according to the Association for Information Systems (AIS)[1,2,3,4] and [31]. Obviously, non-IS journals dominate in investigating cloud computing adoption area with 11 articles each, whereas only one IS journal contributed with three articles. Likewise, non-IS conferences contributed numerously, with 25 articles, whereas IS conferences had 12 articles. However, more published articles were found in IS conference publications than in IS journals.

---

[1] http://aisnet.org/general/custom.asp?page=JournalRankings
[2] http://aisnet.org/?AffiliatedConference
[3] http://aisnet.org/?page=Conferences
[4] http://aisel.aisnet.org/affiliated/

Table 3. Number of articles per outlet type

Outlet type	Outlet name	N
IS Journals	• International Journal of Information Management	3
Non-IS Journals	• Journal of Technology Management for Growing Economies • Journal of Medical Marketing: Device, Diagnostic and Pharmaceutical Marketing • Mathematical and Computer Modelling • Industrial Management & Data Systems • International Journal of Logistics Management • Journal of Enterprise Information Management • IEEE Transactions on Engineering Management • European Management Review • Procedia Technology • Journal of Industry, Competition, and Trade • GSTF Journal on Computing	11
IS Conferences	• International Conference on Information Systems (ICIS) • Americas Conference on Information Systems (AMCIS) • Hawaii International Conference on System Sciences (HICSS) • European Conference on Information Systems (ECIS) • Pacific Asia Conference on Information Systems (PACIS) • Mediterranean Conference on Information Systems (MCIS)	12
Non-IS Conferences	• International Conference for Internet Technology and Secured Transactions (ICITST) • BLED Conference • International Conference on Networked Computing and Advanced Information Management (NCM) • International Conference on Cloud Computing Technology and Science • International Conference on System of Systems Engineering • International Conference on Adaptive Science & Technology (ICAST) • European Conference on Information Management & Evaluation • International Conference on Product Focused Software Development and Process Improvement • International Conference on Information Integration and Web-based Applications & Services (iiWAS) • Annual Allerton Conference on Communication, Control, and Computing (Allerton) • International Conference on Cloud Computing (CLOUD) • International Conference on Advances in Computing, Communications, and Informatics • International Conference on Computing, Management and Telecommunications (ComManTel) • International Conference on Cloud Computing Technologies, Applications and Management (ICCCTAM) • International Conference on Cloud Computing Technologies, Applications and Management (ICCCTAM) • UK Academy for Information Systems Conference • International Conference on Computer and Information Science	25

Table 3. (*Continued*)

- IST-Africa Conference and Exhibition
- International Conference on Research and Innovation in Information Systems (ICRIIS)
- International Conference on ICT for Smart Society
- IEEE World Congress on Services

The findings from the 51 articles are further organized according to theory/framework/model used in each publication. Some articles discuss related concepts (i.e., performance, cost, security, cloud providers, etc.); thus, they are considered to be using "general concepts." Further, other articles use a GT approach to understand cloud computing adoption; these articles built models based on field data. The use of different theories to understand cloud computing adoption factors and processes is quite evident, as per Table 4. Further, articles that tested theories empirically by field data are predominant, but the non-empirically tested theoretical contributions are not slight. General concepts are the most frequently used to explain cloud computing adoption factors and processes.

The use of the technology-organization-environment (TOE) framework is also frequent compared to other theories, followed by diffusion of innovation (DOI) theory and the GT approach, which appear to be the next most frequently used in the reviewed articles. Empirically tested theories/frameworks/models are dominant with 34 articles, whereas studies with no empirical testing were less common: 17 articles. However, the number of articles without empirical testing is still remarkable, which implies the need for more field work. Further, the majority of articles used a combination of multiple theoretical perspectives to gain more insights about cloud computing adoption factors and processes. This implies that cloud computing adoption phenomenon is multifaceted. The majority of articles have used theories/frameworks/models to explain what are the factors that affect the adoption of cloud computing and what are the key considerations in cloud computing adoption processes. Yet, there is a lack of using theories that demonstrate how enterprises react differently to same internal and external factors and why do they react in such a way.

Table 4. Use of theory by reviewed articles

	Theory (T)/Framework(F)/Model(M)	References (Empirical Testing)	References (no Empirical Testing)	Frequency
(M)	Technology Acceptance Model (TAM)	[40], [41], [42]	-	3
(M)	Post-Acceptance Model (PAM) of IS Continuance	[43]	-	1
(T)	Utility Theory	[44]	-	1
(M)	Human-Organization-Technology Fit Model (HOT-fit)	[45]	-	1
(M)	Business Model Factors	[46]	-	1
(M)	Structural Equation Modeling (SEM)	[47]	-	1

Table 4. (*Continued*)

(F)	Technology-Organization-Environment (TOE)	[48], [49], [50], [51], [52], [45], [53], [54], [55]	[56], [23]	11
(T)	Organizational Information Processing Theory	[57]	-	1
-	General Concepts	[58], [59], [60], [61], [62], [63]	[64], [65], [66], [67], [68], [69], [70], [71], [72]	15
(F)	National Outsourcing Association (NOA) Framework for Factors Inhibiting Cloud Computing Adoption	[73]	-	1
(F)	Contextual Usability Framework	[74]	-	1
(F)	Attention Based View (ABV)	[75]	-	1
(T)	Diffusion Of Innovation (DOI)	[76], [40], [74]	[56], [23], [77]	6
(T)	Transaction Cost Economics (TCE) Theory	-	[78], [77]	2
(T)	Resource Dependence Theory (RDT)	-	[77]	1
(T)	Innovation Decision Process Theory (IDPT)	-	[79]	1
(T)	Dynamic Capabilities Theory	[40]	-	1
(T)	Contingency Theory	[40]	-	1
(T)	Mean Field Game Theory (MFG)	-	[80]	1
(M)	Return On Investment (ROI)	-	[81]	1
(T)	Option Pricing Theory	-	[82]	1
(T)	Perceived Attributes Theory	-	[79]	1
(F)	Geoffrey Moore's Technology Adoption Life Cycle	-	[79]	1
(F)	Innovation Value Institute's IT Capability Maturity Framework (ITCMF)	[83]	-	1
(T)	Actor Network Theory (ANT)	[48], [55]	-	2
(M)	Gap Analysis Model	[84]	-	1
(T)	GT Approach	[85], [86], [87], [88], [89]	-	5
Total (without repetitions)		34	17	

As per Table 5, the 51 articles are mapped to cloud computing adoption factors (i.e., external and internal) and processes (i.e., evaluation, proof of concept, adoption decision, implementation and integration, IT governance, and confirmation) identified in this review as well as research methods (RM) employed (i.e., Lab Experiment (LE), Field Study (FS), Case Study (CS), Delphi Study (DS), Survey (SUR), Interviews (INT), Conceptual Paper (CP), Literature Review (LR)). Further, the number of articles (N) per subcategory and research method is provided. The findings, in general, indicate fewer qualitative studies (i.e., case studies, interviews, and field studies) have contributed to the understanding of cloud computing adoption factors and processes, as compared to quantitative studies (i.e., surveys). In some articles, multiple methods are used [42, 44, 50, 57]. Further, external adoption factors are extensively addressed by survey and conceptual articles, and less addressed by in-depth studies. This applies similarly to the internal factors. Among the external factors, investigating government regulations is dominant. Regarding the internal factors, the role of top management in cloud computing adoption is more researched among others. In general, adoption processes, such as evaluation, adoption decision, implementation and integration, IT governance, and confirmation, are not adequately addressed, except for the proof of concept process. However, the number of studies identifying perceived benefits and risks is predominant in proof of concept process and among other cloud computing adoption processes.

Table 5. Mapping of articles to classification scheme and research methods

Cloud computing adoption factors and processes		LE	FS	CS	DS	SUR	INT	CP	LR
External factors	Government regulations (N = 20)	-	[61]	[83], [48], [89], [84]	[57], [87]	[57], [73], [54], [50], [55], [45]	[57], [50]	[23], [77], [69], [78], [68], [79], [72], [70]	-
	IT industry standards institutes (N = 6)	-	-	[83]	-	[76], [54]	-	[77], [78], [71]	-
	Cloud providers (N = 15)	-	-	[51], [48], [89]	-	[75], [86], [76], [85], [55], [53], [46]	-	[78], [79], [68], [77], [72]	-
	Business partners (N = 11)	-	-	[48]	[57]	[52], [76], [57], [75], [85], [85], [55], [74], [42], [53]	[57], [42]	[56]	-
	Competitors (N = 10)	-	-	[51], [48]	[57]	[57], [52], [50], [55], [53], [45]	[57], [50]	[23], [56]	-

Table 5. (*Continued*)

	Cloud service broker (N = 1)	-	-	-	-	-	-	[71]	-
Internal factors	Willingness to invest (N = 11)	-	-	[83], [40], [48], [51]	-	[60], [76], [50], [44], [41]	[50], [44]	[23], [56]	-
	Top management (N = 18)	-	[88]	[40], [51], [83], [49]	[87]	[50], [73], [60], [55], [74], [53], [45]	[50]	[67], [23], [81], [64]	-
	Firm size (N = 9)	-	-	-	-	[52], [50], [60], [55], [53]	[50]	[23], [56], [81], [72]	-
	Organizational culture (N = 5)	-	-	[49], [83]	-	[50], [47]	[50]	[71]	-
	Employees' IT skills (N = 8)	-	-	[49]	-	[60], [50], [52], [55], [45]	[50]	[23], [70]	-
	Prior experience (N = 6)	-	-	[51]	-	[41], [74], [42], [53]	[42]	-	-
Evaluation process	Cost and benefits (N = 10)	-	[61]	[89], [84]	-	[45], [46]	-	[81], [80], [79], [82], [70]	-
	Impact on people and work practices (N = 7)	-	[61]	[83], [89]	-	[42], [41]	[42]	[70], [71]	-
	Internal readiness (N = 7)	-	[88]	[84]	-	[76], [52], [42], [45]	[42]	[23]	-
	Cloud provider selection (N = 6)	-	[61]	[40], [83], [84]	-	-	-	[65], [67]	-
Proof of concept process	Trialability (N = 4)	-	-	[51]	-	[76], [74], [53]	-	-	-

Table 5. (*Continued*)

	Perceived benefits and risks (N = 30)	[62]	-	[51], [40], [49], [48], [89], [84]	-	[50], [86], [63], [75], [54], [76], [85], [73], [59], [41], [55], [74], [42], [53], [45], [46]	[50], [42]	[56], [64], [65], [77], [68], [70], [71]	-
Adoption decision process	Business needs identification (N = 4)	-	[61]	-	-	[76], [53]	-	[64]	-
	Criticality determination (N = 3)	-	-	-	-	-	-	[69], [81], [82]	-
	Strategic value evaluation (N = 3)	-	-	[89]	-	[75], [76]	-	-	-
	Implementation planning (N = 2)	-	-	-	-	[60]	-	[79]	-
	Service model selection (N = 2)	-	-	-	-	-	-	[65]	[66]
	Deployment model selection (N = 2)	-	-	-	-	-	-	[79], [69]	-
	Contract and SLA negotiation (N = 4)	-	-	-	-	[53]	-	[65], [81], [71]	-
Implementation and integration process	Complexity (N = 10)	-	-	[49], [51]	-	[50], [76], [52], [74], [42], [53], [45]	[50], [42]	[23]	-
	Compatibility (N = 9)	-	-	[51]	-	[50], [76], [52], [74], [53], [45]	[50]	[23], [70]	-

Table 5. (*Continued*)

IT governance process	Auditability and traceability (N = 6)	-	-	[49], [83]	-	[50]	[50]	[65], [81], [71]	-
	Risk management (N = 5)	[62]	-	-	-	[63]	-	[69], [71]	[66]
Confirmation process	Usage continuance (N = 2)	-	-	-	-	[43]	-	[79]	-
N per RM		1	2	6	2	24	4	17	1

Cloud Computing Adoption Factors. These comprise internal and external factors that have impact on the cloud computing adoption processes.

External Factors. These comprise factors from the outside social environment in which the enterprise operates and by which its cloud computing adoption process is influenced. These external factors are: 1) government regulations, 2) IT industry standards institutes, 3) cloud providers, 4) business partners, 5) competitors, and 6) cloud service broker. The adoption of cloud computing is arguably surrounded by different levels of environmental and inter-organizational uncertainties [57]. There is a wide emphasis on the importance of *government regulations* at the national and international levels [23, 54, 73, 77]. In spite of their role in facilitating the cloud computing adoption securely, the lack of government regulations can hinder enterprises from adopting the cloud [45, 54, 87]. Some regulations, such as the Sarbanes-Oxley Act (SOX) for corporate accounting data, the Gramm-Leach-Bliley Act (GLBA), and the Health Insurance Portability and Accountability Act (HIPAA) were enacted before cloud computing was becoming increasingly adopted, and they might not be sufficient to facilitate its adoption [69, 72]. However, some countries started to enact laws specific to cloud computing, such as *cloud first policy* and the Health Information Technology for Economic and Clinical Health (HITECH) Act in the USA and *cloud computing strategy* by the Australian government [72, 78].

The inconsistency of international government regulations is a further concern as there is no widely agreed data privacy policy among all governments [72]. Some countries tend to restrict enterprises to store their data in cloud infrastructure only if it is within the national borders [68]. For instance, the EU's privacy laws prohibit the exchange of personal information outside the users' jurisdiction [83]. This is because cloud providers running outside of their home country must comply with the host country's regulations and government surveillance, which can be difficult for enterprises to cope with [61, 78]. An example of the multijurisdictional politics that have negative impact on cloud computing adoption is the USA Patriot Act, which makes countries, especially, the EU countries, skeptical about dealing with US-based cloud providers [70, 72]. However, some cloud providers solved this issue to accord with EU data regulations by allowing enterprises to deploy their IT resources on physical servers located within the EU region [70]. Although government regulations are in place in the developed world, they often conflict with each other, and they are not adequately placed in the developing world [72, 78].

In line with this, *IT standards institutes* are also cited as an important factor for dealing with enterprises' concerns about security and the interoperability of cloud solutions [77, 83]. Although they are still missing pieces in the puzzle of cloud computing for enterprises [54, 76, 78], some efforts to develop security standards have occurred; for instance, Cloud Security Alliance (CSA)'s document Security Guidance for Critical Areas of Focus in Cloud Computing for managing cloud computing risks [83]. *Cloud providers* would have to comply with government regulations and industrial standards to gain liability, reputation, and trustworthiness among their potential and present enterprise users [78]. Additionally, they are required to be transparent in explaining information to enterprises about possible benefits and risks from adopting cloud computing [79]. Cloud providers build their reputations by their experience in managing enterprises' needs and concerns in a responsible manner [68, 75, 77]. This is enabled by delivering the promised benefits from cloud computing to enterprises (i.e., service quality, service availability, and service recovery) and protecting their data from potential threats; for instance, in case the cloud provider went out of business [46, 77, 86]. Further, cloud providers' demonstration of successful business cases and models are likely to increase cloud computing adoption rates [51, 76]. Moreover, the support for implementing and using cloud services made available by cloud services providers is likely to motivate enterprises to adopt cloud computing [53]. however, cloud providers might trigger a major concern for enterprises if they outsource some of their services to another service provider [77]. In this regard, trust issues are not well-explored yet.

Observing that *business partners* perceive benefits from using cloud computing has proven to be an important motive toward its adoption [52, 76]. Another effect of business partners is that they may require an enterprise to adopt cloud computing if they want to remain in collaboration with them [57]. Additionally, *competitors* play an effective role in incentivizing enterprises to adopt cloud computing for gaining market visibility, operation efficiency, and new business opportunities [23, 50]. This especially happens when the enterprise operates in a high-tech, rapidly changing industry [51, 52]. However, competitor pressure may not be relevant to SMEs, as they are more concerned about other cloud computing adoption issues such as cost reduction [51]. There is a lack of studies that explore the important role of the *cloud service broker* or the so-called service integrator in facilitating cloud computing adoption, with only one conceptual article, which described the G-Cloud program initiative in the UK. G-Cloud Authority is an internal cloud service broker that coordinates a managed and assured e-marketplace *CloudStore* of cloud services available to public sector organizations [71]. G-Cloud Authority eliminates the overhead for both cloud providers and consumers; the service makes it easy for cloud providers to sell cloud services, and enterprises do not need to spend a great deal of time in evaluating and selecting cloud providers [71]. The cloud service broker's role is to achieve a predictable end-to-end service outcome for enterprise users; this includes using standards for service management to predict, measure, and sustain cloud service outcomes [71]. Service management tools for cloud service brokers are available through the IT Infrastructure Library (ITIL); however, the ITIL is not mature enough yet [71]. The G-Cloud authority is responsible for providing cloud services once bought from the CloudStore, instantiating cloud services with appropriate business data, integrating the cloud service's management tools into the buying organization's service management framework, and billing coordination [71]. Being commissioned by industry associations enhances the cloud-service brokerage's trustworthiness [71].

Internal Factors. These comprise the enterprise's internal characteristics and capabilities that affect its cloud computing adoption processes; these factors are: (1) willingness to invest, (2) top management, (3) firm size, (4) organizational culture, and (5) employees' IT skills. The enterprise's *willingness to invest* in and use cloud computing both financially and organizationally is claimed to be an important indicator for the adoption of cloud computing [23, 60]. Willingness can be affected by social influences (i.e., subjective norms and image), as enterprises would adopt cloud computing because its managers said cloud computing is a good thing and can enhance the enterprise's status among its social system [41]. Cloud computing adoption is also dependent on the role of the *top management*, as there is a relationship between top management innovativeness (i.e., adopt and accept new technologies) and the willingness to adopt cloud computing [45, 53, 88]. Top management's IT knowledge, competence, and capability of providing the suitable organizational climate for adopting cloud computing in terms of budget, adequate human and IT resources, and time [40, 45, 50, 51] is a cornerstone to the adoption of cloud computing. This involves: (1) understanding of cloud computing and its architecture, service models, and strategic values [23, 60, 67, 73, 81, 87]; (2) identifying enterprise's business needs and aligning IT decisions with business strategies [64, 83]; (3) evaluating the readiness of the existing IT infrastructure, IT knowledge, and skills of the human resources, available resources, and culture [23, 50, 60, 87]; and (4) holding the steering wheel toward cloud computing adoption (i.e., decide on adoption strategy, govern integration and implementation, and evaluate cloud services after use) with the guidance of external regulatory and professional bodies [49, 83].

Additionally, *firm size* is an important factor to cloud computing adoption [23, 50, 52, 56]. A study claims that if the company is spread over many countries, then it is likely controlling its own IT resource and does not need to adopt cloud services [81]. Further, a survey study conducted in Taiwan indicated that large enterprises are likely to adopt cloud computing [52]. On the contrary, a survey study in India indicated that SMEs can benefit the most [60], because large enterprises have sufficient resources to afford on premise solutions [50]. Another survey study reported that large enterprises are likely to proof concept of cloud computing services, and that SMEs can be more flexible in adopting cloud computing [53]. A conceptual article stated that SMEs are likely to be price-oriented and less concerned about performance, whereas large enterprises tend to balance costs against reliability, security, and performance [72].

Furthermore, *Organizational culture* is said to have an impact on the enterprise's adoption of cloud computing [49]. For enterprises that were used to the on premise approach and having full control over their data, it might be difficult for them to accept that the cloud provider will be fully controlling their data. Thus, enterprises would need to further ensure compliance of cloud computing solutions with the internal (i.e., corporate policies) and external (i.e., regulations and standards) constraints [49, 50, 83]. Therefore, culture, capabilities, and processes can be barriers to the realization of cloud computing benefits; thus, cloud service brokers can assist enterprises to overcome these barriers [71]. A survey study advocates the need to identify the way of thinking of organizational elements (i.e., staff, and management) regarding culture that should be adjusted to meet the environmental needs and challenges in the future [47]. Further, *employees' IT skills*, especially non-IT employees', are said to be a crucial factor affecting cloud computing adoption decision, as their understanding of cloud computing is very important [23, 50, 52, 60]. Likewise, IT employees would have to adjust their skills to be able to use cloud solutions [49]. Another factor affecting cloud computing adoption decision is the enterprise's *prior experience* and familiarity with similar technologies, such as virtualization [51].

Cloud Computing Adoption Processes. These comprise processes that enterprises normally follow to adopt cloud computing along with the responsibilities and challenges faced in each process:

Evaluation. This comprises (1) costs and benefits, (2) impact on people and work practices, (3) internal readiness, and (4) cloud provider selection. Prior to cloud computing adoption, the top management is responsible for evaluating the enterprise's suitability for adopting cloud computing as well as the suitability of cloud computing for the enterprise [76, 81]. This includes: *evaluating the costs and benefits* associated with cloud computing in the long and short term, such as profitability, comparing the revenue generated from the firm's IT resources with the revenue expected from cloud computing, ROI, cost of migration and integration, cost of implementation, and hidden costs, such as support and disaster recovery [70, 80, 81]. *Evaluating the impact of cloud computing on people and work practices* is also a must [83], as it may change the role of IT staff and require them to acquire new skill sets (i.e., some jobs may be merged). Regarding the impact, chief information officers (CIOs) may feel they are at risk of losing relevance and, to overcome this, CIOs will need to contribute to business strategy and information management [71], which requires a change in culture and skills across the enterprise led by CIOs [71]. Further, cloud computing is argued to have a job relevance impact, that is, the extent to which cloud computing enhances the enterprise's status and day-to-day operations and provides services applicable to employees' jobs so that they have control over their work and complete their tasks quickly [42].

Evaluating the internal readiness of the enterprise, existing IT infrastructure and IT human resources, for adopting cloud computing [52]—in terms of having sufficient and reliable resources to support the use of cloud computing as well as appropriate learning routines and performance measures is argued to enable the adoption of cloud computing [42, 88]. *Selecting the cloud provider* based on the cloud provider's capability to provide robust security controls, the enterprise's understanding of issues related to the control over the data, the type of service model needed, and the perceived cloud provider's honesty, reputation, and sustainability [40, 65].

Proof of Concept. This comprises (1) trialability and (2) perceiving benefits and risks. *Trialability* is found to have a positive impact on the adoption of cloud computing [51]. Trying cloud services prior to the actual adoption to evaluate its applicability for the enterprise is likely to convince the enterprise to adopt cloud computing [76]. In this process, convincing enterprises to adopt cloud computing can be influenced by how they perceive cloud services. There is a wide agreement on the significant influence of the *perceived benefits and risks* on the adoption of cloud services [51, 86].

This is relatively in line with a survey study's findings that the management's perceptions of security, cost-effectiveness, and IT compliance are likely to have a significant impact on the decision to adopt cloud computing [63]. Cloud computing brings plenty of benefits that are relatively convincing for enterprises to adopt it. This includes cost savings, agility, flexibility, ease of use, scalability, facilitating collaboration between business partners, less operational effort on CIOs, and increased productivity [40, 50, 54, 64, 75, 76, 85].

Even with all these enticing benefits, some SMEs are still negative about adopting cloud computing services [51]. SMEs are concerned with various types of risks [54, 65, 68, 70, 76, 77, 86]:

- Organizational risks, which cover the risk of vendor lock-in as well as the loss of governance within the enterprise.
- Technical risks, which include data leakage, loss of data, downtime, data bottlenecks, and cyber-attacks.
- Legal risks, which include data protection regulations and licensing issues.
- Nontechnical risks, which refer to the misuse of cloud services and natural disasters.
- Performance risks, which are primarily that the moving of huge amounts of data to cloud servers takes a long time, and when moving further in the adoption, this will require increasing bandwidth and connectivity, which is costly [49].

Thus, benefits and risks perceived from trying cloud services will help enterprises to decide whether to adopt or not to adopt cloud computing.

Adoption Decision. This process comprises: (1) identifying business needs, (2) determining criticality, (3) evaluating strategic value, (4) implementation planning, (5) selecting the service model, (6) deploying model selection, and (7) contracting and SLA negotiation. When deciding to adopt cloud computing services, the top management is involved in the following activities: *evaluating core business needs* and competencies (i.e., quick response to market changes and increasing productivity) [61, 76], *determining criticality* in terms of what data and applications should move to the cloud (i.e., critical vs. noncritical data and applications) [69, 81, 82], *evaluating the strategic value* that cloud computing might bring to the enterprise, such as agility by delivering strong coordination IT capabilities, process management maturity, and reduced operational burden on CIOs so they can focus on strategic activities [75], *planning for implementation* of cloud computing systems in terms of the managerial time required to plan and implement cloud solutions was not problematic [60], whereas the problem was the planning for implementation of specific deployment models that suit the current applications [79]).

Furthermore, adoption decision process involves *selecting the right service model* (i.e., SaaS, PaaS, IaaS, or combined choice) that best fits the enterprise's needs [65, 66], *selecting deployment models* based on the sensitivity of the data and applications, if the data and applications are determined to be core, then they should be deployed on a private cloud, and if the applications are determined to be noncore, then they should be deployed on a public cloud [79], whereas another study suggests the core data and applications should not be deployed on the cloud at all [69]. Finally, the adoption decision is dependent on *negotiating the cloud service contract and SLA* with the cloud provider, based on the sensitivity of the data [81], and reaching an agreement on [62, 65, 70, 71]: the modifications to the contract terms, description of services (cost, price, and service content), limitation on the use or reuse of the data, which includes the data sanitization policy to ensure that data are securely removed when the use of cloud services ceases, confidentiality and security requirements in terms of organizational standards for data encryption both at rest and in flight, risk management plans, indemnification, contract terms and renewal, effect of termination, ownership of the data and applications, location of the data, assurance of service availability and expected downtimes, employees access control and protective monitoring, and clarity on roles and responsibilities. These items should be discussed with the cloud provider before proceeding to implementation.

Implementation and Integration. These comprise (1) complexity and (2) compatibility. Compared to the on premise approach, cloud systems can be implemented and running in 24 hours instead of six months [49]. Thus, implementation of cloud systems is not problematic for enterprises, whereas integrating cloud systems with the enterprise's existing IT infrastructure can negatively impact their adoption of cloud computing [49]. Further, the use of cloud system by IT staff is straightforward, while it is challenging for the non-IT staff. This can be attributed to the degree of *complexity* of cloud systems in terms of the ease of understanding, use, and implementation or integration of cloud services. Although cloud computing is considered to be easy to understand and use, it arouses integration complexity issues [50].

Complexity is claimed to be a barrier to the adoption of cloud computing [23, 50, 52, 76]. Integration complexity problems emerge from the less standardized interoperability between cloud systems and the existing IT infrastructure, which triggers integration costs [50]. A survey study reported that the lack of legacy systems allows enterprises to implement cloud computing easily [42]. The lack of *compatibility* of cloud solutions with existing IT infrastructure can be a barrier to the adoption of cloud computing [52]. Interoperability standards can be an enabler or a barrier to the adoption of cloud computing [70]; they are enablers when the enterprise has its data, processes, and systems standardize priori, but as technology evolves, it becomes challenging for the enterprise to catch change in technology. Thus, the enterprise faces a challenge to integrate cloud solutions with already-existing cloud-based or traditional systems. In order to ensure desirable implementation and integration of cloud systems, IT governance initiatives are a required.

IT Governance. This comprises (1) auditability and traceability and (2) risk management. *Traceability and auditability* are cited to have impact on cloud computing adoption, and the former complements the latter [49]. The loss of IT governance within the enterprise can slow down the adoption rates because the data and applications are under the control of the cloud provider [65, 83]. Enterprises are advised to conduct audit trail meetings with the cloud provider to ensure a risk-free implementation of cloud solutions that complies with regulations, standards, and enterprise policies [49]. This is enabled by the top management through IT governance structures and processes [50]. Contrarily, IT governance processes in highly regulated industries will decelerate the adoption of cloud computing [50]. Further, IT governance processes might hinder the adoption if the integration of cloud solutions with the existing infrastructure appears to be difficult [50].

Despite the massive advancements in securing the cloud, security solutions are not tested extensively yet [81]. This matter could be dissolved by IT governance initiatives to ensure that enterprise policies, security standards, and legal requirements are met [49, 50]. Further, IT governance is attained by identifying responsibilities; for instance, the cloud provider may be responsible for the security at the IaaS level, whereas the customer's responsibility is at the SaaS and PaaS levels [83]. However, data security at the level of PaaS and IaaS service models can be a shared responsibility between the cloud provider and the adopting enterprise [66]. Additionally, cloud providers are required to provide traceable access controls to govern who can access what object under which conditions. This has to be validated by the top management for its conformity to internal and external constraints [49]. These controls are used to ensure data integrity and confidentiality [49, 65].

In regard to *risk management* during the planning for cloud computing implementation, a study suggests that the enterprise should consider evaluating the risk of storage damage, data loss, and network security [62]. For instance, the enterprise would maintain an on-site backup of the data moved to the cloud [69]. There is a lack of processes and methodologies that provides guidelines on how to use cloud services to address specific business needs and mitigate associated risks [71]. Eventually, securing enterprise's information from potential risks is more than processes, technical solutions, and people; it is an enterprise-wide security strategy to orchestrate these various elements [63].

Confirmation. This comprises *usage continuance*, about which a study proposed a model for implementation and confirmation stages of cloud computing adoption [79]. This study suggests the evaluation of cloud services based on the perceived attributes from using cloud services (i.e., relative advantage, complexity, compatibility, and trialability) to decide whether to continue using cloud services or not. Further, a survey study argued that perceived usefulness and satisfaction are necessary for IS continuance intention [43]. Apparently, satisfaction is not only related to perceived benefits from using cloud services, it is also dependent on the perception of service fairness from the cloud provider [43]. Service fairness happens when customers feel they are treated equally by the service provider as other customers are treated [43]. Thus, customers can judge how well-structured the cloud provider's system is, and, consequently, customers will likely continue to use the cloud provider's services [43].

4   Discussion and Future Research Avenues

This article sought to review 51 articles to capture the current state of IS research regarding cloud computing adoption in the context of enterprises. The review involved classifying the identified themes in the reviewed articles into cloud computing adoption factors and processes. The findings from the reviewed articles are discussed from three perspectives: theoretical (i.e., theories/frameworks/models utilized), methodological (i.e., research methods employed), and empirical (i.e., cloud computing adoption factors and processes). The contribution of this review is summarized in Fig. 2, where the identified cloud computing adoption factors and processes are depicted in addition to the relationships between them. In general, the review revealed that only three IS journal articles were found contributing to the area of cloud computing adoption issues. Likewise, few IS conference articles appeared to contribute to the understanding of cloud computing adoption. In contrast, articles from non-IS journal and conference outlets are dominant in investigating this phenomenon. Based on the findings, a cloud computing adoption research agenda is drawn accordingly to direct research avenues to towards (1) theoretical, (2) methodological, and (3) empirical studies.

4.1   Theoretical Research Avenues

Articles utilizing the grounded classification and general concepts are dominant, whereas few already-existing theories were utilized to study the adoption of cloud computing. Yet, there is a need for applying more theories (e.g., institutional theory [90, 91]) that fit studying the adoption of IT innovation, to gain more insights regarding cloud computing adoption. Institutional theory captures the notion of irrationality in decision making, as enterprises may or may not adopt the cloud under internal (i.e., cultural resistance and internal readiness) or external pressure (i.e., competitors and business partners) and not because of efficiency and cost reduction. Moreover, institutional theory is helpful in understanding how enterprises respond to external and internal pressures and why [92, 93]. Consequently, this review brings interesting questions to IS researchers' empirical investigation briefcase: what factors (i.e., internal and external) affect the adoption of cloud computing, and how do enterprises form strategies to cope with these factors?

4.2   Methodological Research Avenues

The review indicates a lack of in-depth field and case studies regarding cloud computing adoption processes, as compared to those on cloud computing adoption factors, whereas the quantitative (i.e., surveys) studies and conceptual articles appeared to be dominant. Yet, there are theoretical studies that have not been tested. For instance, a study proposed theoretically a cloud computing adoption assessment model that considers criteria for selecting the cloud provider, but this model has not been tested empirically yet [67]. Thus, further qualitative research needs to be undertaken to explore further issues and test empirically the previous theoretical developments regarding this area.

Consequently, this triggers questions on the IS research round table as to why enterprises adopt cloud computing in spite of its potential risks? Or conversely, why enterprises do not adopt cloud computing in spite of its potential benefits? These questions need to be investigated thoroughly using multiple qualitative case studies in different contexts (i.e., countries and industries) to better understand cloud computing adoption factors and processes.

The majority of reviewed articles study cloud adoption factors and processes in a rather broad perspective. Therefore, there is a need for interpretive case studies to investigate each of cloud computing factors and processes found from this review (i.e., willingness, organizational culture, regulations, cloud providers trustworthiness, evaluation of cloud services, adoption decision, or implementation and integration processes) [94]. These in-depth studies are preferred owing to their implications for both practice and academia.

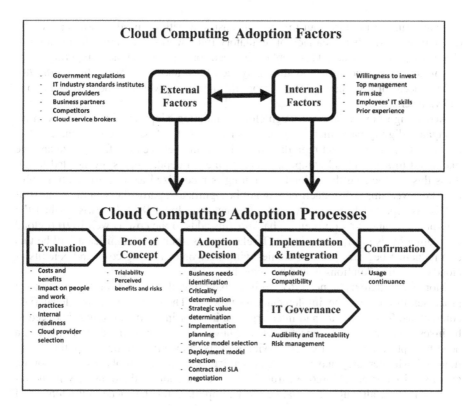

Fig. 2. Cloud computing adoption factors and processes

In spite of the appealing merits that cloud computing brings to enterprises (i.e., cost savings, flexibility, efficiency, agility and so forth), as an innovative IT shared services model [2], cloud computing puts enterprises in a decisive choice between on-premise and on-demand approaches. In this regard, the Delphi method [95–97] would provide insights for IT managers about what are the most important issues, and their priorities, that should be considered when deciding to adopt cloud solutions. Further, this review advocates the need for conducting longitudinal studies to assess the impact of cloud computing implementation on both the technical and managerial capabilities of the enterprise (i.e., integration with existing IT infrastructure, planning, risk management, and IT governance) as well as the impact of the confirmation process on the organizational innovation.

4.3   Empirical Research Avenues

The review shows that cloud computing adoption processes received less attention from IS researchers in terms of exploring the challenges faced in each process and how enterprises cope with these challenges for risk-free adoption of cloud services. Legal issues are taking most of the attention in terms of the adequacy and consistency of government regulations for ensuring security and data privacy needed for using cloud computing services. In the developed world, these regulations, either national or international, are in place, but they are inconsistent with each other, whereas, in the developing, world there is a lack of regulatory frameworks to assure safe adoption of cloud computing services. This implies the need for exploring cloud computing adoption in developing countries, as they may lack legal and IT infrastructures [78, 98], and the need for transferring lessons from the developed world to the developing one and vice versa.

According to the review, although cloud computing adoption factors have been investigated slightly more than the processes have, plenty of issues remain unclear. For instance, there is a conflict regarding the relationship between the firm's size and the likelihood to adopt cloud computing, and further in-depth studies are needed to address this conflict. Further, cloud computing is recognized as a cost-reduction solution; however, this cost reduction may not be significant, particularly in the context of SMEs, as reported by a survey study conducted in India [86]. Likewise, when the enterprise maintains an on premise backup, this adds to the cost as well [69]. If cloud computing helps enterprises reduce IT-related costs, then how significant will be this cost reduction be? Thus, further studies with focus on evaluating costs and benefits of cloud computing solutions would be favorable.

Moreover, there is a need for further exploring the impact of IT governance processes throughout the implementation process. There are still many legal (i.e., contract and SLA), ethical, and inter-organizational or institutional issues that need to be investigated regarding improvements of laws and standards. In addition, there is a need to explore the role of cloud service brokers in enabling cloud computing adoption and whether they have sufficient service management tools for provisioning cloud services or not. Moreover, trust issues are not addressed extensively in the reviewed articles, although it is claimed to be important for the successful adoption of cloud computing [3].

Further, it would be useful to investigate internal readiness and selection of cloud provider issues in the context of SMEs and/or large enterprises. Future studies should explore the compatibility between cloud solutions with enterprises' legacy systems and business needs, as well as the impact of trying or using cloud solutions on organizational culture, staff skills, and work practices. Another issue to consider is whether cloud computing releases enterprises from managing the IT infrastructure so they can focus on their core business activities, and if so, which data and applications should be moved to the cloud and which should remain in-house? Further studies would be appropriate for providing recommendations for practice regarding internal preparation, service model selection, and contract negotiation issues.

5   Conclusion

This study sought to conduct a systematic review of the extant literature on cloud computing adoption by enterprises. This involved identifying the current contributions of IS research regarding the phenomenon and determining the under-investigated issues and the contributions of IS research regarding the phenomenon. The classification of reviewed articles, findings, and implications for future IS research avenues are according to theories, research methods, and cloud computing adoption factors and processes that were identified by using GT approach. Yet, plentiful legal, ethical, technical, and managerial issues are waiting for IS researchers to explore. Thus, the paper suggested a future IS research agenda based on the discussed findings.

This article is not free of limitations; it sought to review only academic articles from seven literature databases, leaving out white papers, magazine articles, other scholarly literature databases, and articles from a forward and backward search, the inclusion of which would help capture more issues about cloud computing adoption by enterprises. The search criterion was limited to article title only; however, including abstracts as a criterion would have revealed more insightful articles. The search phrases were limited; as some articles discuss cloud computing adoption using different words (i.e., utility computing or application service provision) that may not have been included in the search results of this review.

Acknowledgements. This paper is made possible through the help and support from Dr. Eli Hustad, Prof. Dag H. Olsen, Prof. Peter Axel Nielsen, and my colleagues Moutaz Haddara, Fathul Wahid, and Christoph Merschbrock. I owe them thanks for offering valuable advices on the logic and organization of the paper at its early stages. Finally, I sincerely thank the anonymous reviewers for their constructive advices that made the paper appear in a well-presented final shape.

References

1. Elragal, A., Haddara, M.: The Future of ERP Systems: Look Backward Before Moving Forward. Procedia Technol. 5, 21–30 (2012)
2. Su, N., Akkiraju, R., Nayak, N., Goodwin, R.: Shared Services Transformation: Conceptualization and Valuation from the Perspective of Real Options. Decis. Sci. 40, 381–402 (2009)
3. Garrison, G., Kim, S., Wakefield, R.L.: Success Factors for Deploying Cloud Computing. Commun. ACM. 55, 62–68 (2012)
4. Parakala, K., Udhas, P.: The Cloud Changing the Business Ecosystem (2011), http://www.kpmg.com/IN/en/IssuesAndInsights/ThoughtLeadership/The_Cloud_Changing_the_Business_Ecosystem.pdf
5. Herhalt, J., Cochrane, K.: Exploring the Cloud: A Global Study of Governments' Adoption of Cloud (2012), http://www.kpmg.com/ES/es/ActualidadyNovedades/ArticulosyPublicaciones/Documents/Exploring-the-Cloud.pdf
6. Venters, W., Whitley, E.A.: A Critical Review of Cloud Computing: Researching Desires and Realities. J. Inf. Technol. 27, 179–197 (2012)
7. RightScale: RightScale State of the Cloud Report (2013), https://www.rightscale.com/pdf/rightscale-state-of-the-cloud-report-2013.pdf
8. Armbrust, M., Fox, A., Griffith, R., Joseph, A.D., Katz, R., Konwinski, A., Lee, G., Patterson, D., Rabkin, A., Stoica, I., Zaharia, M.: Above the Clouds A Berkeley View of Cloud Computing (2009)
9. Sultan, N.A.: Reaching for the "Cloud": How SMEs Can Manage. Int. J. Inf. Manage. 31, 272–278 (2011)
10. Yang, H., Tate, M.: A Descriptive Literature Review and Classification of Cloud Computing Research. Commun. Assoc. Inf. Syst. 31 (2012)
11. Cummings, M.P., Huskamp, J.C.: Grid Computing. Educ. Rev. 40, 116–117 (2005)

12. Weinhardt, C., Anandasivam, A., Blau, B., Borissov, N., Meinl, T., Michalk, W., Stößer, J.: Cloud Computing – A Classification, Business Models, and Research Directions. Bus. Inf. Syst. Eng. 1, 391–399 (2009)

13. EMA: Hybrid IT Service Management: A Requirement for Virtualization and Cloud Computing (2012),
    `http://www.thinkhdi.com/~/media/HDICorp/Files/`
    `White-Papers/whtppr-FrontRange-Hybrid-ITSM.pdf`

14. Heiser, J., Nicolett, M.: Assessing the Security Risks of Cloud Computing (2008)

15. Hashemi, S.M., Bardsiri, A.K.: Cloud Computing Vs. Grid Computing. ARPN J. Syst. Softw. 2, 188–194 (2012)

16. Susarla, A., Barua, A., Whinston, A.: Understanding the Service Component of Application Service Provision: An Empirical Analysis of Satisfaction with ASP Services. MIS Q. 27, 91–123 (2003)

17. Kern, T., Willcocks, L.P., Lacity, M.C.: Application Service Provision Risk Assessment and Mitigation. MIS Q. Exec. 1, 113–126 (2002)

18. Robison, S.: Everything-as-a-Service: A Blue Sky View of the Cloud (2009),
    `http://www.hp.com/hpinfo/initiatives/eaas/SR_EaaS_viewpoint.pdf`

19. Xin, L., Song, C.: Cloud-Based Innovation of Internet Long Tail. In: The 6th International Conference on Product Innovation Management (ICPIM 2011), pp. 603–607 (2011)

20. Kunesch, U., Reti, M., Pauly, M.: Cloud Computing I. Alternative sourcing Strategy for Business ICT (2010), `http://www.t-systems.com/news-media/white-papers/760948_2/blobBinary/White-Paper_Cloud-Computing-I.pdf`

21. Mell, P., Grance, T.: The NIST Definition of Cloud Computing: Recommendations of the National Institute of Standards and Technology (2011),
    `http://csrc.nist.gov/publications/nistpubs/800-145/`
    `SP800-145.pdf`

22. Hogan, M., Liu, F., Sokol, A., Tong, J.: NIST Cloud Computing Standards Roadmap (2011), `http://www.nist.gov/customcf/get_pdf.cfm?pub_id=909024`

23. Espadanal, M., Oliveira, T.: Cloud Computing Adoption by Firms. In: Proceedings of the Mediterranean Conference on Information Systems, MCIS 2012 (2012)

24. Yang, H., Jing, S., Wang, H.: The Research on ASP-based SMEs Collaborative Platform. In: Proceedings of the 8th International Conference on Computer Supported Cooperative Work in Design, vol. 2, pp. 6–9 (2004)

25. Malathi, M.: Cloud computing Concepts. In: 2011 3rd International Conference on Electronics Computer Technology (ICECT), pp. 236–239 (2011)

26. Salleh, S.M., Teoh, S.Y., Chan, C.: Cloud Enterprise Systems A Review of Literature and its Adoption. In: Proceedings of the Pacific Asia Conference on Information Systems, PACIS 2012 (2012)

27. Marston, S., Li, Z., Bandyopadhyay, S., Zhang, J., Ghalsasi, A.: Cloud computing — The Business Perspective. Decis. Support Syst. 51, 176–189 (2011)

28. Timmermans, J., Stahl, B.C., Ikonen, V., Bozdag, E.: The Ethics of Cloud Computing: A Conceptual Review. In: Proceedings of the Second International Conference on Cloud Computing Technology and Science, pp. 614–620. IEEE (2010)

29. Webster, J., Watson, R.: Analysing the Past to Prepare for the Future: Writing a Literature Review. MIS Q. 26, xiii–xxiii (2002)

30. Vom Brocke, J., Simons, A., Niehaves, B., Riemer, K., Plattfaut, R., Cleven, A.: Reconstructing the Giant: On the Importance of Rigour in Documenting the Literature Search Process. In: The 17th European Conference on Information Systems (ECIS 2009), Verona, Italy, pp. 2206–2217 (2009)

31. Levy, Y., Ellis, T.J.: A Systems Approach to Conduct an Effective Literature Review in Support of Information Systems Research. Informing Sci. J. 9, 181–212 (2006)
32. Dubey, A., Wagle, D.: Delivering Software as a Service (2007)
33. Okoli, C., Schabram, K.: A Guide to Conducting a Systematic Literature Review of Information Systems Research. Sprouts Work. Pap. Inf. Syst. 10 (2010)
34. Orlikowski, W.J., Baroudi, J.J.: Studying Information Technology in Organizations: Research Approaches and Assumptions. Inf. Syst. Res. 2, 1–28 (1991)
35. Galliers, R.D., Land, F.F.: Choosing Systems Appropriate Research Information Methodologies. Commun. ACM. 30, 900–902 (1987)
36. Gonzalez, R., Dahanayake, A.: A Concept Map of Information Systems Research Approaches. In: Proceedings of the IRMA International Conference, pp. 845–849 (2007)
37. Glaser, B.G., Strauss, A.L.: The Discovery of Grounded Theory: Strategies for Qualitative Research. Aldine Publishing Company, Chicago (1967)
38. Wolfswinkel, J.F., Furtmueller, E., Wilderom, C.P.M.: Using Grounded Theory as a Method for Rigorously Reviewing Literature. Eur. J. Inf. Syst. 22, 45–55 (2011)
39. Rich, P.: Inside the Black BoxRevealing the Process in Applying a Grounded Theory Analysis. Qual. Rep. 17, 1–23 (2012)
40. Bharadwaj, S.S., Lal, P.: Exploring the Impact of Cloud Computing Adoption on Organizational Flexibility: A Client Perspective. In: Proceedings of the International Conference on Cloud Computing Technologies, Applications and Management (ICCCTAM 2012), pp. 121–131. IEEE (2012)
41. Opitz, N., Langkau, T.F., Schmidt, N.H., Kolbe, L.M.: Technology Acceptance of Cloud Computing: Empirical Evidence from German IT Departments. In: Proc. 45th Hawaii Int. Conf. Syst. Sci. (HICSS 2012), pp. 1593–1602 (2012)
42. Tjikongo, R., Uys, W.: The Viability of Cloud Computing Adoption in SMME's in Namibia. In: Proceedings of IST-Africa Conference, pp. 1–11 (2013)
43. Lawkobkit, M., Speece, M.: Integrating Focal Determinants of Service Fairness into Post-Acceptance Model of IS Continuance in Cloud Computing. In: Proc. 11th Int. Conf. Comput. Inf. Sci. (2012 IEEE/ACIS), pp. 49–55 (2012)
44. Shin, J., Jo, M., Lee, J., Lee, D.: Strategic Management of Cloud Computing Focusing on Consumer Adoption Behavior. IEEE Trans. Eng. Manag., 1–9 (2013)
45. Lian, J.-W., Yen, D.C., Wang, Y.-T.: An Exploratory Study to Understand the Critical Factors Affecting the Decision to Adopt Cloud Computing in Taiwan Hospital. Int. J. Inf. Manage. 34, 28–36 (2014)
46. Bogataj, K., Pucihar, A.: Business Model Factors Influencing Cloud Computing Adoption Differences in Opinion. In: Proceedings of the BLED 2013, pp. 1–14 (2013)
47. Kusnandar, T., Surendro, K.: Adoption Model of Hospital Information System Based on Cloud Computing Case Study on Hospitals in Bandung City. In: Proceedings of the International Conference on ICT for Smart Society, pp. 1–6 (2014)
48. Saedi, A., Iahad, N.A.: An Integrated Theoretical Framework for Cloud Computing Adoption by Small and Medium-sized Enterprises. In: Proceedings of the Pacific Asia Conference on Information Systems (PACIS 2013), pp. 1–12 (2013)
49. Morgan, L., Conboy, K.: Factors Affecting the Adoption of Cloud Computin An Exploratory Study. In: Proceedings of the 21st European Conference on Information Systems, pp. 1–13 (2013)
50. Borgman, H.P., Bahli, B., Heier, H., Schewski, F.: Cloudrise: Exploring Cloud Computing Adoption and Governance with the TOE Framework. In: Proceedings of the 46th Hawaii International Conference on System Sciences, pp. 4425–4435. IEEE (2013)

51. Alshamaila, Y., Papagiannidis, S.: Cloud computing Adoption by SMEs in the North East of England: A Multi-perspective Framework. J. Enterp. Inf. Manag. 26, 250–275 (2013)
52. Low, C., Chen, Y., Wu, M.: Understanding the Determinants of Cloud Computing Adoption. Ind. Manag. Data Syst. 111, 1006–1023 (2011)
53. Alshamaila, Y., Papagiannidis, S., Stamati, T.: Cloud Computing Adoption in Greece. In: Proceedings of UK Academy for Information Systems Conference, pp. 1–17 (2013)
54. Nkhoma, M.Z., Dang, D.P.T., De Souza-daw, A.: Contributing Factors of Cloud Computing Adoption A Technology- Organisation-Environment Framework Approach. In: Proceedings of the European Conference on Information Management & Evaluation, pp. 180–189 (2013)
55. Saedi, A., Iahad, N.A.: Developing an Instrument for Cloud Computing Adoption by Small and Medium-sized Enterprises. In: Proceedings of the International Conference on Research and Innovation in Information Systems (ICRIIS 2013), pp. 481–486. IEEE (2013)
56. Chang, B.-Y., Hai, P.H., Seo, D.-W., Lee, J.-H., Yoon, S.H.: The Determinant of Adoption in Cloud Computing in Vietnam. In: Proceedings of the International Conference on Computing, Management and Telecommunications (ComManTel 2013), pp. 407–409. IEEE (2013)
57. Cegielski, C.G., Jones-Farmer, L.A., Wu, Y., Hazen, B.T.: Adoption of Cloud Computing Technologies in Supply Chains: An Organizational Information Processing Theory Approach. Int. J. Logist. Manag. 23, 184–211 (2012)
58. Yang, C., Hwang, B., Yuan, B.J.C.: Key Consideration Factors of Adopting Cloud Computing for Science. In: Proceedings of the 4th International Conference on Cloud Computing Technology and Science, pp. 597–600 (2012)
59. Stankov, I., Miroshnychenko, Y., Kurbel, K.: Cloud Computing Adoption in German Internet Start-up Companies. In: Proceedings of BLED Conference, BLED 2012 (2012)
60. Rath, A., Mohapatra, S., Kumar, S., Thakurta, R.: Decision Points for Adoption Cloud Computing in Small, Medium Enterprises (SMEs). In: Proceedings of the 7th International Conference for Internet Technology and Secured Transactions (ICITST 2012), pp. 688–691 (2012)
61. Abokhodair, N., Taylor, H., Hasegawa, J., Mowery, S.J.: Heading for the Clouds? Implications for Cloud Computing Adopters. In: Proceedings of the 18th Americas Conference on Information Systems, AMCIS 2012 (2012)
62. Tsai, C., Lin, U.-C., Chang, A.Y., Chen, C.-J.: Information Security Issue of Enterprises Adopting the Application of Cloud Computing. In: Proceedings of the 6th International Conference on Networked Computing and Advanced Information Management (NCM 2010), pp. 645–649 (2010)
63. Opala, O.J., Rahman, S.(Shawon)M.: An Exploratory Analysis of the Influence of Information Security on the Adoption of Cloud Computing. In: Proceedings of the 2013 8th International Conference on System of Systems Engineering, pp. 165–170 (2013)
64. Subramanian, B.: The Disruptive Influence of Cloud Computing and its Implications for Adoption in the Pharmaceutical and Life Sciences Industry. J. Med. Mark. Device, Diagnostic Pharm. Mark. 12, 192–203 (2012)
65. Onwudebelu, U., Chukuka, B.: Will Adoption of Cloud Computing Put the Enterprise at Risk? In: Proceedings of the 4th International Conference on Adaptive Science & Technology (ICAST 2012), pp. 82–85. IEEE (2012)

66. Bamiah, M., Brohi, S., Chuprat, S., Ab Manan, J.: A Study on Significance of Adopting Cloud Computing Paradigm in Healthcare Sector. In: Proceedings of the International Conference on Cloud Computing Technologies, Applications and Management (ICCCTAM 2012), pp. 65–68. IEEE (2012)

67. Nasir, U., Niazi, M.: Cloud Computing Adoption Assessment Model (CAAM). In: Proceedings of the 12th International Conference on Product Focused Software Development and Process Improvement, pp. 34–37 (2011)

68. Jensen, M., Schwenk, J., Bohli, J.-M., Gruschka, N., Iacono, L.L.: Security Prospects Through Cloud Computing by Adopting Multiple Clouds. In: Proceedings of the 4th International Conference on Cloud Computing (CLOUD), pp. 565–572. IEEE (2011)

69. Kim, W., Kim, S.D., Lee, E., Lee, S.: Adoption Issues for Cloud Computing. In: Proceedings of the 11th International Conference on Information Integration and Web-based Applications & Services - iiWAS 2009, p. 2. ACM Press, New York (2009)

70. Avram, M.G.: Advantages and Challenges of Adopting Cloud Computing from an Enterprise Perspective. Procedia Technol. 12, 529–534 (2014)

71. Bellamy, M.: Adoption of Cloud Computing Services by Public Sector Organisations. In: Proceedings of the IEEE 9th World Congress on Services, pp. 201–208. IEEE (2013)

72. Kushida, K.E., Murray, J., Zysman, J.: Diffusing the Cloud: Cloud Computing and Implications for Public Policy. J. Ind. Compet. Trade. 11, 209–237 (2011)

73. Rawal, A.: Adoption of Cloud Computing in India. J. Technol. Manag. Grow. Econ. 2, 65–78 (2011)

74. Coursaris, C.K., van Osch, W., Sung, J.: A "Cloud Lifestyle": The Diffusion of Cloud Computing Applications and the Effect of Demographic and Lifestyle Clusters. In: Proceedings of the 46th Hawaii International Conference on System Sciences (HICSS 2013), pp. 2803–2812. IEEE (2013)

75. Malladi, S., Krishnan, M.S.: Cloud Computing Adoption and its Implications for CIO Strategic Focus – An Empirical Analysis. In: Proceedings of 33rd International Conference on Information Systems (ICIS 2012), pp. 1–19 (2012)

76. Lin, A., Chen, N.-C.: Cloud Computing as an Innovation: Percepetion, Attitude, and Adoption. Int. J. Inf. Manage. 32, 533–540 (2012)

77. Nuseibeh, H.: Adoption of Cloud Computing in Organizations. In: Proceedings of the 17th Americas Conference on Information Systems, AMCIS 2011 (2011)

78. Bhat, J.M.: Adoption of Cloud Computing by SMEs in India: A study of the Institutional Factors. In: Proceedings of the 19th Americas Conference on Information Systems, pp. 1–8 (2013)

79. Dargha, R.: Cloud Computing From Hype to Reality. Fast Tracking Cloud Adoption. In: Proceedings of the International Conference on Advances in Computing, Communications, and Informatics, pp. 440–445 (2012)

80. Hoe, S.C., Kantarcioglu, M., Bensoussan, A.: Studying Dynamic Equilibrium of Cloud Computing Adoption with Application of Mean Field Games. In: Proceedings of the 50th Annual Allerton Conference on Communication, Control, and Computing (Allerton), pp. 220–224. IEEE (2012)

81. Misra, S.C., Mondal, A.: Identification of a Company's Suitability for the Adoption of Cloud Computing and Modelling its Corresponding Return on Investment. Math. Comput. Model. 53, 504–521 (2011)

82. Kantarcioglu, M., Bensoussan, A., Hoe, S.C.: Impact of Security Risks on Cloud Computing Adoption. In: Proceedings of the 49th Annual Allerton Conference on Communication, Control, and Computing (Allerton), pp. 670–674. IEEE (2011)

83. Mcgeogh, B.T., Donnellan, B.: Factors That Affect the Adoption of Cloud Computing for an Enterprise A Case Study of Cloud Adoption Within Intel Corporation. In: Proceedings of the 21st European Conference on Information Systems, pp. 1–13 (2013)

84. Zhao, F., Gaw, S.D., Bender, N., Levy, D.T.: Exploring Cloud Computing Adoptions in Public Sectors: A Case Study. GSTF J. Comput. 3 (2013)

85. Gupta, P., Seetharaman, A., Raj, J.R.: The Usage and Adoption of Cloud Computing by Small and Medium Businesses. Int. J. Inf. Manage. 33, 861–874 (2013)

86. Iyer, E.K., Krishnan, A., Sareen, G., Panda, T.: Analysis of Dissatisfiers That Inhibit Cloud Computing Adoption Across Multiple Customer Segments. In: Proceedings of the European Conference on Information Management & Evaluation, pp. 145–152 (2013)

87. Luoma, E., Nyberg, T.: Four Scenarios for Adoption of Cloud Computing in China. In: Proceedings of the European Conference on Information Systems, ECIS 2011 (2011)

88. Khanagha, S., Volberda, H., Sidhu, J., Oshri, I.: Management Innovation and Adoption of Emerging Technologies: The Case of Cloud Computing. Eur. Manag. Rev. 10, 51–67 (2013)

89. Kihara, T., Gichoya, D.: Adoption and Use of Cloud Computing in Small and Medium Enterprises in Kenya. In: Proceedings of IST-Africa Conference, pp. 1–12 (2013)

90. Mignerat, M., Rivard, S.: Positioning the Institutional Perspective in Information Systems Research. J. Inf. Technol. 24, 369–391 (2009)

91. Weerakkody, V., Dwivedi, Y.K., Irani, Z.: The Diffusion and Use of Institutional Theory: A Cross-disciplinary Longitudinal Literature Survey. J. Inf. Technol. 24, 354–368 (2009)

92. Oliver, C.: Strategic Responses to Institutional Processes. Acad. Manag. Rev. 16, 145–179 (1991)

93. Deephouse, D.L., Suchman, M.: Legitimacy in Organizational Institutionalism. In: Greenwood, R., Oliver, C., Suddaby, R., Sahlin, K. (eds.) The SAGE Handbook of Organizational Institutionalism, pp. 49–77. SAGE Publications Ltd., Thousand Oaks (2008)

94. Walsham, G.: Interpretive Case Studies in IS Research Nature and Method. Eur. J. Inf. Syst. 4, 74–81 (1995)

95. Dalkey, N.C.: The Delphi Method: An Experimental Study of Group Opinion. In: Dalkey, N.C. (ed.) Studies in the Quality of Life: Delphi and Decision-Making, p. 161. Lexington Books (1972)

96. Okoli, C., Pawlowski, S.D.: The Delphi Method as a Research Tool An Example, Design Considerations and Applications. Inf. Manag. 42, 15–29 (2004)

97. Hsu, C., Sandford, B.A.: The Delphi Technique: Making Sense of Consensus. Pract. Assessment, Res. Eval. 12, 1–8 (2007)

98. Greengard, S.: Cloud Computing and Developing Nations. Commun. ACM 53, 18 (2010)

Here Today, Here Tomorrow: Considering Options Theory in Digital Platform Development

Ted Saarikko

Department of Informatics, Umeå University, Umeå, Sweden
ted.saarikko@informatik.umu.se

Abstract. Past decades have seen business platforms proliferate not only as a means to collaborate, but also decrease time-to-market and promote innovation. However, extant literature tends to dichotomise platforms, perceiving them as either strategic resources or technical systems. Applied to digital platforms, we argue that options theory offers a potential means to reconcile the operand and operant perspectives of platform artefacts. We illustrate our point via a case study of a firm that has gradually developed a product that enables mobile communication into a digital platform that provides a wide range of customers with services from several different suppliers. This study contributes to our understanding of digital platforms as it describes how design choices by a provider can affect flexibility and continued development of new services.

Keywords: Digital platform, digital options, options value, real options, ecosystem.

1 Introduction

In light of increased complexity and competition, firms are increasingly becoming aware of the impracticality of developing the technology to solve all of their problems on a case-by-case basis. One means to manage complexity as well as economise on development is through the use of *platforms*. The platform concept lends itself to several perspectives that may be broadly dichotomised into the platform as a modular core that permits variations on a theme [1] on the one hand, and the platform as a shared structure that facilitates connectivity between parties [2, 3].

As different streams of research tend to pursue their own agenda, they leave in their wake a conceptualisation of platforms that is unclear at best and polysemic at worst. Business literature describes how transactions between actors can be facilitated via multi-sided platforms (e.g. [4, 5]). However, these studies tend to pay little attention to the artefacts we need to enact connectivity. Conversely, IS literature tends to focus on development or governance of the artefact, stopping short of the manner in which they are applied in a business context (e.g. [4], [6]). In essence, there is a tangible divide between studying platforms as operant resources that enable activities, and operand resources as objects of study [7, 8]. As artefacts, platforms are physical (or digital) composite objects of significant complexity. Viewed as operand resources, one is concerned with the prerequisites for creating a platform, e.g. technical requirements,

B. Bergvall-Kåreborn and P.A. Nielsen (Eds.): TDIT 2014, IFIP AICT 429, pp. 243–260, 2014.

design choices, or affordances. However, as platforms are intended to serve as a basis for other applications and uses, it is equally viable to view them as operant resources, i.e. resources that interact with other resources in order to further some ultimate aim. It is therefore not sufficient to study them as either designed artefacts or strategic enablers, but to adopt a composite view whereby both perspectives are equally germane.

We argue that options theory, subdivided into real options and digital options, offers a potentially fruitful means to study the development of platform as an operand resource as well as its appeal for potential users as an operant resource. Although options theory has frequently been applied to information technology (e.g. [9, 10, 11, 12]) and to some extent internal IT platforms (e.g. [13, 14, 15]), it has to the author's knowledge not received any significant attention as a framework for studying the design and diffusion of a platform qua commercial offering. In an effort to address operand as well as operant perspectives, *we seek to explore how options drive the evolution of a digital platform and enable flexibility in application.* We illustrate our reasoning using a case study of a SME located in Northern Europe that has developed and marketed a digital platform in several industries over the past 13 years.

The paper opens with an outline of platform literature with particular emphasis on digital platforms. Following that, we outline the two streams of options theory: Real options and digital options. We then account for the methodological approach and the case studied before moving on to present the results. The paper concludes with a discussion related to our findings.

2   Related Research

The following chapter briefly outlines related research in platforms literature.

2.1   The Platform Concept

The platform concept first came into wide usage in large-scale manufacturing industries where the seemingly incongruent pursuits of mass production and consumer customisation bought about modularisation and the use of standardised components [16]. In a broader sense, the platform concept has attained "wide usage in management literature as a term meaning foundation of components around which an organization [sic] might create a related but differentiated set of products or services" [17, p.36]. Although originally applied predominantly to physical products [1], the discourse has expanded to include distinctly non-material components such as software [18].

Another quality of platforms is their potential to bring multiple actors together around a common structure and thus facilitate connectivity and foster exchange where this would be costly or otherwise impractical [2]. We may distinguish between four platform types depending on their scope: Internal platforms that are used within a firm, supply chain platforms that follow a specific value-added process among several firms, industry platforms that serve as a hub for related or unrelated actors, and multi-sided platforms that are essentially open marketplaces that facilitate transactions [19]. The two latter types, industry platforms and multi-sided platforms, have garnered special attention in relation to novel business models as they are typically accompanied by an ecosystem of backing firms that supply modules or complements that are specific to that platform [18].

A key feature of platforms is their relative stability over time. They have a fixed set of attributes that allows users to interact with the platform and utilise its functionality [20]. Should the manner in which we interact with the platform change on a regular basis, the utility of the platform would diminish as we would no longer have a stable, long-term baseline for which to develop complements [1]. The temporal dimension is also relevant in differentiating between products and platforms. Products are typically isolated entities oriented towards short-term profits and limited life spans, whereas platforms are motivated by the long-term benefit of facilitating the continuous development of new products or services. The distinction between platforms and products has however become increasingly blurry as a physical product may serve as a platform for digital content or services, making the product a stable foundation for complements. This phenomenon has grown increasingly prevalent over the past few years and serves as a basis for a new kind of platform – the digital platform.

2.2   Digital Platforms

The advent of digital technologies has opened up several new possibilities as they allow us to operate upon digital objects that are considerably more pliant than their physical counterparts [21]. The flexibility of digital technologies allows content and services to converge so that we may transmit them using the same standardised channels [22]. Furthermore, devices enabled by digital technologies are no longer limited to a single configuration, but malleable in the sense that their applicability can be altered without interfering with their material properties [23].

Our growing understanding of digital materiality carries with it several corollaries, one of which is that platforms are no longer dependent upon the modularity of physical components. A fixed technical architecture could well be dynamic with regards to the ability to add or replace digital components over time. Hence, artefacts that are static in a physical sense may at the same time be digitally modular, permitting us to consider them digital platforms [24]. While the basic tenets of platform modularity still hold true (i.e. a stable core and interchangeable components), properties such as independence from specific channels of delivery as well as post hoc versatility do have profound bearing on how we can approach digital platforms. Yoo et al. [24] suggest a conception whereby the digital platform encompasses four layers: Device, network, service, and content. The ability to disaggregate the platform into these separate, largely independent layers offers us some idea of the potential afforded by combining digital and physical components. Any one of the four layers of a digital platform could be replaced or upgraded without the necessity to amend or replace the remaining three layers, allowing different aspects of the platform to develop at a different pace. Hence, the platform may be perceived as a stable structure upon which to build common services or business processes while it is at the same time offers significant potential for customisation to suit individual needs and preferences.

The ability of digital platforms to remain stable yet concurrently flexible brings about tremendous potential for different types of innovation [22]. More importantly, they offer favourable conditions for continuous development and complements as digital objects are not dependent upon physical manufacturing facilities or cumbersome logistics. In some cases complements can even be created without involvement from the proprietor of the platform [25]. As such, the owner could conceivably appropriate significant rents in permitting access whilst at the same time incurring moderate expenditures in maintenance and development, as is the case with applications for smartphones or software for computers. The combination of high profit margins for proprietors and easy access to solutions for adopters makes platforms an appealing commodity [4], [17], [23], but it also exposes all concerned to increased complexity as contexts and technologies interact in ways that neither party may be able to predict. In essence, the choices made by providers and adopters affect the viability of a platform as a whole, yet they are made with a limited view of available choices and ensuing consequences. It therefore stands to reason that there is much to gain from elucidating options in a manner that is germane to providers as well as adopters.

3   Options Theory

While options theory represents a diverse field in its own right, we will limit ourselves to the areas of real options and digital options.

3.1   Real Options

Options theory is rooted in financial literature and outlines how firms may pursue investments whilst still minimising risk. Simply put, financial options state that a firm first makes a limited investment which creates an option to acquire an asset. The option grants preferential access to the object of interest and can be activated through a second, larger, investment [26]. Management literature expands upon financial options under the guise of real options, a broader construct that provides insight into how tangible as well as intangible resources can enable options for strategic action [27]. Bowman and Hurry [28] describe the activation of options as a form of incremental decision-making on investments that originate with what they refer to as shadow options – options that are present but not recognised – that only become real options following a process of sense-making [29] or exploration [30]. The identification of real options is to a significant extent subject to contingencies such as technological frames [31], experience [32] and absorptive capacity [33] established by past investments, making the identification of real options virtually unique to every firm. After recognising an option as such, the real option may then be acted upon immediately or left unattended for a considerable amount of time depending upon the situation [28], [14]. Once the holder decides to act, the choices are to either abandon (sell) it or adopt (buy) it. The act of adopting an option may be further subdivided depending upon whether the option represents a continuation of existing strategies or whether it offers flexibility to modify organisational means or ends. Adopted options then give rise to new shadow options that will have to be identified as the cycle begins again.

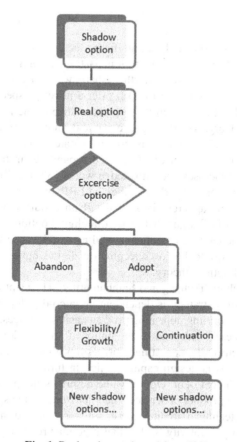

Fig. 1. Real options, adapted from [28]

Real options theory may be transposed onto technology investments insofar as shadow options represent possible avenues of pursuit, real options correspond to developed technologies, and exercising an option equals commercialising or implementing a technology [34]. It is vital to exercise good judgment as moving through this sequence of event cycle too quickly or out of step with technology trends can incur significant liabilities such as infrastructure costs and co-specialised components. The difficulty of evaluation is a perennial feature in IT-investments [35] with particular salience for platforms [13, 14] that primarily serve to enable other functions or services. Under these circumstances, flexibility options may be described as technology positioning investments that represent the cost of attaining a subsequent set of attractive growth options that generate additional options rather than serve current operational needs [34], [36]. While single-purpose artefacts or technologies may be relatively easy to perceive (and evaluate) as a real option, investments in platforms are problematic as they represent significant costs yet only provide vicarious benefits as an infrastructure for further options [13]. The malleable nature of digital technologies may be an additional source of concern as they are ubiquitous yet often require special skills in order to progress beyond unrealised shadow options. With this in mind, we turn our attention to managing options related to digital technologies.

3.2   Digital Options

Information technology is not only a significant factor in overall firm performance, but also a generator of options that help organisations leverage internal and external resources to their advantage. Sambamurthy, Bharadwaj and Grover [37] followed by Overby, Bharadwaj and Sambamurthy [38] offer a novel perspective on real options in the form of digital options which they operationalize as the impact of IT upon the reach and richness of organisational processes and knowledge. Sambamurthy et al. argue that accessing digital options is commensurate to cultivating inimitable resources [39], describing it "a set of IT-enabled capabilities in the form of digitized [sic] enterprise work processes and knowledge work" [37, p.247]. While the concept of digital options has been applied in studies on ERP-systems (e.g. [40]), it has also received criticism for its apparent lack of detail on certain key aspects. Sandberg, Mathiassen and Napier [15] argue that restricting digital options to reach and richness limits the concept's generative potential as well as its relevance to IT capabilities. A preferable alternative would be to conceptualise digital options in a manner more closely related to real options theory.

Woodard, Ramasubbu, Tschang and Sambamurthy [41] adapt digital options to an environment where firm strategy is dependent upon co-development of physical and digital components in forming appealing products and/or services. A salient challenge in operating under these conditions is the ability to promote long-term stability and evolution whilst concurrently extracting short-term profits. The authors argue that the locus for digital options is design capital, which in turn is formed of two qualities: Option value and technical debt. Option value describes the possibilities enabled by the composition of the product or service, encompassing a wide span of features ranging from underlying technical architecture to software-enabled interface. The authors relate option value to generativity [42] in that it permits relatively inexpensive alterations to the original design, e.g. in the form of new product models by the producer or customisation by the consumer. Conversely, technical debt describes limitations in the design that restrict the ability to modify the product or service without incurring significant costs. While restricting the design ultimately serves to limit future development of a product or service, it may be necessary in light of practical considerations such as product cost or R&D expenditures.

Options value and technical debt are not opposites, but rather orthogonal qualities that may be envisioned as a matrix which the firm traverses via design moves. It is possible to alter the options value without incurring or decreasing technical debt – and vice versa. While ostensibly simple, the underlying actions are by no means straightforward as digital business strategies are dependent upon composite physical-digital goods. Each type of materiality offer their own set of possibilities and limitations [21], some of which are emergent and only appear when combined. It is also worth considering that design moves are not necessarily perfectly rational or optimal, but are frequently influenced by external contingencies like availability of resources, influences from partners, or demands from customers.

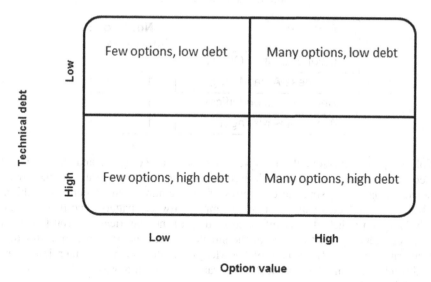

Fig. 2. Design capital [41]

4   Research Method

The objective of the present study is to address the question of how platform evolution relates to the provision of options for application as well as further development. We have pursued this line of inquiry using a single case study [43] centred on a firm that provides a platform for secure communication. As the scope of the study is limited to suggesting means to study a particular phenomenon, the study can be categorised as an explorative study, which is also in keeping with the single-case approach. A qualitative study based on interviews was motivated by the retrospective nature of the study and the unfamiliarity of the researchers with the specific business context. Interviews permit informed answers and access to the expertise of informants, permitting "in-depth studies [...] in plain and everyday terms" [43, p.6]. The object of the study is to garner insight into the actions taken by a firm to meet changing business priorities and technological opportunities. Hence, case study allowed appeared the most viable option as it "studies a phenomenon [...] in its real-world context" [43, p.17].

Empirical data was gathered primarily through five separate interviews with employees, with additional contextual information provided by documentation pertaining to the platform and attention in three meetings with representatives from the firm. Given that the provider is a small firm consisting of some twenty employees, five interviews with high-level staff were deemed sufficient to grasp the aim and scope of the platform.

All interviews were conducted at the offices of the firm and ranged from 45 to 70 minutes in length. The interviews may be considered semi-structured [44] as the interviewer prepared a number of questions beforehand, but also followed up on a priori unexpected or unknown avenues of inquiry that presented themselves.

Table 1. Outline of interviews

Position	No. of interviews
Chief Executive Officer	2
Business Area Manager	1
Chief Operation Officer	1
Area Sales Manager	1

Following transcription, the empirical material was compiled and disassembled guided by the theoretical framework used in this paper. The material was then reassembled thematically using the categories of the framework in an iterative fashion. Analysis was conducted using a bricolage approach where patterns and themes were sought based on a theoretically informed reading of the empirical material [45] with the aim of deducing what aspects of the situated context is amenable to abstraction and contribution to a wider body of knowledge. As the number of interviews conducted is relatively small, no particular software or similar tool was used in the coding and analysis of the empirical material.

5   Case Study

Our study centres on PlatformCo, an enterprise founded in 2000 located in northern Europe that currently houses a staff of 20+ employees. PlatformCo is a branch of a larger firm that is in the business of inventing, developing and selling wired communications systems for emergency use. In its particular niche, the aggregate firm has managed to establish a small yet firm foothold, but profit-margins are relatively low and the competition fierce. With that in mind, PlatformCo pursued an alternative business model and started branching out in the early 2000's by seeking to apply technical skills pertaining to communication in other areas. They sought diversification by developing a communication platform, PlatformCoMobile, which marked two distinct points of departure from the existing business model. First, the platform was designed to facilitate machine-to-machine communication rather than vocal communication between people or interaction between human and system. Second, the idea was to use the platform to sell services as opposed to off-the-shelf products to customers in an effort to increase profit margins. While this upward mobility in the value chain was desirable from a business perspective, it also represented a significant increase in the level of complexity as service-orientation forced closer ties to customers.

In practical terms, PlatformCoMobile is composed of a communications platform that is physically installed into the user's system where it serves as a link to back-office system(s) where services are hosted. The communications platform is composed of a highly customised router and Linux-based software that is intended to provide security and stability. The platform may be integrated into user systems using several means; including common interfaces like Ethernet and Universal Serial Bus (USB) as well as the more specialised Controller Area Network (CAN) Bus which is widely used in automotive applications. PlatformCoMobile also supports a range of wireless communication protocols and is equipped to make use of the Global Positioning System.

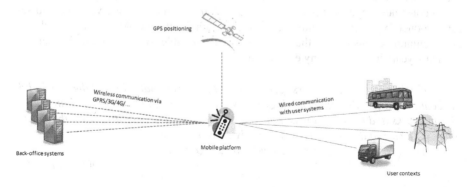

Fig. 3. Platform structure

After installation, the platform allows the customer to access the unit (e.g. vehicle) remotely and gather data from its sensory devices or issue instructions to any on-board control systems. Marketed to business customers, PlatformCoMobile has been adopted in a wide range of industries, including private security, forestry machinery, public transportation and logistics. The majority of application contexts involve supervising vehicles, but there are also customers that prioritise resilience and utilise the platform in situations where physical access is a concern, e.g. for monitoring high-voltage electrical wiring. As customers rely on PlatformCoMobile to continuously transmit data even under extreme conditions, the platform hardware has been certified to comply with several international standards, including those set by the International Electrotechnical Commission (IEC) regarding heat, cold, vibration, shock and humidity.

In addition to services developed by PlatformCo themselves, other suppliers are also able to deliver their services via the platform following a process of certification and testing. PlatformCo typically form partnerships with these external suppliers that utilise their platform, making sure that the partners are able to deliver their service in exchange for a monthly fee. PlatformCo has made it an explicit policy to not develop any services that imitate or infringe upon partner services, instead prioritising the continued existence of the partner and availability of their expertise. While this may limit profits in the short run, it ensures that PlatformCo is able to attract complementors and offer a diverse portfolio of services via its platform.

6   Results

The following chapter presents the results of the study and relates them to theoretical constructs.

6.1   Digital Options in Platform Design

PlatformCoMobile qua device has been redesigned in three major steps; the original iteration developed in 1997 and brought to market in 2000. The original intent was not to construct a platform for services, but rather to offer a robust, versatile and secure product for wireless communications. As such, PlatformCoMobile was marketed as a communications device that was sufficiently durable to withstand active service for many years in virtually any environment.

> *"...if you look back at the first generation...the reason that it looked the way it did is because of the tools and technology that were available at the time. We didn't have 3G-networks and the like. It was limited by the technical possibilities available back then. [...] You could say that it was largely a prototype or proof-of-concept that everything could work together."*
>
> - COO, PlatformCo

The platform was initially a stand-alone solution for communication that offered a highly limited range of functionality and limited prospects for improvements or additions. However, PlatformCo soon began to see the advantages of expanding upon the functionality of the product. The first major step was taken in 2001 when remote access was enabled. The impetus for this move was not a matter of strategy, but rather convenience. Service and configuration of PlatformCoMobile involved significant amount of travelling to remote locations or even neighbouring countries for technical staff. As maintenance is a continuous process, streamlining this activity translates into significant savings, which is particularly important for a relatively small enterprise like PlatformCo. Hence, economising on maintenance was the primary driver for early development of PlatformCoMobile. The following years saw development of platform functionality that was more related to adding value for users, such as the introduction of "managed services" in 2003, which was a basic form of what is commonly referred to as could services today.

Since the first generation of PlatformCoMobile was not intended as a platform for services, it was neither scalable nor expandable. Hence, the transition to the second generation entailed scrapping the entire architecture and starting from scratch with new hardware and software. While costly in terms of time and resources, it was necessary in order to accommodate new components, e.g. an improved GPS transponder and new I/O-ports that were sought by customers. As the second generation of PlatformCoMobile was technically more advanced, PlatformCo took steps to ensure that services followed suit. 2007 saw the introduction of "device management" – a basic maintenance service that facilitates more advanced services. PlatformCo also furthered modularisation of their services by deconstructing the value-chain into four layers: Data transmission, administration and monitoring, data processing and analysing, and high-level services that are often unique to particular business segments. These layers form a kind of hierarchy where data transmission provides the base and high-level services the apex. As the first three layers are closely related to the platform itself, PlatformCo manages these areas in-house whereas high-level services are a blend of services developed by external partners and those developed by PlatformCo. The interdependencies between layers can become bit convoluted as customers sometimes require specialised hardware in order to enable high-level services.

"[...] we've devoted our efforts to infrastructure, a platform where we can add content – content as in services. But in this case the sensors will be plugged in down here in order to add content higher up."

- Business area manager, PlatformCo

While the second generation of the platform was scalable in terms of functionality, it did not scale in terms of performance – meaning that PlatformCoMobile could not run certain desired services simultaneously. The subsequent transition to the third (current) generation of hardware did not entail a complete overhaul, but did require scrapping roughly 50% of the previous architecture.

As it stands, the mobile unit may now be considered a flexible platform that is scalable in terms of functionality as well as performance. More importantly, while the platform can be expressed as a combination of physical components (hardware) and digital components (software), services are merely co-specialised to the software. Hence, it is in some ways accurate to say that the software-component marks the essence of the platform as it stands today. The hardware-product serves as a physical link for communication between the user context and the back-office system, but in terms of the current service model, it is essentially a piece of infrastructure at this point.

"...I see that the product is supposed to enable the services required. So you focus less on how things are performed inside the product, and assume more of a bird's-eye view of what function we're after. Maybe customers also focus less on how things are solved and look to our ability to meet [their] functional requirements. You don't look as much to the product and hardware, but rather the customer that buys a service or functionality and expect it to work. That's what counts."

- COO, PlatformCo

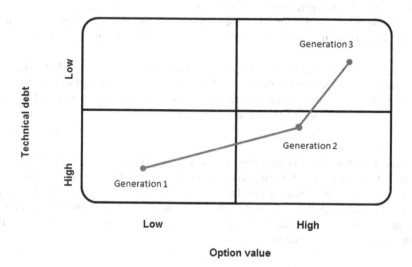

Fig. 4. Design moves at PlatformCo

The software platform can be modified to accommodate virtually any hardware – as is evident by the fact that PlatformCo still has hardware from the first and second generations in active use. It is therefore feasible to run some services on other digital devices, such as smartphones. While this could make quality assurance an issue, PlatformCo has based many features in its platform upon explicit customer requirements or business opportunities. A rough estimate of influences in platform design puts the ratio between explicit customer demands and designer discretion at 40-60, indicating that PlatformCo has cultivated a very pragmatic approach to quality as well as design. All three generations of the physical device have been designed by PlatformCo themselves, but have been based upon readily available standardised components as customisation would be prohibitively expensive. The evolution of the platform is therefore related not only to customer requirements, but also to what technology is available at a competitive price.

6.2   Real Options in Platform Applicability

The idea to utilise PlatfomCoMobile as a platform for services as opposed to a specialised product for wireless communication gradually developed via several interim stages, such as the introduction of managed services in 2003 and a concerted transition from product to systems in 2004. While these events were important for the development of the platform as such, it was still limited to the finite resources of PlatformCo and largely propelled by their core competence, i.e. the development of technical solutions for secure communication. In 2005, PlatformCo adopted a partner strategy whereby they actively sought out firms that offered applications or services that were requested by current or potential platform customers. The advantage of partnering in this manner is bilateral. The partners sought out are highly competent in their respective field, adding cutting-edge services to the portfolio of solutions that PlatformCo can market as part of their platform. Conversely, the communications infrastructure provided via PlatformCoMobile essentially enables partners to black-box the issue of communication and focus on *what* data is being transmitted rather than *how* it is transmitted. Moreover, the aggregated network of partners could handle contracts and clients that are too big for any one supplier to manage on their own.

> *"We see everything that we think and do as a network, and I think…that is the way one should proceed to survive the future. These [big] companies that want it all, they won't be able to pull it off as things are moving too fast […] you have to find the cutting-edge and then fit the puzzle together."*
>
> - CEO, PlatformCo

A salient driving force behind the move towards services was the recalcitrance of customers towards paying for infrastructure (i.e. hardware). Explaining the merits of a platform can often be a challenge as the term does not readily convey a sense of benefit or utility. Familiarising oneself with different industries – or finding partners with the requisite knowledge – has proven to be a significant factor in the ability to successfully market services rather than products.

"...nobody is really in the market for a platform. What they want is a solution. [...]
If you then look at public transportation – the bus-ecosystem – there we've learnt how
the industry works in the Nordic countries in order to supply the functionality that
they actually want from this platform. In doing so it has suddenly turned into a solu-
tion."

- Business area manager, PlatformCo

The transition from product to services has involved working in closer proximity to customers, trying to comprehend the mind-set of a wider range of stakeholders. The business is no longer comprised of engineers who sell products to other engineers, but rather engineers developing services that everyday users can comprehend. Engaging with customers under these circumstances often entails working in close proximity to clarify a problem, deconstruct it, identify relevant causal factors, and then conceptualise feasible services that can alleviate or resolve the issue. Once services have been identified, they are matched to the current offerings available via partners. In cases where obvious match is found, PlatformCo scans the market for providers who offer services that conform to the perceived requirements. If a supplier is found, the company initiates contact and investigates the possibility of a partnership using the business opportunity as a tangible motive. If no suitable solution is found, then the engineers at PlatformCo can fill this "gap" themselves by developing a new service based on the capabilities of their platform.

"The classic example is the children's room with pieces of [building blocks] all
over the ground. You can build anything with it, but you need to know what to build,
how to do it, where you find the pieces and so on. The next step is to package it in a
box. The third step is to categorise the different models with a description and a pic-
ture. It's about knowing the industry – for instance what the bus driver needs. Before
you know that you cannot package a solution."

- Business area manager, PlatformCo

Learning how an industry works and what it needs is a time-consuming and laborious process. It does however leave in its wake the added boon of naturalising the interactions with customers in that business segment. The need to go into technical detail diminishes, leaving PlatformCo and customers free to stick with the practical concern of how to integrate the solution into the business rather than debate technologies and communication protocols. While PlatformCo strives to package their services as ready-to-order solutions, the practical reality of adapting to a variety of customers and industries limits the applicability of this approach. The efficacy of the platform is dependent upon the ability to integrate it into a given context (e.g. a vehicle) and relay desired data to a corresponding back-office system. As it is not uncommon for customers to employ an eclectic variety of hardware and machinery, the engineers and developers at PlatformCo often find themselves working alongside customers in solving novel problems related to localised integration.

"It's always tough to 'productify' solutions. For instance, one particular solution is intended to work with a truck – we've done that before. But it's pulling a salt spreader from the 1980's. We need signals from that as well, so we're back to customisation again. [...] That's the way it is with our customers – machinery from the 80's meets tablets from last year."

- Business area manager, PlatformCo

The initial installation of the platform always requires a certain amount of man-hours depending on the context. However, following the initial integration of the platform, services are activated and managed remotely via back-office systems as per customer request. In many cases, this is tantamount to enabling remote connectivity in machinery that was never designed to facilitate this feature. The sudden reality of taking a fleet of vehicles to an online-world can foster new perspectives as one improvement can snowball into new ideas of how to utilise the new infrastructure. It is therefore not uncommon for the customer to come up with several new ideas or suggestions on how they would like to use the platform in the months and years after the initial installation.

7   Discussion

The application of digital platforms as a means to facilitate modularity of physical products holds great potential, but also significant complexity. In the present study, we have illustrated the evolution of PlatformCoMobile in three major design moves, originating as a stand-alone solution for communication that offered a highly limited range of functionality, evolving to a connected product able to deliver a range of services, and ending up as the current scalable service-platform for customers operating in several industries.

The significance of digital options is of particular relevance when taking the leap from product evolution to platform evolution. A product is a stand-alone device that alleviates or solves current problems. You may use such a device to deliver services to customers who want simple, purposeful solutions that meet their present needs. Product providers may improve upon their product in relative isolation as improvements are typically implemented in the form of a new version of the product. Platforms differ in at least two respects. First, the underlying motivation for having platforms is to afford changes to individual components that allow the structure as a whole to evolve as needed. Second, (industry) platforms are intended to serve as a hub or shared structure that enables or simplifies interactions between parties. As such, the platform may be regarded as an infrastructure [46] that connects supplier offerings to customer needs.

The difficulty in evaluating platforms is inherent in its vicarious nature. Set against the basic premise of financial options, platforms ostensibly behave in an inverse manner. Rather than a small amount, adopters pay a significant portion of the investment up front in order to access the platform. As suggested by Taudes et al. [13], one way to justify the investment is to evaluate each function permitted by the platform in isolation and tally the result. The present study illustrates that the platform provider

can facilitate this through either pre-packaged offerings as real options, or by participating in a process of sense-making to develop nascent shadow options present in the
operating environment of the adopter. Additionally, the fluid nature of digital materiality is highly commensurate with the mobility of financial assets that provide part of
the underpinnings for real options. Digital platforms allow adopters to either consciously hold an option (e.g. on a particular service or application) for a lengthy
period of time before acting upon it, or gradually develop shadow options into real
options as they come to better understand the platform or identify new organisational
needs. Hence, digital platforms can be said to promote incremental decision-making
with the notable exception of the physical artefact that houses the digital content.

Digitalisation allows physically non-modular devices to be modified with new
software and content, potentially granting them some of the versatility of platforms.
That being said, the platform provider must weigh design moves more carefully when
developing a platform. A product may to a greater extent be viewed as an independent
device with fixed properties, enabling the designer to limit the scope of variables. A
(digital) platform may allow the designer considerable leeway with regards to amend-
ing those aspects that are obscured to the outside, but cannot redesign physical interfaces or enabling software with the same sense of carte blanche. Alterations must take
into consideration an installed base of complementors and users that integrate the
platform in a wide variety of local systems for an equally wide variety of purposes. In
effect, myopic design moves made to improve the operations of the device could simultaneously incur technical debt for the platform if they are not in keeping with
what partners expect or customers require.

Last but not least, evaluating investments on an individual basis may be disadvan-
tageous as it limits one's ability to see the whole picture [47]. This is especially salient when applied to IT as one must usually take compatibility with extant systems
into consideration [15]. Options theory ostensibly flies in the face of this reasoning as
it advocates incremental decision making under conditions where each option is to
some degree perceived as an encapsulated entity. However, when applied to a platform as in the present case study, a case-by-case perception of the different individual
services appears a feasible approach as it provides a clearer case for acceptance or
rejection when compared to a whole suite of services. Furthermore, the digitised
nature of the services makes them inherently flexible. Once the platform qua infrastructure is in place, services can be switched on and off with short notice. Hence,
adoption or cancellation of services enabled by digital platforms offers the malleabil-
ity presupposed by options theory. If anything, an options perspective may be advan-
tageous when seeking to balance a "portfolio" of different services that can enhance
the firm's processes or knowledge.

8   Conclusions

In this paper, we argue that options theory can contribute to our understanding of
digital platforms both as phenomena as well as enabling tools. We employ two con-
ceptions of options theory, real options and digital options, and apply them to case
study of a digital platform developed over the course of 13 years by an SME operating in Northern Europe. Using digital options in the form of design capital, we are

able to plot the evolution of the artefact as an operand resource and see how design moves impact the transition from product to platform. Real options theory provide the other half of the discourse by showing that options are unavailable until they emerge into consciousness following a process of sense-making. In establishing a nascent platform, there is much to be gained by the platform provider in facilitating this sense-making as each new realisation is another potential sales argument.

Objects and services enabled by digital platforms ostensibly lend themselves to the end-user simplicity of real options due to the flexibility of digital materiality. A possible avenue for future research would be to further explore the relation between design and application, e.g. by studying the relationship between real options and technology affordances.

References

1. Baldwin, C., Woodard, J.: The Architecture of Platforms: A Unified View. In: Gawer, A. (ed.) Platforms, Markets and Innovation, pp. 19–44. Edward Elgar, Cheltenham (2009)
2. Eisenmann, T., Parker, G., Van Alstyne, M.W.: Strategies for Two-sided Markets. Harvard Business Review 84(10), 92–101 (2006)
3. Eisenmann, T., Parker, G., Van Alstyne, M.: Platform Envelopment. Strategic Management Journal 32(12), 1270–1285 (2011)
4. Eisenmann, T., Parker, G., Van Alstyne, M.W.: Opening Platforms: How, When, and Why? In: Gawer, A. (ed.) Platforms, Markets and Innovation, pp. 131–162. Edward Elgar, Cheltenham (2009)
5. Bodreau, K.J., Haigu, A.: Platform Rules: Multi-sided Platforms as Regulators. In: Gawer, A. (ed.) Platforms, Markets and Innovation, pp. 163–191. Edward Elgar, Cheltenham (2009)
6. Wareham, J., Fox, P., Cano Giner, J.L.: Technology Ecosystem Governance. ESADE Business School Research Paper 225-2 (2013)
7. Vargo, S.L., Lusch, R.F.: Evolving to a New Dominant Logic for Marketing. Journal of Marketing 68(1), 1–17 (2004)
8. Nambisan, S.: Information Technology and Product/Service Innovation: A Brief Assessment and Some Suggestions for Future Research. Journal of the Association for Information Systems 14(4), 215–226 (2013)
9. Dos Santos, B.: Justifying Investment in New Information Technologies. Journal of Management Information Systems 7(4), 71–89 (1991)
10. Benaroch, M., Kauffman, R.J.: Justifying Electronic Banking Network Expansion Using Real Options Analysis. MIS Quarterly 24(2), 197–225 (2000)
11. Benaroch, M., Jeffery, M., Kauffman, R.J., Shah, S.: Option-based Risk Management: A Field Study of Sequential Information Technology Investment Decisions. Journal of Management Information Systems 24(2), 103–140 (2007)
12. Ghosh, S., Li, X.: A Real Options Model for Generalized Meta-Staged Projects-Valuing the Migration to SOA. Information Systems Research 24(4), 1011–1027 (2013)
13. Taudes, A., Feurstein, M., Mild, A.: Options Analysis of Software Platform Decisions: A Case Study. MIS Quarterly 24(2), 227–243 (2000)
14. Fichman, R.G.: Real Options and IT Platform Adoption: Implications for Theory and Practice. Information Systems Research 15(2), 132–154 (2004)

15. Sandberg, J., Mathiassen, L., Napier, N.: Digital Options Theory for IT Capability Investment. Journal of the Association for Information Systems (forthcoming, 2014)
16. Suarez, F., Cusumano, M.: The Role of Services in Platform Markets. In: Gawer, A. (ed.) Platforms, Markets and Innovation, pp. 77–98. Edward Elgar, Cheltenham (2009)
17. Cusumano, M.A.: Platforms Versus Products: Observations from the Literature and History. History and Strategy 29, 35–67 (2012)
18. Tiwana, A., Konsynski, B., Bush, A.A.: Research Commentary—Platform Evolution: Coevolution of Platform Architecture, Governance, and Environmental Dynamics. Information Systems Research 21(4), 675–687 (2010)
19. Gawer, A.: Platform Dynamics and Strategies: From Products to Services. In: Gawer, A. (ed.) Platforms, Markets and Innovation, pp. 1–18. Edward Elgar, Cheltenham (2009)
20. Le Masson, P., Weil, B., Hatchuel, A.: Platforms for the Creation of Platforms: Collaborating in the Unknown. In: Gawer, A. (ed.) Platforms, Markets and Innovation, pp. 273–375. Edward Elgar, Cheltenham (2009)
21. Kallinikos, J., Aaltonen, A., Marton, A.: The Ambivalent Ontology of Digital Artifacts. MIS Quarterly 37(2), 357–370 (2013)
22. Tilson, D., Lyytinen, K., Sørensen, C.: Research Commentary—Digital Infrastructures: The Missing IS Research Agenda. Information Systems Research 21(4), 748–759 (2010)
23. Yoo, Y., Boland, R.J., Lyytinen, K., Majchrzak, A.: Organizing for Innovation in the Digitized World. Organization Science 23(5), 1398–1408 (2012)
24. Yoo, Y., Henfridsson, O., Lyytinen, K.: Research Commentary—The New Organizing Logic of Digital Innovation: An Agenda for Information Systems Research. Information Systems Research 21(4), 724–735 (2010)
25. Tilson, D., Sorensen, C., Lyytinen, K.: Platform Complexity: Lessons from the Music Industry. In: Proceedings of the 46th IEEE Hawaii International Conference on System Sciences, Maui, USA (2013)
26. Black, F., Scholes, M.: The Pricing of Options and Corporate Liabilities. The Journal of Political Economy 81(3), 637–654 (1973)
27. Adner, R., Levinthal, D.A.: What is Not a Real Option: Considering Boundaries for the Application of Real Options to Business Strategy. Academy of Management Review 29(1), 74–85 (2004)
28. Bowman, E.H., Hurry, D.: Strategy through the Option Lens: An Integrated View of Resource Investments and the Incremental-choice Process. Academy of Management Review 18(4), 760–782 (1993)
29. Weick, K.E., Sutcliffe, K.M., Obstfeld, D.: Organizing and the Process of Sense-making. Organization Science 16(4), 409–421 (2005)
30. March, J.G.: Exploration and Exploitation in Organizational Learning. Organization Science 2(1), 71–87 (1991)
31. Orlikowski, W.J., Gash, D.C.: Technological Frames: Making Sense of Information Technology in Organizations. ACM Transactions on Information Systems 12(2), 174–207 (1994)
32. Ciborra, C.U.: The Platform Organization: Recombining Strategies, Structures, and Surprises. Organization Science 7(2), 103–118 (1996)
33. Cohen, W.M., Levinthal, D.A.: Absorptive Capacity: A New Perspective on Learning and Innovation. Administrative Science Quarterly 25(1), 128–152 (1990)
34. McGrath, R.G.: A Real Options Logic for Initiating Technology Positioning Investments. Academy of Management Review 22(4), 974–996 (1997)
35. Brynjolfsson, E.: The Productivity Paradox of Information Technology. Communications of the ACM 36(12), 66–77 (1993)

36. Fichman, R.G., Keil, M., Tiwana, A.: Beyond Valuation: "Option Thinking" in IT Project Management. California Management Review 47(2), 74–95 (2005)
37. Sambamurthy, V., Bharadwaj, A., Grover, V.: Shaping Agility Through Digital Options: Reconceptualizing the Role of Information Technology in Contemporary Firms. MIS Quarterly 27(2), 237–263 (2003)
38. Overby, E., Bharadwaj, A., Sambamurthy, V.: Enterprise Agility and the Enabling Role of Information Technology. European Journal of Information Systems 15(2), 120–131 (2006)
39. Barney, J.: Firm Resources and Sustained Competitive Advantage. Journal of Management 17(1), 99–120 (1991)
40. Karimi, J., Somers, T.M., Bhattacherjee, A.: The Role of ERP Implementation in Enabling Digital Options: A Theoretical and Empirical Analysis. International Journal of Electronic Commerce 13(3), 7–42 (2009)
41. Woodard, C.J., Ramasubbu, N., Tschang, F.T., Sambamurthy, V.: Design Capital and Design Moves: The Logic of Digital Business Strategy. MIS Quarterly 37(2), 537–564 (2013)
42. Zittrain, J.L.: The Generative Internet. Harvard Law Review 19(7), 1974–2040 (2006)
43. Yin, R.K.: Case Study Research – Design and Methods, 4th edn. Sage Publications, Thousand Oaks (2009)
44. Creswell, J.W.: Qualitative Inquiry & Research Design - Choosing among Five Approaches, 2nd edn. Sage Publications, Thousand Oaks (2007)
45. Kvale, S., Brinkmann, S.: Interviews: Learning the Craft of Qualitative Research Interviewing, 2nd edn. Sage Publications, Thousand Oaks (2009)
46. Star, S.L., Ruhleder, K.: Steps Toward an Ecology of Infrastructure: Design and Access for Large Information Spaces. Information Systems Research 7(1), 111–134 (1996)
47. Teece, D.J.: Explicating Dynamic Capabilities: The Nature and Microfoundations of (Sustainable) Enterprise Performance. Strategic Management Journal 28(13), 1319–1350 (2007)

Rethinking the Roles of Actors in the Mobility of Healthcare Services

Tiko Iyamu[1], Suama Hamunyela[2], and Sharol Sibongile Mkhomazi[3]

[1] Polytechnic of Namibia, Department of Business Computing, Windhoek, Namibia
connectvilla@gmail.com
[2] Namibia University of Science and Technology,
Department of Informatics, Windhoek, Namibia
slhamunyela@polytechnic.edu.na
[3] Tshwane University of Technology, Department of Office Management and Technology,
Pretoria, South Africa
mkhomaziss@tut.ac.za

Abstract. Patients seek attention and treatments to various types of diseases and symptoms. Diseases infection and symptoms are often not predictive. Normally, there is a spread and movement of people across the geographical locations, of both the rural and urban communities, in countries including Namibia. As such, healthcare could be needed at any location, and at anytime. There is significant mobility of individuals and groups within a country. Unfortunately, the healthcare services are not always as mobile at the level and speed that individuals and groups does in Namibia. Hence, there is need for the mobility of healthcare services at both primary and secondary healthcare levels, particularly in the developing countries, such as Namibia.

The population of Namibia is scantly spread among its towns and cities. The major towns and cities are situated, in the average of 175km far apart from each other, in the country's 825, 418km square landscape. The spread necessitates movements of individuals and groups, particularly the old, poor, and nomadic people. Unfortunately, healthcare records in the country are not centralised and virtualised, making accessibility into patients' records difficult or impossible, from any location. As a result, healthcare service delivering is challenged. This study therefore explored and examined the possibility of mobility of healthcare services to those who live in the country.

The study employed the qualitative research method, within which data was gathered from primary healthcare service providers, using open-ended questionnaires. The Moments of Translation from the perspective of actor network theory (ANT) was used as a lens in the analysis of the data, to examine and understand the power and factors, which influences mobility of healthcare service in Namibia. Categorisation of Patients, Response Time, Understanding the Actors, Actors' participatory to service delivery, and Actors' Alliance were found to be the influencing factors in the provision of mobility of healthcare services.

Keywords: Healthcare services, Actor Network Theory.

B. Bergvall-Kåreborn and P.A. Nielsen (Eds.): TDIT 2014, IFIP AICT 429, pp. 261–276, 2014.
© IFIP International Federation for Information Processing 2014

1   Introduction

The movement and spread of the population in developing countries is argued to impact healthcare service provision [1]. To ensure effective healthcare services provision, states and healthcare organisations are engaged in transforming the industry. According to [2], to improve the quality and efficiency of healthcare many hospitals are involved in extensive efforts to substitute electronic patient records for paper records. Another effort that has been made by some organisations is the integration of health information systems to improve quality of healthcare service.

Also, the shift from curative to planning and preventing of disease outbreaks and control has significantly necessitated the need for healthcare data management, efficient service delivery, healthcare information flows between health practitioners and patients, as well as information sharing between healthcare levels of operandi [3]. The mission of curative, preventing and disease control can only be made possible if the information of the whole population based is made available to policy makers, healthcare profession, administrators, donors and all healthcare organisations.

However, different categories of patients exist in the healthcare sector and the needs for healthcare services are diverse. There is the nomadic patient. This inflates the need to investigate different dimensions of healthcare service provisions processes in a country. In [4] argument, there is a scenario where the patient may visit a different healthcare organisation, either because the patient is dissatisfied with the treatment of his or her previous visit or the patient moves to a different location. Distinctively in this case is the mobility of healthcare services in Namibia.

Mobility in this paper refers to the state of easy accessibility of health services from any geographical location. The essentiality of mobility of healthcare is centred on factors such as portability, transferability and availability of healthcare information including real-time interaction between healthcare providers and the needing [5]. In healthcare, mobility is typically associated with mobile healthcare systems and applications, the use of health public kiosk, cellular phone devices, and other portable computing devices [6]. This paper argues that mobility can also be classified by the availability of healthcare services at different levels of healthcare operandi.

Mobility of healthcare services could be translated by various human actors (patients and healthcare workers), based on the different moments. Translation is a key tenet of actor network theory [7]. In actor network theory (ANT), translation is influenced by interest of the actors [8]. Translation takes place between the object and the actors it encounters as the initial program or script is altered through interaction.

ANT is popular for its ability to provide a rich and dynamic way of bringing together the socio-technical and non-technical aspects of the organization [9]. In ANT, society and organisations are a formation of different agents, and the agents interact to form heterogeneous networks [10]; [11], [12]. Networks define, describe and provide substance to agents. ANT then, deeply question and provide retorts to the existence of strong and weak (thus power) networks.

The Namibian healthcare levels of operandi cover both rural and urban areas following the thirteen political and administrative regional demarcations of the country. As a developing country, majority of Namibians still resides in rural areas. There is a significance movement of people between urban and rural areas.

The remainder of the paper in divided into five main sections. The first and second sections cover the literature review and research methodology, respectively. The third section presents the data analysis, which the findings. Based on the findings, the implications for the mobility of healthcare services in Namibia context are discussed in the fourth section. Finally, a conclusion is drawn.

The research was guided by two main questions: (i) what are the factors which influence the mobility of healthcare services in Namibia? (ii) What are the roles of human and non-human actors in the mobility of the mobility of healthcare services?

2   Healthcare Service

The healthcare sector in many countries consists of a large contingence of institutions and organisations, ranging from centres, small and medium to large and technologically advanced hospitals [13]. The institutions are classified differently in many countries. In Namibia for example, the healthcare centres are classified according to geographical areas, namely, community (constituency) and district level, regional level and national level [14]. The levels of categories cover both rural and urban geographical locations. As in many developing countries, in Namibia, 58% of the population resides in rural areas while the remaining percentage resides in urban areas [15].

Due to the essentiality of healthcare, different studies have been conducted in pursuit to establish and describe health services to different healthcare seekers. [16] examined how mobile health could be used as an innovative solution, to providing healthcare services to patients who reside in remote locations. The later stated that locality influences healthcare service delivery, therefore Mobile healthcare services are essential. This is affirmed by [5] stating that, Mobile health greatly benefits patients who reside in remote areas.

Due to the geographical spread of citizens, mobile healthcare is highly essential, however, challenges do exist. According to [16], healthcare providers in rural areas face numerous challenges in providing coherent and integrated services as compared to those in urban areas, which results from lack of mobile healthcare facilities. Also, the approaches that are often used by primary healthcare service providers in the rural areas are primitive and obsolete [17]. This also could be attributed to the fact the recipients of the services do question or protest the act by the service providers.

[5] emphasised that mobility means the use of mobile technologies to access healthcare service, from different places, at the same time; different places, at the different times; different time, different places; and same time, same place. Mobile of healthcare services includes electronic records, shared and accessed via mobile devices among healthcare providers and receivers. It is assumed that, with the mobile health technologies, healthcare problems, such as inadequacy of doctors and poor clinical examination as a result of insufficient skilled workers and scarcity of centre are eradicated [18]. Since available healthcare providers can now remotely interact with patients and conduct analysis remotely. According to [19], M-health offers a variety of benefits, such as timely access, monitoring patients remotely, and improved quality of patients care, to healthcare organisation, providers and patients.

The need for accessibility and quality of health information particularly in developing countries such as Namibia necessitates refection and attention. Thus, there is need for investigation on the mobility of services to improve delivering of healthcare. It has been empirically unveiled, it is important to have healthcare services at the communities' disposal, and at any location, as opposed to the difficulty of accessibility due to distances. The investigation to ensure achieving this objective was carried through a study. The methodology that was applied in the study is explained next.

3   Methodology

The case study research approach and the qualitative interpretive research method were employed. The case study approach was selected mainly because of its focus on real-life situation. According to [20], a case study can be described as the investigation of a contemporary phenomenon within a real-life context. The Namibian Ministry of Health and Social Services (MoHSS) was used as the case, in the study. In addition the MoHSS, the general populace were allowed to participate in the study.

Questionnaires and interviews were used, from the perspective of qualitative method. This was to allow the participants to share their subjective view of how they provide and receive healthcare services in the country. [21] argued that the qualitative method recognises and focuses on the subjective meaning which the participants bring to the context of the study. Upon completion of the questionnaire, follow up telephonic interviews were conducted to establish deeper understanding of the formation of networks and build of alliances. The two techniques are well established forms of data collection in social science studies.

The participants in the study were identified. A total of 23 people participated in the study. The participants included nurses (6), doctors (4), and patients (8) and non-patients (5), across the country. As at the time of the study, each of the participants had been in service, in their profession for at least five years. This was to ensure the quality of data obtained from them, in terms of the services that they render to nomadic patients of the country.

The data analysis was carried out, using the moments of translation from the perspective of actor network theory (ANT). ANT was selected mainly because it allows us to examine the process of change, and the interaction that take place between technical and non-technical actors. Without the use of ANT, it would have been difficult or impossible to understand and exhume the processes and actors' influences in the mobility of healthcare services in Namibia. Translation occurs when actors start to define roles, distribute and redistribute roles and power, describe a scenario to form alliances of technical and non-technical. Translation stage involves a process of change, which occur via four major moments. The ANT translation stage involves a process of change, which occur via four major moments: problematization, interessement, enrolment and mobilization. This occurs when actors start to define roles, distribute and redistribute roles and power, describe a scenario to form alliances of technical and non-technical.

The Moments of Translation elements can be summarised as follows: (i) Problematization is the stage which reveals what necessitate the network formation. [22]

elaborated that during problematisation, actors establish themselves as an obligatory passage point (OPP) between them and the network for indispensability. (ii) Interessement: at this stage, actors consciously or unconsciously reveal their individual or groups' interest on the item that has been problematized by the focal actor. (iii) Enrolment: process begins with a primary agent imposing their will on others for actions to be executed; this act requires yielding from different actants. (iv) Mobilization: an enrolled actor speaks on behalf of the network, and tries to an interest to persuade others to partake in the activities of the network.

3.1 Namibian Ministry of Health and Social Services (MoHSS): The Case Studied

As it is in many countries, the Ministry of Health and Social Services (MoHSS) of Namibia coordinates and oversee the activities of the medical and health sectors in the country. The MoHSS is mandated to provide an integrated, affordable, accessible, quality health and social welfare services, which is responsive to the needs of the Namibian population [17]. The population seeks services from the available healthcare facilities which are located at different levels of operandi in the Namibia [14]. Processes and activities of the MoHSS are mostly performed manually (paper-based) or through health information systems (HIS). This can be a huge setback for the services which the MoHSS provides to the communities in the country such as distribution of the HIV treatment and immunisation against contiguous decease's outbreaks. Worse, the manual approach significantly delays centralisation of processes and activities [14]. This indeed is dangerous to patient needs, particularly those who are of intensive and chronic nature and nomadic patients.

In addition, there is mobility of individuals and groups within a country. Hence, there is need for the inclination of centralizing healthcare services at both primary and secondary healthcare levels in developing and developed countries. In Namibia, the geographical spread of the population, the widely held image of the healthiness of people in rural area, different groups with needs for healthcare (the old, the poor, nomadic people est.) necessitates the mobility of healthcare services.

4 Data Analysis

As mention earlier in the methodology section, the analysis of the data was done, using the lens of actor network theory. The components of ANT that were followed in the analysis include Actor-Network, and Moments of Translation. In each of the sections of the analysis, the findings are presented and discussed.

Patients are attended to when seeking for health services at the centre, where a discussion (Translation) between the patient and the healthcare takes place. It is procedural to bring along a medical passport (a form of identity which issued by healthcare service providers) when seeking for health services and routine for the healthcare provider to note in the health passport the diagnosis taken and prescriptions. Interactions between healthcare and patients can be classified as part of a durable network that exists to offer services. It is a durable network because a fixed health centre exists and there are actants stationed at each centre.

Currently there are no records readily available when attending to in transit patients except for the health pass port and the medication labels which might not be available at times or lost. For example HIV patients who have been under the care of private doctors and wish to move to state hospitals might not be attended to or attended to after a long time due to communication break down between public and private centres. One of the common challenges encountered by the healthcare providers was a repetition of treatment course which were not effective. There were no records to show that the same treatment or test was carried out, and that it was not effective. One way to overcome these issues is implementation of an Electronic Patient Monitoring System (EPMS) and Electronic Dispensary Tool (EDT) linked to all health facilities providing HIV care for patients to be helped without relying on hard copies only.

4.1   Actor-Network

The human actors in the healthcare sector includes healthcare needing people, healthcare professionals (Doctors and Nurses), and the government MoHSS. The non-human actors consist of processes, ICT artefacts and other medical tools. As at the time of this study, different networks existed, some of them were in the categories of nurses' professionals, urban patients, rural patients, and tribal patients.

The actors had different interest. Each of the actors made a difference, either as a receiver or provider of healthcare service. The difference was based on the impact that the actors had on each other. For example, the knowledge a professional acquired in the course of providing health service to a patient.

Currently, there exist different networks to which actors belong. The enrolment of actors in the different networks was influenced by their interests. As gathered from the participants in the study, the primary interest of the general actors were, to receive service from the practitioners, and to render service to the patients. These interests were however, influenced and manifested by other factors and interests, which included spoken language, culture, and accessibility.

Findings: Categorisation of Patients

Categorisation of patients was found to be significant, due to the different healthcare services they require, and how the services could be provided and by whom. The categorisation is divided into grouping and indexing:

i.   Grouping – the actors require groupings, in terms of networks. The different networks, formed in accordance to categories, such as health related challenge, gender, spoken language, and resident location. This will help in terms of referral of patients, to specialist.

ii.   Index key – indexing of patients' record is critical. This is to enable searches, in the different categories, such as spoken language, tribal origin, current location, and illness type. This will help improve response time.

Some of the patients could only enrol in the network where there preferred language was used as the medium of communication. Even though interpreters were readily available, they preferred to express themselves than the use of translation. Enrolment into a network by many patients in some parts of the country was influenced by their culture. According to some of the participants, their tradition does not allowed them to be treated by professional of opposite sex.

4.2   Moments of Translation

The moments which consist of four stages, namely problematisation, interessement, enrolment and mobilisation was employed in the analysis primarily to examine and understand the interactions which happen amongst the actors. This was to further understand the suitability, and transformation of the current *status quo* to era of mobility of service within the healthcare environment.

- **Problematisation**

The activities of the healthcare sector were initiated, problematised through two primary channels, patient and the government. The patients problematise an activity through illnesses, which were often varied. While the other focal actor, the government does same, problematise its healthcare related activities through the Minister of the Ministry of Health and Social Services (MoHSS).

The patients or their representatives (guardian) report incidents of illness, including vehicle accident involving human at the nearest healthcare centre. The incidents were recorded by the front-office professional, who normally were the Nurses. The Nurses escalate the incidents to the appropriate or respective specialist for further and detailed attention. Another criterion that was used for the referral of patients was language, to enable communication and precise understanding between actors (patient and specialist). The Nurses does so, record and escalate incidents based on the power bestowed on them by the authority of the organisation, which comes from their qualification to practice.

The government problematises all initiatives relating healthcare in the country through the Minister of health. The Minister further problematises the initiatives to heads of units and departments of agencies and organisation within the health sector, through workshops and strategic meetings. Unfortunately, the initiatives are not fit for the districts and rural communities, where they are considered needed most e.g. Unavailability of medical reports 'breaks' the continuity of HIV care between health districts.

Healthcare service providers are stationed at different locations of operands. The spread of the operands are far apart, of about 150kms in average. The travelling and nomadic people are therefore forced to seek healthcare service from the nearest location of medical operand. There is a national policy which is intended to address the challenges of patients who are "on-transits" within the country. The policy defines "on-transit" as a maximum duration of three months stay from original or residence location. The implication is that, a patient who exceed that period may be denied the privilege which the on-transit healthcare service offers.   Also, on-transit patient require a letter or medical passports in other to receive medical attention. The requirement is be able to access medical history, which includes previous diagnoses, treatments, and consultations. Unfortunately, some healthcare service providers are adamant on the requirement before service. The challenge is that many people inevitably lose or damage their medical passport. Some people do not always have the passport with them as the medical incidents are not always predictive. Even though the health passport is replaceable, the process is not real-time. As such, it delays treatment to the patient, worst, if the incident is severe.

Findings: Response Time

Following the process of problematization, from the moment of translation, we found *Response Time* to be crucial in delivering healthcare service to patients. This is even more critical because of the distances the patients have to travel to get the services. Response time is further viewed from two perspectives of significance, in the mobility of healthcare services in Namibia. The factors include the impact of bureaucracy and lack of access to real-time medical data:

i.   Bureaucracy – the process of initiating medical attention is too bureaucratic for incidents which are health related. It is worst if the incident is severe, or become live-threatening. The situation can be more challenging in rural areas, and where there is no next of kin to provide relevant information about the patient.

ii.   Real-time data – there is lack of real-time data of patients' record. This makes it difficult for healthcare providers to provide relevant and instance services to patients, or to know of *previous diagnosis and prescriptions.*

Our interpretation of the findings indicates that the impact of bureaucracy and lack of access to real-time medical data requires cloud computing solution, as shown in Figure 1.

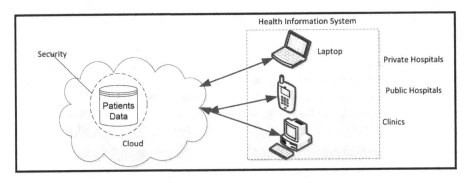

Fig. 1. Patients data in the cloud

Cloud Computing – Figure 1, depict the use of cloud computing solution to store, and access patients' data for health services in Namibia. [23] referred to cloud computing as *both the applications delivered as services over the Internet and the hardware and systems software in the data centers that provide those services.* This allows personnel or specialists to store and access patients' data from Private and Public hospital, including clinics, using different devices, such as laptop, mobile phones, and desktop. The architecture (Figure1), using the cloud solution, enables all healthcare medical personnel in the country to have access to real-time data for their services.

The overall problem is the provision of healthcare services to the nomadic patients of the country. The MoHSS aim to provide effective services to all patients regardless of their dwelling status are currently a challenge, as many of the patients are given too much responsibility in addition to their individual illness. In response to the need for a more effective health services, highly qualified and skilled workforce is enrolled in this activities. Furthermore, procedures to deliver or receive healthcare services are enforced (e.g. only registered nurses can attend to patients or patients should carry their healthcare passport in case looking for healthcare services). This in turn leads to the consideration of suitable healthcare provision, healthcare received and medical history for patients. For healthcare service innovation by the MoHSS, the problematisation proposed by the instigators is that to improve healthcare services to all patients including the nomadic patients, there must be service innovations that enable the desired outcomes.   This is seen as an OPP by the MoHSS to remain a competent healthcare service provider in the country. In the case of the patients, they need to be certain that they will receive adequate services at any time anywhere.

- **Interessemment**

As earlier revealed in the analysis, the actors had different interests. The actors were categorised into two main groups, healthcare service recipients and providers, which consist of patients and professionals, respectively. The interests of these groups were diverse, even though the primary goal was healthcare services.

The interest of the healthcare recipients were influenced by factors such as locations, type of health related service that was required, and the affordability of services. Proximity was a hindrance to many of the people who lived in the rural areas of the country. The healthcare facilities were far apart from each other. As a result, there were few options to those who need services such as Human Immunodeficiency Virus (HIV) patients, who needed to get their Antiretroviral (ARV) medications from healthcare centre.   Due to the fewness of the facilities, the common ones were "General Practitioners". This made it difficult or impossible to access specialists and certain services.

The MoHSS for instance, interest concern its public mandate and social responsibility visible in different directorates and divisions that formed up the MoHSS. The MoHSS also has directorates and division managers in different roles that oversee the execution of duties (e.g. delivery of services), managing healthcare centres, recruit healthcare providers, procurement of necessary medications and other equipment's. These individuals set themselves up as the focal actors and as such, making rues for obligatory passage point.

The healthcare providers' interests were of professional progress, income, status and job descriptions. Healthcare providers in service benefited differently during the course of their duties, depending on the location and the responsibilities that they were assigned. Some of the benefits included flexibility and shifts working hours, housing subsidy, and free medical aid. Also, exposure to different health related cases which in long term can be attributed to experience gained.

ICT artefacts were used differently in the healthcare organisations to support the delivery of services, such as diagnostics and documentation of individual and group records. The use of ICT artefacts were also based on the interest of the users.

The interests were informed by their technical skill and know-how of the technologies, and what they needed them for. Another factor was whether the technologies were supported for use in the environment that they were deployed. This played a critical factor in individual and group interest to make use of available technologies for healthcare services in Namibia. As a result, many of the professional anchor their interests on paper-based processes, which they were more comfortable with in delivering services. Paper technology is crucial to nomadic patients thus; it is required for them to forward the healthcare passport to receive the necessary services.

Findings: Understanding the Actors

In our examination of the empirical data, using the interessment tenet of the Moments of Translation, we found Understanding of the Actors to be significantly useful. In that, only through understanding of the involving actors mobility of healthcare services can be influenced. Understanding of the actors was shared from the perspective of awareness and technology know-how:

i. Awareness – the actants (healthcare providers and patients) took part in the healthcare services, including in the ways in which the services were provided and received, were based on their levels of awareness. For example some health professionals were became health professionals for personal benefits; and some patients' preference for healthcare services centres were influenced by factors, such as their knowledge of the type of services provided by the centres, the types of their illness, and knowledge of proximity to the centres.

ii. Technology know-how - healthcare providers made use of the technologies that they were familiar and comfortable with. For example, some professional could hardly use computer systems to record or access patients' data. However, different technological tools are applicable in diagnosis and other services provision

As already established, the lack of awareness and technology know-how has detrimental implication on the mobility of healthcare services. Thus, a mobile kiosk provides a redress. The use of mobile kiosk will help to reduce or eradicate factors, such as proximity, as it changes location. Also, it could assist patients to garner more information that are offered and available in the different centres, as the patients visit the kiosk in their locations.

As shown in Figure 2, the mobile kiosk is intended to continually, move from one location to another. The kiosk is expected to move within cells (geographical location covered by base station), so it could access, and be accessed by hospitals and clinics, at any location, using any mobile device. According to [24], mobiles devices include microwave ovens, Bluetooth devices, and cordless phones. However, personnel from the hospitals and clinics need to be able to make of mobile devices in order to access the mobile kiosk.

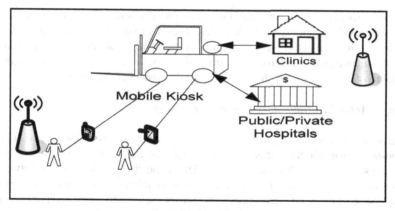

Fig. 2. Mobile Kiosk

- **Enrolment to the Network**

This process begins with a primary agent (in this case the MoHSS management) imposing their will on others in attempt to achieve for common goal. This was mainly because of the significant of participation of all key stakeholders, which determines the success of failure of healthcare initiatives in Namibia. However, participation was always a challenge, as a result, definition of roles and responsibilities were seen as critical.

The ministry defines the regulations, roles and responsibilities to healthcare providers, and standards of service deliveries at public healthcare centres. This process centred on negotiation and alignment of actants' interests within the different networks. The process was challenging in that it was always lengthy and difficult, and so many conflicts arose. The challenges were manifestation of the different cultural background, interests' focuses, as well as recording keeping. For example, some patients had relocated, and others had lost their health passport, and they needed medical attention. In such cases provision was made to create a new health passport for them through negotiation.

Even though health services were considered essential and critical, some patients would not enrol or reluctantly enrolled in the health related programs. This challenge was prevalence in the rural parts of the country. Many of the communities' members cited the same reason for their lack of participation in the health programs. Some of the reasons included accessibility, literacy, and affordability. For example, some of the participants in this study claimed that many needing healthcare are not literate enough to understand the messages which were used as medium of communication to them. Inscription occurs in this case in the sense that the primary interest of the MoHSS at different healthcare centres was to provide efficient services to all patients including the nomadic patients. Interest of all actants has been aligned and now there is a need to maintain the network. This results into a durable or not durable network.

Existence of conscious and unconscious networks of people, and their enrolments which were created overtime and space across the country signifies that there is need for durability and mobility of healthcare services. Thus, patients communicate their healthcare complains to healthcare providers, provide the healthcare passport if in possession, healthcare providers carry out the diagnosis process and offer prescriptions, again healthcare providers communicates the different cases encountered at reporting intervals to supervisors which in return reports to management (regional, district or national). Or though healthcare providers have power in durability of the network, MoHSS management have the most power to ensure the existence and the growth of the network.

Findings: Actors' Participatory to Service Delivery

The analysis revealed that actors' participatory, drawing from the connection and relationship between human actors and interactive systems, is essential to the mobility of healthcare services in the Namibian context. The connection and relationship between the actors is enacted by different tools and devices, to enable and encourage participation in the MoHSS initiatives on health programs, across the country. The components of the participatory factor, connectivity of the actors and interactive system:

i.   Connectivity of actors – connectivity will foster actors' enrolment in the mobility of healthcare services. As shown in Figure 2, users (healthcare service providers and patients) need to have application on their devices, which will enable them to easily access the mobile kiosks. The application should be symmetrical, in that it is user friendly to both literate and illiterate actors in their needs to access the kiosks. The application will enable users to easily access the kiosks, from any location including at impromptu times.

ii. Interactive system – the interactive system establishes a step-by-step conversation, with the caller. The system is intended to scrutinize calls from the communities, thereby narrow the request or inquiring towards a specific need of the caller. This is purposely for efficiency and effectiveness of the mobile kiosks, in response to the community needs.

- **Mobilisation**

Due to the essentiality of health services in the country, it was vital for some actors from both MoHSS and the community to mobilise the healthcare service providers and recipients towards a common goal.

During mobilisation, some actors were assigned the role of new initiators by becoming delegates or spokesperson for the focal actor [25]. In this case, hospital matrons, and supervisors at different healthcare centres tried to mobilise healthcare providers to actively participate in the network (carry out their duties). This resulted to a stability of the process of delivering healthcare services in some areas, particularly in the urban areas.

As a result of the stability through adequate services, more patients became spokespersons to different healthcare centres. The self appointed spokespersons encouraged others with the same or different health issue to seek healthcare services from designated locations of their preference. Also, the altitude and tribal inclination were the others factors which influenced mobilisation and of patients. For example, some patients recommended others to visit or seek assistance from health centres where majority of the health professional were on their tribal origin and spoke the same language as them.

Findings: Actors' Alliance

The actors formed formal and informal alliances. The alliances were significantly helpful in understanding the challenges factors in the quest to provide healthcare services to the various communities in the country. The alliances were seen as forms of collaboration and political affiliation:

i.   Collaboration –mobility of healthcare services require collaboration between community members and healthcare providers. The collaboration could be driven by an agent, but it is the responsibility of all that are involved in the mobility of healthcare services. The collaboration could happen at different levels, such as community members, health professional, and the government (MoHSS).

Political affiliation – the mobility of healthcare services in Namibia is endangered by tribal preference for services. This manifests from political affiliation of individuals and groups. Political inclination has potentials of influencing mobilisation of actors, to participate in the mobility of healthcare service in their communities. Political inclination is critical as some actors are heterogeneous in the networks, as shown in Figure 3.

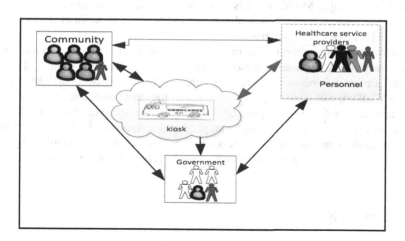

Fig. 3. Collaboration

Social Networking – the social networking approach will help to bring all actors together, in fostering the mobility of healthcare services in Namibia. According to [26], ssocial networking is a type of virtual community that has grown tremendously in popularity over the past few years. Social networking has no boundaries, in terms of spoken language, and tribal origin. It brings people of common interest together in the same network.

Another important factor of social networking is that, an actor can be heterogeneous in that the actor can belong to more than one network, as shown on figure 3. In this instance, the actor is able to influence and connect the networks to each other. This help to eradicate or silence tribal or political inclination which has potential to hamper the common goal, of the mobility of healthcare services.

5   Mobility of Healthcare Services in Namibia

People, technology and procedures are the actors in the process of healthcare service delivery. ANT's translation process that was followed in this study defines the formation of networks, which helped to identify the groupings and how they were created. The process starts with the main actor who defines the roles through problemitisation of the issue or item. This was done by localization of the issue, so as to foster relationship, and get more and regional actors to be interested, and partake in the initiative.

Although the employment of technical actants can be viewed as the consequences of the action of all actants to an extent, the ministry of health in this case has power to hire healthcare providers and extend the provision of services to all health service level of operation. This signifies authority to define procedures of service delivery e.g. change the national policy of the in transit patients or implement an Electronic Patient Management System (EPMS) at health centers. By so doing, associations of technical and non technical actants are strengthen.

Moreover, the mobility of healthcare services is enabled and constrained within network such as community by the actions of actors, which often based on individual or group knowledge. Mobilisation is necessary to educate and inform actants about the services. Patients need to know about their rights to health services at any location and the importance of a health passport.

A health passport, referral letter or medication container was issued to patients by medical personnel at different locations or health centres across the country. Thus, the patients present whenever they needed health related treatment anywhere in the country. Challenge of presenting the above is that they are vulnerable to loss or results to unclear information on the passport or letter. The consequence of such loss and unclear information make services complex and complicated to both healthcare service providers and the patients. Hence it is critical to enforce electronic systems, which allow access to patients' health related records from anywhere across the country, and on real-time.

6   Conclusion

This paper presents a critical analysis of the role and account of actors in the mobility of healthcare services in Namibia. The analysis is of vital important to the Namibia, and other countries which has similar setup and challenges, in that it unveiled issues that the State government and many healthcare professional are not aware of, take for granted.

In the past, and continuous (before this study), the state Government as in many developing countries continue to invest and focus on technical issues, which often become "white elephants" due to lack of usefulness. This study revealed fundamental and primary issues, which makes technology useful and ease of use in the mobility of healthcare services across Namibia.

The paper emphasises on the importance of relationships between the actors (health professional and patients), and as well the significance of networks in the mobility of healthcare services at different health operandis. As at the time of the study, patients in transit were handled in accordance to the national health policy as promulgated by the MoHSS. The study revealed how healthcare service providers, through the use of spoken language and tribal origin, enable, and at the same time, constrain the services that they are supposed to render to the patients for better healthcare. These factors were often conscious, and sometimes unconsciously exhibited by the actors.   However, little or nothing was known of the impact, the service providers of healthcare in Namibia.

References

1. Rygh, E.M., Hjortdahl, P.H.: Continuous and integrated health care services in rural areas. A literature study. The International Electronic Journal of Rural and Remote Health Research, Education Practice and Policy 7(766), 1–10 (2007)
2. Sander-Granlien, M., Hertzum, M.: Confirmatory factor analysis of service quality dimensions within mobile telephony industry in Ghana. The Electronic Journal Information Systems Evaluation 15(2), 197–227 (2007)
3. Chaulagai, C.N., Moyo, C.M., Koot, J., Moyo, H.B.: Design and implementation of a health management in Malawi: issues inovation and results, pp. 2–10. Published by Oxford University Press in association with The London School of Hygiene and Tropical Medicine (2005)
4. Chang, P.: Modeling the Management of Electronic Health. Records in Healthcare Information Systems. In: 2011 International Conference on Cyber-Enabled Distributed Computing and Knowledge Discovery (2011)
5. Fardoun, H., Cipres, A., Alghazzawi, D., Oadah, M.: KAU e-Health Mobile System. In: 13th International Congress on Human Computer Intercation. ACM (2012)
6. Cisco.: Mobility solution for healthcare: voice, text, images and information, delivered to the point of care (2007),
   http://www.cisco.com/web/strategy/docs/healthcare/
   07cs1084-MobForHC_062708.pdf
7. Latour, B.: Technology is society made durable. In: Law, J. (ed.) A Sociology of Monsters: Essays on Power, Technology and Domination, pp. 103–131. Routledge, London (1991)
8. Iyamu, T.: Underpinning Theories: Order-of-Use in Information Systems Research. Journal of Systems and Information Technology 15(3), 1–13 (2013)
9. Wickramasinghe, N., Bali, R., Goldberg, S.: Using S'ANT for facilitating superior understanding of key factors in the design of a chronic disease self-management model. Actor Network Theory and Technology Innovation: Advancements and New Concepts Journal, Information Science Reference, Hershey, NY (2011)
10. Law, J.: Notes on the theory of the Actor Network: ordering, strategy and heterogeneity (1992), http://comp.lancs.ac.uk/sociology/soc054jl.html
11. Tatnall, A., Gilding, A.: Actor-Network theory and Information Systems Research. In: Proceeding of the 10th Australian Conference on Information Systems (ACIS), Wellington, Victoria University of Wellington (1999)
12. Creswell, K., Worth, A., Sheikh, A.: Actor-Network theory and its role in understanding the implementation of information technology developments in healthcare. BMC Medical Informatics and Decision Making, 10–67 (2010)
13. Braa, J., Hanseth, O., Heywood, A., Mohammed, W., Shawn, B.: Developing information systems in developing country: The flexible standards strategy. MIS Quartely (31), 1–22 (2007)

14. Hamunyela, S., Iyamu, T.: Readness Assessment model for the deployment of health information systems in the Namibian MoH. In: International Federation for Information Processing, 12th Internation Conference on Social Implications of Computer in Developing Countries, Jamaica (2013)

15. NPC: Namibia 2011 population and housing census (2012),
    http://www.npc.gov.na

16. Rygh, E.M., Hjortdahl, P.: Continuous and integrated health care services in rural areas: a literature study. Rural and Remote Health 7, 766 (2007)

17. MoHSS.: Integrated healthcare delivery the challenge and implementations (2012),
    http://www.healthnet.org.na/documents.html

18. Narang, J.K.: Quality of Healthcare Services in Rural India: The User Perspective. VIKALPA, 51–60 (2011)

19. Istepanian, R.J.: Guest Editorial Introduction to the Specialon M-Health: Beyond Seamless Mobility and Global Wireless Health-Care Connectivity. IEEE Transactions on Information Technology in Biomedicine, 405–414 (2004)

20. Yin, R.K.: Case Study Research Design and Methods, 3rd edn. Sage Publications, UK (2003)

21. Hovorka, D.S., Lee, A.S.: Reframing Interpretivism and Positivism as Understanding and Explanation: Consequences for Information Systems Research. In: International Conference on Information Systems, Paper 188 (2010)

22. Uden, L., Francis, J.: Service Innovation using Actor Network theory. Actor Network Theory and Technology Innovation: Advancements and New Concepts Journal, Information Science Reference, Hershey, NY (2011)

23. Armbrust, M., et al.: A view of Cloud Computing. Communications of the ACM 53(4), 50–58 (2010)

24. Haeberlen, A.: Practical Robust Localization over Large-Scale 802.11 Wireless Networks. In: Proceedings of the 10th Annual International Conference on Mobile Computing and Networking (2004)

25. Iyamu, T., Tatnull, A.: The impact of netwrork of actors on the infomation technology. Actor Network Theory and Technology Innovation: Advancements and New Concepts Journal, Information Science Reference, Hershey, NY (2011)

26. Dwyer, C., Hiltz, S., Passerini, K.: Trust and privacy concern within social networking sites: A comparison of Facebook and MySpace. In: The Proceedings of the Thirteenth Americas Conference on Information Systems (2007)

A Mechanism-Based Explanation
of the Institutionalization of Semantic Technologies
in the Financial Industry

Tom Butler and Elie Abi-Lahoud

University College Cork, Ireland
TButler@afis.ucc.ie

Abstract. This paper explains how the financial industry is solving its data, risk management, and associated vocabulary problems using semantic technologies. The paper is the first to examine this phenomenon and to identify the social and institutional mechanisms being applied to socially construct a standard common vocabulary using ontology-based models. This standardized ontology-based common vocabulary will underpin the design of next generation of semantically-enabled information systems (IS) for the financial industry. The mechanisms that are helping institutionalize this common vocabulary are identified using a longitudinal case study, whose embedded units of analysis focus on central agents of change—the Enterprise Data Management Council and the Object Management Group. All this has important implications for society, as it is intended that semantically-enabled IS will, for example, provide stakeholders, such as regulators, with better transparency over systemic risks to national and international financial systems, thereby mitigating or avoiding future financial crises.

Keywords: Institutional Theory, Social mechanisms, Institutional mechanisms, Semantic technology, Web Ontology Language, OWL, Financial Industry Business Ontology.

1   Introduction

Forty four years ago, Wall St. had to close its doors on Wednesday each week to do paperwork—such was the volume of paper-based data produced in conducting business in the stock market alone [1]. The financial industry faces similar difficulties today; but instead of manual systems that produce paper, it is computer-based information systems that generate big data. While the volume of data being processed has grown, so too has number of information systems. Our unpublished research found that CitiGroup Inc. alone has over 70,000 computer-based information systems supporting its business operations globally, many of which are similar and replicating the same tasks in different geographical locations. Even small financial services organizations typically possess between 5-12 poorly-integrated information systems. Thus, organizations both large and small face significant data management problems [2], the solutions to which involve addressing the root cause—the so called 'vocabulary problem' [3].

B. Bergvall-Kåreborn and P.A. Nielsen (Eds.): TDIT 2014, IFIP AICT 429, pp. 277–294, 2014.
© IFIP International Federation for Information Processing 2014

The financial industry responded to the above problem by institutionalizing a 'common vocabulary', enabled by semantic technologies, to manage better not only the mountains of data, but also financial risk, and to enable comprehensive compliance reporting [2] [4]. Semantic technologies, such as OWL-based ontologies, provide the ability for organizations to consolidate, integrate and federate both structured data in legacy database silos and also the increasing volume of unstructured data that is now being generated electronically [5]. Inter alia, the benefits then identified were to: (1) Identify patterns and insights in data; (2) Integrate heterogeneous data; and (3) Optimize enterprise search and navigation. Thus, semantic technologies are argued to enable improved data processing and management, in addition to search, visualization, and information exchange for organizations in the financial industry [5, 6].

This paper operates from an IS perspective and applies a mechanism-based conceptual framework to study the institutional initiatives that are producing novel approaches to data and risk management using semantic technologies, for the purpose of modelling, federating, and integrating diverse operational and risks data in and across financial services organizations. The remainder of this paper is structured as follows. The second major section presents the theoretical background, the objective of which is present a mechanism-based conceptual framework to help explain institutional change. The third section describes the research method. The fourth section applies the aforementioned framework in our case study of the institutionalization of semantic technologies in the financial industry. The final section then offers some concluding thoughts.

2   Theoretical Background

Institutional theory explains how the regulative, normative, and cultural-cognitive influences shape societal and organizational fields and organizations [7]. In an IS context, researchers maintain that institutional theory can explain "how regulative processes, normative systems, and cultural frameworks shape the design and use of technical systems" [8, p. 153]. Theories developed from the conceptual framework offered by intuitional theory usually explain how regulative, normative, or cultural-cognitive forces shape institutional environments and organizational fields, while influencing organizational structures and processes. At a macro-level such outcomes result from, and can be explained by, the action of coercive, normative and mimetic (cultural-cognitive) mechanisms [7, 9]. However, a range of other mechanisms, operating at different levels, are at play. Take, for example, that actors apply mechanisms in an institutional environment to influence the formation and structure of organizational fields: such actors include governments, industry associations, dominant organizations, and social movements. An organizational field is typically defined as consisting of organizations with similar business, commercial, or public service interests: also included are suppliers of services, resources, and/or products, customers and consumers, government agencies, and other stakeholders [7, 9]. These actors also apply endogenous mechanisms to shape and influence structure and process in and across the field [10].

2.1   Social, Institutional and Organizational Mechanisms

A social, institutional or organizational mechanism may be a structure or a process [11], it may be observable or unobservable, and/or it may be formal or substantive in nature [12]. According to Hedström [13, p. 25], mechanisms describe "a constellation of entities and activities that are organized such that they regularly bring about a particular type of outcome." We adopt Gross' [12] conceptualization of mechanisms as consisting of a configurations of actors, their habits of cognition and action, related resources, and the responses they make when faced with problem situations. Researchers have identified a range of social, institutional or organizational mechanisms that operate at macro- meso- and micro-levels to explain social phenomena [cf. 12, 13, 14, 15]. Micro-level mechanisms employed by individual actors translate into social and organizational mechanisms that operate at meso- and macro-levels [10] [16]. According to Elster [16, p. 42] "atomic" mechanisms are "elementary psychological reactions that cannot be reduced to other mechanisms at the same level." Such atomic mechanisms might form the "building blocks in more complex 'molecular' mechanisms" [16, p. 43], whether micro-level individual, meso-level or macro-level. Hedström's [13] Desires (D), Beliefs (B) and Opportunities (O) or DBO theory describes three fundamental atomic mechanisms that shape individual and collective Action (A). Institutional theorists broadly categorize meso- and macro-level mechanisms as coercive, normative or mimetic [9, 10]. Hedström and Swedberg [11] posit three categories of social mechanisms: situational mechanisms are macro-or meso-level social, institutional or organizational structures and processes that shape desires and beliefs; micro-level action-formation mechanisms link desires, beliefs, and opportunities with resultant actions; and transformational mechanisms explain individual and collective action as a cascade/network/constellation of individual mechanisms, leading from micro- to meso- to macro-level. Finally, it is important to note that mechanisms operate in tandem, in cascade and/or in combination with each other to bring about observed outcomes [10] [13].

2.2   The Role of Mechanisms in Institutional Theory

Institutional theory has as its subject "the formal and informal rules, monitoring and enforcement mechanisms, and systems of meaning that define the context within which individuals, corporations, labor unions, nation-states, and other organizations operate and interact with each other" [10, p. 1]. Scott [7, p. 35] argues that "regulatory processes involve the capacity to establish rules, inspect another's conformity to them, and as necessary, manipulate sanctions – rewards or punishments – in an attempt to influence future behavior. These processes may operate through diffuse, informal mechanisms, involving folkways such as shaming or shunning activities, or they may be highly formalized and assigned to specific answers, such as the police or the courts." Thus the coercive mechanisms that underpin institutional change may, for examples, be instituted and employed by governments, dominant organizations, and social movements and operate through governance or power systems—their origins may also be within an organization, however. Normative mechanisms typically draw upon values and norms that "introduce a prescriptive, evaluative, and obligatory dimension" to organization life in a field [7, p. 37].   Values indicate what is preferred or desirable, while norms specify the means by which what is desirable should be achieved. In an organizational field, normative mechanisms typically originate in and are applied by professional and standards bodies, non-government organizations (NGOs), consulting organizations, professional bodies, academic institutions and publications etc. Cultural-cognitive or mimetic mechanisms operate with reference to symbolic systems, cultural rules, and shared perceptions and understandings. Cultural-cognitive mechanisms emanate from societal actors, NGOs, social movements, community groups, investors, and other stakeholders. Di Maggio and Powell [9] argue that over time organizations in a field tend to become homogenous in terms of both their processes and structures—this they term isomorphism. Competitive isomorphism arises from market forces in an organizational field, while institutional isomorphism arises out of coercive, normative, and mimetic mechanisms that underpin political and organizational legitimacy in the field [7] [9].

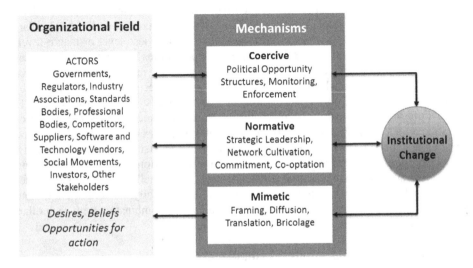

Fig. 1. Mechanisms Underpinning Institutional Change

Campbell [10] [14] employs both macro- and meso-level social and institutional mechanisms to help explain institutional change in a variety of research contexts, whether it is mechanisms involved in shaping organizational reproduction, or change due to globalization, or collective action in organizations and social movements in organizational fields. These mechanisms are: (a) Framing, which involves the use of metaphors and symbols which influence how issues are perceived and which inform social action in the context of socially constructed realities; (b) Diffusion, which refers to the dissemination of concepts, social structures, and practices, mainly through social networks; (c) Translation, which refers to how diffused concepts and ideas are transformed for application in new social contexts; (d) Bricolage, which involves the recombination of concepts, practices, etc. from other social contexts to produce new forms of social activity; (e) Network cultivation, which involves creating social and institutional movements and associations; (f) Strategic leadership (or institutional entrepreneurship), in which social actors decide on which, direction a social, institutional or organizational entity should take; and (g) Political Opportunity Structures, include regulations, laws, governance policies, and informal unwritten rules. Campbell [10] also makes reference to 'monitoring and enforcement mechanisms'. Our previous research indicates that these are important sub-categories of coercive mechanisms in that they are required to provide full explanations of institutional processes and change.

Figure 1 places the mechanisms described above into a conceptual framework which posits that such mechanisms operate at different levels to bring about the institutional change observed in organizational fields. The upcoming case study section applies this conceptual framework to explain how the organizational field of the financial industry is being shaped by exogenous and endogenous mechanisms with the objective of instituting a common vocabulary using semantic technologies. The next section describes the research design and method through which this research objective was met.

3   Research Method

An exploratory/explanatory, longitudinal case study design was chosen for the study [17]. The case study design permitted the development of a mechanism-based theory of institutional change in the financial industry by applying previously identified mechanisms associated with institutional change [10] [14] with empirical insights gathered from a case study of this organizational field in the United States and Europe. Two embedded units of analysis were purposively selected—the Enterprise Data Management Council (EDM Council) and the Object Management Group (OMG). The first is an industry association whose members are drawn from the financial industry and related sectors. The second is an international software industry standards consortium. The exploratory aspect of this study is important, as this topic is novel and has not previously been the subject of research in the social sciences. The explanatory dimension arises as we seek to illustrate the combination of mechanisms that are instituting change in this important industry sector, which, more than any, impacts on the daily lives of individuals globally. Participant observation was chosen as the primary research technique as the process of institutional change in organizational fields is often "obscured from the view of outsiders" [18, p. 12]. Participant observation of, and data gathering from, social actors in the embedded units of analysis occurred at OMG technical meetings, industry conferences, and through a series weekly and monthly teleconferences and webinars, with the EDM Council, the Open Financial Data Group (OFDG), the OMG's Financial Domain Task Force (FDTF), the OMG's and Smart Regulation Initiative, and related meetings with key informants from the EDM Council on FIBO. Each of the on-site or teleconference meetings lasted from between 1-1.5 hours each. A research team of 5 actively participated in the data gathering activities and took field notes of their observations, formal and informal discussions. Data gathering began in March 2012 and continues into and throughout 2013. This gave a total of over 350 hours of direct data gathering. Also as members of the OMG and the EDM Council, the research team had unrestricted access to all relevant documentation. Detailed field notes were taken throughout the research process and these were reflexively analyzed and recorded by the researchers.

A wealth of documentary evidence was also gathered. While observation was the primary data source, supplemental and confirmatory information was acquired through documents and formal and informal conversations during meetings. Data analysis involved the use of the Campbell's [10, 14] coercive, normative and cultural-cognitive/mimetic mechanisms as 'seed' or a priori categories for coding, constant comparative analysis and rigorous coding procedures [19].

4   Case Study: The Institutionalization of Semantic Technologies in the Financial Industry

The business need for a common vocabulary and semantic technologies in the financial industry was first comprehensively articulated at the Demystifying Financial Services Semantics Conference on March 13, 2012 in New York. This event was viewed as a critical incident [19] in our study of the institutionalization of a common vocabulary and related semantic technologies in the financial industry and is therefore of particular relevance to this case study. First, however, we explain the ongoing development of this common vocabulary/semantic technologies and their institutionalization by focusing on the agents of change—the Enterprise Data Management (EDM) Council and Object Management Group (OMG)—and the critical incidents that marked the changes in the institutionalization process. The second section focuses on the critical incident of note, the Demystifying Financial Services Semantics Conference. The third section focuses on the development of the semantic technologies and common vocabulary around which the institutional change in the financial industry revolves.

4.1   Strategic Leadership and the Enterprise Data Management Council

The Enterprise Data Management (EDM) Council was founded in 2005 by IBM, SunGard, and GoldenSource. The council was established to provide solutions to data-related problems in the financial industry. The Council is governed by a board of 24 members. The council currently presents its program of work in four categories; standards, industry best practices, industry relations and business networking. It structures on-going activities around six projects: FIBO Standard, Legal Entity ID, Data Management Maturity, Benchmarking, Data Quality and Regulation. Such programs resulted in its establishment as an industry leader in enterprise data management in the financial industry and beyond. In the following, we describe how the EDM Council leveraged its strategic leadership position towards institutionalizing semantic technologies across the financial industry in general and the ongoing development and application of its semantics repository in particular.

From the outset, network cultivation operated to secure the participation and sponsorship of leading organizational actors in the field, Bank of America, Citigroup, Deutsche Bank, UBS. In 2006, the EDM Council conducted over 60 interviews with different field actors to read the "EDM pulse and define core priorities"; here, they identified the lack of enterprise-wide EDM and the dangers of short sighted project-oriented EDM. In 2007, the council published (diffused) a series of reports on EDM case studies (Mellon Financial, JPMorgan Chase, Daiwa Securities, SMBC Europe, HBOS,

Barings Asset Management, M&G Investments, etc.) identifying major issues, success stories and current best practices. In April 2007, the council proceeded to frame the lessons learned in an EDM scoreboard. This scoreboard provides a common framework for evaluating the issues associated with EDM. It used the mechanisms of translation and bricolage to build on the framework presented by CitiGroup's Chief Data Officer to the Financial Information Management (FIMA) conference in 2007. Furthermore, continuing its efforts to establish EDM as a business priority, and itself in a strategic leadership position, the EDM Council diffused its findings through an important report on July 6th 2007 and subsequently briefed the Department of Defense on the benefits and challenges of EDM.

The EDM Council relied again on network cultivation to take leadership on a new topic: Entity Identification, which is recognized as a shared need by organisational actors. Capitalising on its strategic leadership, the council briefed, upon invitation, the US Securities & Exchange Commission (SEC) on the status of legal entity identification and data attribute tagging on January 18th 2008. Later on, the council acting as "global facilitator, neutral and trusted" brought together, using network cultivation, 22 financial industry members, 10 software vendors, regulators and standards bodies, such as the SEC, FSA, CESR, and BaFIN, to frame and diffuse Business Entity Identification as testified in the EDM Council February 2008 report to its members. Also in 2008, the EDM Council leveraged its strategic leadership position to diffuse novel concepts such as Business Semantics and the Web Ontology Language (OWL).

4.2   The Emergence of Semantic Technologies as a Solution to EDM Problems

The financial industry faces data integration problems that are unique in nature [2]. Business processes and transactions span multiple functions and sophisticated supply chains, with several trading entities and with data being exchanged in a range of formats and message protocols. Add to this a multiplicity of systems involved in risk and compliance management, general ledger and reporting and so on. The major problem here is that the same data is defined differently across systems, with divergent data models and database schemes—this is a classical 'vocabulary problem' (Furnas 1987). It was with this in mind that the EDM Council decided to commission a semantics model and repository for Security terms and definitions to help begin to address the aforementioned problems with multiple meanings of data stored in heterogeneous databases. This would then be extended into other areas. Thus, the EDM Council recognized that the major problem facing the industry was not, necessarily, the huge volumes of data, but the different meanings attributed to the real world objects and data entities that represent them both within and across a multiplicity of organizational information systems. Hence, in order to begin to manage the mountains of data effectively, it was recognized that the first task would be to provide a common vocabulary for the industry globally—a semantic approach was therefore adopted in order to arrive at unambiguous concept and relationship definitions for all financial industry data. Bennett (2011, p. 440) reports that what was needed was "a resource in which there was one entry per meaningful concept, with a written definition that could be agreed by business domain experts, and any number of synonyms for that term. This would provide the needed common point of reference for message and database integration across the supply chain." To achieve this goal a pilot implementation was conducted to model terms used in trading and analysis of derivative-based mortgage and asset-backed securities. Here the EDM Council again leveraged it strategic leadership position and engaged in network cultivation to have IBM Research, the European Central Bank, US regulatory agencies, several financial institutions and risk analytics vendors participate in finding a solution—or at least a viable proof of concept (PoC). The goal of this initiative was to prove, from a regulatory perspective, the relevance of semantic technologies. This proof of concept was demonstrated (diffused) to several major financial institutions on Wall Street in September 2008, as the financial system unraveled due the very problems that the proof of concept was meant to solve.

This endogenous critical incident had the EDM Council advance the development of the Financial Industry Business Ontology (FIBO). This ontology is currently being proposed as an industry standard through the Object Management Group (OMG), one of the software industry's influential standards body. The OMG has been shaping the Software industry since 1989 with standards like the predominant Unified Modeling Language (UML) for creating, inter alia, visual models of object-oriented systems. The OMG task forces produce "enterprise integration standards" for different technologies used in several domains such as manufacturing, healthcare, government and finance. Between the EDM Council and the OMG, the nascent FIBO standard is being used to both frame the meaning of common financial concepts in a knowledge model (i.e. the common vocabulary) and diffuse this model as an OMG standard specification. The institutional actors which is playing a pivotal role in applying these mechanisms is the Financial Domain Task Force (FDTF), which is a sub-group of the OMG; FDTF members share the same desires and beliefs regarding the role and application of semantic technologies. The FDTF mission is to "promote the notion that Data and its Semantics are the DNA of financial services". It brings together industry practitioners (banking, securities, funds, compliance, etc.), technologists and academics to collaborate on a series of projects focusing on interoperability between financial information systems. The co-optation of the OMG provided the EDM Council with the opportunity to use, within the OMG-FDTF, a combination of framing, translation and bricolage mechanisms on technologies developed for the semantic web (RDF, RDFS, OWL2, Graphs, Common and Description Logic) and on OMG legacy standard specifications such as the Unified Modeling Language (UML), and on more recent ones such as the Semantics of Business Vocabulary and Business Rules (SBVR, OMG's Business Natural Language specification), to develop semantic repositories and a family of ontologies. In this context, the OMG is also using co-optation mechanisms to have semantic modeling experts from a range of other disciplines and industry sectors to participate in this venture. Members of other OMG Task Forces (TF), Special Interest Groups (SIG) and Working Groups (WG) were invited to the FDTF. The latter partnered with 8 different OMG sub-groups such as the Ontology SIG, Business Modeling and Integration TF (managing SBVR) and the Regulatory Compliance SIG. Members of those sub-groups are active on a set of projects and use cases framing the need for a "common vocabulary" like FIBO and translating its implementation possibilities. The FDTF also partnered with several non-OMG groups to leverage domain expertise (CFTC, OFR, BIAN), co-opt legacy industry standards (ISO, FIX, XBRL), ensure future co-optation of FIBO, and expand its diffusion network. The joint,

OMG-Data Transparency Coalition (DTC), SMART Regulation initiative clearly illustrates how this co-optation benefits from network cultivation, framing, translation and diffusion to promote data standards and semantic technologies. Figure 2 helps illustrate the role of mechanisms in shaping institutional structures and processes—that is in bringing about the FTDF and the adoption and diffusion of UML and SBVR standards in the expression of the common vocabulary.

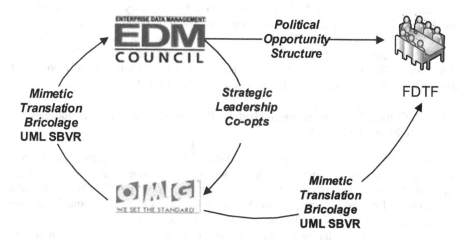

Fig. 2. An Example of the role of mechanisms in shaping institutional structure and process

4.3   The EDM Council and Political Opportunity Structure Mechanisms

In order to further its aims, the EDM Council is actively engaging in creating political opportunity structure mechanisms with US regulators to legitimize [7] the use of semantic technologies in the financial industry. Take, for example the evidence provided to the US SEC and the Commodity Futures Trading Commission by Michael Atkin, Managing Director, of the EDM Council, in 2010. The SEC/CFTC study "explores whether the collection, reporting, and management of risk exposures can be aided by the computer-readable descriptions - a common dictionary with standardized, electronic "spelling" for each aspect of a derivative." The aim of the SEC here is to enhance greater understanding of risk by both regulatory and financial industry actors. We reproduce part of the introductory statement by the EDM Council, which indicates the power of semantic technologies for GRC–related data management in the financial industry:

"To summarize, complete, accurate and consistent data is relevant at three distinct levels: facts about contracts, facts about positions and holdings within a financial institution, and facts about the wider system. Tagging each of these kinds of terms semantically with reference to contract, party, market events and the mathematics of cash flow would ensure accuracy and consistency across different data sources and different reporting mechanisms."

Hence, in collaborating with the SEC and Commodity Futures Trading Commission, the EDM Council is shaping future political opportunity structure mechanisms by framing the solution to the problem in semantic terms to legitimize its position on the use of semantic technologies in the sector. Its submission proved influential, as the report cited in the above footnote indicates. Other initiatives aimed at creating or influencing political opportunity structure mechanisms are that the Managing Director of the EDM Council (along with several member organizations of the council) sits on the Office of Financial Research's (OFR) Financial Research Advisory Committee. He is also the Chair of the FRAC Data and Technology Subcommittee, a member of the Financial Stability Board's LEI Private Sector Participatory Group; a member of the financial industry's LEI Steering Committee within GFMA, a member of the CFTC's Data Standardization Subcommittee; sits on the Board of Advisors for the Data Transparency Coalition, and is a member of both ISO TC68/SC4 and ANSI/X9D. This is also evidence of the use it is making of network cultivation and diffusion mechanisms at various levels and to a variety of audiences.

4.4   A Critical Incident in the Institutionalization of Semantic Technologies for the Financial Industry

The stated objective of the Demystifying Financial Services Semantics Conference was to help conference participants "better understand the role of semantics in meeting both business processing and regulatory oversight objectives". This conference was convened by the Enterprise Data Management Council (EDM Council) and the Object Management Group (OMG), with the OMG being responsible for the conference organization (i.e. the two embedded units of analysis). In setting the stage, the OMG pointed out the financial industry is characterized by organizations who use "common business terms that have different meanings, common meanings that use different terms and vague definitions that don't capture critical nuances." In an organizational field where transactional data is captured in real-time by complex processes/workflows and stored in and across heterogeneous systems in different formats, where governance policies, risk management and compliance reporting on business processes and transaction outcomes is becoming increasingly difficult in the face of ever increasing and more complex and onerous regulations, then the "precision of data matters." This introduces a huge issue for data management, integration, and analytics, to say nothing of risk assessment and analysis. The purpose of this conference was to highlight the business value and role of semantics and semantic technologies for the financial industry. Semantic technologies in the financial industry will be used to capture business and regulatory terms, their definitions and meanings, the relationships that exist between them, and business and other rules that govern their application, and the contexts in which they are applied. The conference's importance in bringing institutional change to the financial industry cannot be understated, as will be now explained.

It is clear from our analysis that the objective of the EDM Council and the OMG in jointly convening and hosting this conference was to widen and deepen the interest in the adoption and implementation of semantic technologies, specifically the Financial Industry Business Ontology (FIBO) across the organizational field to solve the regulatory and data management problems described herein. The structure of this one day event, which was attended by several hundred members of the financial industry, US regulators, and IT vendor organizations, focused on panel discussions of several general themes: The business case for data semantics in financial services, the need for a business natural language (BNL) for financial services (based on the OMG's Semantics of Business Vocabulary and Business Rules, SBVR standard), regulatory reporting using XBRL, and the implications of semantic models for the challenges posed by big data. The conference included two formal presentations on FIBO, the first was a brief overview of this family of ontologies, the second focused on the operational application of FIBO using a proof of concept on over the counter (OTC) derivatives. This was followed by a panel that shared perspectives on semantic metadata provided by FIBO, a critical view of the capabilities of such semantic technologies, and the future application of FIBO. Primary actors from across the organizational field participated in the remaining panels and in the debates that ensued on the topics discussed.

As indicated earlier, DBO theory posits that desires, beliefs and opportunities for action are three fundamental atomic mechanisms that shape individual action. Actors employ molecular, meso-, or macro-level mechanisms to alter the desires and beliefs of others [13]. Viewed from this paper's conceptual framework, actors on the conference stage employed a combination of strategic leadership, framing, network cultivation and diffusion mechanisms to alter the desires and beliefs of, and present opportunities for action to, attendees from the financial industry. The panels and breakout networking are clearly general network cultivation and diffusion mechanisms; however, in framing the central issues, Mike Atkin, managing Director of the EDM Council stated:

"First, it's about the development of a common vocabulary so we can deal with the requirements for the precision of contracts that drive all of our activities. It is also a common vocabulary that is required for us to do analytics in a complex and interconnected industry. The second thing is about combining the precision of that language with business tools, straightforward definitions of how things work together and the power of computers to do inferences and to do analysis and to make connections."

The other members of the panel repeatedly used the phrase 'common vocabulary'. In order to help diffuse this message, Atkin stated that the conference was going to employ 'Use Cases' that illustrated the power of semantics good and that illustrated "the challenges of adopting these things into real environments and what we have to do to overcome them." After a short introduction, he then put a question to John Bottega, Chief Data Officer, Bank of America. The mechanism of strategic leadership operates at several levels; at the macro-level the EDM Council is, as indicated, leading the field in endeavoring to solve enduring problems using semantic technologies; at a micro-level, individuals such as John Bottega in his capacity as Chief Data Officer are changing the beliefs and desires of organizational actors, while also providing them with opportunities for action. In explaining his position Bottega stated the "Chief Data Officer is still relatively new, its position in a firm is being recognized now as important, more from the perspective – and this is probably more linked to the meaning of Data linked to technology – the Chief Data Officer does not replace the Chief Technology Officer, or the CIO." He went on to explain that Bank of America's:

"focus is on concepts and meaning [in solving] one of the key business problems we face every day; In large institutions in Finance, multiple areas of a Bank or Financial Institution will perform transactions and activities with common data.

That data, although it may start out in 5, 6, 10, 12 different areas funnels its way into the bank's core control function where we have to look at risk, we have to look at regulatory requirements and reporting...there is an opportunity now to start bringing meaning to that data, minimize those transformations, minimize the cost of doing that aggregation and actually get a result in analytics that makes sense".

Eric Chacon, Global Head of Business Data Management at CitiGroup, New York echoed and elaborated on the points made by Bank of America's CDO. Again the theme of a need for a common vocabulary emerged. He stated that the most challenging problem is "how do we get everyone to speak a common vocabulary?" In order to put the common vocabulary issue into contact, the panel pointed out that the financial industry funds and finances the economy and creates and trades complex financial instruments. Chacon stated that "the challenge has always been that business experts have to translate what is in their head's to a technologist to substantiate that into a system, and that has not traditionally worked that well. There is the lost in translation type of activity that goes on, and what often happens is that the business people are so involved working with a client and making the trade, that that responsibility gets delegated to the technologists, now there is another layer of lost in translation as the technologists try to do this." According to Chacon the problems arise because there is no common vocabulary. Both he and the Bank of America CDO argued that semantics can provide "a language that both parties speak." Of course agreeing on what that common vocabulary is needs to be resolved—that, he indicated, was the purpose of the conference. Referring to CitiGroup, he stated that:

"We have to come to agreement within the firm on what do we mean by terms like 'contract', 'transaction', 'customer', 'product'. Those foundational terms and everything underneath them are used ubiquitously but they are used in different ways by different silos. We have conservatively speaking, hundreds of silos within Citigroup. We have silos around product lines, silos within markets and countries, we have arbitrary management, barriers; we also have regulatory imposed barriers. "

CitiGroup's solution was to develop a set of semantically defined, data standards that Chacon stated was "essentially an ontology, although we don't usually describe it with that term." CitiGroup are using a data dictionary and an underlying model that defines the business language, naturally, formally and completely. As with Bank of America, CitiGroup are not doing "a massive integration or a large scale gate linkage or data analysis; that would be overwhelming...we're starting in small areas, we're building." In this scheme of things, we subsequently learned through engagement with CitiGroup, that its Chief Data Officer was promoting SBVR as a platform for the emergent common vocabulary that would help bridge the 'silos' mentioned above.

Joseph Bugajski, Managing SVP at Gartner Inc., and former VISA's Chief Data Officer, broadened the debate and highlighted the need for such a common vocabulary across the organizational field to help solve the problems of the "perfect spaghetti pot" of data that had been created by the growth of heterogeneous data silos within and across financial services organizations. He pointed out that "every single financial institution maintains bilateral agreements with almost every other major financial institution and with many, many minor financial institutions; and inside Financial Institutions, each one of which can have its own set of goals on how those relationships are maintained etc." Building on observations by Mike Atkins and John Bottega that retail and investment banks face huge 'reconciliation' problems with internal data, the transactions that take place between banks and other financial institutions require additional data reconciliation, Bugajski estimated that over "40% of total costs that goes into maintaining interfaces between systems and between companies" could be reduced by half. He opined that "that's just the beginning, better communications means better information therefore for our clients. It means better information for use in investment; it means better information for use in risk management. So all along the way we see improvements, so the rising tide that rises all ships in this case are the ontologies".

In order to look at other areas of the organizational field that might benefit, Mike Atkins asked Con Crowley Director of Standards, Office of Financial Research at the US Treasury for his thoughts on how a common vocabulary could help regulators manage better systemic risk. The Director of Standards stated that "the same silos that you're dealing with internally, regulators are dealing with on an industry-wide basis. So the ability to aggregate that information, to be able to improve the quality, the ability to compare the data, will get you better systemic analysis. The review of systemic risk across the industry is critically dependent on the quality of data that is received and the ability to view it in a common vocabulary so you can compare that data." CitiGroup's Global Head of Business Data Management pointed out that this work had already commenced, specifically with complex instruments such as derivatives and swaps: "Right now reporting our swaps and derivatives trades, there are a lot of attributes that describe those instruments that we've had trouble defining the meaning of. Semantics is going to give us an opportunity to bring technology and business to the table and agree upon those terms and again reduce that lost in translation and transformation that governs regulators." Thus, the role that was socially constructed (framing) for semantic technologies is not limited to data management, but ultimately one of managing systemic risk in order to avoid future financial crises.

To further reinforce their message the EDM Council had scheduled two presentations from vendors of semantic technologies; however, the most influential use case of the application of common vocabulary- based semantic technologies was that provided by Dennis Wisnosky, then Chief Technology Officer and Chief Architect, Business Mission Area, U.S. Department of Defense.

The U.S. Department of Defense had significant problems implementing its Defense Integrated Military Human Resources System (DIMHRS) to get its personnel data in order by consolidating personnel records. The failed DIMHRS platform cost the U.S. taxpayer $850 million. Dennis Wisnosky disclosed how the Department of Defense leveraged semantic technologies such as RDF, OWL, and SPARQL with Business Process Model and Notation (BPMN) to deliver an enterprise-wide HR system for the DoD based on its Business Enterprise Architecture (BEA). Using a semantic approach, the DoD was able to solve legacy HR data integration and problems. Now the DoD employs a 'Model-Data-Implement' semantic technology pattern to design and deploy the semantic version of its HR system in up to 90 days. Prior to this it had taken over 11 years to develop the monolithic HR system at the aforementioned cost of $850 million. He demonstrated the capabilities of the system which could now perform complex ad-hoc queries using the reasoning power of ontologies. For example, Mr. Wisnosky stated that "after the earthquake in Haiti, we wanted to find out how many service members there were who spoke Creole or Haitian French, who could be deployed in 24 hours and had at least 12 months' service time remaining."

These examples and others like them impressed the delegates at the conference, as the follow up questions illustrated. There was evidence across attendees that their DBO about the relevance of semantic technologies was reinforced by this use case. It also impressed the EDM Council.

In a statement released on February 14th 2013, the EDM Council announced that it had appointed "Dennis E. Wisnosky to lead the standards implementation process for the Council's Financial Industry Business Ontology (FIBO) suite of standards. In this role, Wisnosky will provide technical strategy and operational guidance to help the Council finalize and implement FIBO standards. Wisnosky brings extensive experience with enterprise architecture, ontology development and semantic deployment and is poised to help the Council address the political and technical realities associated with the FIBO standard." In commenting on his new role, Wisnosky argued that for data management purposes, records of securities share many similarities with military personnel records. Semantic technologies could determine with great accuracy relevant parties of interest in a particular transaction, right back to the entity that first issued a loan that forms one asset in a mortgage-based security.

In terms of this study's theoretical perspective, the strategic leadership provided by the US government, and the innovations they made in implementing semantic solutions—through a combination of translation and bricolage of W3C and OMG standards and the DoD's BEA—are being used by the EDM Council to influence the DBO of council members and others across the organizational field. The object of diffusing these concepts is stimulating mimetic responses across the financial industry.

4.5   The What and How of the Financial Industry Business Ontology

Up until now, we have explained why and how semantic technologies are being institutionalized across the financial industry. We now explain briefly what it is that this industry desires and believes in respect of the proposed common vocabulary and its expression using semantic repositories and related modeling techniques. The Financial Industry Business Ontology (FIBO) aims to "bridge the language gap between business and technology". It captures business meanings (rather than a being a mere data dictionary or a taxonomy) in business language for business people. It also provides definitions and explanations with no technical representations or new languages to learn (EDM Council, Head of Semantics, Mike Bennett). The main components of FIBO are: (i) a Business Conceptual Ontology, (ii) a web-accessible business presentation layer, (iii) a set of operational ontologies, and (iv) the FIBO Object Management Group Specifications. The FIBO Business Conceptual Ontology (FIBO-BCO) is a family of ontologies that describe the major concepts (Things) relevant to financial services and what type of conceptual abstractions they derive from (i.e. facts about those Things). It describes common definitions and illustrates how they relate to each other. FIBO-BCO revolves around two main elements: (i) Financial and Entity concepts and (ii) a Basic Business Ontology. The Financial and Entity concepts are grounded in commitments, obligations, transactions, legal contracts etc. The Basic Business Ontology captures the "most primitive of each concept abstracted and maintained in a formal semantic structure". The EDM Council aims to align its Basic Business Ontology with formal industry-led semantics where available. FIBO covers the following subject areas: (1) FIBO-Foundations (Global Terms and modelling framework); (2) Business Entities; (3) Tradable Securities; (4) Derivatives; (5) Loans; (6) Pricing/Market Data; (7) Corporate Events and Actions and (8) Payments.

The web-accessible business presentation layer is the EDM Council Semantics Repository. It presents FIBO-BCO, alongside its RDF/OWL representation, in a business readable format that avoids technical representations or the need to learn new languages. The EDM Council uses (i) "boxes and lines" in OMG UML-like diagrams to present the modelled business concepts and their relationships, and (ii) tabular spreadsheets to capture the definitions in natural language. The focus on accessibility for business people remains a major concern for the EDM Council, who tries to avoid technical representations or the need to learn new languages. Following the same rationale, the council recently expressed its intention to leverage OMG's Business Natural Language specification Semantic of Business Vocabulary and Rules (SBVR) to present FIBO's knowledge model in the form of a business vocabulary.

Several operational ontologies could be derived from FIBO-BCO. An operational ontology is often a subset of the BCO. It is oriented towards solving a given business problem or task. Technically, a FIBO Operational Ontology is described in a machine readable language thus rendering automatic algorithmic reasoning (inferencing in particular) possible. It contains concepts and their attributes, relationships between concepts and axioms governing business activities related to those concepts. A team headed by David Newman - Strategic Planning Manager, Vice President Enterprise Architecture, Wells Fargo Bank is building an operational ontology for Business Entities, with a use case of LEI (Legal Entity Identifier) data processing. This project falls under Operational FIBO for OTC Derivatives Proof of Concept (PoC). The PoC's main objective is to demonstrate to the financial industry and the regulatory community how FIBO can help achieve data standardization, integration, linkage and automatic classification in securities firms and investment banks.

In regard to the how of constructing a common vocabulary, Subject Matter Experts (SMEs) play a central role in building FIBO. The financial services professionals and software engineers from the members of the EDM Council and the OMG insure that FIBO-BCO sections "represent a full and factual view of the world as seen by the business". When the EDM Council drafts a section of FIBO, it is presented to SMEs for validation. The purpose of this validation is to ensure that the modelled section is "True" so that it captures the business reality. The review process can take two forms: (1) individual reviews, where an SME reviews offline a section of FIBO and reverts to the EDM Council with comments and suggested changes or (2) group teleconferences, where a community of SMEs joins a weekly teleconference by the EDM Council on which a section of FIBO is deeply discussed. The authors and this paper and their co-researchers are participating in these activities, as indicated, to contribute to the development of two family members to the FIBO ontology. It is through this iterative process that the EDM Council, its members, and other stakeholders are socially constructing a common vocabulary for the financial industry.

5   Conclusions

This paper offers an explanation of the why and how the financial industry is rethinking the design and integration of financial information systems, to say nothing of the way it views data. The CIOs, CTOs and CDOs in industry now realize that data is all about meaning, and, accordingly, that they need a common vocabulary to describe that meaning—to humans and to machines. This is a field level phenomenon which involves the institutionalization of new micro-level desires, beliefs and opportunities for action (DBO) [13] among financial services and IT professionals through the application of meso- and macro-level mechanisms. These DBO relate to the need for a common vocabulary and the use of semantic technologies to manage financial and GRC data across multiple silos in, across, and between organizations and on to government departments and regulators.

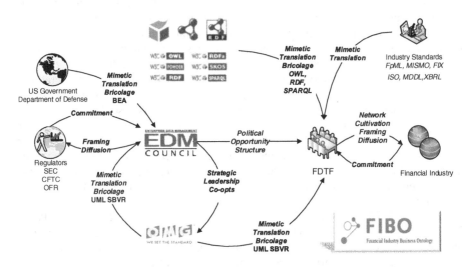

Fig. 3. Institutional Actors, Mechanisms and the Institutionalization of FIBO

We have adduced the benefits of such vocabulary-based technologies and provided an example of one—the Financial Industry Business Ontology (FIBO)—which is about to become an industry standard. As indicated, FIBO is being developed incrementally by subject matter experts from across the financial industry under the sponsorship of the Enterprise Data Management (EDM) Council and with the assistance of the industry standards body the Object Management Group (OMG) and its Financial Domain Task Force (FDTF). Figure 3 builds on Figure 2, and the forgoing empirical findings, to illustrate how mechanisms are shaping the development and institutionalization of FIBO.

The powerful and influential EDM Council, which is not widely known outside of this organizational field, has, over the past 8 years, used a combination of macro- and meso-level mechanisms to achieve its objectives in relation to enterprise data management. This paper extends the conventional conception of coercive, normative, and mimetic mechanisms previously used to explain IS-related phenomena, with meso-level mechanisms (i.e. political opportunity structure, strategic leadership, network cultivation, framing, diffusion, translation, and bricolage mechanisms) used to explain field-level phenomena such as the institutionalization of semantic technologies. The paper also bridges these situational mechanisms to micro-level DBO mechanisms, which are used to inform action (action-formation mechanisms) and transform (transformational mechanisms) social and institutional contexts [13]. It is outside the scope and length of this paper to explain the latter in detail; however, we have observed translation and bricolage mechanisms in operation as social actors adopted semantic web technologies such as OWL, and adapted design standards such as UML and SBVR, to create the aforementioned common vocabulary, which is represented in FIBO (see Figure 3). We have also observed senior financial services executives commit, because of changes to their desires and beliefs due to the EDM Council's framing and diffusion mechanisms, to the use of semantic technologies to manage risk and compliance for securities trading in one US-based Fortune 100 organization.

We argue that the EDM Council and the OMG have achieved the semi-institutionalization [21] of sematic technologies in the organizational field of the financial industry. Thought leaders in this industry expect that the adoption of standards such as FIBO will bring profound changes to the design and development of IS, as traditional data management approaches give way to semantic modelling, and radical innovation around semantic technologies leads to a new generation of semantically-enabled IS. Such radical innovations will permit organizations across the industry to bring added value to, and enhance the delivery of, financial services. On the other hand, regulators such as the SEC argue that the institutionalization of a common vocabulary and related semantic technologies will permit them to better assess systemic risks across the financial industry and to detect a potential financial crisis in the early stages, thereby avoiding catastrophes like the global economic meltdown that occurred in 2008.

Acknowledgement. This research study was supported by the Irish Government through funding provided by Enterprise Ireland and the Irish Development Authority under the Technology Centres Programme.

References

1. Gordon, R.S.: The Solution Became the Problem. The Long View (August 25, 2012), http://online.barrons.com/article/SB5000142405311190488140457603452851756694.html (accessed February 2013)
2. Bennett, M.: Semantics standardization for financial industry integration. In: Collaboration Technologies and Systems (CTS), May 23-27, pp. 239–445. IEEE (2011)
3. Furnas, G.W., Landauer, T.K., Gomez, L.M., Dumais, S.T.: The vocabulary problem in human-system communication. Commun. ACM 30(11), 964–971 (1987)
4. Rodier, M.: OMG and Enterprise Data Management Council to Develop Data Standards for Financial Reform. Wall Street and Technology (March 15, 2011), http://www.wallstreetandtech.com/data-management/omg-and-enterprise-data-management-counc/229301007 (accessed March 2013)
5. Stephens, S.: The Enterprise Semantic Web: Technologies and Applications for the Real World. In: Hepp, M., Lytras, M., Cardoso, J. (eds.) Semantic Web and Beyond Computing for Human Experience, vol. 6, pp. 17–37. Springer, NY (2008)
6. Lara, R., Cantador, I., Castells, P.: Semantic Technologies for the Financial Domain. In: Hepp, M., Lytras, M., Cardoso, J. (eds.) Semantic Web and Beyond Computing for Human Experience, vol. 6, pp. 41–74. Springer, NY (2008)

7. Scott, W.R.: Institutions and Organizations. Sage Publications, Thousand Oaks (1995)
8. Orlikowski, W.J., Barley, S.R.: Technology and Institutions: What Can Research on Information Technology and Research on Organizations Learn from Each Other. MISQ 25, 145–166 (2001)
9. DiMaggio, P.J., Powell, W.W.: The Iron Cage Revisited - Institutional Isomorphism and Collective Rationality in Organizational Fields. Am. Sociol. Rev. 48, 147–160 (1983)
10. Campbell, J.L.: Institutional Change and Globalization. Princeton University Press, Princeton (2004)
11. Hedström, P., Swedberg, R.: Social Mechanisms: An Analytical Approach to Social Theory. Cambridge University Press, New York (1998)
12. Gross, N.: A Pragmatist Theory of Social Mechanisms. Am. Sociol. Rev. 74, 358–379 (2009)
13. Hedström, P.: Dissecting the Social. Cambridge University Press, Cambridge (2005)
14. Campbell, J.L.: Where do we stand? Common mechanisms in organizations and social research. In: Davis, G.F., McAdam, D., Scott, W.R., Zald, M.N. (eds.) Social Movements and Organization Theory, pp. 41–68. Cambridge University Press, New York (2005)
15. Davis, G.F., Marquis, C.: Prospects for Organization Theory in the Early Twenty-First Century: Institutional Fields and Mechanisms. Organ. Sci. 16, 332–343 (2005)
16. Elster, J.: Explaining social behavior: More nuts and bolts for the social sciences. Cambridge University Press, Cambridge (2007)
17. Yin, R.K.: Case Study Research Design and Methods. Sage Publications, California (2003)
18. Jorgensen, D.L.: Participant Observation: A Methodology for Human Studies. Sage Publications, California (1989)
19. Patton, M.Q.: Qualitative Evaluation and Research Methods. Sage Publications, California (1990)
20. Chell, E.: Critical incident technique. In: Symon, G., Cassell, C. (eds.) Qualitative Methods and Analysis in Organizational Research, pp. 51–72. Sage Publications, London (1998)
21. Tolbert, P.S., Zucker, L.G.: Institutionalization of Institutional Theory. In: Clegg, S., Hardy, C., Nord, W. (eds.) Handbook of Organizational Studies, pp. 175–190. Sage Publications, London (1996)

Diffusion and Innovation Theory: Past, Present, and Future Contributions to Academia and Practice

Richard Baskerville[1], Deborah Bunker[2], Johan Olaisen[3], Jan Pries-Heje[4],
Tor. J. Larsen[3,*], and E. Burton Swanson[5]

[1] Georgia State University, Atlanta, USA
Baskerville@acm.org
[2] The University of Sydney Business School, Sydney, Australia
Deborah.Bunker@sydney.edu.au
[3] BI Norwegian Business School, Oslo, Norway
{Johan.Olaisen,Tor.J.Larsen}@bi.no
[4] Roskilde University, Roskilde, Denmark
Janph@ruc.dk
[5] UCLA Anderson School of Management, Los Angeles, USA
Burt.Swanson@anderson.ucla.edu

Keywords: Diffusion theory, Innovation theory, Theory development, Value, Academia, Practice.

1   Background

The field of information systems (IS) has throughout its history experienced extensive changes in technology, research, and education. These renewals will continue into the foreseeable future [10]. It is recognized that IS is a key force in the ongoing societal and organizational renewal and change [2, 8, 14]. For example, in the US business sector, IS continues yearly to consume about 30% of total investments made [5]. Recent research document that IS supports the creation of business value, with particular emphasis on an organization's innovation and change capabilities [1, 3]. Traditionally, research in IS has been interdisciplinary in nature – since it draws on innovation theory, models of value creation, actors' roles and behaviors, the creation and running of task oriented groups, and how these relate to organizational structures and mechanisms [24]. Throughout its history the question of benefits from investing in IS has been lively discussed.

It is emphatically true that IS software creators, consultancies, and organizations taking IS into use have done what they deem is necessary to carry through IS-related development, implementation, and usage processes. As we know, these actors have developed methods, techniques, procedures for securing competence, and tools for supporting the creation and maintenance of the IS portfolio. Although the path of IS development and use has been winding and full of potholes, it is equally apt to

---

[*] Panel Moderator.

B. Bergvall-Kåreborn and P.A. Nielsen (Eds.): TDIT 2014, IFIP AICT 429, pp. 295–300, 2014.

observe that despite of setbacks IS has over its decades of existence consistently en-joyed a staggering level of success.

Within the umbrella of innovation and change, what have been the contributions of academia? Indeed, Silicon Valley is a success story. Yet, in theoretical terms, what are the contributions in theory that have enjoyed wide use among software creators and user organizations?

IFIP WG8.6 was in 1993 created to bring together researchers and practitioners with a particular interest in diffusion of technology issues. In the group's early days Rogers' [25] theory of diffusion of innovation played a major role, resulting in a se-ries of conference contributions (see, e.g., [17, 19]). The introduction of Davis' Tech-nology Acceptance Model [7] in 1989 over time virtually killed the interest in Rogers' diffusion theory. We can safely say that TAM has enjoyed wide and intense attention with hundreds of publications (see, e.g., [18, 30]). Yet, it is exceedingly difficult to find evidence of practical application of TAM, that is, that TAM one way or other has been concretely included in IS projects and that TAM has worked as a vehicle for practitioners in understanding aspects of IS use. Diffusion theory and TAM address phenomena on the individual level of analysis. Examples of contributions on the or-ganizational level are the Capability Maturity Model [11] and Swanson's [26, 29] explorations of innovation theory. Yet, it is unclear whether these have resulted in further theory developments or have enjoyed wide use in practice. These questions are also raised about process oriented approaches, such as Soft Systems Thinking [6].

The panel is put together to address these and related issues. We ask, what have been major contributions within the umbrellas of diffusion and innovation theory related to IS since the mid 1990ies? Are these still alive, and if not, what would it take to re-invoke them? If what we in academia have addressed so far are dead ends, what other approaches to theory building should we cultivate, and what would those diffu-sion and innovation theories actually be? Who would benefit from our endeavors; practitioners or academicians?

2   Position Statements

2.1   Baskerville: No Silver Canon-Ball – Dodging the Limits of Theory

Each Diffusion and Innovation Theory allows us to explain different aspects of the events under inspection. For example, technology push-pull is an early, but well known theory, often used to explain how production and market forces affect innovation and diffusion. Each such theory is limited to its explanatory scope. When used strategically, such theories will only provide part of the strategy: the core aspect selected in hopes this chosen strategic core will drive the entire setting in the desired direction. These are high hopes given the complexity with which such events unfold. A strategy for diffusion and innovation creates something of a synthetic collision: a kind of engineered complex event that almost immediately exceeds theoretic control. Such a collision creates lots of interesting (and useful) noise, changing everything associated with the events: individuals, societies, cultures, organizations, the technology itself, and even its utility. Theories that successfully explain aspects of such events may prove unsuccessful in strategizing them simply because the scope of the resulting strategy is insufficient to deal with the range of the unfolding complexity.

2.2 Bunker: Diffusion and Innovation Theory – Real or Just an Illusion?

There have been many major contributions to diffusion and innovation theory since 1990. The IFIP WG8.6 has accepted papers on the aggregate contributions in this area since 2008. By way of example, Dwivedi, Levine, Williams, Singh, Wastell, and Bunker [9] reviewed the evolution IFIP WG8.6 since its inception in 1993, as a means of understanding the research themes and approaches that have occupied the group during this time. Most frequently researched topics have included 'organizational impact, technology transfer, diffusion, software engineering and adoption' whilst research approaches such as 'actor-network theory, diffusion of innovation, and institutional theory' have been the most utilized by researchers within the group.

The real crux of the argument is, however: is diffusion and innovation theory real and relevant or just an illusion?

The core of our work is alive to our academic colleagues. For example, we still see the influence of Fred Davis [7] and his work on the technology acceptance model (cited in 18.650 instances to date) especially in the formative work of many of our research students. We still fail, however, to effectively address the issue of usefulness of such ideas within society and business, and their relevance to our practitioner colleagues. The original mission of the WG8.6 was to address this very issue, by actively engaging with practitioners, but this problem transcends mere "engagement" to the need for a model of knowledge and systems co-creation and co-production. True diffusion, innovation and technology transfer must occur "on location" where theory makers and theory users can work though practical/practice based implications of diffusion and innovation theory and their relevance [4].

Within IFIP WG 8.6 we have completed some rigorous and relevant research. However, we need to do more to co-produce diffusion and innovation theory, frameworks and approaches with our practitioner colleagues, in order to overcome the illusory nature of what it is we do. This would mean that both academics and practitioners (ably supported with funding from government) would need to set a suitable and practical agenda that addresses such issues as: research themes of importance, co-location of academic and practitioner researchers, shared research language, agreed to methods of: representation, categorization and research; and workable IP models.

If we were able to effectively tackle this issue then both practitioners and academicians would be able to harness mutual and complimenting strengths to produce useful, relevant, rigorous and robust theory, frameworks and approaches as well as a reinforcing "learning loops" to ensure continuous improvement of both theoretical and practical outcomes of our work.

2.3 Olaisen: Value Creation in a Philosophy of Science Perspective – Subjective Pluralism or Objective Trivialism

My position is an integrated view of IS. For an organization IS will include people, processes, structures, technology/tools and the context. The context includes both the internal and external parts of an organization. This means that the global customers, partners and networks are included. IS will then be handling both global efficiency and effectiveness -- likewise standardization and specialization of production and services. IS are then handling an increasing degree of internal and external complexity. IS logistics are then a primary requirement for any kind of value creation. Any business innovation and entrepreneurship capabilities include IS. To work smarter and greener is an IS issue. The edge of the research and development for this reality in any respect is today found in the business world and not in the academic world. Why? The academic IS world produce trivial empirical research without any relevance than for the academic world itself. IS are not anymore an important part of the business schools curriculum. The academic world do not participate in the IS business world or vice versa. The only way to do research upon IS will be a in a holistic perspective where the value creation is understood as a part of the whole business reality. This requires research paradigms as action research and clarified subjectivity research describing the past and present predicting the future. The empirical IS research and theoretical models of IS are outdated and irrelevant. We need a rebirth of IS research based upon clarified subjectivity exploring the present and future. We need subjective sensitizing research concepts not definitive objective empirical concepts. That might give us a brave new academic IS world!

2.4   Pries-Heje: A Broad Unifying Perspective on Diffusion and Adoption

Many theories look at a small and detailed part of diffusion and adoption. However, organizational change requires much more than a "view through a straw". I argue that we need to look broadly and across theories to find what is needed to design effective diffusion and adoption. I present a first draft that starts out with the people involved in different roles [21, 32, 33, 34]. Look at phases that change goes through [15, 16, 20]. Distinguish between forced and voluntary change [25]. Aim at planning for change with end in mind [13]. And finally - based on contingencies of the situation – recommend an organizational change strategy [12, 22].

2.5   Swanson: Meeting the Institutional Challenge

While much research on the diffusion of IT innovation has focused on the uptake of technology by first, individual users, and second, individual organizations, rather little has focused on the technologies themselves and their institutional trajectories and histories. Considerable opportunities exist for impactful research at this broader level of analysis (see, e.g., [31, 35]), though there are challenges in building a community committed to it. My own research [27, 28] has promoted the concept of the organizing vision as a way to understand certain IT innovation in an institutional context, and while others have built on this work, the cumulative effort has not yet opened a gate through which many are attracted to enter and join (for one call, see [23]). More widely, the IS academic community's engagement of its research subject matter at the institutional level remains rather weak, with the consequence that narrower findings are often presented out of historical context, curiously, as if they were somehow invariant with the passage of time and IT innovation itself.

References

1. Aral, S., Brynjolfsson, E., Wu, L.: Three-way Complementarities: Performance Pay, Human Resource Analytics, and Information Technology. Management Science 58(5), 913–931 (2012)
2. Baskerville, R.L., Myers, M.D.: Information Systems as a Reference Discipline. MIS Quarterly 26(1), 1–14 (2002)
3. Brynjolfsson, E., McAfee, A.: Race Against the Machine: How the Digital Revolution is Accelerating Innovation, Driving Productivity and Irreversibly Transforming Employment and the Economy. Digital Frontier Press, Lexington (2011)
4. Bunker, D., Campbell, J.: A Perspectival Punctuated Action Approach to Policy Development in Information Technology and Systems. In: Proceedings of the 16th Australasian Conference on Information Systems, Sydney, Australia, November 29-December 2 (2005), http://aisel.aisnet.org/
5. Centre for the Study of Living Standards (2012), http://www.csls.ca/ (last accessed on November 12, 2012)
6. Checkland, P., Holwell, S.: Information, Systems and Information Systems – Making Sense of the Field. John Wiley & Sons, Chichester (1998)
7. Davis, F.D.: Perceived Usefulness, Perceived Ease of Use, and User Acceptance of Information Technology. MIS Quarterly 13(3), 319–340 (1989)
8. Davis, G.B.: Information Systems Conceptual Foundations: Looking Backward and Forward. In: Baskerville, R., Stage, J., DeGross, J.I. (eds.) Proceedings of the IFIP WG8.2 Conference on The Social and Organizational Perspective on Research and Practice in Information Technology, Aalborg, Denmark, June 9-11, pp. 61–82. Kluwer Academic Publishers, Boston (2000)
9. Dwivedi, Y.K., Levine, L., Williams, M.D., Singh, M., Wastell, D.G., Bunker, D.: Toward an Understanding of the Evolution of IFIP WG 8.6 Research. In: Pries-Heje, J., Venable, J., Bunker, D., Russo, N.L., DeGross, J.I. (eds.) IFIP WG. IFIP AICT, vol. 318, pp. 225–242. Springer, Heidelberg (2010)
10. Galliers, R.D., Currie, W.L.: The Oxford Handbook of Management Information Systems: Critical Perspectives and New Directions. Oxford University Press, Oxford (2011)
11. Herbsleb, J., Zubrow, D., Goldenson, D., Hayes, W., Paulk, M.: Software Quality and the Capability Maturity Model. Communications of the ACM 40(6), 30–40 (1997)
12. Huy, Q.N.: Time, temporal capability, and planned change. Academy of Management Review 26(4), 601–623 (2001)
13. Jackson, P.Z., McKergow, M.: The Solutions Focus. Nicholas Brealey Publishing, London (2007)
14. Kebede, G.: Knowledge management: An Information Science Perspective. International Journal of Information Management 30, 416–424 (2010)
15. Kotter, J.P.: Leading Change: Why Transformation Efforts Fail. Harvard Business Review 73(2), 59–67 (1995)
16. Kotter, J.P.: Accelerate! Harvard Business Review 90(11), 43–58 (2012)
17. Larsen, T.J.: The Phenomenon of Diffusion: Red Herrings and Future Promise. In: Ardis, A.M., Marcolin, B.L. (eds.) Proceedings of the IFIP WG8.6 Conference on Diffusing Software Product and Process Innovations, Banff, Canada, April 7-10, pp. 35–50. Kluwer Academic Publishers, Boston (2001)
18. Legris, P., Ingham, J., Collerette, P.: Why do People Use Information Technology? A Critical Review of the Technology Acceptance Model. Information & Management 40(3), 191–204 (2003)

19. Lyytinen, K., Damsgaard, J.: What's Wrong with the Diffusion of Innovation Theory? In: Ardis, A.M., Marcolin, B.L. (eds.) Proceedings of the IFIP WG8.6 Conference on Diffusing Software Product and Process Innovations, Banff, Canada, April 7-10, pp. 173–190. Kluwer Academic Publishers, Boston (2001)
20. Moore, G.A.: Inside the Tornado. Harper Business (1995)
21. Pries-Heje, J.: Role Model for the Organisational IT Diffusion Process. In: Damsgaard, J., Henriksen, H.Z. (eds.) Networked Information Technologies: Diffusion and Adoption, pp. 115–129. Kluwer Academic Publishers (2003)
22. Pries-Heje, J., Baskerville, R.: The Design Theory Nexus. MIS Quarterly, Special Issue on Design Science Research 32(4), 731–755 (2001)
23. Ramiller, N.C., Swanson, E.B., Wang, P.: Research directions in information systems: Toward an institutional ecology. Journal of the AIS 9(1), 1–22 (2008)
24. Roberts, N., Galluch, P.S., Dinger, M., Grover, V.: Absorptive Capacity and Information Systems Research: Review, Synthesis, and Directions for Future Research. MIS Quarterly 36(2), 625–648 (2012)
25. Rogers, E.M.: Diffusion of Innovations, 5th edn. Free Press, New York (2003)
26. Swanson, E.B.: Information Systems Innovation among Organizations. Management Science 40(9), 1069–1092 (1994)
27. Swanson, E.B.: Illuminating Organizing Vision Careers through Case Studies. In: Proceedings of the Americas Conference on Information Systems, Chicago, IL (2013)
28. Swanson, E.B., Ramiller, N.C.: The Organizing Vision in Information Systems Innovation. Organization Science 8(5), 458–474 (1997)
29. Swanson, E.B., Ramiller, N.C.: Innovating Mindfully with Information Technology. MIS Quarterly 28(4), 553–583 (2004)
30. Venkatesh, V., Morris, M.G., Davis, G.B., Davis, F.D.: User Acceptance of Information Technology: Toward a Unified View. MIS Quarterly 27(3), 425–478 (2003)
31. Wang, P., Ramiller, N.C.: Community Learning in Information Technology Innovation. MIS Quarterly 33(4), 709–734 (2009)
32. Weinberg, G.M.: Quality Software Management. First-Order Measurement, vol. 2. Dorset House, New York (1993)
33. Weinberg, G.M.: Quality Software Management, Volume 3, Congruent Action. Dorse House, New York (1994)
34. Weinberg, G.M.: Quality Software Management. Anticipating Change, vol. 4. Dorset House, New York (1997)
35. Williams, R., Pollock, N.: Moving Beyond the Single Site Implementation Study: How (and why) We Should Study the Biography of Packaged Enterprise Solutions. Information Systems Research 23(4), 1–22 (2012)

Entrepreneurial Value Creation in the Cloud: Exploring the Value Dimensions of the Business Model

Jyoti M. Bhat and Bhavya P. Shroff

Indian Institute of Management, Bangalore, India
{jyoti.bhat,bhavya.ps}@iimb.ernet.in

Abstract. Cloud computing's potential in creating and capturing business value is being increasingly acknowledged. Existing empirical studies of business value in cloud computing have focused on user organizations and large enterprises with legacy systems. Acknowledging the innovation opportunities created by cloud, we study entrepreneurial cloud service providers. In this paper we conduct an exploratory study of six cloud-based start-up firms in India. We examine the value dimensions of the business model concept to study entrepreneurial value creation in the cloud. We find that cloud is a key resource in the structural configuration of their business model and enables the value proposition.

Keywords: Cloud computing, entrepreneurship, start-ups, value creation, business model.

1   Introduction

Cloud computing brings in new market players and value networks [1] with different business values for the various players [2]. The access, affordability and fast setup of IT infrastructure provided by cloud computing enables firms to focus on core competencies, addresses issues of IT inefficiency [3]; lowers the entry barriers for entrepreneurs [4] and acts as a catalyst for innovation [5]. Literature reviews of academic publications find that empirical studies related to business issues and business value of cloud computing is limited [6]. The limited empirical studies on the business impact of cloud computing have focused on service providers' value creation with cloud [7] and benefit patterns that organizations achieve by leveraging cloud capabilities [8]. Venters and Whitley [9] found that cloud was being used by start-ups to innovate, but how cloud-computing supports innovation and value creation is largely an unexplored area in empirical research. Business value of cloud-computing for adopter organizations is apparent with benefits related to cost and efficiency, but value creation by cloud service providers is an unexplored area.

The tremendous growth of the cloud computing market has brought in a significant number of cloud start-ups. Hence entrepreneurial value generation in the cloud is relevant in this growing market space. Investigating the value of cloud computing faces the typical challenges highlighted in IT value research, as the economic impact and competitive benefit depends on several firm level factors [10]. We attempt to

B. Bergvall-Kåreborn and P.A. Nielsen (Eds.): TDIT 2014, IFIP AICT 429, pp. 301–310, 2014.

explore the following research questions - *How do firms leverage cloud computing to create and derive business value?* We use an exploratory approach and study value creation by six cloud based start-ups. A business model is "the rationale of how an organization creates, delivers and captures value" [11]. Hence we use the business model concept to examine value creation through exploitation of opportunities provided by cloud computing.

In the next section we describe the theoretical background and the framework used in the study. We then outline the case study data and the method adopted for the study. Section 4 details the findings and analysis of the case studies. In section 5 we discuss our findings with respect to other studies and conclude with directions for future research.

2   Theoretical Background

2.1   Business Model Concept

The business model (BM) concept is gaining importance in IS, strategy and technology management research, particularly when studying ICT-enabled businesses [12]. The BM concept has been used to study e-business [11], [13], telecommunication [14] and other IT innovations like ERP implementation [15]. Viet et al. [16] review the BM literature in IS and identify BMs in IT industries as one of the pillars for future BM research within IS. BM is identified as crucial to value creation not only for the focal firm but also for its suppliers, customers and partners [13]. The success and sustainability of the firm is dependent on the underlying business rules and several exogenous factors such as the value created for the consumer, value chain position, capturing the market, industry factors, etc. Therefore, the design of the BM model is said to be a very important decision for new firms [17].

Amit and Zott [13] argue that in e-business BMs can create value through efficiency, novelty, complementarities, and lock-in. Hedman and Kalling [15] propose a more generic BM concept based on strategy literature and integrate RBV, five forces model, generic strategies of the firm, value chain analysis and process research. Afuah and Tucci [18] examine internet business models and identify the components of the BM and provide guidelines for evaluating a BM. From an entrepreneurial point of view the BM helps narrow down entrepreneurial ideas to specific opportunity and establishes the goals of the firm [19].

A conceptual framework proposed by Al-Debei and Avison [20] based on a comprehensive literature review of the BM concept identifies 4 primary value-based dimensions. We use the V4 ontological structure of BM for our study of the cloud-based start-ups as it provides clarity to the BM concept from a value creation perspective.

2.2   The Fundamental Elements of a Business Model

The four value dimensions of 'V4 Business Model'- value proposition, value-network, value-architecture, and value-finance are the aspects which need to be examined when designing, evaluating, and managing BMs. A detailed description of the dimensions and elements is available in [14]. The operationalization of the BM elements depends on the context; hence we define below the dimensions and elaborate the concepts being used in the proposed study from an entrepreneurial perspective. Figure 1 shows the V4 BM dimensions and elements considered for this study.

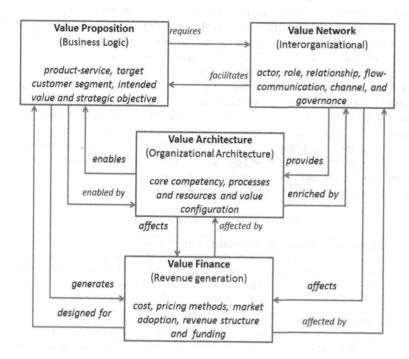

Fig. 1. V4 Business Model Dimensions for Cloud-based start-ups (Adapted from [14])

- *Value proposition* demonstrates the business logic of creating value through products/offerings targeted to specific market segments. The strategic objective of the product/service is also an important aspect of this dimension.
- *Value architecture* specifies the holistic structural design of the organization which includes the technological architecture and organizational infrastructure. Value configuration is an important element as it enables the combinatorial innovation capabilities required for cloud-based start-ups [5].
- *Value network* represents the interorganizational perspective and shows how value flows across the actors. Customers, complementaries and partners are expected to be the key actors in the network. Competitors are not pertinent in an opportunity-centric view [19].
- *Value finance* describes the cost and pricing methods, and the revenue structure that ensures the economic viability of the offering. In the context of start-ups the focus is more on market penetration than on immediate financial returns. Also the pricing methods and revenue models for start-ups can be volatile in their early days.

3   Research Method and Data

3.1   Research Method

We adopted a multiple case study method to explore how technology start-ups leverage cloud computing for value creation. The case studies method is a good strategy to study contemporary phenomenon in its real-life context [21]. To meet the needs of the exploratory study the cases were purposefully chosen to span across all layers of the cloud - software-as-a-service(SaaS), platform-as-a-service(PaaS), and infrastructure management. Some of the criteria for choosing the cases were: 1) cloud-based offering is the predominant focus of the company 2) the cloud services are offered to businesses (B2B space). We also ensured that the start-ups have a viable business potential by verifying that they have a product which has been used by some paying customers or the venture has the backing of an investor or incubation cell.

The six companies are based out of Bangalore, India and provide different products in the cloud environment for global customers. All the companies chosen have been around for 1 to 3 years and have less than 25 employees.

Table 1 provides details of the individual case studies.

Table 1. Start-ups for the case study

C1. Cloud Manager*: (Technology/ Infrastructure Management) A cloud management product which helps consume and manage any cloud service from any cloud provider. Their product provides a self-service portal which integrates with a firm's workflow systems and enables centralized control of cloud service consumption and governance across the enterprise. The product is offered in SaaS and in-house hosted models.
C2. PrivateCloud: (Technology/ Infrastructure Management) A cloud engine that helps medium sized enterprises to migrate existing IT infrastructure to a private cloud. Their platform provides tools for monitoring and allows the virtualization of IT infrastructure.
C3. CloudALM: (Software / Development Platform & PaaS) A development platform for cloud based agile software development. The platform orchestrates and manages the various software development tools and the cloud infrastructure services procured by their customers. The product is primarily a hosted solution, but is also offered on the cloud to small companies.
C4. VC-on-demand: (Technology/ SaaS) A cloud based video bridge as a widget on the customer's website. The product integrates video conferencing with the workflow of the firm and provides certain intelligence and analytics of the video call.
C5. e-voucher: (Accounting/SaaS) A cloud based pre-accounting and compliance product which allows firms to define financial rules, prevent data errors and creates an intelligent digital voucher. E-voucher leverages the global access of cloud to connect remote stakeholder of firms and eliminate data errors at the point of entry.
C6. MicroAnalytics: (Analytics/SaaS) A sophisticated analytics which can be run on small datasets. The product offers affordable analytics to SMEs.

* All names are pseudonyms to ensure anonymity.

3.2   Data Collection and Analysis

The data collection was primarily through semi-structured interviews with the founders of the six firms. As the business model reflects the management/entrepreneur's hypothesis about the value proposition and customer requirements [22], interviews were conducted with the entrepreneur/founders. We adopted face-to-face interviews as it allows delving deeper into the areas of importance [21]. Each interview lasted between 45 to 80 minutes. We used 20 open-ended questions based on the V4 BM dimensions to guide the interview. In addition to the notes taken by two researchers, each interview was audio-recorded with the interviewee's consent to further aid data analysis. Supporting documents obtained from the interviewees and their firm websites included brochures, demos, firm related information and social media entries.

For each interview we prepared the answers to our framework elements from the interview notes, recording and documents available. The data was initially coded using an open approach to identify the main ideas which were emerging. These ideas were then grouped using the V4 dimensions to identify categories. The ideas were also grouped using interactions between the V4 dimensions. The data was analyzed and observations discussed between the two researchers to reach an agreement about the findings. We first analyzed each case using the V4 dimensions and then conducted a cross-case analysis to identify the role of cloud in the BM.

4   Findings and Analysis

We present our findings and analysis along the value dimensions of the V4 BM. We associate individual findings with specific cases (C1 to C6 from Table 1) to bring clarity.

4.1   Value-Proposition

Value proposition is a critical dimension of the business model for most technology organizations. The growth of cloud technologies which created *new markets* for cloud resource management was leveraged by the start-ups (C1,C2,C3). The SaaS startups (C3,C4,C5,C6) productize the entrepreneurs' domain expertise and deliver them using cloud technologies. Their businesses exist because the capabilities, reach and affordability of cloud helped them implement their ideas to cater to unsatisfied needs of the customer. *"...all traditional industries are moving to the cloud...there is compute,... network...and a lot of things are falling in place which makes it* (this idea) *possible now"* –Founder, C4.

The cloud-based start-ups focus on providing *new niche capabilities* (such as microanalytics, accounting, agile development, etc.) and are not trying to replace existing capabilities or change existing processes in their customer organizations. The offerings plug on to existing enterprise systems and IT infrastructure. The features consider local infrastructure conditions (like 200kbps or 2G connection, prepaid billing plans, etc.) (C4,C5,C6). The start-ups provide different usage scenarios of their products as the value proposition in technology products depends on the context of its use (C1,C4,C5,C6). *"The framework is one... right, but the use cases of this product is a lot and that's why we are pitching it to different players"* – Founder, C1. All the start-ups said that they did not have any direct competitors and their focus is on increasing the size of the targeted market.

4.2   Value-Architecture

Cloud is an important resource for the start-ups as it enables product development with minimal IT investment. For SaaS products cloud is the channel for product delivery and usage (C4,C5,C6). For start-ups providing on premise hosted services, the IT infrastructure and cloud based services at their customer site are necessary resources for their product (C1,C2,C3). The SaaS products have a dependency on complementary products used by the customer organizations (such as enterprise systems, web browsers, etc). "...we verified the products they [SME customers] use and built data adaptors for those..." – C6. Though technical skills is an important resource, most of the start-ups have a lean development team (C1,C2,C4,C6).

The core-competency of the start-ups is the skills and expertise of the founders. Though a differentiated product strategy is adopted, a cloud based model forces a low-cost requirement from the start-ups. "...customer pays 10 bucks for the cloud services, so why will he pay me 10 more bucks to manage it for him?" – C1. Hence resource optimization and customer relationship becomes important for the start-ups. Most of the start-ups continuously evaluate the resources and cloud services which were being used to deliver their products (C1,C3,C4). Product enhancement and resource optimization are the main drivers of this continuous review.

4.3   Value-Network

All the start-ups interviewed mentioned leveraging external networks for value creation. The start-ups use expert groups or online social networks as intermediaries to gain access into customer organizations. They use their free version to create awareness in the expert group through which they can connect to the decision makers in the enterprise (C1,C3,C5). The products have globally relevant features and added capabilities to cater to India specific infrastructure requirements. The low price points allow these products to compete with global products having similar or less features. "...our input costs are 100 times lower, we can directly compete on price and can give high quality work...but I can't tie up with cloud service providers in US, I need the system integrators and consultants... who can bring in their connects to make it happen" – C1. C5 uses its professional contacts within the network of accountants to acquire customers in US, Middle East, Africa and India. Hence developing value networks and partners is very critical for the cloud-based start-ups.

Some start-ups maintain a free and paid version of the product (C1,C3,C5). The free customers are valuable resources for product testing and feedback. None of the start-ups leverages the multiple-tenancy of their products. All of them mentioned that data is owned by the client and they do not plan to use data across tenants. Most start-ups leverage the brand value and trust of the large cloud providers (Microsoft, Amazon, IBM), especially when it comes to security and reliability aspects with their customers.

4.4   Value Finance

Subscription based pricing with slabs was the popular model adopted by the start-ups. Even on premise products adopt this model, *"renting even if on premise"*, due to customers' expectations. This reduces the variability for themselves and their customers. The SaaS subscriptions have a base price range of $15 to $25, which is *"...less than the monthly mobile phone bill"* – C6. Such low price points are possible only due to cloud and the reduced input costs in India. The main costs for the start-ups are the cloud services and human resources; but most of the start-ups are not too concerned about both these costs. But not all start-ups pursued a low-cost model; start-ups with higher input costs or niche products adopt a value-based pricing.

Market penetration and acquiring customers is the focus of the startups, hence they have not explored revenue structures in detail. But availability of funding was critical for many of them. *"The subscription based model requires upfront investment whereas the revenue has a long tail."* – C4. Some of the startups have explored different revenue flows like build domain specific solutions (C4,C6) and embed the SaaS product in other products.

The key findings across the four BM value dimensions are summarized in Table 2.

Table 2. Key Findings across the value dimensions of the BM

BM Value Dimension	Key Findings
Value Proposition	• Infrastructure management and platform start-ups exploited markets created due to cloud • SaaS players created a new/niche market which was enabled by cloud.
Value Architecture	• Have a dependency on complementary products and resources owned by customers • Need to respond rapidly to new trends and continuously innovate in the cloud environment
Value Network	• Use experts and social networks as intermediaries for customer acquisition • Cloud B2B start-ups do not aggregate across customers
Value Finance	• Subscription based pricing (Flat rates) with slabs is the popular model, but complex and niche products use value-based pricing • Only mature start-ups have explored multiple revenue flows

5   Discussion

Cloud-based entrepreneurial ventures offer functionalities which are at the boundaries of the firm and integrate into the existing enterprise systems. Though they do not replace existing enterprise capabilities, their value propositions include enabling new business models, decision support, real time data/process transparency, etc. Cloud computing has created new markets for specialized knowledge like accounting and analytics [23] which previously required expensive resources like IT investments and consultants. Chen and Wu [4] show that on-demand services are more profitable for firms with differentiated products, we found that the cloud start-ups were all focused on differentiating their products on features. All the start-ups position their products into market segments where large CSPs and product vendors currently do not operate and hence their BM increases the size of the market [17]. We found cloud technology is an enabler of the BM in cloud-based start-ups. This aligns with the functionalist perspective of BM (at the firm level) where technology complements the BM as an enabler and the core logic of the BM deals with the value proposition to the customer, value capture and revenues for the firm [12].

The low-priced subscription based billing model may not be a sustainable model as the cloud-based product offerings matures with more features based on complementors and network partners. The "utility model" which was popularized by the cloud infrastructure providers may not be adequate to handle the complex architecture and networks of cloud offerings [5]. Koehler et al. [24] find three types of cloud computing customers based on their preference for different billing models (pay-per-use, flat rate and one-time), which provides an opportunity for price discrimination. This is an opportunity which the cloud-based start-ups can explore.

In line with previous empirical studies [1], [7], [8], the importance of partner network for value creation was reiterated in the current study. Unlike [7] who found human resources as the biggest cost for CSPs, the cloud-based start-ups in India did not mention this as an issue. Hence India based cloud start-ups may have a unique value proposition of low price- high quality in the emerging cloud-based market. All the entrepreneurs in the study used the global CSPs when it came to storage and compute services. India based IaaS may make infrastructure cheaper and can create more opportunities for value creation for the cloud-based start-ups and their customers. This calls for action from the Indian government to ensure suitable policy and support for cloud computing.

6   Limitations, Conclusion and Future Work

Deviating from the larger stream of research focusing on technical aspects and capabilities of cloud the current study explores business value creation in cloud computing. We find that cloud computing created markets for cloud management which was exploited by start-ups; also the characteristics of cloud enabled start-ups to create new opportunities and markets for niche products. The start-ups derive value from two aspects of cloud –1) access to affordable IT infrastructure for product development 2) Ability to deliver products and services by making cloud part of their BM. This reiterates the importance of BM in unlocking the value of new technologies.

There are several limitations in this study. As an exploratory study with a small sample of six start-ups, our findings cannot be generalized without further study. This study provides insights for a detailed study as it highlights many aspects where more clarity is required. The start-ups we interviewed experience steady loads in their activities as they onboard customers in a planned manner. Hence some of the technological features of cloud (like elasticity) are not fully experienced by these start-ups. The combination of technological features and BM-enabling features could not be investigated in this study. The BM is a function of its environment; hence the country context has an influence on some of the findings which we have highlighted. Future studies can explore newer themes such as the innovation-enabling role of cloud technologies in the start-ups, new cloud-enabled business model taxonomies, cloud enabled BM innovation in adopter organizations.

References

1. Leimeister, S., Riedl, K., Krcmar, H.: The Business Perspectives of Cloud Computing: Actors, Roles and Value Networks. In: ECIS (2010)
2. Weinhardt, C., Anandasivam, A., Blau, B., Borissov, N., Meinl, T., Michalk, W., Stößer, J.: Cloud Computing – A classification, business models, and research directions. Business & Information Systems Engineering 1(5), 391–399 (2009)
3. Armbrust, M., Fox, A., Griffith, R., Joseph, A.D., et al.: A view of cloud computing. Communications of the ACM 53(4), 50–58 (2010)
4. Chen, P.Y., Wu, S.Y.: The Impact and Implications of On-Demand Services on Market Structure. Information Systems Research 24(3), 750–767 (2013)
5. Brynjolfsson, E., Hoffman, P., Jordan, J.: Cloud Computing and Electricity: Beyond the Utility Model. Communications of the ACM 53(5) (2010)
6. Yang, H., Tate, M.: A Descriptive Literature Review and Classification of Cloud Computing Research. Communications of the Association for Information Systems 31(2) (2012)
7. Morgan, L., Conboy, K.: Value Creation in the Cloud: Understanding Business Model Factors Affecting Value of Cloud Computing. In: AMCIS (2013)
8. Iyer, B., Henderson, J.C.: Business Value from Clouds: Learning from Users. MIS Quarterly Executive 11(1) (2012)
9. Venters, W., Whitley, E.A.: A critical review of cloud computing: researching desires and realities. Journal of Information Technology 27(3), 179–197 (2012)
10. Kohli, R., Grover, V.: Business Value of IT: An Essay on Expanding Research Directions to Keep up with the Times. Journal of the Association for Information Systems 9(1) (2008)
11. Osterwalder, A., Pigneur, Y., Tucci, C.L.: Clarifying Business Models: Origins, Present and Future of the Concept. Communications of AIS 15, 751–775 (2005)
12. Zott, C., Amit, R., Massa, L.: The business model: recent developments and future research. Journal of Management 37(4), 1019–1042 (2011)
13. Amit, R., Zott, C.: Value Creation in E-Business. Strategic Management Journal (22), 493–520 (2001)
14. Al-Debei, M.M., Fitzgerald, G.: The design and engineering of mobile data services: developing an ontology based on business model thinking. In: Pries-Heje, J., Venable, J., Bunker, D., Russo, N.L., DeGross, J.I. (eds.) IFIP WG. IFIP AICT, vol. 318, pp. 28–51. Springer, Heidelberg (2010)
15. Hedman, J., Kalling, T.: The business model concept: theoretical underpinnings and empirical illustrations. European Journal of Information Systems 12(1), 49–59 (2003)
16. Veit, D., Clemons, E., et al.: Business Models. Bus & Information Systems Engineering 6(1), 45–53 (2014)
17. Zott, C., Amit, R.: Business model design: an activity system perspective. Long Range Planning 43(2), 216–226 (2010)
18. Afuah, A., Tucci, C.: Internet Business Models and Strategies. McGraw-Hill International Editions, New York (2001)
19. George, G., Bock, A.J.: The business model in practice and its implications for entrepreneurship research. Entrepreneurship Theory and Practice 35(1), 83–111 (2011)

20. Al-Debei, M.M., Avison, D.: Developing a unified framework of the business model concept. European Journal of Information Systems 19(3), 359–376 (2010)
21. Yin, K.: Case Study Research: Design and Methods, 3rd edn. Sage Publications, London (2003)
22. Teece, D.J.: Business models, business strategy and innovation. Long Range Planning 43(2), 172–194 (2010)
23. Mircea, M., Ghilic, B., Stoica, M.: Combining Business Intelligence with Cloud Computing to Delivery Agility in Actual Economy. Economic Computation and Economic Cybernetics Studies and Research 45(1), 39–54 (2011)
24. Koehler, P., Anandasivam, A., Dan, M., Weinhardt, C.: Customer Heterogeneity and Tariff Biases in Cloud Computing. In: ICIS (2010)

mGovernment Services and Adoption: Current Research and Future Direction

Mehdi Hussain and Ahmed Imran

UNSW, Canberra
Australia
mehdiwpu@gmail.com

Abstract. With the unprecedented growth of mobile technologies, governments of both developed and developing countries have started adopting mobile services in the form of m-government. While the vendors and practitioners are heavily engaged in this transformation, the scholarly world is lagging to keep pace with the progress and to provide clear theoretical guidance for successful adoption. This paper takes a stock of scholarly publications on m-government adoption since the year 2000 and reports findings and future directions based on meta-analysis of secondary data. The articles were classified into research themes, delivery mode, theory and methods. The paper identifies the dearth of scholarly work and calls for more in-depth work to make important contribution in this area.

Keywords: mGovernment, Literature review, Web-based, Non-web based (SMS), Public Sector ICT, Cross country study, m-services, IT adoption.

1   Introduction

With the wide spread growth of mobile devices in the recent past, consumer activities across the globe began to extend from electronic (e-business, e-commerce, e-government) to mobile (m-commerce, m-government) services. Mobile phones have become an essential personal possession for daily activities with a high percentage of active mobile phone subscribers both in developed and developing world [e.g. Australia, 106.19%, Bangladesh, 63.76%, world approaching to 100% [6,7]. To keep pace with this unprecedented explosion of mobile devices, government of different countries are also seeking to expand their citizen services through mobile technology in the form of m-government [29].

mGovernment has the potential to provide greater access to information for citizens, business organizations and government employees compared to any other channels of information and service delivery because of its convenience, mobility, portability and ubiquitous nature and characteristics. mGovernment services and applications can be 'web-based' and 'non-web based' [19]. Web-based platforms generally are web-portals made to suit mobile applications and m-apps which requires Internet connection; whereas, in the non-web based platforms, short message services (SMS) and interactive voice response (IVR) are used. It has been found in the review

B. Bergvall-Kåreborn and P.A. Nielsen (Eds.): TDIT 2014, IFIP AICT 429, pp. 311–323, 2014.

that many mGovernment services are delivered through web-based and particularly SMS for non-web based giving more emphasis on the former in developed countries and the latter in developing countries.

This review paper considers m-portals and m-apps as 'web based' and SMS as 'non-web based' for the analysis. Socio-cultural, technical, economic, political factors of developed and developing country context stretch the web-based m-government in developed countries and non-web based (SMS) in developing countries. Internet penetration and access in developing country is still very low compared with mobile penetration and growth. In developed countries, internet penetration is higher than that of developing countries and also the cost to connect is affordable. Scarcity of power supply, both interruption and absence, is also another issue in developing countries. Browsing the web through mobiles will require more frequent charging. Computer literacy rate is also higher in developed countries comparing that of developing, which permits more people in the former to browse web through mobile. Moreover, both developed and developing countries differ in terms of history and culture, technical aspects, infrastructure, internet accessibility and computer literacy [2]. In the developed countries, most of the nations' government and economy developed early, immediately after independence; have more technical knowhow abilities and good infrastructure with high internet access; decent computer literacy rate. These contextual characteristics offer greater variety of mGovernment services in the developed countries mostly through mobile web-based for the mass comparing to non-web based.

On the other hand, the opposite characteristics of developing countries offer various mGovernment services mostly through non-web based particularly SMS. mGovernment development worldwide so far has been uneven and still evolving in some contexts [15],[18]. Success stories and best practices are insufficient in comparison to its wide application and demand. The implementers and practitioner world are still struggling to find a workable model in this area. On the other hand, research on mGovernment is also scarce and in its early stage. It is found from the review that most of the research works on mGovernment have been carried out in the last five years, which shows it is a recent phenomenon. Researchers are yet to address many critical issues surrounding mGovernment, such as security, privacy, trust, user readiness, information overload, user need analysis in different socio-cultural and technical contexts [14,15].

In this paper, we attempt to review articles on mGovernment services published from the year 2000 to date in order to provide the current landscape of scholarly work on mGovernment services and also to propose future directions. This paper presents a review of 48 relevant articles that exclusively focuses on m-government, synthesized and shortlisted from wider range of literature. The main purpose of this paper is to critically evaluate previous m-government research to develop a comprehensive understanding towards its trends, limitations and opportunities for future research. The paper is structured as follows. In the next section, it introduces mGovernment applications and services. Section 3 outlines the method and approach used to extract the data from the literature review. Section 4 provides the findings in terms of research themes and focus, delivery mode and theoretical frame of knowledge. Section 5 provides an analytic discussion and future direction followed by limitation and conclusion at the end.

2   Overview on mGovernment

Mobile Government or mGovernment is conducted over mobile or wireless networks which extends the reach of e-government for public service delivery. mGovernment also includes the strategy and its implementation of all kinds of wireless and mobile technology, applications and services by the government or public institutions for the purpose of providing information and services to the citizen, business world, non-profit organizations and for themselves [11], [13,14]. Fig. 1 shows four major domains of mGovernment: m-administration, m-communication, m-services and m-democracy [3], [11], [13], [32]. mGovernment can be again classified into four types in terms of its interaction between entities. These are mGovernment to citizen (mG2C),   mGovernment to business (mG2B),   mGovernment to employee (mG2E) and mGovernment to government (mG2G) [3], [13], [23].

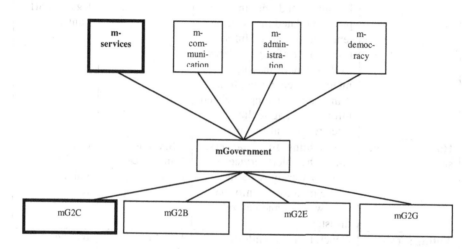

Fig. 1. mGovernment domains and levels

Out of above stated classifications, 'm-services' and 'mG2C' categories appear to be most important one in terms of its wide application and scope (highlighted in fig. 1, referred from table 1). Currently different governments of the world are offering variety of m-government services and applications. Table 1 depicts the list of various m-government application and services in different parts of the world. As a part of the m-government overview, the purpose of this table is to provide idea of variety of mGovernment services to the readers. To broaden the list, examples from [8] published books on mGovernment were also used. To gain further insight and a comparison, the table includes the column with examples of both developed and developing countries where these services are adopted and used. For the sake of this study 'Advanced economies' identified by IMF has been considered as 'developed countries'.

Table 1. List of mGovernment application and services offered by developed and developing countries

mGovernmnet services	Examples	Developed Countries	Developing countries
mG2C services			
Tourism and recreation ser-vices		Canada, Esto-nia	Bahrain
Information services	Contact information of Member of Parliament; public office address, assessment of services, comments with other citizens leveraging on a social check-in paradigm; lost and found, missing people; job related information, tender information, Information about different services to President or mayor, mGovernment portal, limited drinking water supply related information; agricultural price related information	Canada, Italy, The Republic of Korea, Sweden	Philippines, Brazil, Oman, Mexico, Turkey, Malaysia, Rwanda, Uganda, Sri Lanka
Hazard related services	Fire fighting, flood dangers; emergency alert services / security warnings; earthquake monitoring information, weather and natural disaster	USA, UK, Canada, Denmark	China, Mexico, Turkey, Italy, Hong Kong
Voting services	General election information, results of election, voter registration, finding polling station for voting	UK, France, Estonia	Indonesia, Kenya, Venezuela, Malaysia
Transportation services	Traffic flow, city maps, ferry, bus, metro schedules and services, guide to city services, ticket payment, vehicle detailed system, traffic offence; parking facilities, season parking, parking payments; street incidences; train mobile web services, drivers' m-portal, alerts of delay in public transport; m-parking	Spain, Finland, Singapore, Canada, Estonia, UK, Italy, Australia, Austria, Japan, Sweden, Korea	Turkey, Indonesia, Saudi Arabia, Kenya

Table 1. (*continued*)

Law enforcement	Information on policies, laws/regulations, statistics, URL of the public organization	The Republic of Korea, USA	
Tax services		Spain, Singapore, Ireland, Norway, Korea	China, India, Africa, Japan
Health services	Medical appointment scheduling & cancellation and alert, m-hospital	Spain, Malta, Finland	Africa, Saudi Arabia
Education services	School services, exam results, scholarship decisions, m-library	Italy, Malta, Finland	South Africa, Philippines, Saudi Arabia, Hungary, Africa
Criminal offence services	Reports relating crime, illegal waste deposits, corruption, complaints about govt. agencies' actions, parking offences; police services offences; tract suspect' move, m-police	Germany, the Netherlands, Malta, Korea	Tanzania, Philippines
Other services	Baby care; take-off and landing at airports, airport information; emergency cash transfer; Id card and passport related services; license renewal services; anti pollution	USA, Spain, Canada, Singapore, Finland	Malawi, Kenya, Philippines
mG2G services			
	Fire department mobile inspection services; Traffic and earthquake information system; Disaster management information systems; agriculture services, insecticide control	Ireland, USA	Brazil, Turkey, Bangladesh
	Electoral data process	Spain	
	Information on failure alerts, maintenance status and results	Korea	

Table 1. (*continued*)

mG2B			
	Agribusiness		Brazil, India, Uganda, Ghana
	Business support services	The Republic of Korea	
	Inspection and reporting information	USA	
mG2E			
	Mobile field inspection system	China	China
	m-signature	Spain	

As reflected in table 1, examples from handful countries from both developed and developing countries are documented in the literature which is far less than its actual application and growth. A wide ranging innovative approaches and applications in many developed and developing countries are not studied and captured for further knowledge building and sharing. The absence of contextual knowledge provides an opportunity for researchers to tap into this important area. Application in mG2G, mG2E and mG2B services are also scanty, which is another niche area for further exploration.

3   Method

We performed a systematic approach prescribed by Okoli & Schabram (2010, p.7) [25] to conduct the literature review on mGovernment services adopting studies from a range of IS Journals and conference papers (fig. 2). Data extraction was carried out using a guide-sheet, highlighting criteria to screen out the 'research themes', 'approaches' and 'out of scope' study. Key words used in the search were "mobile government", "mGovernment", "m- government" to search the relevant articles covered a period of 2000 - Present (Sep, 2013). Also, the Boolean characters 'AND/OR' were used in different combination of 'citizen', 'services', 'adoption' with the key words. These keywords were selected because mG2C is the dominantly used services among the four offered levels (refer table 1).

Articles screened, selected were then organized for further analysis. A content analysis was conducted to extract mGovernment research themes based on a conceptual framework (a granular categorization) [30]. Then framework and theoretical part on previous mGovernment research work was examined through the categories of theoretical frame of knowledge adapted from [4]. The analysis under study was used to examine the presence or absence of theories on accumulation of and consistency in knowledge in mGovernment studies.

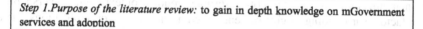

Step 1.Purpose of the literature review: to gain in depth knowledge on mGovernment services and adoption

↓

Step 2. Protocol and training: a guide-sheet was developed and shared highlighting criteria to screen out 'research themes', 'approaches' and 'out of scope' study

↓

Step 3. Searching for the literature: above stated key words with Boolean characters used to search the relevant articles in the journal and conference segments covering a period of 2000 - Present (Sep, 2013). Eliminating duplications, 90 articles were found, in which there were e-government articles as well

↓

Step 4. Practical screen: further screening was conducted on the basis of 'topics' including "mobile government, m-government, mobile government services, m-government services, mGovernment" resulting 48 articles that exclusively dealt with mGovernment services and adoption

↓

Step 5. Quality appraisal: In the refining process after selecting 90 articles, 'out of scope' articles were excluded

↓

Step 6. Data extraction: In the data extraction stage, sole purpose was given to understand why the article is written, which country is included in the analysis, whether 'web-based' or 'non-web based' strengths are reflected in the paper

↓

Step 7. Synthesis of studies: few synthesized tables were shown

↓

Step 8. Writing the review: written in the report.

Fig. 2. Stepwise systematic guideline followed to conduct the literature review

4   Findings

Findings and observations from the analysis of meta data are presented in the following sub-sections.

4.1   Research Themes and Focus

Majority of the studies focused on design and implementation (48%) followed by context-based (21%) studies out of the four themes we considered (table 2). High percentage of design/implementation study is not surprising as m-government is still at its primary stage of innovation and development. While most of these studies did not have a strong theoretical foundation and pure research method, they used some model or schema to address some design issues and describe factors, challenges affecting the design and implementation. Most of the papers describe the general design and implementation issues; however, few papers describe particular issues, such as, design architectural issues for m-police, disable groups. Context theme covers a broad range factors surrounding m-government including m-services or applications related studies. Several contextual challenges and barriers are identified in different studies. [10] identified barriers from the broader organizational, technical, governance and social context. [16] identified factors for m-government management, [12] identified constructs of efficient transaction. Some of these studies tend to overlap with factors affecting design and implementation, e.g. design issues for m-participation [26].

However, researchers found less interested to focus on m-government adoption study. The limited studies includes identification of various determinants of adoption and attempted to extend the existing individual adoption models such as TAM, TRA, TPB, UTAUT , DOI except one mathematical model with wider dimensions by [17] and a case study by [9]. Four studies specifically used required 'theoretical framework' [20,21], [28], [31] to identify the constructs. Two articles [9], [17] identified factors affecting adoption of mGovernment discussing appropriate methodology but without using any theoretical framework. 'Impact' and 'evaluation' studies were combined together, where impact assessment tools described in the study were also included in this category apart from actual assessment. The focus and attention in this area is low, which limits our understanding of m-government potential and broader impact for the government and societies. Only two studies make use of a derived framework, out of which one applied grounded theory. Studies identified performance assessment criteria or developed a model for mGovernment assessment. One study utilized task-technology fit framework to assess the performance.

Table 2. Various themes and focus of mGovernment services and adoption related papers

Themes	Frequency (%)
Design/implementation (D/I) - dealt with the design and implementation of mGovernment (such as mGovernment in agriculture, payments, banking etc.)	23 (48%)
Adoption (A) - dealt aspects of mGovernment adoption, such as its factors, processes, barriers	8 (17%)
Impact and evaluation (IE)- report actual assessment while implementing mGovernment or developing mGovernment service measurement framework; and evaluate the success and performance of mGovernment	7 (14%)
Context (C) - examine mGovernment issues from technical, organization, or social contexts and also include broad mGovernment related issues such as detailing mGovernment services, mGovernment applications, mGovernment management.	10 (21%)

From technological perspective, m-government services can be offered through both 'web-based' and 'non-web based' (SMS) medium [19]. However, most of the mGovernment services make use of a broader spectrum of technologies being available on mobile phones rather relying only on web based e-government services [24]. In order to determine the degree of emphasis of 'web-based' or 'non-web-based' approaches and to understand their comparative use in developed and developing countries, we had to select only those papers (29 in this case) where country names were mentioned. We found that 42% of 'web-based' and 58% of 'non-web' mGovernment services discussion mentioned in the studies (Fig. 3). The degrees of emphasis are classified based on the volume of discussions on 'web-based' or 'non-web based' in the articles. Each article was marked independently on 'web-based' and 'non-web based' services through separate columns identified with 'x+' for high emphasis; 'x' for mid emphasis and 'x-' for low emphasis.

Degree of emphasis	Developing Country (Web) (SMS)		Developed Country (Web) (SMS)		Web-based & Non-web based (SMS)
High emphasis	7%	21%	15%	3%	Web-based (42%)
Medium emphasis	3%	14%	3%	3%	And Non-web based (SMS)
Low emphasis	7%	7%	7%	10%	(58%)

Fig. 3. Degree of emphasis on web-based and non web-based m-government services in developing and developed country

It can be conjectured that m-government adoption in developed countries are happening as part of e-government maturity and expansion of its existing service channels, whereas in developing countries m-government adoption seem to be following a different adoption curve skipping several generation of technology. Many applications in the area of m-government in developing countries emerged out of local need and innovation. For example, the digital sugarcane procurement system, e-Purjee was established in Bangladesh to replace paper-based supply process communications with a SMS based digital method. Comparing traditional paper-based system, e-Purjee allows timely delivery of purchase order to 1500,000 sugarcane growers and also timely delivery of sugarcane to the mills creating win-win situation (also profit for farmers and almost double the production of all the mills in 2010 comparing previous year output) [5].

4.2 Theoretical Frame of Knowledge

Following the categories of theoretical frame of knowledge provided by [4], we examined the research approach of m-government research as per Table 3. There were situations where a paper had more than one elements of the theoretical knowledge framework, in that case only the highest frame of knowledge was recorded.

Table 3. mGovernment research work according to theoretical frame of knowledge - Adapted from [4]

Categories	Frequency (%)
Theory based (theory used either to apply or test)	5 (10%)
Framework based (framework used taking from a body of theoretical work)	7 (15%)
Model based (model presented without referring any deeper frame of knowledge)	4 (8%)
Schema based (schema of techniques are highlighted)	7 (15%)
Concept based (some concept is used such as, micro/macro payment, m-participation)	3 (6%)
Category based (presented list of factors or a set of categories only)	7 (15%)
Non-framework-based (no use of any perceptible framework of knowledge; provides a set of data and ideas)	15 (31%)

Table 3 shows a highest percentage of research works on m-government are non-framework-based, which may be acceptable at this stage being m-government relatively a new and growing area. Only twelve (25%) articles are theory and framework based which indicates that majority of the scholars have attempted to present what is happening in mGovernment rather offering any understanding of why is happening. 39.6% papers (both 'non-framework-based' and 'model based') lack coherence and accumulation of knowledge due to their absence and inadequacy of developing common base for further work.

4.3   Methods Followed

Of the reviewed papers, twenty five articles (58.30%) did not have any specific 'method(s)' or 'methodology' section. Among the rest twenty-three articles, three papers [17], [21,22] embedded the method discussion under heading 'materials and methods', 'empirical section', 'sampling' respectively. Survey method was used in 20.8% of the studies whereas case study was done in 6.2% of the papers. Two papers used both survey and interviewing which we considered under survey method. Moreover, there were technical papers and mathematical modeling papers which have been grouped as 'others' along with a paper used meta-synthesis method.

5   Discussion and Future Directions

The in-depth literature review and meta analysis of existing data provided a good insight on m-government research landscape. It was evident that present research works on mGovernment services and adoption are still scattered and in its preliminary stage. We noticed that much of the research works in m-government are done from the year 2010 onwards, which indicates it is a recent and emerging phenomena.

In order to bring the coherence in knowledge accumulation in m-government arena, future studies should attempt to apply or test proper theoretical framework and preferably not mix 'web-based' and 'non-web based' m-government services, especially in adoption studies. IS adoption theories were not applied or tested at the individual or organization level adoption studies. It is also found that there are lacks of interpretive research in adoption studies, where 75% of the adoption studies applied quantitative research method focusing on answering 'what' questions. Often constructs were used without proper justification of their inclusion, for example Mohamedpour, Faal & Fasanghari (2009). On the other hand, some studies adapted constructs from several IS adoption theories and justifies the adoption but does not empirically test the model, for example Wang et.al., (2011). For the impact and evaluation study, in different contexts, longitudinal research design can be proposed. Action Design Research (ADR) can also be a relevant for this type of evaluation study which carries out iterative process in a target environment intertwining the building of the IT artefact, intervention in the organization and evaluation [27]. Future adoption studies should be conducted both at the individual and firm level using appropriate theories for example, TOE framework by Tornatzky & Fleischer (1990) or UTAUT theory by Venkatesh et.al. (2003) or institutional theory by Scott (1995). At the individual level, the newly derived UTAUT2 theory of Venkatesh, Thong and Xu (2012) may also be relevant in different contexts for mGovernment adoption. In order to find out the 'why' association in different contexts among the human and non-human actors considering the 'social' and the 'technical' as inseparable, Actor-Network-Theory (ANT) by Callon (1991); Latour (1996); Law (1992) can be a good candidate. Moreover, the involvement of multiple stakeholders: different governmental agencies/ department, telecommunications carriers, supporting value chain members and most importantly, the citizens who are the ultimate end users [1] may be included in future studies to gather rich insight from multiple perspectives.

6   Conclusions and Limitations

mGovernment will continue to grow both in developed and developing countries through 'web-based' and 'non-web-based' services especially in the mG2C level. But only a handful of rigorous research have addressed some of the challenges and problems surrounding m-government services and its adoption. Information System researchers are requested to engage in more empirical and theory building research in this area in order to make valuable contribution. A very noteworthy issue is to separate the 'web-based' or 'non-web based' mGovernment services which will provide further scope for detail analysis and understanding of adoption trajectories. The review excludes papers written in other languages and disciplines such as, public administration.

References

1. Aloudat, A., Michael, K.: Toward the regulation of ubiquitous mobile government: a case study on location-based emergency services in Australia. Electronic Commerce Research 11(1) (2011)
2. Chen, Y.N., Chen, H.M., Huang, W., Ching, R.K.H.: E-government strategies in developed and developing countries: an implementation framework and case study. Journal of Global Information Management 14(1), 23–46 (2006)
3. Georgiadis, C.K., Stiakakis, E.: Extending an e-Government Service measurement framework to m-government services. In: Ninth International Conference on Mobile Business and 2010 Ninth Global Mobility Roundtable, Athens, June 13-15, pp. 432–439 (2010)
4. Heeks, R., Bailur, S.: Analyzing e-government research: perspectives, philosophies, theories, methods, and practice. Government Information Quarterly 24(2), 243–265 (2007)
5. Imran, A., Gregor, S., Turner, T.: eGovernment Management for Developing Countries. Published by National Centre for Information Systems Research (NCISR), ANU College of Business and Economics, The Australian National University, Canberra, ACT 2000, Australia (2013)
6. ITU: Mobile cellular subscriptions report (2012), http://www.itu.int/en/ITU-D/Statistics/Pages/stat/default.aspx
7. ITU: ICT facts and figures (2013), http://www.itu.int/en/ITU-D/Statistics/Documents/facts/ICTFactsFigures2013.pdf
8. ITU, OECD: M-Government: Mobile technologies for Responsive Governments and Connected Societies (2011)
9. Khamasey, A., Lawrence, E.: Mobile Government in actions at local councils: A case study. Digital Society (2010)
10. Kiki, T.E.: mGovernment: A reality check. In: Sixth International Conference on the Management of Mobile Business, July 9-11 (2007)
11. Kiki, T.E., Lawrence, E.: Government as a mobile enterprise: Real-time, ubiquitous government. In: Proceedings of the Third International Conference on Information Technology: New Generations (ITNG), Las Vegas, Nevada, April 10-12, pp. 320–327 (2006)
12. Kiki, T.E., Lawrence, E.: Mobile user needs: Efficient transactions. In: Fifth International Conference on Information Technology: New Generation, Las Vegas, April 7-9 (2008)
13. Kim, Y., Yoon, J., Park, S., Han, J.: Architecture for implementing the mobile government services in Korea. In: Wang, S., et al. (eds.) ER Workshops 2004. LNCS, vol. 3289, pp. 601–612. Springer, Heidelberg (2004)
14. Kushchu, I., Kuscu, H.M.: From E-government to M-government: Facing the inevitable. In: The Proceeding of European Conference on E-Government (ECEG), Trinity College, Dublin, Ireland (2003)
15. Lee, S.M., Tan, X., Trimi, S.: M-government, from rhetoric to reality: Learning from leading countries. Electronic Government 3(2) (2006)
16. Li, X.J., Guan, Z.L., Fan, L.: Analysis of mobile Government's influence on government managements. In: International Conference on Management and Services Science, pp. 1–4, Wuhan (2009)
17. Madden, G., Bohlin, E., Oniki, H., Tran, T.: Potential demand for m-government services in Japan. Applied Economics Letters 20 (2013)
18. Mengistu, D., Zo, H., Rho, J.J.: M-Government: Opportunities and challenges to deliver mobile government services in developing countries. In: Fourth International Conference on Computer Sciences and Convergence Information Technology, pp. 1445–1450. Seoul (2009)

19. Misra, D.C.: E-government: The New Frontier in Governance, New Delhi (2010),
    `http://mgovworld.org/libra/mgovernance/papers`
20. Mohamedpour, M., Faal, Z.M., Fasanghari, M.: A proposed framework for effective mobile services acceptance factors. In: Sohn, S., et al. (eds.) 4th International Conference on Computer Sciences and Convergence Information Technology, Seoul, Korea, pp. 250–255 (2009)
21. Nan, Z., Xunhua, G., Guoqing, C., Gang, S.: A MCT acceptance model from the cultural perspective and its empirical test in the mobile municipal administrative approach. In: Hu, X., Scornavacca, E., Hu, Q. (eds.) 8th International Conference on Mobile Business, Dalian, China, pp. 319–323 (2009)
22. Nkosi, M., Mekuria, F.: Mobile government for improved public service provision in South Africa. In: IST-Africa 2010 Conference Proceedings, Durban, South Africa, May 19-21 (2010)
23. Ntaliani, M., Costopoulou, C., Karetsos, S.: Mobile government: A challenge for agriculture. Government Information Quarterly 25(4), 699–716 (2008)
24. Oghuma, A.P., Park, M.C., Rho, J.J.: Adoption of mGovernment service initiative in developing countries: A citizen-centric public service delivery perspective. In: 19th ITS Biennial Conference, Bangkok, Thailand, November 18-22, pp. 1–27 (2012)
25. Okoli, C., Schabram, K.: A guide to conducting a systematic literature review of Information System Research (2010),
    `http://papers.ssrn.com/sol3/papers.cfm?abstract_id=1954824`
26. Reuver, M., Stein, S., Hampe, F., Bouwman, H.: Towards a service platform and business model for mobile participation. In: Ninth International Conference on Mobile Business and Ninth Global Military Roundtable, Athens, Greece, pp. 305–311 (2010)
27. Sein, M.K., Henfridsson, O., Purao, S., Rossi, M., Lindgren, R.: Action design research. MIS Quarterly 35(1), 37–56 (2011)
28. Shareef, M.A., Kumar, V., Kumar, U., Dwivedi, Y.K.: e-Government adoption model (GAM): Differing service maturity levels. Government Information Quarterly 28(1) (2011)
29. Waema, T.M., Musyoka, J.M.: Shifting shores: investing now the shift from electronic to mobile government interacts with the development practice in Kenya. In: Proceedings of the 3rd International Conference on Theory and Practice of Electronic Governance, pp. 191–197. ACM, NY (2009)
30. Wahid, F.: Themes of research on eGovernment in developing countries: Current map and future roadmap. In: Sprague Jr., R.H. (ed.) 46th Hawaii International Conference on System Sciences, HICSS, Wailea, HI, USA, January 7-10 (2013)
31. Wang, C., Lu, Z., Feng, Y., Fang, R.: M-government use: Technology, context, and environment determinants. In: International Conference on Information Technology, Computer Engineering and Management Sciences, Nanjing, Jiangsu, China, vol. 3 (2011)
32. Wu, H., Ozok, A.A., Gurses, A.P., Wei, J.: User aspects of electronic and mobile government: Results from a review of current research. Electronic Government: An International Journal 6(3), 233–251 (2009)

Human Interaction in the Regulatory of Telecommunications Infrastructure Deployment in South Africa

Sharol Sibongile Mkhomazi[1] and Tiko Iyamu[2]

[1] Tshwane University of Technology,
Department of Office Management and Technology, Pretoria, South Africa
mkhomaziss@tut.ac.za
[2] Polytechnic of Namibia, Department of Business Computing, Windhoek, Namibia
connectvilla@gmail.com

Abstract. Telecommunications is increasingly vital to the society at large, and has become essential to business, academic, as well as social activities. Due to the necessity to have access to telecommunications, the deployment requires regulations and policy. Otherwise, the deployment of the infrastructures would contribute to environment, and human complexities rather than ease of use.

However, the formulation of telecommunication infrastructure deployment regulation and policy involve agents such as people and processes. The roles of the agents are critical, and are not as easy as it meant to belief. This could be attributed to different factors, as they produce and reproduce themselves overtime.

This paper presents the result of a study which focused on understanding how non-technical factors enable and constrain the development and implementation of telecommunications infrastructure sharing regulations. In the study, the interactions that take place amongst human and non-human agents were investigated. The study employed the duality of structure, of Structuration Theory as lens to understand the effectiveness of interactions in the formulation of regulations, and how policy is used to facilitate the deployment of telecommunications infrastructure in the South African environment.

Keywords: Regulatory Authority, Telecommunications, Infrastructure sharing, Structuration Theory, Human Interaction.

1   Introduction

Globally, telecommunications infrastructures (broadband) are deployed in urban and rural areas and these infrastructures can be shared. Infrastructure sharing is a concept that advocates on negotiated terms the sharing of network resources within geographical locations by two or more telecommunications network service providers [1]. Sharing telecommunications infrastructure limits duplication and, enhances investment, product innovation and improved customer services [2], and reduces the

B. Bergvall-Kåreborn and P.A. Nielsen (Eds.): TDIT 2014, IFIP AICT 429, pp. 324–333, 2014.
© IFIP International Federation for Information Processing 2014

infrastructure deployment costs for network service providers. It is further supported by [1] that building shared networks will lower the operators' capital investment and increase infrastructure roll-out speed. However, the amount that an operator can save depends upon the depth of sharing arrangements [2].

The deployment and performance of shared telecommunications infrastructure (such as broadband) is significantly influenced by different national regulatory institutions, political processes and regulations [3]. These network infrastructures need to be managed and maintained with sound regulatory systems. In one of its strategic documents of [4] stated that the rapid rate, at which broadband technologies are deployed, requires regulations and policies for its guidance. INTEL's articulation and proposal for regulations and policies are mainly to avoid irregularities in the deployment, as well as to improve the technologies' efficiency and effectiveness.

Regulation plays an important role in the telecommunication industry. Regulatory structures represent key factors for innovative processes in the infrastructure sectors as they guide the direction of development and deployment of technology infrastructure [5]. These include price regulation, rules on network accessibility and environmental regulations. Therefore its sustainability relies on the legislation and regulatory structures of the country [6]. With distributed infrastructure and innovative regulations, telecommunication infrastructures such as broadband can provide high-end services to the business sector, as well a range of low-cost, high-quality services to all [7].

This article presents the use of duality of structure from the perspective of Structuration Theory to understand the effectiveness of regulatory in facilitating the deployment of shared telecommunications infrastructure. The focus is to understand how non-technical factors enable and constrain the development and implementation of telecommunications infrastructure sharing regulations.

2   Research Approach

To understand the factors that influence the formulation of regulations and policies which guided the telecommunications infrastructure deployment, a real-world situation was solicited through the case study and qualitative methods. [8] described the case study as method for eliciting natural setting. Qualitative research is a good inquiry process of understanding a social context [9]. In this vain, [10] described the method as a process which allows experience or perceptions to be shared. Based on the objectives of the research which was to understanding how non-technical factors enable and constrain the development and implementation of telecommunications infrastructure sharing regulations, probing of response was essential. The qualitative method allows for follow-up such was "why", "how", and "what" [11].

Capricon Regulatory Authority (CRA) was selected for the study. CRA is the main regulatory body in the South Africa. The organisation was instituted under the South African act of 1994. A total of four employees were interviewed within the organisation. The interviewees included two senior managers and two junior staff members. Owing to the current processes of formulating and amendment of broadband and infrastructure sharing regulation, the researcher was limited to only a few interviewees. This also contributed to the adoption of interviews as the single source of data collection.

The interviews approach was used in the data collection [12]. [13] described the interviews approach as a data collection method that produces first-on-hand accounts of experience, opinion, and perception from the respondents. The interviews were carried out by closely following the interview guide as follows:

i.   the purpose of the study was explained to each participant before the interview started;
ii.   the interviewees were informed that their confidentiality and anonymity were assured;
iii. the interviewees' rights for participating in the study were explained to each of them;
iv.   contact details were given to the participants for any queries regarding their rights.

The interview guidelines were to ensure consistency and uniformity in the data collection. This was followed by presenting all participants with the same demographic interview questions regarding the individual's position in the organisation and occupation. The use of an interview guide ensured that there was some structure and consistency to the interviews, even though the interviews were treated as conversations during which the interviewer elicited detailed information and comments from the respondents.

Data was analysed using Structuration Theory's (ST) duality of structure as a lens to understand how and why interactions amongst actors were carried out in the manner that they did, in attempt to develop and implement telecommunication infrastructures sharing regulations. ST is a theory which constitutes agents and structure within a social phenomenon. The social structure is drawn upon by agents, to consciously or unconsciously produce and reproduce their actions [14]. [15] argued that ST allows us to examine how people (agents) enact structures which shape their emergent and situated use of technology as they interact with it in their ongoing practices. For this study ST provided the steps that needed to be followed in terms of understanding why things happen the way they do within the development and implementation of telecommunications infrastructure sharing regulations. This was instrumental for following the necessary and sequence of steps to understand why certain things are considered significant; how the available facilities are used to enable and constrain processes and activities during regulatory development and implementation.

3   Telecommunication Infrastructure Deployment Regulation

The deployment of telecommunications' infrastructures includes technologies that enable high speed transfer of multi-media and high bandwidth information [16]. The deployment of telecommunications' infrastructures is socio-technical in nature [5]. This is primarily because of the technical and non-technical such as people and process components that are in involved in the deployment. Many countries, including South Africa ensure that legal requirements are met as part of the processes for telecommunication's regulatory matter [7].

Regulation is critical role on how and where telecommunications infrastructure are deployed and shared. Apart from the geographical location, regulatory structures have a major impact not only on the functioning and performance of national telecommunications but also on the comparative global performance of telecommunications [17]. [18] argued that the role of regulations is important in investment decision making of telecommunication companies as it helps to determine or shape the direction of their return on investment (ROI).

In South Africa regulatory and policy activities in telecommunication markets are strictly regulated by CRA. It is the sole telecommunications regulator in the country maintaining a competitive and socially responsive communications industry. South Africa derives its legislative mandate from the country's Telecommunications Act of 1996, Competition Act of 1998, the Broadcasting Act of 1999, the CRA Act of 2000 and the Electronic Communications Act of 2005 (ECA) [7]. The CRA develops regulations and policies, issues licenses to telecommunications companies, and also manages the frequency spectrum [19].

Telecommunication infrastructures are increasingly unconditional for information societies across the world. Telecommunication infrastructure facilitates, support and enable transparent system, wider dissemination of information, as well as guarantees freedom of speech for technology users [20]. Therefore the effectiveness of regulatory policies is critical in facilitating infrastructure deployment and sharing arrangements among the telecommunication companies, and the communities. The expansion of telecommunication infrastructure through sharing of infrastructure is a strategic process that necessitates co-operation among competitors, and it is subject to explicit involvement by telecommunication regulatory authorities to enforce implementation.

4   Structuration View of Telecommunication Regulatory Development

The formulation of regulations for telecommunications infrastructure was carried out within rules and regulations of the country. The regulations facilitate the telecommunications operations in terms of infrastructure deployment. The resources required in the formulation and implementation of telecommunications regulations included technology and people. There were also processes involved.

The organisation, CRA employed both internal and external rules and regulations when formulating the governance and guidance for telecommunication's activities. The internal rules and regulations (standards and procedures) were based on the organisation's objectives and strategy. The external rules and regulations were mainly from the stakeholders including the National Government and Municipal authorities of the country. This made the formulators of the regulations and policies to be powerful.

- **Duality of Structure: Signification and Communication**

The CRA formulation of regulations for telecommunications infrastructure was carried out within rules and regulations of the country. One of the criticalities for the development and implementation of regulations and policies was to guide against telecommunication service providers deploying infrastructures in locations as they so wish. The regulations and policies were considered to be of important to the service providers as it provides an umpiring status amongst them. This controlled competitiveness in the deployment of their infrastructures, particularly in areas considered to be strategic. However, there seemed to be a gap in CRA's infrastructure deployment regulations. The implications of the gap in the regulations and policies resulted in inappropriate deployment of telecommunications infrastructure in the different locations across the country. One of the employees of CRA briefly explained that *"the incumbents are using the limitation of regulations to their defence for not deploying telecommunications infrastructure appropriately"*.

There are also external rules and processes such as municipality bylaws that were regarded as critical to the deployment of telecommunications infrastructure. However the challenge is that these rules are not formulated in conjunction with the organisation (CRA), and has a major impact on how telecommunications infrastructure could be deployed in the country. This could be attributed to lack of information sharing or different interpretations of shared information. One of the managers, explained that *"There are different municipal bylaws guiding the deployment of infrastructure, and that the inconsistencies in municipalities' bylaws created a complicated process for operators deploying telecommunications infrastructure in different locations"*.

This lack of communication among agents involved in the development and implementation if telecommunication regulatory was considered to be an integral part of regulatory development and implementation plans. The stakeholders who were involved in formulating telecommunications regulations and policies were expected at all times, to understand the importance of regulating the telecommunications industry. The structures and channels that were required were also understood by the stakeholders. However, the structures amongst other factors gave some individuals and groups certain power, and source of domination.

- **Duality of Structure: Domination and Power**

As already established, the formulation of regulations and policies for the deployment of telecommunications infrastructures in the country was the responsibility of the CRA by virtue of the mandate bestowed upon them by the Ministry of Communications, as allowed by the constitution of the country. The CRA therefore formulated regulations to facilitate and manage the deployment of shared telecommunications infrastructures.

The organisation had policy that guided how telecommunications infrastructure could be shared among the telecommunications companies. The policy was named or tagged *"Facility Leasing"*. The *Facility Leasing* regulations was formulated to help facilitate efficient and appropriate infrastructure deployment. One of the employees explained that: *"the facility leasing regulation defines the essential facilities that network operators (telecommunications companies) could use or apply in the deployment of their telecommunications infrastructure"*. However, there seem to be some challenges in the finalisation of the *Facility Leasing* regulations. As a result, the telecommunications companies have not been able to apply the regulation in some areas such as sharing of the spectrum technology. The challenges include technical know-how to properly define and articulate technologies terms of reference for the telecommunications companies. One of the employees expressed himself as follows: *"there are many challenges with the Facility Leasing regulation, as a result, it is not executable. This is because it was not properly developed"*. The challenge was attributed to lack of availability of sufficient resources such as skilled people. The lack of available skilled personnel was attributed to insufficient funds. Two of the interviewees explained that *"the organisation do not receive enough funds which would enable them to recruit qualified skilled personnel. This therefore impacted the quality of regulations and policies that we formulate"*.

Unfortunately the organisation depended on the Government for funding in order to carry out their mandates. The implication of such dependent led to control and political manipulation of the organisation's activities. Through this type of funding model, the government asserted its power and dominance over CRA and the telecommunications companies in the country. At the time of this study, this was the norm and was legitimised and accepted by the stakeholders such as the telecommunications companies, the communities and CRA.

- **Duality of Structure: Legitimation and Sanctions**

As already established above, CRA provided governance, and were the custodian of all regulatory development and implementation in the telecommunication industry. However, legitimation and approval of CRA activities which were driven through three-way dimensional approach: the CRA, Department of Communications, and the Minister of Communications had an impact on the efficiency of regulatory and policy by CRA. One of the managers tried to explain the process and rational for the approach as follows: *"the Department of Communication was the bridge between the CRA and the Minister. That the communication between CRA and the Minister has to go through the Department of Communication, this was based on the 1994 government on which the CRA was established"*.

The formulation and implementation of regulations and policies were also guided by external and internal rules and interests. The bylaws were fundamental in that each of the geographical location across the country had its unique requirements. One of the interviewees pointed out: *"It was a very complicated process for the telecommunications operators to deploy infrastructure in different locations, and that the challenge was due to lack of coordination in addressing the different bylaws set by municipalities"*. Despite the challenges, the CRA, government and the communities accepted the development and implementation of the regulations that facilitated the telecommunications' activities in the deployment of infrastructures in the country.

5   Factors Influencing Telecommunication Regulations and Policies

From the analysis presented above, some factors were found to influence the formulation of regulations and policing which guided the telecommunications infrastructure deployment as depicted in Figure 2, and discussed below.

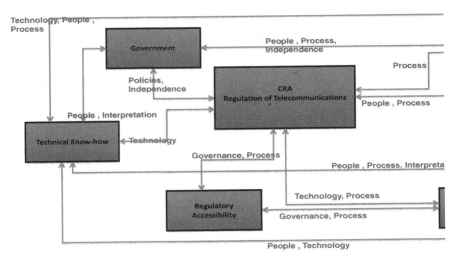

Fig. 1. Components of telecommunication regulatory

- ## Government

The interest and role of the government was defined around power to control the activities of the telecommunication through the establishment of CRA. By so doing, the government created obligatory passage point for CRA, meaning the organisation could not act based on its own assertion. This had negative impact on the operations of the organisation. For example, their privilege to access funds for its operations was not based on their scope of activities, but on the discretion of the Minister of Communication, which sometimes created uncertainty. However, there were some positive implications of government interference in CRA activities. It gave the organisation the political strength and muscle to manage and get the telecommunication to adhere to its regulations and policies. The government interference was a manifestation of politics which emanated from interactions amongst the agents of the stakeholders.

- ## Organisational Politics

The organisational politics as experienced by CRA was influenced by many different factors, such as power to control and signification of presence, from both internal and external sources. The politics were driven by the government interests in the activities of CRA. This in-turn impacts the types and quality of service that the communities get from the telecommunication companies overtime and space of occurrence.

Also, the manifestation of politics ignited the decision to sometime withheld fund, which deprived the CRA from recruiting qualified personnel, which sometimes derailed activities, as revealed in the analysis. Organisational politics and organisational structure influence, and depend on each other to exist and make a difference. As such, it is difficult, or lack of sustenance to address one without the other.

- **Organisational Structure**

The organisational structure of CRA was relied upon in the distribution and allocation of tasks when it came to formulation of regulations and policies for the deployment of telecommunication infrastructures. On another hand, the structure of the organisation shaped the both interaction and relationship between CRA and the government, as well as the telecommunication companies.

Somehow, the structure of the organisation was not clear and transparent, at least to external stakeholders. The organisational structure of CRA was interpreted by some stakeholders as complicated, and as well undermined by some influencing factors or agent such as the government. This was attributed to ineffectiveness in CRA performance of its activities because the Minister of Communication played a dominant role in the organisation's recruitment process. The Minister appointment of CRA's Council member made it difficult for the organisation to make decisions that were contrary to Government's interest. Also, the organisational structure influenced and shaped the technical know-how in the formulation of regulations and policies in the deployment of telecommunications' infrastructures in the country.

- **Technical Know-How**

To implement sufficient and efficient regulations it was crucial to have skilled and competent employees within the organisational structure. The organisation lacked sufficient skilled people to carry out its strategic objective. Although the people formulate regulation, they cannot implement it. There was a need for skilled people with the appropriate technical know-how as it is a lack of such knowledge that causes problems with regulations such as spectrum sharing.

Another factor contributed to lack of technical know-how was the Government's intervention and the organisation dependence on government for funding. These have led to CRA not being able to employ the appropriate skilled persons to fulfil the role of regulating and implementing telecommunications regulations and policies.

- **Communication**

The effect of the organisational politics shaped and influenced how information was communicated, and interpreted by employees as well as the stakeholders. Some employees including stakeholders shared and interpreted information in accordance to their personal interests. In the same vain, others understood their roles and responsibilities based on their interest. Unfortunately, the information and their interpretations were followed in executing their daily activities.

Another critical aspect was that the communication within the organisation took a different shape from the communication which happened externally, between the CRA, and the government, as well as the telecommunications companies. Due to factors such as organisational politics, and organisational structure, communication channels were not effective, messages did not reach audiences accurately. This has an impact on the deployment of shared telecommunications infrastructure in the country.

- **Regulatory Accessibilities**

The communication channels had an impact on how information was shared in the organisation. Based on our empirical evidences, it is fair to say that information sharing, and access to processes and procedures were limited in CRA. This had impact on the end-product, regulations and policies procedures which resulted in some regulation such as Facility Leasing not being easy to implement by telecommunications organisations.

6   Conclusion

The study has empirically proven and revealed that the role played by non-technical factors such as people, processes and politics are critical to the development of telecommunication regulations and policies. The factors have a major impact on the effectiveness and efficiency in regulatory development and implementation. The study would therefore be important to telecommunications managers, the regulatory authority, government, as well the communities at large to gain better understanding of the impact and implications of the actions of non-technical factors.

The use of duality of structure from the perspective of Structuration Theory (ST) was useful in understanding how events and activities were produced and reproduced overtime and space in the formulation of regulations policies for the deployment of telecommunication infrastructures in the country. Within the frame of the duality of structure, it was possible to follow the interactions which took place amongst the agents, and understand how significant was associated to facilities, and how events transformed themselves and become norm. This would be difficult or impossible to achieve without ST.

References

1. Berkers, F., Hendrix, G., Chatzicharistou, I., De Haas, T., Hamera, D.: To Share Or Not To Share? Business aspects of network sharing for Mobile Network Operators. In: ICIN, BMMP Workshop, Berlin (2010)
2. Chanab, L., El-Darwich, B., Hasbani, G., Mourad, M.: Telecom Infrastructure sharing: Regulatory Enablers and Economic Benefits (2007),
   http://www.boozallen.com/media/file/Telecom_In
3. Naidoo, R., Kaplan, D., Fransman, M.: The South African Telecoms Innovations Systems and teh Diffusion of Broadband (2005),
   http://radian.co.za/docs/BROADBAND_paper_final.pdf
4. INTEL.: Realising the benefits of Broadband. White Paper (2009),
   http://www.intel.com/content/dam/www/publications
5. Markard, J.: Characteristics of infrastructure sectors and implications for innovation processes. Discussion paper for the Workshop on Environmental Innovation in Infrastructure Sectors (2009)
6. Roman, E.S.: Bringing broadband access to rural areas: A step-by-step approach for regulators, policy makers and universal access program administrators. Paper presented at the Nineth Global Symposium for Regulators, Beirut, Lebanon (2009)

7. Gillwald, A.: Case Study: Broadband the case of South Africa. Paper presented at the ITU Regulatory Implications of Broadband Workshop (2001), http://www.itu.int/osg/spu/ni/broadband/workshop/southafricafinal.pdf
8. Yin, R.K.: Case study research: Design and methods, 4th edn., California (2009)
9. Cresswell, J.W.: Research designs: Qualitative, quantitative and mixed methods approaches, 2nd edn. Sage Publications, Thousand Oaks (2003)
10. De Vos, A.S., Strydom, H., Fouche, C.B., Delport, C.S.L.: Research at Grass Roots: For the social sciences and human service professions. Pretoria, Van Schaik (2002)
11. Saunders, M., Lewis, P., Thornhill, A.: Research Methods for Business Students, 4th edn. Prentice Hall, Harlow (2007)
12. Babbie, E.: The basic of social research, 3rd edn. Thomson, Canada (2005)
13. Polkinghorne, D.E.: Language and meaning: Data collection in Qualitative research. Counselling Psychology Journal 52(2), 137–145 (2005)
14. Giddens, A.: The Constitution of society: Outline of the theory of Structuration. University of California Press, Berkely (1984)
15. Orlikowski, W.J.: Using technology and constituting structures: A practice lens for studying technology in organisations. Organisational Science 11(4), 404–428 (2000)
16. Papacharissi, Z., Zaks, A.: Is Broadband the future? An analysis of broadband technology potential and diffusion. Telecommunications Policy 30, 64–75 (2006)
17. Fransman, M.: Global broadband battles: Why the US and Europe lag while Asia leads. Standford University Press, Standford (2006)
18. Sutherland, D., Aranjo, S., Egert, B., Kozluk, T.: Infrastructure Investment: Links to growth and the role of public Policies. OECD Economic department Working Papers, No 686. OECD Publishing (2009)
19. Tweheyo, A.: Spectrum Management Policy framework for mobile communication: A case study of Uganda (2009), http://dspace.mak.ac.ug/bitstream/123456789/600/3/twehenyo=asaph-cit-pgd-report.pdf
20. Chinn, M.D., Fairlie, R.W.: The Determinants of the Global Digital Divide: A cross-country analysis of computer and Internet penetration. Institute University of Wisconsin, Madison (2004)

A Theoretical Framework for Examining IT Governance in Living Laboratory Ecosystems

Trevor Clohessy, Lorraine Morgan, and Thomas Acton

Business Information Systems, Whitaker Institute,
National University of Ireland Galway, Ireland & Lero -
The Irish Software Engineering Research Centre, Ireland
{t.clohessy2,l.morgan,thomas.acton}@nuigalway.ie

Abstract. In recent years Living Labs, which embody an open innovation milieu, have gained currency as representing a salient catalyst for Smart City research and development. However, the current body of Living Lab research, in conjunction with the fragmented isolated nature of existing Living Labs dispersed across the European Union (EU), indicate that a lack of common standardised IT governance procedures are currently being operationalised. While cross border pan European Living Lab initiatives are emerging to rectify this issue, further research is warranted to better understand the role of IT governance in Living Labs and identify how varying IT governance mechanisms impact the effectiveness of open innovation processes. Thus, this paper begins a theory building process for examining IT governance in living labs. The paper concludes by presenting a conceptual framework for future testing.

Keywords: Smart City, Living Laboratory, Open Innovation, IT Governance.

1   Introduction

A "smart city", also known in the guises of intelligent city, information city, digital city, e-city and virtual city, has been identified as being an exemplary example of a response to address the current and future complex challenges of increasing resource efficiency, reducing emissions, sustainable health care services for ageing populations, empowering youth and integrating minorities [1, 2]. Kanter and Litow [3] profess their vision for future smart cities in which world leaders combine technological capabilities and social innovation to enable the development of a smarter, sentient even, world comprising smarter communities that sustain the eudaemonia of all citizens. Cities however "can only be smart if there are intelligence functions that are able to integrate and synthesise data to some purpose, ways of improving the efficiency, equity, sustainability and quality of life in cities"[4]. Batty, et al. [4] propose a typology which delineates the typical functions inherent in a smart city comprising smart economy (competitiveness), smart people (social and human capital), smart governance (participation), smart mobility (transport and information, communication and technology), smart environment (natural resources) and smart living (quality of life).

B. Bergvall-Kåreborn and P.A. Nielsen (Eds.): TDIT 2014, IFIP AICT 429, pp. 334–344, 2014.

The requirement for participatory government, a concept which refers to the empowerment of cities citizens, a form of "democratic innovation", first popularised by Von Hippel [5], denotes the increasing ability of enterprises and consumers, utilising software products and services, to innovate for themselves. Nam and Pardo [6] affirm that "as urban planning is based on governance with multiple stakeholders is pivotal to smart growth, smart city initiatives necessitate governance for their success". The use of emerging nascent IT computing can enable the "development of smart governance infrastructures which provide transparency of public efforts, promotes cultural flourishing and can increase accountability [7].

The concept of a Living Laboratory (Living Lab) has emerged as an exemplar of an integrated open innovation user-driven ecosystem approach in the advancement of smart city research, enabling the foundation for the establishment of large, open and federated experimental facilities, which are required prior to the deployment and operationalisation of real-life smart urban infrastructure and services [1, 8, 9]. Living Labs require new forms of IT governance which reflect the characteristics of emerging IT solutions and open source ecosystems that "favour wide knowledge sharing and communication, networking and partnering" [10]. Currently, there is a paucity of research that examines governance mechanisms in living labs and their impact on open innovation effectiveness. Thus, we respond to this research gap by theorising the role of IT governance in Living Lab ecosystems.

The remainder of the paper is structured as follows. The next section builds the theoretical background for our analysis. The subsequent section delineates the resulting theoretical model of relationships and constructs underlying this study. The final section presents concluding remarks.

2   Theoretical Background

2.1   The Open Innovation Process

It has been argued that organisations that actively engage in an open innovation process may be rewarded with valuable strategic innovations [11]. Chesbrough [12] opines that the design and subsequent management of end user open innovation driven communities will play a pivotal role in the future of open innovation. An organisation's capability to mould strategic innovations is enabled by utilising technology created by others, or by allowing others to use their technology [13]. Thus, open innovation may be defined as a process of "systematically relying on a firm's dynamic capabilities of internally and externally carrying out the major technology management tasks, i.e., technology acquisition and technology exploitation, along the innovation process" [14]. According to van de Vrande et al., [15] as open innovation is a consequence of managerial practices that encompass integrative innovation management activities such as business strategy, collaborative agreements and innovation partners, further research is required into the open innovation domain with regard to external technology acquisition and cooperation amongst stakeholders. Feller et al., [44] argue that "dramatic reductions in innovation cycles and increasing globalisation will continue to force organisations to explore more avenues for leveraging external entities to enhance their ability to innovate." To that end, we explore the concept of a Living Lab as an avenue for leveraging open innovation capabilities.

2.2   The Living Lab Approach

A Living Laboratory is defined as "a user-centred open innovation ecosystem integrating concurrent research and innovation processes" [16] within public-private-civic partnerships where IT "innovations are created and validated in collaborative multi-contextual empirical real-world environments"[10]. It is this multi-contextual dimension which bestows the Living Lab concept a distinct advantage over traditional user-centric methodologies [17]. The European Network of Living Labs (ENoLL) is the international federation of benchmarked Living Labs in Europe and worldwide and currently provisions strategic guidance to over 300 Living Labs. Living Labs, which embody open business models of collaboration, represent a fundamental methodology for the manner in which open innovation user-driven ecosystems should be organised [1].

The Living Lab concept is similar in its approach to other open methodologies such as open innovation [18], communities of creation [19], democratic user - driven innovation [5], crowdsourcing [20] and also contains characteristics inherent in user centric approaches such as participatory design and socio-technical design [21]. In recent years, Living Labs have "proved to be an effective means to close the gap between innovative research and development (R&D) in the smart city arena and market take-up, and make the innovation process more effective" [9]. They facilitate the engagement of users to tackle specific salient R&D issues which are relevant to the development of smart cities such as multi-stakeholder participation, organisational processes and structures, behavioral change and innovation, IT governance, business modelling change and impact assessment and cultural specificities [9].

3   Building the Theoretical Framework

In order to address our research questions, we engage in a process of theory building as proposed by Dubin [22], Whetten [23] and Reynolds [24] whereby we analyse the extant research and delineate constructs and relationships between them in the form of theoretical propositions.

3.1   Delineating IT Governance

According to Brown and Grant [25] the concept of IT governance has its origins as early as the 1960s where researchers attempted to address a number of fundamental concepts which directly mirror modern day definitions of IT governance. Weill [26] proclaim that "effective IT governance encourages and leverages the ingenuity of all enterprise personnel in using IT, while ensuring compliance with the enterprise's overall vision and principle...good IT governance can achieve a management paradox: simultaneously empowering and controlling". Additionally, effective IT governance has been identified as being a critical issue for preventing financial, operational and strategic impairment [27]. However, IT governance has been described as being a "ephemeral and 'messy' phenomenon, emerging in ever-new forms with increasing complexity" [28]. This author utilises an ancient Indian fable, 'the blind men and the elephant', to highlight how the complexity of IT governance systems in conjunction with the blinkered focused strategic objectives of principal stakeholders can impede effective governance of IT. It is now widely recognised that "getting IT right" does not stem merely from the technology, but stems principally from effective (distributed) IT governance [28]. According to De Haes and Van Grembergen [29] three levels of IT governance exist: strategic level (board of directors), management level (executive management) and operational level (IT and business management). The authors argue that whilst some IT governance practices can be applied solely on one specific level, other practices can be applied at multiple levels. In terms of concreting an IT governance definition, sufficient consensus has not been reached, mainly due to the divergence in IT governance research over the last decade on an accepted definition [30]. However, for the purpose of the study, we have selected a definition which appropriately embodies the concept of a Living Lab, an ecosystem which encapsulates a multitude of stakeholders whose decisions on strategic IT are articulated, where IT governance is defined as "the distribution of IT decision-making rights and responsibilities among stakeholders...the procedures and mechanisms for making and monitoring strategic decisions regarding IT" [28].

3.2   Living Lab IT Governance

According to Ballon, et al. [9] existing European based Living Lab initiatives are largely isolated and fragmented, mainly as a consequence of the operationalisation of varying IT governance processes within Living Lab environments which is compounded by language and regional barriers. These deficiencies are culminating in the failure of Living Labs, not only to effectively promote and share innovation across European public sectors, but also failing to address the ramifications that these siloed IT governance procedures may have on the effectiveness of open innovation processes and on the development of future smart city IT governance policies. Peterson [28] argues that "emerging paradigms for IT governance, are based on collaboration, not control, where the need for distinct competencies is recognized, developed, and shared adaptively across functional, organizational, cultural and geographic boundaries". The emergence of open, pan European platform initiatives such as the European Platform for Intelligent Cities (EPIC) are paving the way for smarter cities to exchange practical reference models that may be operationalized in real life contexts. Nonetheless, further research is warranted to identify how suitable IT governance mechanisms facilitate effective open innovation activities in Living Lab ecosystems. It is envisaged that Living Lab ecosystems with successful governance will have proactively designed a cogent combination of governance mechanisms (e.g., IT organisational structures, committees, monitoring procedures, active stakeholder relationship management, aligned incentives and so on) that stimulate behaviours, which are in keeping with the ecosystem's mission, strategy, culture, norms and values [26]. The process of determining the correct IT governance architecture is a "complex endeavour and it should be recognised that what strategically works for one organisation does not necessarily work for another, even if they work in the same industry sector" [29].

3.3   IT Governance Capabilities

IT governance capabilities have been defined as the "managerial ability to direct and coordinate the multifaceted activities associated with the planning, organisation and control of IT" [28]. According to the collective works of Peterson (2000, 2004), Weill and Woodham (2002), and Van Grembergen, De Haes and Guldentops (2005), three distinct governance capabilities include structures (connection), processes (coordination) and relational mechanisms (collaboration). Moreover, Grant et al. (2007) propose two further IT governance dimensions: temporal and external influences, which we believe are also important to consider in the context of a Living Lab.

3.3.1   Structures

The structures dimension represent formal and informal mechanisms that "encourage contacts and socialisation between stakeholder groups" [31]. Structures concern the existence of clearly defined roles and responsibilities and the establishment of steering committees and IT strategy committees [29]. Typically an "IT steering committee is situated at executive or management level and has the specific responsibility for overseeing major projects or managing IT priorities, IT costs, IT resource allocation, etc."[29]. Grant, et al. [30] describes the structures dimension as constituting "tangible planning and organisational elements outlined by high-level governance strategy". These authors outline several forms of governance structures which are typically embodied within the structural capability: i) roles and responsibilities, ii) IT organisational archetypes and iii) management and steering committee structure. The establishment of competence and excellence centres, which enable the pooling of knowledge from different functional areas and enable an increased focus on developing valued business and IT skill sets, constitute a salient dimension of structural capability [28].

3.3.2   Processes

The processes dimension has been articulated as describing the "formal and informal activities that are planned and emerge during business IT initiatives e.g., organisation and evaluation of IT initiatives" and "the formalisation and institutionalisation of strategic IT decision making or IT monitoring procedures" [28]. The process dimension is primarily focused on the "integration of business and IT decisions, or the alignment of strategic IT investments with the strategic goals and objectives of the firm" [28]. The author outlines four levels of IT decision making process integration: administrative (budgets and schedules are amalgamated between business and IT), sequential (business decisions provide guidance for IT decision making), reciprocal (business and IT decisions carry collective credence) and full (concurrent operationalisation of IT and business decisions) integration. According to Grant et al., (2007) "the underlying principle of the process view is the recognition that IT governance is based on lateral decision making that extends beyond the walls of the traditional IT function into all parts of an organization...organisations must engage all levels of internal and external stakeholders in the establishment of an appropriate IT governance framework". These authors argue that the appropriate operationalisation of "ex post" monitoring mechanisms e.g., IT maturity alignment model, scorecards, cost benefit analysis, charge backs, service level agreements and so on, enables the ongoing control and evaluation of the IT governance structure.

3.3.3   Relational Mechanisms

The structural and process IT governance capabilities working in tandem are not suited, given the mandatory tangible nature of both capabilities, for the design of effective IT governance architectures in dynamic and complex environments [31]. However, the operationalisation of the two aforementioned capabilities in conjunction with the intangible and tacit nature of relational capabilities can be quite cogent [28]. Relational mechanisms are "crucial in the IT governance framework and paramount for attaining and sustaining business-IT alignment, even when the appropriate structures and processes are in place" [29]. The relational capability dimension represents the requirement for the operationalisation of suitable mechanisms for ensuring effective relationship management amongst principal stakeholders. Relational mechanisms also incorporate unstructured strategic IT dialogues between principal stakeholders which can facilitate "rich conversation and communication to resolve diverging perspectives and stakeholder conflicts" [28]. Feurstein, et al. [17] posit that further research is warranted to determine how best to integrate society and citizens into Living Lab open innovation ecosystems. The authors argue that "as private persons become a source of ideas and innovations, an appropriate rewarding and incentive mechanism needs to be put in place which simultaneously secures pay-back to all the actors involved whilst adopting fair and suitable mechanisms for the handling of IPR (Intellectual Property Rights) and other ethical issues". In a distributed open innovation environment, it is important to create a 'cognitive minimum common denominator' amongst all the participant stakeholders in order to promote the development of shared values, shared trust and reciprocity [19]. Based on the analysis above the following propositions are delineated:

Proposition 1: Effective Living Laboratory IT governance is dependent on formalisation and institutionalisation of a high-level governance strategy, an appropriate IT organisational structure and the predefining of roles and responsibilities within the ecosystem.

Proposition 2: Effective Living Laboratory IT governance is dependent on the formalisation and institutionalisation of appropriate IT monitoring procedures/tools and also on the distribution of strategic IT decision making amongst internal and external stakeholders.

Proposition 3: Effective Living Laboratory IT governance is dependent on appropriate relational mechanisms which facilitate internal and external relationship management.

3.3.4   Temporal

The essence of the temporal dimension reflects that IT governance is a dynamic and continually evolving mechanism which must be continually monitored, controlled and evaluated to ensure that the IT governance remains aligned with the overall objective of the Living Lab initiative [30]. According to Grant et al., [30] the temporal dimension contains three separate elements: maturity (IT governance maturation model), life cycle (IT governance implementation will vary according to the stage in the life cycle of the governance process) and rate of change (IT governance approaches will differ depending on the stability or the agility of the Living Lab initiative). IT governance "develops over longer periods of time and credibility accumulation of experience and learning. Interpersonal relationships, coalitions through between stakeholders may take years to develop, to be able to effectively exploit information technology" [31]. For example, there is evidence to suggest that relational mechanisms are more influential at the initiating stages of IT governance [32], however no longitudinal research exists to confirm whether or not individual IT governance mechanisms have a more prominent role to play than others over time.

3.3.5   External Influences

It is generally accepted that the most cogent IT governance architecture for a given organisation is contingent on a variety of factors [33, 34]. Early research exploring how contingencies actively influenced IT governance arrangements identified factors such as corporate governance, economies of scope and absorptive capacity [35]. The IT governance institute identified a number of contingencies which consider size (computed by calculating turnover or staff numbers) industry type and geographical location [29]. More recently, the concept of an external influences dimension has been described as the manner in which the dynamics of environmental factors (e.g., socio-cultural, technological, legal/regulatory, political, economic, organisational and so on) mould IT governance arrangements and execution in real-world settings [30]. When designing a Living Laboratory IT governance architecture comprising structures, processes, temporal and relational mechanisms, it is important to note that these mix of mechanisms may be dependent on a multitude of externally influenced contingency factors which can influence the shaping of these mechanisms and subsequently impact on the IT governance outcome [29]. Given the absence of research in the area of Living Lab IT governance temporal mechanisms and external influencers, the following research can provide salient insight into not only the manner in which governance mechanisms have been moulded by contingency factors and the subsequent impact on the governance outcome, but also elucidate how IT governance has evolved over a period of time. Thus, two more propositions are presented.

Proposition 4: Effective Living Laboratory IT governance is time and context dependent as stakeholder experience, perceptions and expectations can lead to a realignment of IT governance.

Proposition 5: The chosen mix of structures, processes, temporal and relational mechanisms is dependent on multiple external influencers.

3.4   Open Innovation Effectiveness

Recent research into open innovation has focused on identifying select aspects of open innovation activities which make them effective e.g. vertical cooperation [36], costs of openness [37] and so on. There are differing opinions pertaining to what constitutes open innovation effectiveness. Cheng and Huizingh [38] explored whether the implementation of various open innovation activities resulted in greater innovation performance and concluded that effectiveness may be a multi-dimensional construct comprising multiple factors. Effectiveness may also include benefits such as offering an organisation a platform with which to measure an innovation's real value or to identify their core competencies [39]. The effectiveness of open innovation may also be determined by the resource endowments of the partnering organisation [40]. More importantly, Huizingh [41] argues that future research into open innovation effectiveness must venture beyond the "obvious consequences of lower costs, shorter time to market and more sales". This author also calls for research into case organisations where the open innovation process was ineffective. Despite the competitive advantage opportunities afforded by open innovation [18, 42], there are a number of risks which are inherent in the management of open innovation processes, for example, Morgan et al., [43] surmise that "the level of commitment, volume of knowledge exchange and successful alignment of objectives depends on the effective governance of resources and capabilities of all participants in a [collaborative open innovation] network." Likewise, the concept of a Living Lab encompasses multiple stakeholders working in close partnership and thus, the management of these relationships, through robust governance mechanisms, constitutes an essential component in the successful implementation of open innovation processes [44]. Thus, we present our final proposition:

Proposition 6: Open innovation effectiveness in living labs is dependent on the implementation and subsequent institutionalisation of an effective IT governance architecture.

We conclude our process of building a preliminary research model from extant research by presenting the constructs and relationships between them in Figure 1.

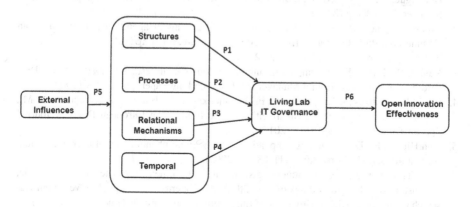

Fig. 1. Theoretical Model of Relationships and Constructs

4   Conclusion

Given the importance of IT governance in contemporary Living Lab initiatives, steering committees are faced with the challenge of how best to operationalize an IT governance mechanism that will facilitate effective open innovation processes. The theorising process employed in this study proved to be highly effective as the framework builds a basis for executing research on how Living Lab ecosystems are implementing IT governance and elucidate on the relationship between IT governance and open innovation effectiveness. Thus, in terms of future research we will concentrate on providing an empirically validated version of the research model proposed in this study, stipulating whether each dimension of the research model is applicable in the context of a Living Lab and if it can be substantiated. We believe an empirically validated research model will assist existing and new Living Lab initiatives reduce the risks encountered and support the management of emergent pathways that result as a consequence of operationalizing a particular IT governance mechanism.

Future research could also build on the findings to i) verify how IT governance implementations evolve over time ii) identify the core individual elements of effective IT governance mechanisms and iii) determine whether current Living Lab IT governance mechanisms are conducive for the future deployment of technologies in a smart city IT governance scenario.

Acknowledgment. This work was supported, in part, by Science Foundation Ireland grant 10/CE/I1855 to Lero – The Irish Software Engineering Research Centre (www.lero.ie).

References

1. Schaffers, H., Komninos, N., Pallot, M., Trousse, B., Nilsson, M., Oliveira, A.: Smart cities and the future internet: Towards cooperation frameworks for open innovation. In: Domingue, J., et al. (eds.) Future Internet Assembly. LNCS, vol. 6656, pp. 431–446. Springer, Heidelberg (2011)

2. Kroes, N.: The critical role of cities in making the digital agenda a reality. European Commission. Press Release (2010), http://europa.eu/rapid/press-release_SPEECH-10-272_en.htm

3. Kanter, R., Litow, S.: Informed and interconnected: A manifesto for smarter cities. Harvard Business School General Management Unit Working Paper, pp. 09-141 (2009)

4. Batty, M., Axhausen, K., Giannotti, F., Pozdnoukhov, A., Bazzani, A., Wachowicz, M., Ouzounis, G., Portugali, Y.: Smart cities of the future. The European Physical Journal Special Topics 214(1), 481–518 (2012)

5. Von Hippel, E.: Democratizing innovation: The evolving phenomenon of user innovation. Journal für Betriebswirtschaft 55(1), 63–78 (2005)

6. Nam, T., Pardo, T.A.: Conceptualizing smart city with dimensions of technology, people, and institutions. In: Proceedings of the 12th Annual International Digital Government Research Conference, Digital Government Innovation in Challenging Times. ACM (2011)

7. Johnston, E.W., Hansen, D.L.: Design lessons for smart governance infrastructures. American Governance 3 (2011)

8. Hernández-Muñoz, J.M., Vercher, J.B., Muñoz, L., Galache, J.A., Presser, M., Gómez, L.A.H., Pettersson, J.: Smart cities at the forefront of the future internet. In: Domingue, J., et al. (eds.) Future Internet Assembly. LNCS, vol. 6656, pp. 447–462. Springer, Heidelberg (2011)

9. Ballon, P., Glidden, J., Kranas, P., Menychtas, A., Ruston, S., Van der Graaf, S.: Is There a Need for a Cloud Platform for European Smart Cities? In: eChallenges e-2011 Conference Proceedings, pp. 1–7 (2011)

10. Eriksson, M., Niitamo, V.-P., Kulkki, S.: State-of-the-art in utilizing Living Labs approach to user-centric ICT innovation-a European approach. Center for Distance-spanning Technology. Lulea University of Technology Sweden, Lulea (2005), http://www.vinnova.se/upload/dokument/verksamhet/tita/stateoftheart_livinglabs_eriksson2005.pdf
11. Lichtenthaler, U., Ernst, H.: Attitudes to externally organising knowledge management tasks: A review, reconsideration and extension of the NIH syndrome. R&D Management 36(4), 367–386 (2006)
12. Chesbrough, H.: Open Innovation: Where We've Been and Where We're Going. Research Technology Management 55(4), 20–27 (2012)
13. Chesbrough, H., Vanhaverbeke, W., West, J.: Open Innovation: Researching a New Paradigm. Oxford University Press, Oxford (2006)
14. Lichtenthaler, U.: Open innovation in practice: An analysis of strategic approaches to technology transactions. IEEE Trans. Eng. Manage. 55(1), 148–157 (2008)
15. van de Vrande, V., Vanhaverbeke, W., Gassmann, O.: Broadening the scope of open innovation: past research, current state and future directions. Int. J. Technol. Manage. 2(3-4), 221–235 (2010)
16. Pallot, M.: The Living Lab Approach: A User Centred Open Innovation Ecosystem. Webergence Blog 2010 (2009)
17. Feurstein, K., Hesmer, A., Hribernik, K., Thoben, K., Schumacher, J.: Living Labs: A new development strategy. In: Schumacher, J., Niitamo, V.-P. (eds.) European Living Labs: A New Approach for Human Centric Regional Innovation, Wissenschaftlicher Verlag (2008)
18. Chesbrough, H.: Open Innovation: The New Imperative for Creating and Profiting from Technology. Harvard Business School Press, Boston (2003)
19. Sawhney, M., Prandelli, E. (eds.): How organizations learn: Managing the search for knowledge, p. 271. Cengage Learning EMEA (2004)
20. Howe, J.: The rise of crowdsourcing. Wired Magazine 14(6), 1–4 (2006)
21. Bergvall-Kareborn, B., Stahlbrost, A.: Living Lab: An open and citizen-centric approach for innovation. International Journal of Innovation and Regional Development 1(4), 356–370 (2009)
22. Dubin, R.: Theory building. Free Press (1978)
23. Whetten, D.A.: What constitutes a theoretical contribution? Academy of Management Review 14(4), 490–495 (1989)
24. Reynolds, P.: Primer in theory construction, An a&b classics edition. Allyn & Bacon, Needham Heights (2006)
25. Brown, A., Grant, G.: Framing the frameworks: A review of IT governance research. Communications of the Association for Information Systems 15 (2005)
26. Weill, P.: Don't just lead, govern: How top-performing firms govern IT. MIS Quarterly Executive 3(1), 1–17 (2004)
27. Singh, H.: A Practice Theory View of IS Governance. In: Proceedings of the JAIS Theory Development Workshop - SPROUTS: Working Papers on Information Systems, vol. 9(52) (2009)
28. Peterson, R.: Crafting information technology governance. Information Systems Management 21(4), 7–22 (2004)
29. De Haes, S., Van Grembergen, W.: IT governance structures, processes and relational mechanisms: Achieving IT/business alignment in a major Belgian financial group. In: Proceedings of the 38th Annual Hawaii International Conference. IEEE (2005)
30. Grant, G., Brown, A., Uruthirapathy, A., McKnight, S.: An Extended Model of IT Governance: A Conceptual Proposal. In: AMCIS Proceedings (2007)

31. Peterson, R.: Emerging Capabilities of Information Technology Governance: Exploring Stakeholder Perspectives in Financial Services. In: Proceedings of the 8th ECIS, pp. 667–675 (2000)
32. De Haes, S., Van Grembergen, W.: An exploratory study into IT governance implementations and its impact on business/IT alignment. Information Systems Management 26(2), 123–137 (2009)
33. Brown, C.V., Magill, S.L.: Alignment of the IS Functions with the Enterprise: Toward a Model of Antecedents. MIS Quarterly 18(4), 371–404 (1994)
34. Brown, C.V.: Examining the emergence of hybrid IS governance solutions: Evidence from a single case site. Information Systems Research 8(1), 69–94 (1997)
35. Sambamurthy, V., Zmud, R.W.: Arrangements for information technology governance: A theory of multiple contingencies. MIS Quarterly, 261-290 (1999)
36. Tomlinson, P.R.: Co-operative ties and innovation: Some new evidence for UK manufacturing. Research Policy 39(6), 762–775 (2010)
37. Laursen, K., Salter, A.: Open for innovation: The role of openness in explaining innovation performance among U.K. manufacturing firms. Strategic Management Journal 27(2), 131–150 (2006)
38. Cheng, C., Huizingh, K.: Open innovation to increase innovation performance: Evidence from a large survey. In: Proceedings of the XXI ISPIM International Conference, vol. 6(9) (2010)
39. Rigby, D., Zook, C.: Open-market innovation. Harvard Business Review 80(10), 80–93 (2002)
40. Dahlander, L., Gann, D.M.: How open is innovation? Research Policy 39(6), 699–709 (2010)
41. Huizingh, E.K.: Open innovation: State of the art and future perspectives. Technovation 31(1), 2–9 (2011)
42. Enkel, E., Gassmann, O., Chesbrough, H.: Open R&D and open innovation: Exploring the phenomenon. R&D Management 39(4), 311–316 (2009)
43. Morgan, L., Feller, J., Finnegan, P.: Open source innovation networks: Exploring high and low-density models. In: Proceedings of PACIS (2012)
44. Feller, J., Finnegan, P., Hayes, J., O'Reilly, P.: Institutionalising information asymmetry: Governance structures for open innovation. Information Technology & People 2(4), 297–316 (2009)

Examining Contextual Factors and Individual Value Dimensions of Healthcare Providers Intention to Adopt Electronic Health Technologies in Developing Countries

Yvonne O' Connor[1,*], Stephen Treacy[2], and John O' Donoghue[1]

[1] Health Information System Research Centre, University College Cork, Ireland
{y.oconnor,J.odonoghue}@ucc.ie
[2] Business Information Systems, University College Cork, Ireland
s.t.treacy@umail.ucc.ie

Abstract. Despite substantial research on electronic health (e-Health) adoption, there still exist vast differences between resource-rich and resource-poor populations regarding Information Technology adoption. To help bridge the technological gulf between developed and developing countries, this research-in-progress paper examines healthcare providers' intention to adopt e-health technologies from two perspectives 1) contextual factors (i.e. specific to developing world settings) and 2) individual value dimensions (i.e. cultural, utilitarian, social and personal). The primary output of this paper is a theoretical model merging both the contextual factors and value dimensions; this forms a strong baseline to examine and help ensure the successful adoption of e-Health technologies within developing countries. Future research will be performed to validate the model developed in this paper, with a specific focus on mobile Health in Malawi, Africa.

Keywords: Contextual Factors, Individual Value System, Developing Countries, Theoretical Model.

1 Introduction

A vast array of research exists which examines the adoption of Information Technology (IT) at various levels of analysis in both developed and developing regions, with the former dominating extant Information Systems (IS) research. In recent years, academics have focused their research attentions on the implementation of IT in developing regions, i.e. countries operating within Information and Communication Technology (ICT) resource-constrained conditions and where the population has limited knowledge in utilising ICT solutions [1]. Adoption levels of IT in resource-poor regions continue to lag behind their richer region counterparts [2, 3], particularly in the health care domain [4]. The need for reforming the delivery of healthcare services to accommodate the needs of modern societies is driven by unprecedented health inequities between the poor and wealthy economies.

---

[*] Corresponding Author.

B. Bergvall-Kåreborn and P.A. Nielsen (Eds.): TDIT 2014, IFIP AICT 429, pp. 345–354, 2014.

A significant amount of literature focuses on intentions to adopt technology in the e-health domain. Despite the contributions of such studies, there still remains a high failure rate of e-health technologies in developing regions [5], due to the lack of adoption [6]. Understanding why people accept or reject information technology is the first step toward finding a solution to the problem [7]. Such failure rates imply that more effort is required to fully understand this research domain and that additional factors exist which were previously undocumented in extant literature. However, more attention is required to examine the human, as opposed to technical, aspects associated with e-health implementation initiatives [8].

Extant research shows that factors which effect the adoption of IT in western societies may not have the same influential impact on IT adoption in developing regions [9, 10]. The rationale is that the contextual landscape and individual values differ across both populations [11, 12]. First, the very concept of value has been defined as "the worth, desirability or utility of a thing" [13] and it has been measured and explored at various levels of analysis. However few authors would contend that the search for value has reached a point where both theoreticians and practitioners are satisfied with its outcomes [14], as the worth/desirability/utility to a targeted user depends on many factors [13], for example transparency and ease of access. A review of extant literature also shows a wide array of opinions as to what value actually entails, with no unanimously accepted definition. As a result, authors often seek to interchange the term with other concepts such as impact [15], influence [16], quality [17], success [18], and effectiveness [19]. It should not be surprising therefore that investigating value creation from emerging ICTs is a complex phenomenon, involving the simultaneous presence and interaction of various exogenous and endogenous factors.

Developing from the various disagreements between authors surrounding their approach of theorising value, there is a consensus that value creation starts with identifying the perceived value that is being offered to the end user by the project in question [14]. Hu et al. [20] define perceived value as the intended user's "perception of the net benefits gained in exchange for the costs incurred in obtaining the desired benefits" (p.4). Despite various definitions of perceived value, there exists general acceptance that it: a) is linked through the use of some product, service or object; b) is subjectively perceived by users, rather than objectively determined; and c) involves a trade-off between what the user receives and gives to acquire and use the product or service [21]. From this synopsis, the locus of potential value in e-health technologies can be identified where there exists the opportunity for the users involved to obtain desired results. Multiple loci (cultural, utilitarian, social and personal) have been therefore identified for the successful adoption of e-health technologies in developing countries.

Second, when examining an end users' rationale for adopting e-health technologies in developing countries it is important that the contextual landscape along with the perceived value is taken into account. For example, existing researchers [cf. 22] argue for the significance of examining context but rarely portray its importance. Exploring the contextual landscape is imperative as it reflects external elements that comprise the environment or conditions for decision making tasks [23], which may be outside of the researchers' control. Yet, a dearth of research exists which examines the impact contextual landscape and individual values have on behavioural intentions to adopt e-health technologies in developing countries. The authors argue that it is imperative to examine this unexplored area in extant literature to obtain richer insights into the intentions to adoption e-health technologies in resource poor countries.

The objective of this study is to develop a theoretical model which explores the drivers of e-health technology adoption from a contextual and value dimensions perspective. The authors observe that exploring contextual factors in association with an individual's value system may help enhance current knowledge on health care providers' intentions to adopt e-health technologies in developing countries.

This paper is structured as follows: In an effort to bridge the research gap highlighted previously, a theoretical model and three propositions are presented in Section 2. This theoretical model, which draws upon and extends extant literature, is proposed for future research. Section 3 outlines the proposed research methodology which will empirically examine the newly established theoretical model and associated propositions. Section 4 concludes by presenting the key implications of this study for theory and practice.

2   Theoretical Model Development and Propositions

This paper seeks to provide richer insights into healthcare providers' (referred to as Health Surveillance Assistants in rural Malawi, Africa) intentions to adopt e-health technologies. A theoretical model (see Figure 1) is presented which will be used to explore this phenomenon. This model, developed by adopting and extending extant literature will be explained in the following section, beginning with the rationale underpinning each construct and proceeding to the development of three propositions.

2.1   Contextual Factors

Contextual factors have been found to influence the intentions to adopt an innovation at various levels of analysis (i.e. individual, firm/organisational, and national). Contextual factors influence one's decision making behaviour [23] which can vary across populations and industries.

According to extant literature [24, 25, 26, 27], important differences exist between healthcare and other industries (e.g. manufacturing, financial, aerospace). First, Chiasson et al. [25] argue that healthcare represents a markedly different social and technical context compared with many of the industries where IS research is conducted. Second, it is argued that the special characteristics of healthcare functions, processes and organisations are another difference which distinguishes it from any other service sectors or industries, with healthcare being a highly customised, complex relationship (person-to person), contrary to banking or insurance industries [24].

The healthcare context in resource-poor regions is more complex than developed countries due to uncertainty surrounding lack of resources (financial, technical and human). Therefore, the contextual factors for e-health technology adoption in developing countries differentiate this research from previous studies examined in developed countries. Several authors have concluded that value conceptualisations may vary depending on a study's context [28, 29, 30]. As a result, it is proposed that:

P1: Contextual factors in developing countries impact Healthcare Surveillance Assistants' value system.

P2: Contextual factors impact Healthcare Surveillance Assistants' to adopt e-health technologies in developing countries.

2.2   Individual Value System

Defined as "an organized set of preferential standards that are used in making selections of objects and actions, resolving conflicts, invoking social sanctions, and coping with needs or claims for social and psychological defenses of choices made or proposed" [31], an individuals' 'value system' comprises of a cluster of combined values which influences individual behavior [32]. For this paper, an individual value system comprises of cultural, utilitarian, social and personal values (each dimension is described in Table 1). An 'individual' in the context of this paper refers to Health Surveillance Assistants (HSA), whose role in society is described in Section 2.

Culture diversity between developing and developed countries can be observed based on "Individualism versus Collectivism", "Power distance", and "Masculinity versus Femininity" [43]. For instance, resource-rich environments (such as Europe and U.S.A) are driven by individualist approaches whereas developing countries are concerned with collectivist strategies [44].

Utilitarian values reflect functional values which are relevant for task-specific use and are characterised as instrumental and extrinsic [35]. E-health technologies offer an array of services which can assist HSAs in their tasks. For instance, electronic health records provide a digital collection of clinical accounts and diagnostic reports pertaining to an individual patient [46, 47] which can assist HSAs when assessing and diagnosing patients. When individual users' perceive that the technological tool could facilitate them when accomplishing tasks, their behavioural intentions towards adopting the IT increases [48, 49].

Social value, as defined in the context of this study, is closely linked to the [37] motivational construct; namely, introjected motivation. This type of motivation identifies the social needs of individuals to obtain social approval from other individuals in society to improve/maintain feelings of worth. Individuals often adopt IT solutions in pursuit of recognition among other individuals and/or based on the influence of 'others', for instance, the social influence of peers, superiors, and family members has been found to directly affect individuals' decision to adopt IT [49],[50],[54].

Table 1. Value Dimensions Definition

Value Dimension	Definition used for the purpose of this study	Relevance to Behavioural Intentions to Adopt e-Health technologies
Cultural Value	A set of beliefs and norms that are both consciously and subconsciously held by HSA in the given society (adapted from [33]).	It is unlikely that cultural values can be easily changed or adjusted to conform to any changes introduced by new technology. This conformity, therefore, may have an impact on individual users' intentions to adopt e-health technologies [9].
Utilitarian Value	The degree to which a HSAs believe that using e-health technologies will assist in accomplishing his/her goals (i.e. delivering healthcare services to patients) in terms of effectiveness and efficiency (adapted from [34, 35]).	The utilitarian view is concerned with the effectiveness and efficiency that result from the potential use of an IT application [34]. HSAs perceive utilitarian value from e-health technologies when such technological tools facilitate healthcare providers to deliver healthcare services to patients without impacting their daily routines.
Social Value	The degree to which HSAs perceive social utility acquired from the potential adoption of e-health technologies (adapted from [36]).	It is argued [36] that social value represents "the preference for certain outcome distributions between the self and the interdependent other." As a result, social value is often established from the use of a product or service which is shared with other people [51],[53]. This perspective may have an impact on HSAs' intentions to adopt e-health technologies.
Personal Value	Conscious valuing of a behavioural goal such that the action is accepted or owned as personally important to HSAs (based on [27]).	Individual perception that the values associated with an IT project are similar with his/her personal goals and identity, thus viewing the action as personally important [56], thus increasing likelihood of e-health technology adoption by HSAs.

Personal values are conceptualised as deeply-embedded motivational sources and often defined as goals that vary in their importance and serve as guiding principles in people's lives [55]. Personal values therefore are similar to the concept of identified motivation [37]. With an identified motivation, an individual consciously values the collective goal of the IT project and perceives it as his or her own [37],[56], which ultimately can influence e-health technology adoption.

It is evident from the previous sections and Table 1 that healthcare providers' intentions towards e-health technologies can be attributed to various value dimensions which form an individual's value system. As a result, it is proposed that:

P3: Healthcare Surveillance Assistants' Value System impacts their intentions to adopt e-health technologies in developing countries.

Based on this review of extant literature a theoretical model is developed, consisting of three propositions (Figure 1).

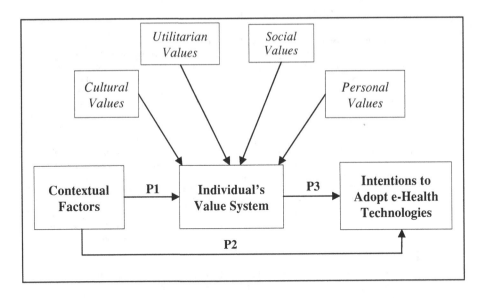

Fig. 1. Theoretical Model

3   Proposed Methodology

Future work will empirically examine the theoretical model (Figure 1) by obtaining quantitative data from HSAs (sometimes referred to as Community Healthcare Workers) in Malawi, Africa. HSAs are deployed in rural settings with an assigned catchment area, responsible for preventive health in children. Presently, HSAs utilise a paper-based set of guidelines known as the Case Community Management (CCM), which is a stepwise and structured approach towards assessing and managing children. Attempts are currently underway to digitise this paper-based approach.

To obtain the necessary quantitative data, a paper-based survey is the data collection technique which will be implemented. The survey will be designed adhering to existing guidelines in the IS literature. Measures for each construct highlighted in Figure 1 are reflective in nature and will be obtained from extant literature. The Partial Least Square [PLS] (Structural Equation Modelling [SEM]) approach will be employed to analyse the data. All statistical analysis of the quantitative results will be conducted using SmartPLS (Version 2.0.M3). All reliability and validity test will be performed meeting the integral criteria and their associated threshold levels documented in the IS literature.

4   Discussion and Conclusions

The technological gulf between resource-rich and resource-poor populations still exists. To assist in overcoming this real-world problem, developing countries need to leverage their existing ICT resources. To help ensure that a successful adoption of ICT is achieved, greater attention is required to assess contextual factors and individual value dimensions of a healthcare provider's intention to adopt e-health technologies. Therefore the objective of this study is to develop a theoretical model which explores the drivers of e-health technology adoption intentions from both a contextual and value perspective.

Values can be difficult to interpret, considering the complexity, significance and meaning that differs from one context to another. There is a real need to examine individual values under a clear set of contextual factors. The primary contribution of this paper is the construction of a theoretical model which will enable multiple individual values to be assessed under different contexts. From this baseline, researchers will be able to assess more accurately a user's intentions to adopt e-health technologies under a variety of contextual factors. The framework is supported by three propositions which are supported based on existing research:

- P1: Contextual factors in developing countries impact Healthcare Surveillance Assistants' value system.
- P2: Contextual factors impact Healthcare Surveillance Assistants' intention to adopt e-health technologies in developing countries.
- P3: Healthcare Surveillance Assistants' Value System impacts their intentions to adopt e-health technologies in developing countries.

While the proposed model has been rigorously developed based on extant literature, its principal limitation is that it has not been empirically examined against a developing world context. Moreover it solely focuses on human/environmental as opposed to technological dimensions, which have been reported to impact intentions to adopt IT in extant literature. Once the data is collected and assessed the proposed theoretical model may be refined to reflect the real-world impact (a) contextual factors in the developing world and (b) associated values have on the intentions to adopt e-health technologies. This research will serve as a basis for future adoption based research within developing countries.

Acknowledgement. The Supporting LIFE project (305292) is funded by the Seventh Framework Programme for Research and Technological Development of the European Commission www.supportinglife.eu.

References

[1] Ssekakubo, G., Suleman, H., Marsden, G.: Issues Of Adoption: Have E-Learning Management Systems Fulfilled Their Potential In Developing Countries? In: Proceedings of the South African Institute of Computer Scientists and Information Technologists Conference on Knowledge, Innovation and Leadership in A Diverse, Multidisciplinary Environment, pp. 231–238. ACM (2011)

[2] Dasgupta, S., Gupta, B.: Impact of Organizational Culture on Technology Use in a Developing Country. In: ECIS 2012 Proceedings. Paper 240 (2012)

[3] Greenhalgh, T., Procter, R., Wherton, J., Sugarhood, P., Shaw, S.: The Organising Vision for Telehealth and Telecare: Discourse Analysis. BMJ 2, E001574 (2012)

[4] Li, J., Moore, N., Akter, S., Bleisten, S., Ray, P.: Mhealth For Influenza Pandemic Surveillance in Developing Countries. In: IEEE 43rd Hawaii International Conference on System Sciences, pp. 1–9 (2010)

[5] Heeks, R.: Information Systems and Developing Countries: Failure, Success, and Local Improvisations. The Information Society 18, 101–112 (2002)

[6] Wouters, B., Barjis, J., Maponya, G., Maritz, J., Mashiri, M.: Supporting Home Based Health Care in South African Rural Communities Using USSD Technology. In: AMCIS 2009 Proceedings. Paper 410 (2009)

[7] Al-Gahtani, S.S.: Computer Technology Adoption in Saudi Arabia: Correlates of Perceived Innovation Attributes. Information Technology for Development 10, 57–69 (2003)

[8] Cocosila, M., Archer, N.: Adoption of Mobile ICT for Health Promotion: An Empirical Investigation. Electronic Markets 20, 241–250 (2010)

[9] Al Sukkar, A., Hasan, H.: Toward a Model for the Acceptance of Internet Banking in Developing Countries. Information Technology for Development 11, 381–398 (2005)

[10] Vatanasakdakul, S.: Introducing Cultural Fit Factors to Investigate the Appropriateness of B2b Technology Adoption to Thailand. In: 21st Bled Econference Ecollaboration: Overcoming Boundaries Through Multi-Channel Interaction (2008)

[11] Ahern, D.K., Kreslake, J.M., Phalen, J.M.: What Is Ehealth (6): Perspectives on the Evolution of Ehealth Research. Journal of Medical Internet Research 8 (2006)

[12] Fischer, M.A., Vogeli, C., Stedman, M.R., Ferries, T.G., Weissman, J.S.: Uptake of Electronic Prescribing In Community-Based Practices. Journal of General Internal Medicine 23, 358–363 (2008)

[13] Cronk, M.C., Fitzgerald, E.P.: Understanding "IS Business Value": Derivation of Dimensions. Logistics Information Management 12, 40–49 (1999)

[14] Davern, M., Kauffman, R.: Discovering Potential and Realizing Value from Information Technology Investments. Journal of Management Information Systems 16, 121–143 (2000)

[15] Gable, G.: Re-Conceptualizing Information System Success: The IS-Impact Measurement Model. Journal of The Association For Information Systems 9, 377–408 (2008)

[16] Mason, R.O.: Measuring Information Output: A Communication Systems Approach. Information and Management 1, 219–234 (1978)

[17] Day, E., Crask, M.R.: Value Assessment: The Antecedent Of Customer Satisfaction. Journal of Consumer Satisfaction Dissatisfaction and Complaining Behavior 13, 52–60 (2000)

[18] Delone, W.H., Mclean, E.R.: Information Systems Success: The Quest for the Dependent Variable. Information Systems Research 3, 60–95 (1992)

[19] Iivari, J., Ervasti, I.: User Information Satisfaction: IS Implementability and Effectiveness. Information and Management 2, 205–220 (1994)

[20] Hu, F.L., Chuang, C.C.: A Study of the Relationship Between the Value Perception and Loyalty Intention Toward an E-Retailer Website. Journal of Internet Banking & Commerce 17 (2012)

[21] Woodruff, R.B.: Customer Value: The Next Source for Competitive Advantage. Journal of the Academy of Marketing Science 25, 139–153 (1997)

[22] Meijers, J.M., Janssen, M.A., Cummings, G., Wallin, L., Estabrooks, C.A., Halfens, R.Y.: Assessing the Relationships Between Contextual Factors and Research Utilization in Nursing: Systematic Literature Review. Journal of Advanced Nursing 55, 622–635 (2006)

[23] Fjerrnestad, J., Hiltz, S.R.: Experimental Studies of Group Decision Support Systems: An Assessment of Variables Studied and Methodology. In: Proceedings of the Thirtieth Hawaii International Conference on System Sciences, pp. 45–65. IEEE (1997)

[24] Rigby, M., Roberts, R., Thick, M.: Taking Health Telematics into the 21st Century. The Radcliffe Press (2000)

[25] Chiasson, M.W., Davidson, E.: Pushing the Contextual Envelope: Developing and Diffusing IS Theory for Health Information Systems Research. Information and Organization 14, 155–188 (2004)

[26] Lyons, M., Woloshynowych, M., Adams, S., Vincent, C.: Error Reduction in Medicine. Final Report to the Nuffield Trust (2005)

[27] Kay, M.J.: Healthcare Marketing: What is Salient? International Journal of Pharmaceutical and Healthcare Marketing 1, 247–263 (2007)

[28] Chiu, C.M., Hsu, M.H., Sun, S.Y., Lin, T.C., Sun, P.C.: Usability, Quality, Value and E-Learning Continuance Decisions. Computers and Education 45, 399–416 (2005)

[29] Sanchez-Fernandez, R., Iniesta-Bonillo, M.A.: The Concept of Perceived Value: A Systematic Review of the Research. Marketing Theory 7, 427–451 (2007)

[30] Halinen, A., Jaakkola, E.: Marketing in Professional Services Firms: Turning Expertise into Customer Perceived Value. In: Handbook of Research on Entrepreneurship in Professional Services, vol. 219 (2012)

[31] Williams, R.: Change and Stability in Values and Value Systems: A Sociological Perspective. Free Press, New York (1979)

[32] Fritzsche, D., Oz, E.: Personal Values' Influence on the Ethical Dimension of Decision Making. Journal of Business Ethics 75, 335–343 (2007)

[33] Adler, N.J.: International Dimensions of Organizational Behavior. South-Western College Publishing, Cincinnati (2002)

[34] Holbrook, M.B.: The Nature of Customer Value: An Axiology of Services in the Consumption Experience. Service Quality: New Directions in Theory and Practice 21, 21–71 (1994)

[35] Babin, B.J., Darden, W.R., Griffin, M.: Work and/or Fun: Measuring Hedonic and Utilitarian Shopping Value. Journal of Consumer Research 20, 644–656 (1994)

[36] Chou, T.C., Chen, J.R., Pu, C.K.: Exploring the Collective Actions of Public Servants in E-Government Development. Decision Support Systems 45, 251–265 (2008)

[37] Ryan, R.M., Deci, E.L.: Self-Determination Theory and the Facilitation of Intrinsic Motivation, Social Development, and Well-Being. American Psychologist 55, 68–78 (2000)

[38] Leidner, D.E., Kayworth, T.: Review: A Review of Culture in Information Systems Research: Toward a Theory of Information Technology Culture Conflict. MIS Quarterly 30, 357–399 (2006)

[39] Schein, E.H.: Organizational Culture and Leadership: A Dynamic View. Jossey-Bass, San Francisco (1985)

[40] Straub, D., Keil, M., Brenner, W.: Testing the Technology Acceptance Model Across Cultures: A Three Country Study. Information and Management 33, 1–11 (1997)

[41] Anandarajan, M., Igbaria, M., Anakwe, U.P.: IT Acceptance in a Less-Developed Country: A Motivational Factor Perspective. International Journal of Information Management 22, 47–65 (2002)

[42] Bankole, F.O., Bankole, O.O., Brown, I.: Mobile Banking Adoption in Nigeria. The Electronic Journal of Information Systems in Developing Countries 47 (2011)

[43] Hofstede, G.: Culture's Consequences: International Differences in Work-Related Values. Sage, Beverly Hills (1980)

[44] Hofstede, G.: The Cultural Relativity of Organizational Practices and Theories. Journal of International Business Studies 14, 75–89 (1983)

[45] Van Der Heijden, H.: User Acceptance of Hedonic Information Systems. MIS Quarterly 28, 695–704 (2004)

[46] Safran, C., Golberg, H.: Electronic Patient Records and the Impact of the Internet. International Journal of Medical Informatics 60, 77–83 (2000)

[47] Hunt, D.L., Haynes, R.B., Hanna, S.E., Smith, K.: Effects of Computer-Based Clinical Decision Support Systems on Physician Performance and Patient Outcomes. JAMA: The Journal of the American Medical Association 280, 1339–1346 (1998)

[48] Miller, R.A., Gardner, R.M., Johnson, K.B., Hripcsak, G.: Clinical Decision Support and Electronic Prescribing Systems. Journal of the American Medical Informatics Association 12, 403–409 (2005)

[49] Venkatesh, V., Thong, J., Xu, X.: Consumer Acceptance and Use of Information Technology: Extending the Unified Theory of Acceptance and Use of Technology. MIS Quarterly 36, 157–178 (2012)

[50] Venkatesh, V., Morris, M.G., Davis, G.B., Davis, F.D.: User Acceptance of Information Technology: Toward a Unified View. MIS Quarterly 27, 425–478 (2003)

[51] Sheth, J., Newman, B., Gross, B.: Consumption Values and Market Choices: Theory and Applications. South-Western, Cincinnati (1991)

[52] Pura, M.: Linking Perceived Value and Loyalty in Location-Based Mobile Services. Managing Service Quality 15, 509–538 (2005)

[53] Sweeney, J.C., Soutar, G.N.: Consumer Perceived Value: The Development of a Multiple Item Scale. Journal of Retailing 77, 203–220 (2001)

[54] Venkatesh, V., Morris, M.G.: Why Don't Men Ever Stop to Ask For Directions? Gender, Social Influence, and their Role in Technology Acceptance and Usage Behavior. MIS Quarterly 24, 115–139 (2000)

[55] Schwartz, S.: Universals in the Content and Structure of Values: Theoretical Advances and Empirical Tests in 20 Countries. In: Advances in Experimental Social Psychology. Academic Press, San Diego (1992)

[56] Ke, W., Zhang, P.: The Effects of Extrinsic Motivations and Satisfaction in Open Source Software Development. Journal of the Association for Information Systems 11, 784–808 (2010)

Personalized Support with 'Little' Data

Peter Bednar[1], Peter Imrie[2], and Christine Welch[3]

[1] University of Portsmouth, School of Computing, Buckingham Building, Lion Terrace,
Portsmouth, PO1 3HE, UK
peter.bednar@port.ac.uk
[2] University of Portsmouth, School of Computing, UK
pch.imrie@gmail.com
[3] Portsmouth Business School, Richmond Building, Portland Street,
Portsmouth, PO1 3DE, UK
christine.welch@port.ac.uk

Abstract. In this paper we look at opportunities to support the creation of value for all through the use of end-user-owned Virtual Personal Assistant. We use a chat-bot as example of technology with a possibility for transferring and diffusing new functionality, features and capabilities. This category of software can create potential value through its AI and natural language processing combined with emulation and imitation of emotional engagement which is personal, private and as such allows for intimate contextual relevance to be developed.

Keywords: Personalized support, End-user owned, Knowledge worker, Little data, chat-bot, Emotional engagement, Contextual dependency, Natural Language Processing.

1 Introduction

How could we help to support the creation of value for all through IT? We reflect on the use of Virtual Personal Assistant (VPA) as an example of future technology with a potential to create value by transferring and diffusing new functionality, features and capability. The VPA we are looking at as an example (Kari) is not just an intelligent program with natural language processing capabilities. This software has potential value through its AI and natural language processing combined with emulation and imitation of emotional engagement [10]. This is contextualized and private in the form of an end user controlled VPA. As a contrast to large scale AI based personalized DSS which draw upon centralized systems [8] and / or cloud computing [1]. Kari (used as an example in this paper) is completely independent from central systems and costs the equivalent of a typical computer game. Kari could run on handheld computers (e.g. smartphones) without needing any additional processing or database. It can also interact with other devices (internet-of-things) on behalf of its user (local owner).

"We are witnessing a shift in human attention, from physical to dynamic instances in which digital and physical blends emerge" [6].

B. Bergvall-Kåreborn and P.A. Nielsen (Eds.): TDIT 2014, IFIP AICT 429, pp. 355–358, 2014.
© IFIP International Federation for Information Processing 2014

Kari is not a front end to a larger centralized system so avoids focusing on Big Data. The system is not a top down managed systems due to the human enhancement being provided to and from the true user, where the true user is the expert involved in the situational problem space. All metadata analysis and pattern analysis etc. is consequently developed locally and not shared with other devices or databases. It is a bottom up approach and appropriately described as 'Little Data'.

The personality and capabilities of Kari is developing through interaction with its unique user via natural language processing. It expands its database and constantly evolves its behaviour and interaction model through pattern recognition and metadata analysis, both on heuristics and behavioural analysis of user interaction (not just content analysis). This makes it adapting to increasingly complex, uncertain and differentiated contexts, as it develops a unique behavioural personality as a consequence of its evolving analysis and meta-analysis of end user interactions [9]. Kari is capable of analysing similar data and creates different outputs which may be inconsistent with each other. This para-consistent logic [2] allows for the expert to reflect upon their own perspective and personal 'bias' [4].

2   Discussion

In an era of 'Big Data', it could be said that professionals are supported by organizational systems that will capture all aspects of working life and can be interrogated and used to perform analysis. However, we suggest that this is to ignore the need for 'Little Data' that is both immediate and context specific (even if incomplete) [5]. As deZeeuw [13] puts it:

"An alternative is to invite the user to become a proper user, one who uses results in a way which makes them useful. An example is the development of professional organizations." [13,p837]

This is relevant in the context of knowledge organizations and society.

When engaging complex problem spaces we want to support a move from uncertainty to ambiguity. One example of usefulness is when support for reflection is necessary but alternative interpretations and viewpoints are not imagined. To have more than one alternative description opens the potential to reflect and contrast alternatives with each other. In other words when choices are available decisions can be reflected upon.

"In the case of ambiguity, people engage in sense making because they are confused by too many interpretations, whereas in the case of uncertainty they do so because they are ignorant of any interpretations" [12, p91].

Croon-Fors [7] highlights two aspects of life with which individuals seek help. First, people perceive that the use of universal theories misses most of their experience of 'reality'. Secondly, there is a necessity for human beings to take responsibility for social relations of science and technology. We benefit from embracing the skillful task of reconstructing the boundaries of daily life, in partial connection with others, in communication with all our parts including technologies. A VPA (such as Kari) in the form of a metaphorical human avatar could contribute to enhance our understanding of, and reflection over, our situated problem experiences. It also makes it possible to criticize the idea of a person as a coherent subject individual, and so helps us as users with our self-exploration. As such, a VPA emulates *"moodiness"* and multiple emotional behaviour patterns. It expresses a variety and incompleteness of control mechanism as part of its natural language processing and interaction.

With the VPA we can engage with the three principal responses as mentioned by Croon-Fors, i.e. disclosure, performativity and *'the real'*. Disclosure is related to the provocation ability of the VPA, its demands on personal attention and affectionate interaction. Performativity is related to the ability to simulate emotional behaviour, such as *'being'* moody, bitchy, humorous etc., and its ability to explore alternative and even inconsistent avenues and subjects for conversation. The reality aspect of the VPA is related to the intimate and physical interaction between a unique real user and the software imitation of a metaphorical human (avatar).

As Croon-Fors [7,p55] states, *"… we acknowledge the existence of various interrelationships between self and otherness, interrelationships that are constantly changing in various sense-making and interpretative processes. Such view also suggests the real to be constituted by an indefinite number of on-going sense-making processes."*

A user-owned service running a VPA (as opposed to an interface to *'Big.Data'*) changes the focus of the supporting system to the contextual sphere of the user [3]. E.g. Kari can function as a virtual *'girlfriend'* [10] because it communicates with the user using similar methods of natural language processing and also tries to provoke social conversation with the user. This purpose of social interaction is closely related to the one developed by Kiribo.

"Earth's first talking robot to go off world, is en route to the International Space Station - and its prime directive is to tackle loneliness." [11].

3   Conclusions

Kari is social, intimately private and personal to the user. The software aims to give personal companionship, and to replicate human interaction as nearly as possible with the assistance of algorithms designed to enable the program to learn from its inputs. As Kari develops new libraries and metadata based on conversation with the user, the patterns of use and subject content developed are uniquely personal and in a way contextually relevant. This reflects on how today's new trends are creating value for all through development of new technology, focusing on innovation of human enhancement through a personal, user owned decision support systems.

This category of VPA has a potential as a sophisticated self-service support system. Its great benefit is that it constantly develops as a self-user generated service. Software such as Kari is versatile, running on hand-held devices and costing no more than a typical gaming package. Adaptable for many differing purposes, and therefore providing new opportunities in professional life, everyday activities or leisure applications. It could create value for all, potentially supporting the evolution of a democratizing society.

References

1. Apple. (n.d.). Siri. Your wish is its command,
   `http://www.apple.com/uk/ios/siri/` (accessed April 15, 2013)
2. Bednar, P.M., Anderson, D., Welch, C.: Knowledge Creation and Sharing – Complex Methods of Inquiry and Inconsistent Theory. In: Proceedings of 6th European Conference on Knowledge Management, September 8-9. University of Limerick (2005)
3. Bednar, P.M., Welch, C., Graziano, A.: Learning Objects and their implications on Learning: A case of developing the foundation for a new Knowledge Infrastructure. In: Harman, K., Koohang, A. (eds.) Learning Objects: Applications, Implications & Future Directions, ch. 6, pp. 157–185. Informing Science Press, NY (2007)
4. Bednar, P.M., Welch, C.: Bias, Misinformation and the Paradox of Neutrality. Informing Science 11, 87–106 (2008)
5. Berger, J.: Contagious: Why Things Catch on (2013), reported at
   `http://www.linkedin.com/today/post/article/20130908184001-5670386-is-little-data-the-next-big-data` (accessed March 5, 2014)
6. Croon Fors, A.: The beauty of the beast: The matter of meaning in digitalization. AI & Society 25, 27–33 (2010)
7. Croon Fors, A.: The Ontology of the Subject in Digitalization. In: Luppicini, R. (ed.) Handbook of Research on Technoself: Identity in a Technological Society, pp. 45–63. IGI Global, Herschey (2013)
8. IBM. (n.d.). The DeepQA Project, `http://www.research.ibm.com/deepqa/deepqa.shtml` (accessed February 2, 2013)
9. Imrie, P., Bednar, P.: Virtual Personal Assistant. In: Martinez, M., Pennarolaecilia, F. (eds.) Proceedings of 10th Conference of the Italian Chapter of AIS, Empowering Society Through Digital Innovations. Università Commerciale Luigi Bocconi in Milan, Italy (2013)
10. Lhandslide Studios, Advanced Virtual Girl with Artificial Intelligence (2012), `http://www.karigirl.com/` (accessed April 22, 2013)
11. Parnell, B-A.: World's First Talking Space Robo-Chum Blasts Off to the ISS: Domo arigato, Mr Roboto ... また会う日まで, `http://www.theregister.co.uk/2013/08/05/talking_robot_iss/` (accessed August 5, 2013)
12. Weick, K.: Sense-making in Organizations. Sage, Thousand Oaks (1995)
13. de Zeeuw, G.: Knowledge Acquisition in changing realities. Kybernetes 26(6/7), 837–847 (1997)

The "PantryApp": Design Experiences from a User-Focused Innovation Project about Mobile Services for Senior Citizens

Anna Sigridur Islind

University West, Sweden
anna-sigridur.islind@hv.se

Abstract. This experience report aims to reflect on a design initiative conducted as a user-focused innovation. It is based on a research and development project about mobile commerce. Herein, I include various forms of mobile services that accumulate the core function of mobile payments. The target group of the design was senior citizens who need to have their grocery shopping done in a more safe and convenient way. In this report I will particularly focus on the design process and the design product.

Keywords: Design Experiences, Senior Citizens, Mobile Application and Services, Mobile Payments.

1   Introduction

This experience report aims to reflect on a design initiative conducted as a user-focused innovation. It is based on an action design research project about mobile services and mobile payments [1]. The target group of the design is senior citizens and other caretakers that need their grocery shopping done in a more safe, sufficient and convenient way. The focus in this report lies on the design process and the design product.

1.1   The Problem

People need food and grocery shopping is a part of everyday life. For people with disabilities, diseases, impaired vision, high age or other problems that render them unable to take care of themselves completely, going grocery shopping is out of the picture. These citizens belong to the home care system and receive help from caregivers that tend to their needs and see to that they get fresh groceries. The actual situation in the case of the studied municipality, the caregivers collect handwritten shopping lists and money and then shop for five caretakers at a time. This quite often results in mistakes and the caregivers have a tendency to bring home the wrong groceries. Problems have also occurred during the payment process. To hand money or a payment card over to a caregiver, which a caretaker might be meeting for the first time, is precarious since time to establish important trust is not always available. Furthermore,

B. Bergvall-Kåreborn and P.A. Nielsen (Eds.): TDIT 2014, IFIP AICT 429, pp. 359–362, 2014.

the caregivers do not consider it optimal to handle money and having the forced responsibility of bringing the right change back to the five caretakers.

Some caretakers have portrayed mistrust towards the caregivers and have occasionally made allegations against the caregivers, accusing them of stealing. These kinds of incidents usually have a logical explanation and are resolved in a good manner but put unnecessary stress on all parties involved. Additionally, the caregivers have educated themselves in care or nursing and should not be forced to go grocery shopping.

Consequently, this is a process with a lot of human factors that can easily go wrong. Nevertheless, after almost one and a half year of working with this project and this problematic process, it is obvious that as long as the money factor is involved in this process, there will be mistrust.

2   The Design of the PantryApp

The design of the PantryApp was reflected by the steps: investigation, exploration, composition and evaluation [2].

2.1   Investigation

The investigation has included extensive empirical research, in terms of interviews in focus groups in addition to individual interviews. As this is a project with user focus, the key-persons in the interview phase were the senior citizens (caretakers), a group of retired citizens that do not yet belong to the Swedish home care system as well as the caregivers. The caregivers have tacit knowledge so they were able to, through interviews, distinguish how they perceived their daily work tasks into the tiniest detail. The owners and employees in the store that delivers the groceries have also been interviewed regularly. The caretakers have shed light on their specific needs and wants. Their lack of technology knowledge implied that they all in fact belonged to digital divide as presented by Selwyn, et al. (2003). These user groups have had the biggest influence, both in the interface design and in the usability design.

Leaders from all levels in the municipality in addition to politicians have been involved as well through giving feedback on the applications impact on the organizational structure. They helped crystalize how the organization works on a higher level.

2.2   Exploration

From being a software developer for six years to becoming a more user-focused designer has been a learning journey for me. My role as a project leader in this complex project has been the greatest experience yet. I have developed real passion for helping the caretakers and caregivers as I felt compelled to use my education for some greater good: to help those in need, and these wonderful senior citizens are certainly in dire need. This helped develop a sense of possibilities and led to the realization of what can be, rather than putting emphasis on what is (Nelson and Stolterman, 2012). At a certain point there was a shift in focus to how things could be done in the perfect world, full of possibilities. The first draft of this "perfect world" did not correspond to what the application later evolved into, since aiming for the perfect scenario is neither relevant nor realistic. This was merely a learning process for all parties and led to an even closer collaboration.

This close cooperation with the end-users resulted in a functional co-produced prototype, which has been redesigned for the next phase, a full-scale artifact. It answers the needs of today, but it requires nurture as well as careful and continuous cooperation to answer the needs of the future users. What we have today might not look or feel anything like what the future will hold but is certainly a start of something. This start of something has already, according to the caregivers themselves, shown improvement possibilities in their daily work. Consequently, their role should evolve into a more meaningful care taking and nurturing one and resulting in them having more pride in their profession.

With the implementation of the PantryApp, both in its prototype stage and in the full-scale version, the handwritten shopping lists from the seniors are history. They now pick their products out in the PantryApp, which presents all products with pictures and sit in the comfort of their home alongside their caregiver that help them choose and order selected products.

The implementation has generated further needs and wants such as a guidance role for the caregivers that have been asked to provide nutrition advice. The caretakers have progressed as well. They have expressed curiosity towards what others buy, so a function that presents the most popular choices amongst all buyers has been implemented. The prototype version was only an android application but the full-scale PantryApp is platform independent at the request of both user groups. Taking this user-focused perspective has generated these new innovative user ideas continuously and thus made the application richer.

2.3   Composition

The application was designed and programmed in harmony with the organizational changes. This organizational development included designing a new schedule for the caregivers to go between the caretakers' homes in a more efficient manner to grocery shop via the PantryApp. The grocery store involved picks and packs the groceries and sent out an invoice directly to the senior citizens during the pilot phase. In the full-scale PantryApp, the caretakers pay directly within the application using mobile payments. The groceries are then picked up and delivered to the seniors' homes, by another party.

2.4   Evaluation

The users have expressed satisfaction towards the project as a whole and shown fulfillment regarding the new design of the full-scale application. Their gratitude gets me excited and enthusiastic to get to the next stage in the project. The anticipation is that a large group of caretakers alongside caregivers will find the artifact facilitating and useful and that the application will be implemented in numerous municipalities.

The money factor, already eliminated in the prototype phase, has influenced trust-creation between the caretaker and the caregivers to a great deal. The implementation of mobile payments in the full-scale application is expected to result in an even greater impact on the trust factor.

The application allows the caretakers to gain control over their own economy and spending decisions again, that most of them lost years ago. The PantryApp even allows the caretakers to make the final decision about their grocery selection. Being in need of care, should not mean loss of control.

3   Conclusions and Lessons Learned

L1. End User Involvement: The concrete and direct involvement of senior citizens in the design process was essential. During that process it became clear that the senior citizens especially had difficulties seeing how things are possible without having an artifact right in front of their eyes. This may be due to the digital divide.

L2. Mediating Artifact: Before, there was a lack of caring communication between the caretakers and the caregivers. At present, the application is considered as a conversation starter as the caretakers now sit closer to their caregivers and they seem more relaxed with each other than they did before. There is no pressure to know each other beforehand or get to know each other on a personal level. The artifact actually links these two groups together in a community-of-practice kind of way.

L3. Professional Values: Daily problems in the professionals' practices regarding trust factor and handling money are accommodated through the artifact. The focus is now shifting from the role of a personal assistant towards the professional role of nursing and caring.

References

1. Sein, M.K., et al.: Action Design Research. MIS Quarterly 35(1) (2011)
2. Nelson, H., Stolterman, E.: The design way: Intentional change in an unpredictable world, 2nd edn. MIT Press, Cambridge (2012)
3. Selwyn, N., Gorard, S., Furlong, J., Madden, L.: Older adults' use of information and communications technology in everyday life. Ageing and Society 23, 561–582 (2003)

Author Index

Printed in the United States
By Bookmasters